Research Methods in Clinical Linguistics and Phonetics

Guides to Research Methods in Language and Linguistics

Series Editor: Li Wei, Birkbeck College, University of London

The science of language encompasses a truly interdisciplinary field of research, with a wide range of focuses, approaches, and objectives. While linguistics has its own traditional approaches, a variety of other intellectual disciplines have contributed methodological perspectives that enrich the field as a whole. As a result, linguistics now draws on state-of-the-art work from such fields as psychology, computer science, biology, neuroscience and cognitive science, sociology, music, philosophy, and anthropology.

The interdisciplinary nature of the field presents both challenges and opportunities to students who must understand a variety of evolving research skills and methods. The *Guides to Research Methods in Language and Linguistics* addresses these skills in a systematic way for advanced students and beginning researchers in language science. The books in this series focus especially on the relationships between theory, methods and data – the understanding of which is fundamental to the successful completion of research projects and the advancement of knowledge.

Published

1. *The Blackwell Guide to Research Methods in Bilingualism and Multilingualism*
   Edited by Li Wei and Melissa G. Moyer

2. *Research Methods in Child Language: A Practical Guide*
   Edited by Erika Hoff

3. *Research Methods in Second Language Acquisition: A Practical Guide*
   Edited by Susan M. Gass and Alison Mackey

4. *Research Methods in Clinical Linguistics and Phonetics: A Practical Guide*
   Edited by Nicole Müller and Martin J. Ball

Forthcoming

Research Methods in Sociolinguistics: A Practical Guide
Edited by Janet Holmes and Kirk Hazen

Research Methods in Sign Language Studies: A Practical Guide
Edited by Eleni Orfanidou, Bencie Woll, and Gary Morgan

Research Methods in Language Policy and Planning: A Practical Guide
Edited by Francis Hult and David Cassels Johnson

Research Methods in Clinical Linguistics and Phonetics

A Practical Guide

Edited by Nicole Müller and Martin J. Ball

WILEY-BLACKWELL

A John Wiley & Sons, Ltd., Publication

Library of Congress Cataloging-in-Publication Data
Research methods in clinical linguistics and phonetics: a practical guide / edited by Nicole Müller and Martin J. Ball.
    p.   cm.
    Includes bibliographical references and index.
    ISBN 978-1-4443-3583-5 (cloth) – ISBN 978-1-4443-3584-2 (pbk.)
1. Speech disorders.   2. Communicative disorders.   3. Language disorders.   4. Phonetics.
5. Applied linguistics.   I. Müller, Nicole, 1963–   II. Ball, Martin J. (Martin John)
    RC423.R455 2013
    616.85′5–dc23
                                                                        2012010361
A catalogue record for this book is available from the British Library.

Cover image: Goreme National Park, Turkey © Carson Ganci/Design Pics/Corbis
Cover design by www.cyandesign.co.uk

Set in 10/13pt Sabon by SPi Publisher Services, Pondicherry, India
Printed in Singapore by Ho Printing Singapore Pte Ltd

1   2013

Contents

Notes on Contributors

Marcy Adler-Bock is a speech-language pathologist who works with preschool children with communication difficulties in Vancouver, British Columbia. She completed her BA at Simon Fraser University and her MS at the University of British Columbia. She has collaborated on various research projects within the School of Audiology and Speech Sciences at the University of British Columbia since 2004, in particular, with use of ultrasound. Her Master's thesis was an ultrasound treatment study with two adolescents who had difficulty with /r/.

Penelope Bacsfalvi is an instructor for Linguistics and Audiology and Speech Sciences at the University of British Columbia. She received her PhD in 2007 on the use of visual feedback in speech habilitation. She is a speech-language pathologist and researcher at the Provincial Resource Programme for Auditory Outreach (PRP-AO). Her clinical work focuses on hearing loss in children, cochlear implants, visual feedback technology, and a team approach to auditory verbal intervention. Her research continues on visual feedback in speech habilitation.

Martin J. Ball is Hawthorne-BoRSF Endowed Professor at the University of Louisiana at Lafayette. He is co-editor of the journal *Clinical Linguistics and Phonetics* (Taylor & Francis), and the book series Communication Disorders across Languages (Multilingual Matters). His main research interests include sociolinguistics, clinical phonetics and phonology, and the linguistics of Welsh. He is an honorary Fellow of the Royal College of Speech and Language Therapists, and a Fellow of the Royal Society of Arts. Among his recent books are *Handbook of Clinical Linguistics* (co-edited with M. Perkins, N. Müller, and S. Howard, Wiley-Blackwell, 2008), and *Phonology for Communication Disorders* (co-authored with N. Müller and B. Rutter, Psychology Press, 2010).

Scott Barnes is a speech-language pathologist and postdoctoral research fellow with the Centre for Clinical Research Excellence in Aphasia Rehabilitation, based at the University of Sydney. His doctoral dissertation examined topic talk during everyday interactions involving a person with aphasia, and was undertaken via Macquarie University, Sydney. He is currently using CA to investigate everyday interactions involving people with acquired communication disorders.

B. May Bernhardt has been a speech-language pathologist since 1972 and on faculty at the School of Audiology and Speech Sciences, University of British Columbia, since 1990. Her main focus has been phonological and other language development, assessment and intervention, with application of nonlinear phonology and use of visual feedback in intervention. She was awarded Honours of the BCASLPA Association in 2006 for her collaborative research projects involving practitioners in British Columbia. Recently, her interest in collaboration has led to two final career projects: (1) speech, language and hearing support for First Nations, Métis and Inuit people in Canada and (2) crosslinguistic investigation of phonological development.

Stuart Cunningham is a Lecturer in the Department of Human Communication Sciences at the University of Sheffield. He has a PhD in computer science and his primary research interests are in robust automatic speech recognition and the application of speech technology in the field of assistive technology. He has recently led work on the development of new approaches to the automatic recognition of dysarthric speech. Dr Cunningham has also conducted research into ways of producing personalized synthetic voices for people with speech disorders for use in voice output communication aids.

Paula S. Currie is an Associate Professor and the Assistant Dean of the College of Nursing and Health Sciences at Southeastern Louisiana University. She received her BA from Louisiana State University; her Master of Communication Disorders from the Louisiana State University Medical Center in New Orleans; her PhD from the University of New Orleans. She has worked as a speech-language pathologist in a variety of settings including public schools, private practice, and universities. Her areas of interest include administration, assessment of communication disorders, and intervention for people with complex communication disorders.

Alison Ferguson is Professor of Speech Pathology at the University of Newcastle, Australia. Her main research interests are in the application of linguistics to the assessment of people with aphasia and to understanding the processes of therapy for aphasia.

Margaret Forbes studied English at Randolph College (BA) and Carnegie Mellon University (MA) and received her training in Communication Sciences and Disorders at the University of North Carolina at Chapel Hill and the University of Pittsburgh (MA). She treated adults with cognitive and communication disorders at the University of Pittsburgh Medical Center hospitals for 10 years. She has been involved in communication disorders research at the Alzheimer Disease Research Center of the University of Pittsburgh, Western Psychiatric Institute and Clinic, and Carnegie Mellon University, where she is currently a research faculty member working on the AphasiaBank project directed by Brian MacWhinney. Her research interest is neurogenic communication disorders in adults.

Davida Fromm did her training in speech-language pathology at the University of Michigan (BA), the University of Wisconsin (MS), and the University of Pittsburgh

(PhD). Between 1990 and 2007, she taught courses in Communication Science and Disorders at the University of Pittsburgh and Duquesne University. In 1999, Dr Fromm co-authored the revised Communicative Abilities in Daily Living (CADL-2) test with Audrey Holland and Carol Frattali. Currently, she is a Research Faculty member at Carnegie Mellon University in the Department of Psychology. Her research interests have focused on adults with acquired neurogenic communicative disorders.

Angela Granese is a doctoral student in the Applied Language and Speech Sciences program at the University of Louisiana at Lafayette. She received a BA in Mass Communication from the University of South Florida in 2006. She is in the process of earning the Certificate of Clinical Competence in Speech-Language Pathology (CCC-SLP). Her research interests include clinical phonetics and phonology, bilingualism, and autism.

Jacqueline Guendouzi is a clinical linguist who received her PhD from Cardiff University. Currently she is a Professor in the Communication Sciences and Disorders department at Southeastern Louisiana University. Her research interests include psycholinguistics and discourse analysis. Her publications include: J. Guendouzi and N. Müller (2006) *Approaches to Discourse in Dementia*, Lawrence Erlbaum Associates; J. Guendouzi, F. Loncke, and M. Williams (2011) *Handbook of Psycholinguistics and Cognitive Processes: Perspectives in Communication Disorders*, Psychology Press.

Audrey Holland is Regents' Professor Emerita of Speech and Hearing Sciences at the University of Arizona. Her areas of expertise include working with adults who have aphasia and other neurologic communication disorders, aspects of aging, and counseling individuals with disabilities. She has served on the Advisory Council for the US National Institute on Deafness and other Communication Disorders (NIH), the Secretary's Advisory Committee on Prosthetics and Special Disabilities, US Department of Veterans Affairs, and was a member of the Advisory Committee of the National Center for Medical Rehabilitation Research. She is a recipient of the Honors of the American Speech-Language-Hearing Association. She also received the Clinical Achievement Award from the Academy of Neurologic Communication Disorders and Sciences, and the Professional Achievement Award from the Council of Graduate Programs in Communication Sciences and Disorders.

Sara Howard is Professor in Clinical Phonetics in the Department of Human Communication Sciences at the University of Sheffield and an ESRC Research Fellow. As well as degrees in phonetics and linguistics, she has a professional qualification as a speech-language therapist. Her research interests span clinical phonetics and phonology (with a particular interest in phonetic transcription and electropalatography) and developmental speech disorders, including cleft palate. Her most recent books are *Cleft Palate Speech: Assessment and Intervention* (Wiley-Blackwell, 2011), co-edited with Anette Lohmander, and *The Handbook of Clinical Linguistics* (Wiley-Blackwell, 2008), co-edited with Martin Ball, Mick Perkins, and Nicole Müller. She is currently President of the International Clinical Phonetics and Linguistics Association.

Mark Huckvale is Senior Lecturer in Speech Sciences in the Division of Psychology and Language Sciences at University College London. He has a degree in physics from Warwick University, and a PhD in human communication from the University of London. He has over 25 years of experience in research and teaching in speech and hearing sciences. His research activities have included speech recognition, speech synthesis, and speech signal processing. He is the main author of the Speech Filing System toolkit for speech analysis and is a recipient of the Provost's Teaching Award for his contributions to phonetics teaching at UCL.

Louise Keegan is Assistant Professor in Communication Sciences and Disorders at Appalachian State University, North Carolina. She is originally from Limerick, Ireland, and graduated as a speech and language therapist from University College Cork. She completed her PhD in applied language and speech sciences in the University of Louisiana at Lafayette in 2012. Her research interests lie in the social use of language especially in populations with acquired language disorders, and her PhD dissertation focused on the linguistic construction of identity in individuals with traumatic brain injury.

Sharynne McLeod is Professor of Speech and Language Acquisition at Charles Sturt University in Australia. She is editor of the *International Journal of Speech-Language Pathology*, vice president of the International Clinical Linguistics and Phonetics Association, and a Fellow of both the American Speech-Language-Hearing Association and Speech Pathology Australia. She has been received national awards for her teaching and research. Recent co-authored and co-edited books include *The International Guide to Speech Acquisition*, *Speech Sounds*, *Interventions for Speech Sound Disorders in Children*, and *Multilingual Aspects of Speech Sound Disorders in Children*.

Brian MacWhinney, Professor of Psychology, Computational Linguistics, and Modern Languages at Carnegie Mellon University, has developed a model of first and second language acquisition and processing called the Competition Model which he has also applied to aphasia and fMRI studies of children with focal lesions. He has also developed the CHILDES project for the computational study of child language transcript data, the TalkBank system for the study of conversational interactions, AphasiaBank for the study of aphasia, and the E-Prime and PsyScope programs.

Vesna Mildner is a Professor and Chair of Applied Phonetics at the Faculty of Humanities and Social Sciences, University of Zagreb. Her research and teaching areas of interest are neurophonetics, bilingualism, speech perception, speech acquisition, and clinical phonetics. She is the author of two books and dozens of peer-reviewed articles and chapters and has edited a number of books, proceedings, and journal special issues; she is editor-in-chief of the journal *Govor* and on the editorial board of several journals. She has organized more than 20 conferences and presented invited talks and courses in Austria, Brazil, China, Croatia, France, Hungary, Italy, and Slovenia. Mildner is active on several research projects and is a member of IPA, IASCL and ICPLA.

Geetanjalee Modha is a speech-language pathologist with the Acquired Brain Injury program at GF Strong Rehabilitation Centre in Vancouver. She has also worked with preschool children and at the Provincial Autism Resource Centre. She is a clinical educator and has instructed a course in phonology and labs at UBC. Her Master's research was a case study of a teenager with /r/ challenges and providing treatment using ultrasound. She is currently involved in a study at GF Strong to explore communication strategies in stroke.

Nicole Müller is a Professor of Communicative Disorders at the University of Louisiana at Lafayette, and holds a Hawthorne-BoRSF Endowed Professorship. Among her teaching and research interests are phonetics and speech output disorders, as well as Systemic Functional Linguistics and its applications to various data genres in the context of communicative disorders, such as conversation in dementia and traumatic brain injury. She also co-edits the journal *Clinical Linguistics and Phonetics* and the book series Communication Disorders across Languages.

Judith D. Oxley is a speech-language pathologist and Assistant Professor at the University of Louisiana at Lafayette. Her current clinical and research interests include language and speech development in children who use augmentative and alternative communication, cognitive demands of using alternative communication modalities for adults following traumatic brain injury, and the emergence of metastrategic insight into clinical practice in preprofessional speech-language pathology students.

Thomas W. Powell is Professor of Rehabilitation Sciences in the School of Allied Health Professions at the Louisiana State University Health Sciences Center – Shreveport, USA. His research interests include clinical phonetics and phonology, measurement, and ethics. Dr Powell is co-editor of *Clinical Linguistics and Phonetics*, the official journal of the International Clinical Phonetics and Linguistics Association. He edited, with Martin Ball, a four-volume compendium entitled *Clinical Linguistics*, part of the Critical Concepts in Linguistics series published by Routledge. He also co-authored *Ethics for Speech-Language Pathologists: An Illustrative Casebook*.

Barbara Purves is an Assistant Professor in the School of Audiology and Speech Sciences at the University of British Columbia (UBC). She received a PhD in Interdisciplinary Studies in 2006 at UBC and has over 25 years' clinical experience working as a speech-language pathologist with people with acquired communication disorders. Concerning speech communication, she has researched the area of comprehensibility in adult dyads. A recent Aphasia Mentoring Project involved people with aphasia providing information and learning opportunities for students from a variety of disciplines.

Joan Rahilly is Senior Lecturer in Phonetics and Linguistics at Queen's University, Belfast, Northern Ireland. Her research interests are wide ranging, and include segmental and suprasegmental aspects of speech variability in Irish English, speech acquisition, and clinical linguistics. Her publications in all of these areas are united by a particular focus on the interactive effects of speech and language variation and breakdown within and between speech communities.

Eleonora Rossi received her Master's and PhD from the Linguistic Department at the University of Groningen (the Netherlands). Her dissertation focused on investigating morpho-syntactic disorders in speakers with agrammatic aphasia and in bilingual aphasic speakers. She is currently working within the Center for Language Science – CLS – as a post-doctoral research associate at Pennsylvania State University, where she is investigating bilingual language processing in healthy populations utilizing behavioral and neuroimaging methods, such as eye-tracking, Event-Related Potentials (ERPs), and functional Magnetic Resonance Imaging (fMRI).

Ben Rutter is a university teacher in the Department of Human Communication Sciences at the University of Sheffield. His research interests focus on the application of phonetics and phonology to the study of speech and language disorders. He has published research adapting methods in acoustic phonetics to the study of dysarthria, progressive speech degeneration, and phonological acquisition. He holds a PhD in clinical linguistics from the University of Louisiana at Lafayette.

1 Linguistics, Phonetics, and Speech-Language Pathology: Clinical Linguistics and Phonetics

Nicole Müller and Martin J. Ball

1.1 A Brief Historical Overview of Clinical Linguistics and Phonetics

The speech-language sciences and arts have, of course, informed speech-language pathology for a long time; for example, the knowledge of normal articulation was imported from phonetics, the use of terms for word classes (such as nouns and verbs) from traditional grammar. However, the more recent close interaction between linguistics and communication disorders started only in the 1970s. Kent (2011), in a review of the development of the journal *Clinical Linguistics and Phonetics*, points to Duchan's online survey of the development of speech-language pathology, where she refers to the period from 1965 to 1975 as the "linguistic era" (see Duchan, 2011).

In the 1970s and 1980s David Crystal and his colleagues developed linguistically based profiling techniques for the analysis of normal and disordered syntax and morphology (Crystal, 1979; Crystal, Fletcher, and Garman, 1976), and then phonology, prosody, and semantics (Crystal, 1982). At the same time an interest in the clinical application of modern phonological theory began to emerge, with publications by Grunwell (1982), Ingram (1976, 1981), Edwards and Shriberg (1983), and Elbert and Gierut (1986), among others. Interestingly, however, the appearance of the term "clinical linguistics" dates to the end of this period, with the publication of the book of that title by David Crystal (1981). Crystal defines clinical linguistics as "the application of linguistic science to the study of communication disability, as encountered in clinical situations" (Crystal, 1981: 1). He added to this definition: "clinical linguistics is the application of the theories, methods and findings of linguistics (including phonetics) to the study of those situations where language

Research Methods in Clinical Linguistics and Phonetics: A Practical Guide,
First Edition. Edited by Nicole Müller and Martin J. Ball.
© 2013 Blackwell Publishing Ltd. Published 2013 by Blackwell Publishing Ltd.

handicaps are diagnosed and treated" (Crystal, 1984: 31). Limiting the direction of application from linguistics to language disorder is intentional: "the orientation ... should be noted. It may be contrasted with the approach of neurolinguists, for example, who study clinical language data in order to gain insights into linguistic or neurological theory" (Crystal, 1984: 30–31). Nevertheless, despite Crystal's wish for clinical linguistics to be a unidirectional hybrid discipline, many researchers working in the field have adopted a bidirectional approach. For example, Ball and Kent (1987: 2) wrote that they preferred a definition that allows "either applying linguistic/phonetic analytic techniques to clinical problems, or showing how clinical data contribute to theoretical issues in linguistics/phonetics." The work of Grodzinsky and colleagues (e.g. Grodzinsky, 1986, 1990) illustrates the use of data from language disorder to inform syntactic theory.

Clinical linguistics developed through the publication of a number of important books (some noted above), the drawing up of analysis procedures and the development of instrumental techniques (to which we return below). An important milestone for this new field of study was the launching of a new academic journal, *Clinical Linguistics and Phonetics*. This took place in 1987, with an initial volume of just two issues (soon increased to four). Now in its twenty-fifth year, the journal publishes 12 issues a year, testimony to the increase in interest and work in clinical linguistics.

1.2   The Role of Clinical Linguistics and Phonetics in Speech-Language Pathology

In this section we will look at some of the contributions made from clinical linguistics and phonetics to clinical practice and research in speech-language pathology, starting with the investigation of speech output impairments as informed by clinical phonetics. The description of disordered speech has benefitted in several ways from the input of clinical phonetics, not least in phonetic transcription, which forms the foundation on which much of both clinical decision-making and clinical speech research builds. Phonetic transcription using the IPA (International Phonetic Alphabet) has long been the norm in data analysis in disordered speech. However, it became clear fairly early on that the range of sounds encountered in the clinic appeared to be larger than the range encountered in natural language. At first ad hoc symbolizations were devised by speech-language pathologists (SLPs) to deal with sounds that could not be denoted through the use of IPA symbols or diacritics because they did not occur in natural language (Grunwell, 1982). In 1983 the King's Fund in the UK published a paper describing a proposed range of additional symbols for just these atypical sounds: the Phonetic Representation of Disordered Speech (PRDS; PRDS, 1983). While a step forward, these PRDS symbols had limited currency, being little known, for example, in North America. The 1989 meeting of the International Phonetic Association in Kiel instituted a committee to examine the symbolization of atypical sounds found in disordered speech. It considered the PRDS symbols and other suggestions and eventually recommended a set of Extensions to the International Phonetic Alphabet (extIPA) for clinical use. This was described in Duckworth *et al.* (1990), and has been updated since (see, e.g. Ball, Müller, and Rutter (2010) for the most recent (2008) revision).

The provision of the extIPA symbols set (and later on the VoQS voice quality symbols; see Ball, Esling, and Dickson, 2000; Ball and Müller, 2005) is a good example of how insights from phonetics have influenced developments in communication disorders. However, it is also arguable that the needs of speech pathology (in this case the description, through transcription, of atypical speech) have informed phonetics. While it is true that Pike (1943) contained descriptions of a wide range of sounds (both linguistic and nonlinguistic), it is only since the development of extIPA that phoneticians seem to have recognized this range of sounds not found in natural language (for example, through the inclusion of the extIPA symbols in publications of the International Phonetic Association).

Another example of a two-way interaction between speech science and speech pathology can be found with instrumental analyses of speech. A wide range of these exist (see, e.g. Awan, 2008; Ball and Code, 1997; Gibbon, 2008; Kent and Kim, 2008; Whitehill and Lee, 2008; and Chapters 4, 12, and 13 in this volume). Some of these techniques examine speech production processes, some the acoustic signal, and others the perception of speech. While these techniques were mainly developed for the investigation of normal speech, some of them were given a special impetus through their use in the speech clinic. We can point to two of these in particular: electropalatography (EPG) and electroglottography (EGG) (also known as electrolaryngography, ELG). The work by Gibbon and colleagues on "covert contrasts" using EPG is a good illustration of this clinic–research interaction. Gibbon investigated articulatory contrasts made by a speaker that are not perceptible by the listener. For example, in Gibbon (1990) the author reports that one of two sisters is transcribed as backing alveolars to velars, but the other is not. EPG patterns recorded for both sisters had tongue contacts at both alveolar and velar positions at the onset of target alveolars, but the EPG tongue–palate contact patterns at the point of release differed. One sister released her velar contacts before her alveolar ones (thereby producing a release burst that was acoustically similar to that of the control subject), whereas the other released her alveolar contacts first and velar ones last, thereby producing a release burst that sounded like that of [g].

As Fourcin (2000) has pointed out, ELG (or EGG) can help establish links between objective measurement using laryngograph-type signals and the use of subjective auditory dimensions of voice quality description. This is because ELG measurement techniques are able to provide a way of escaping from the current clinical bias towards the utilization of data that are convenient for the researchers, because they are easy to measure (sustained vowels for example), but that are rather less relevant to real-life voice use.

Clinical linguistic research has also informed development of the application of phonology to disordered speech. As Bowen (2009) notes, insights from early phonological theory began to be applied clinically in the 1960s. Many researchers working within clinical linguistic tradition helped spread later theoretical developments within phonology to clinical situations. For example, Grunwell used Stampe's framework of natural phonology in clinical assessment (Grunwell, 1987, 1997; Stampe, 1979).

Bernhardt and Stemberger, and Gierut and Dinnsen applied nonlinear models of phonology, and more recently Optimality Theory, to disordered speech data (Bernhardt and Gilbert, 1992; Bernhardt and Stemberger, 2000; Dinnsen, 1997; Dinnsen and Gierut, 2008), and the current authors have used more functional and cognitive models of phonology for the analysis of clinical data (Ball, Rutter, and Code, 2008; Müller, Ball, and Rutter, 2008). Ball, Müller, and Rutter (2010) describe a range of phonological approaches and how these can be used to analyze disordered-speech data and also to help plan intervention.

Concrete outcomes from clinical phonology include a range of assessment instruments based on different models of phonology, or combining several such approaches. Arguably, the two such assessments most within the clinical phonology tradition are the PACS procedure (Grunwell, 1985) and PROPH, a profile developed by David Crystal (Crystal, 1982) (see Ball and Müller, 1997, for a comparison of the two profiles). Both these assessments rely on naturalistic speech data and provide profiles of the speaker's phonological abilities, using a range of phonological analyses, rather than standardized scores derived from a limited set of tokens.

1.3   Research Philosophies, and the Rest of this Book

Clinical linguistics and phonetics is far from a homogenous field in terms of research traditions, philosophies, and methods adopted by its practitioners. In fact one might go so far as to say that the one thing all clinical linguists and phoneticians have in common is an interest in data related to language or speech disorder, which in turn represents a rather wide remit, and not one that is entirely straightforward in definition (for instance, do we describe the communicative sequelae of dementia as primarily *cognitive* or *linguistic*, and indeed, what difference does it make?). Some clinical linguists would describe their work as, essentially, a branch of applied linguistics, where the application is the (eventual) translation of linguistic and phonetic analyses into clinical assessment and intervention, while others take theorizing about the nature of human language, speech, and cognition as their inspiration, and wish to investigate how impairments of speech and language inform such theories.

In all branches of science that ultimately take human conditions as their object of investigation, there is a potential tension between different scientific orientations (and at times, priorities). Thus, confronted with any one person with aphasia, one may ask numerous questions, such as, but not limited to, "what can this person's history of stroke and the effects on her language processing tell me about human language?"; "what characteristics of aphasia do I see in this person?"; "which specific language skills are impaired by a stroke such as the one experienced by this person?"; "how does aphasia affect this person's life?"; "what tools do I need to effectively assess the language skills and deficits in this person?"; "what do I need to know in order to plan effective intervention for this person?"; "what does this person have to tell me about how aphasia affects her life?", and so forth.

The starting point for research in clinical linguistics and phonetics is always going to be a person with impaired language or speech, whether he or she is a participant in a group study, or a single "case." While ethical conduct is of course a prerequisite of all good research, working with vulnerable populations such as children or people with a variety of impairments of communication and cognition imposes particularly stringent requirements. In Chapter 2 of this book, Thomas W. Powell discusses research ethics in the clinical arena, from the planning stage to the eventual dissemination of research results.

In order to situate different approaches to research in clinical linguistics and phonetics, and the role of the individual in them, it is useful to make reference to Luria's distinction between *classical* and *romantic* science (Luria, 1987a, 1987b; see Sabat, 2001, for discussion, with specific reference to dementia research). Classical science is reductionist in philosophy and approach, and aims to find general and generalizable insights. Phenomena are analyzed into component parts which are investigated using standardized procedures. A classical researcher aims at discovering the, ideally, context-free essence of the object investigated, a "truth" or general characteristic that transcends any one individual case. Classical reductionist science is typified by experimental group studies. Thus, research aiming for explanations of "the nature of," for instance, language impairment in aphasia, or Specific Language Impairment, or phonological delay tends towards experimental or quasi-experimental studies. Given the difficulty in finding large groups of people exhibiting sufficiently similar constellations of symptoms of speech or language impairment (in the absence of confounding variables, and well enough matched for the purposes of an experiment), many quasi-experimental studies in this field are case studies intended to contribute, by a process of accumulation, to a generalizable body of knowledge. Such clinical case studies have a long and proud history in medicine, psychology, and indeed the clinical speech and language sciences (see, e.g. Code *et al.*, 1996, 2003).

Chapter 3 in this volume, by Vesna Mildner, is something of a *tour de force* of principles of experimental and quasi-experimental research as relevant to clinical linguistics and phonetics. Mildner discusses steps in experimental research design, the concepts of reliability and validity, the choice of appropriate design variants (including pre- and non-experimental designs), and questions of subject selection, data collection, and interpretation. May Bernhardt and colleagues (Chapter 4) use the International Classification for Function (ICF; WHO, 2007) as a framework for their chapter on experimental and quasi-experimental research on speech production and (re)habilitation. A researcher's beliefs and assumptions are what underlie that researcher's constructs of what constitutes, for example, "disorder," and how it can be investigated. Judith Oxley's chapter on experimental and quasi-experimental research on disordered language (Chapter 5) includes a discussion of nosological constructs, and of theories accounting for language development and change that drive research. At the heart of data analysis and interpretation in experimental and quasi-experimental research is the application of appropriate statistical methods, since statistical significance serves as a determinant of whether the hypothesis investigated is to be accepted or rejected. Statistical methods as applicable to clinical linguistics and phonetics are the topic of Chapter 14, by Eleanora Rossi.

With classical reductionist science, Luria contrasts what he calls *romantic* science, which is holistic in approach and philosophy and attempts to *not* reduce phenomena to abstract component parts and generalizable characteristics, but rather to "preserve the wealth of living reality" (1987b: 6). Clinical linguists and phoneticians oriented towards this goal often tend towards qualitative approaches, which involve a flexible approach to research design and the avoidance of a priori hypothesis formation. Qualitative studies in clinical linguistics are also often based on single cases, and include the layering of multiple types of data in an attempt to capture complexities embedded in, and emergent from, the real-life and individual concerns and priorities of the participant(s) (see Chapter 6, on qualitative research). Chapters 7 and 8 are dedicated to two strands of qualitative research, namely the Ethnography of Communication (by Jacqueline A. Guendouzi), and Conversation Analysis (by Scott Barnes and Alison Ferguson). Clinical sociolinguistics, which in Chapter 9 (by Martin J. Ball and Louise Keegan) is operationalized as the application of sociolinguistic methods (specifically the investigation of sociolinguistic variation) to the clinical context, is another branch of clinical linguistics that aims at capturing the complexity of the living reality of human communicative encounters; in this case, interactions with and between persons with speech and language impairments.

The core of any linguistic or phonetic analysis is a solid body of high-quality data, and many studies involve the processing of audio or video data. Chapter 10, by Benjamin Rutter and Stuart Cunningham, deals with audio and video data, the analytical purposes for which they are useful, and their recording and storage. Data recording is a first step in analysis, since the data recorded will constrain, and thereby help to focus, an analysis. Impressionistic approaches have long been a mainstay in clinical phonetics and linguistics. For such analyses, researchers employ a variety of transcription methods to transform audio or video data into a graphic source for and record of analyses. Such methods, their applicability to different areas of research, and their role in data analysis are the topic of Chapter 11, by Martin J. Ball and colleagues. While transcription-based approaches essentially rely on the transcriber's perceptual and transcription skills to filter the data into usable units, acoustic data processing methods remove this particular filter from the analysis and base interpretation on acoustic measurements. Mark Huckvale (Chapter 12) presents an introduction to acoustic measures of voice pitch, voice quality, segmental characteristics, and prosody relevant for use in clinical phonetics. A further avenue of analysis in clinical phonetics is speech imaging, that is, a variety of techniques that produce visual representations of movements of the vocal tract. Such methods, their applicability in clinical phonetics, and the technical requirements involved are the topic of Chapter 13, by Joan Rahilly. In Chapter 15, Brian MacWhinney and colleagues present a branch of research that is becoming increasingly prominent in linguistics in general, and clinical linguistics in particular, namely corpus-based approaches. Given the rapid advances in storage and processing capacity of mainstream computing in recent years, it is now feasible for researchers to access and investigate large corpora of language data without having to invest in expensive specialist computer hardware (the same is also true of acoustic analysis; see Chapter 12). MacWhinney and colleagues base their chapter on the AphasiaBank project, which to our knowledge is the largest and fastest-growing corpus of language data relating to language impairment in the world.

Doing research in clinical linguistics and phonetics is, in our humble opinion, fun while it lasts. However, it would not warrant the label of "research," nor would it warrant inconveniencing research participants, unless the ultimate goal of the research endeavor is dissemination, that is, the publication of our investigations for scrutiny by the research community, and for the purpose of contributing to the available body of knowledge in our field. Writing and disseminating research can follow many avenues, including theses and dissertations in fulfillment of degree requirements, edited books, journal articles, conference presentations, and more. The writing and dissemination of research is discussed in the final chapter of this book (Chapter 16, by Sharynne McLeod).

References

Awan, S. (2008). Instrumental analysis of phonation. In M. J. Ball, M. R. Perkins, N. Müller, and S. Howard (eds), *The Handbook of Clinical Linguistics*. Oxford: Wiley-Blackwell, pp. 344–359.

Ball, M. J. and Code, C. (eds) (1997). *Instrumental Clinical Phonetics*. London: Whurr.

Ball, M. J., Esling, J., and Dickson, C. (2000). Transcription of voice. In R. D. Kent and M. J. Ball (eds), *Voice Quality Measurement*. San Diego, CA: Singular Publishing, pp. 49–58.

Ball, M. J. and Kent, R. D. (1987). Editorial. *Clinical Linguistics and Phonetics*, 1, 1–5.

Ball, M. J. and Müller, N. (1997). A comparison of two phonological profiles. *Journal of Communication Disorders*, 30, 171–204.

Ball, M. J. and Müller, N. (2005) *Phonetics for Communication Disorders*. Mahwah, NJ: Lawrence Erlbaum.

Ball, M. J., Müller, N., and Rutter, B. (2010). *Phonology for Communication Disorders*. New York: Psychology Press.

Ball, M. J. Rutter, B., and Code, C. (2008). Phonological analyses of a case of progressive speech degeneration. *Asia-Pacific Journal of Speech, Language and Hearing*, 11, 305–312.

Bernhardt, B. and Gilbert, J. (1992). Applying linguistic theory to speech-language pathology: the case for non-linear phonology. *Clinical Linguistics and Phonetics*, 6, 123–145.

Bernhardt, B. H. and Stemberger, J. P. (2000). *Workbook in Nonlinear Phonology for Clinical Application*. Austin, TX: Pro-Ed.

Bowen, C. (2009). *Children's Speech Sound Disorders*. Oxford: Wiley-Blackwell.

Code, C. F. S., Wallesch, C.-W., Joanette, Y., and Lecours, A. R. (1996). *Classic Cases in Neuropsychology*. Hove, UK: Psychology Press.

Code, C. F. S., Wallesch, C.-W., Joanette, Y., and Lecours, A. R. (2003). *Classic Cases in Neuropsychology*, vol. II. Hove, UK: Psychology Press.

Crystal, D. (1979). *Working with LARSP*. London: Edward Arnold.

Crystal, D. (1981). *Clinical Linguistics*. Vienna and New York: Springer.

Crystal, D. (1982). *Profiling Linguistic Disability*. London: Edward Arnold.

Crystal, D. (1984). *Linguistic Encounters with Language Handicap*. Oxford: Blackwell.

Crystal, D., Fletcher, P., and Garman, M. (1976). *The Grammatical Analysis of Language Disability*. London: Edward Arnold; 2nd edn, 1989, London: Whurr.

Dinnsen, D. (1997). Non-segmental phonologies. In M. J. Ball and R. D. Kent (eds), *The New Phonologies: Developments in Clinical Linguistics*. San Diego, CA: Singular Publishing, pp. 77–125.

Dinnsen, D. and Gierut, J. (2008). Optimality theory: a clinical perspective. In M. J. Ball, M. R. Perkins, N. Müller, and S. Howard (eds), *The Handbook of Clinical Linguistics*. Oxford: Wiley-Blackwell, pp. 439–451.

Duchan, J. (2011). Getting here: a short history of speech pathology in America. Twentieth century. Retrieved 22 January 2011, from http://www.acsu.buffalo.edu/~duchan/history.html.

Duckworth, M., Allen, G., Hardcastle, W., and Ball, M. J. (1990). Extensions to the International Phonetic Alphabet for the transcription of atypical speech. *Clinical Linguistics and Phonetics*, 4, 273–280.

Edwards, M. L. and Shriberg, L. (1983). *Phonology: Applications in Communicative Disorders*. San Diego, CA: College Hill Press.

Elbert, M. and Gierut, J. (1986). *Handbook of Clinical Phonology: Approaches to Assessment and Treatment*. Austin, TX: Pro-Ed.

Fourcin, A. (2000). Voice quality and electrolaryngography. In R. D. Kent and M. J. Ball (eds), *Voice Quality Measurement*. San Diego, CA: Singular Publishing, pp. 285–306.

Gibbon, F. (1990). Lingual activity in two speech-disordered children's attempts to produce velar and alveolar stop consonants: evidence from electropalatographic (EPG) data. *British Journal of Disorders of Communication*, 25, 329–340.

Gibbon, F. (2008). Instrumental analysis of articulation in speech impairment. In M. J. Ball, M. R. Perkins, N. Müller, and S. Howard (eds), *The Handbook of Clinical Linguistics*. Oxford: Wiley-Blackwell, pp. 311–331.

Grodzinsky, Y. (1986). Language deficits and the theory of syntax. *Brain and Language*, 27, 135–159.

Grodzinsky, Y. (1990). *Theoretical Perspectives on Language Deficits*. Cambridge, MA: MIT Press.

Grunwell, P. (1982). *Clinical Phonology*. London: Croom Helm.

Grunwell, P. (1985). *The Phonological Assessment of Child Speech (PACS)*. Windsor: NFER-Nelson.

Grunwell, P. (1987). *Clinical Phonology*, 2nd edn. London: Churchill Livingstone.

Grunwell, P. (1997). Natural phonology. In M. J. Ball and R. D. Kent (eds), *The New Phonologies: Developments in Clinical Linguistics*. San Diego, CA: Singular Publishing, pp. 35–75.

Ingram, D. (1976). *Phonological Disability in Children*. London: Edward Arnold.

Ingram, D. (1981). *Procedures for the Phonological Analysis of Children's Language*. Baltimore: University Park Press.

Kent, R. D. (2011). The birth and growth of a scientific journal. *Clinical Linguistics and Phonetics*, 25, 917–921.

Kent, R. D. and Kim, Y. (2008). Acoustic analysis of speech. In M. J. Ball, M. R. Perkins, N. Müller, and S. Howard (eds), *The Handbook of Clinical Linguistics*. Oxford: Wiley-Blackwell, pp. 360–380.

Luria, A. R. (1987a). *The Man with a Shattered World*. Cambridge, MA: Harvard University Press.

Luria, A. R. (1987b). *The Mind of a Mnemonist*. Cambridge, MA: Harvard University Press.

Müller, N., Ball, M. J., and Rutter, N. (2008). An idiosyncratic case of /r/ disorder: application of principles from Systemic Phonology and Systemic Functional Linguistics. *Asia-Pacific Journal of Speech, Language and Hearing*, 11, 269–281.

Müller, N. and Mok, Z. (2012). Applying Systemic Functional Linguistics to conversations with dementia: the linguistic construction of relationships between participants. *Seminars in Speech and Language*, 33, 5–15.

Pike, K. (1943). *Phonetics: A Critical Analysis of Phonetic Theory and a Technique for the Practical Description of Sounds*. Ann Arbor: University of Michigan Press.

PRDS (1983). *Final Report. The Phonetic Representation of Disordered Speech*. London: The King's Fund.

Sabat, S. R. (2001). *The Experience of Alzheimer's Disease: Life through a Tangled Veil*. Oxford: Blackwell.

Stampe, D. (1979). *A Dissertation on Natural Phonology*. New York: Garland.

Whitehill, T. and Lee, A. (2008). Instrumental analysis of resonance in speech impairment. In M. J. Ball, M. R. Perkins, N. Müller, and S. Howard (eds), *The Handbook of Clinical Linguistics*. Oxford: Wiley-Blackwell, pp. 332–343.

World Health Organization (WHO) (2007). International Classification of Functioning, Disability and Health. Retrieved December 5, 2010 from www.who.int/classifications/icf/en/.

2 Research Ethics

Thomas W. Powell

2.1 Introduction

The scientific method entails the collection of data to answer carefully formulated questions in a valid, replicable, and impartial manner. As explored throughout the present volume, a variety of methodologies exist for studying speech and language phenomena from clinical populations. In this chapter, basic ethical considerations will be considered relative to the planning, implementation, and dissemination of research within the discipline of clinical linguistics and phonetics.

2.2 Basic Concepts

Traditionally, the field of ethics has been characterized as a branch of philosophy that addresses issues of right and wrong (e.g. Ross, 1930). In research contexts, the term *ethics* has come to encompass policies, procedures, and practices that are intended to ensure fair and humane treatment of participants and associates throughout the investigative process (Elliott and Stern, 1997). Ethical principles also guide the dissemination of scholarly works by providing guidelines for honesty in reporting results and for impartial and fair peer review of work submitted for publication or presentation.

There have been many attempts to distil ethics down to a small number of underlying principles. Ross (1930), for example, recognized the ethical principles of *fidelity, reparation, gratitude, justice, beneficence, self-improvement,* and *non-maleficence*. These general principles overlap considerably with those proposed in Beauchamp and Childress's (1979) influential work, which identified four principles of bioethics: *respect for autonomy, beneficence, nonmaleficence,* and *justice.*

Research Methods in Clinical Linguistics and Phonetics: A Practical Guide,
First Edition. Edited by Nicole Müller and Martin J. Ball.
© 2013 Blackwell Publishing Ltd. Published 2013 by Blackwell Publishing Ltd.

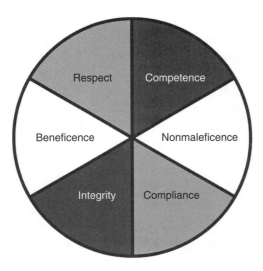

Figure 2.1 An ethics model for clinical linguistics and phonetics.

Although certain ethical principles are robust throughout the literature, it is important to consider the specific ethical issues that are germane to each discipline. Within the field of clinical linguistics and phonetics, six ethical constructs have been proposed (Powell, 2007). These constructs were identified from a review of an international sample of ethical codes from professional and scientific associations in related disciplines, including applied linguistics, speech and language therapy, and forensic phonetics:

- *beneficence*: acting in the best interest of others;
- *nonmaleficence*: minimizing risks and harm to others;
- *competence*: accepting responsibility for quality of work;
- *integrity*: avoiding conflicts of interest and communicating honestly;
- *compliance*: working in accordance with rules and regulations;
- *respect*: protecting individual autonomy and accepting differences.

These principles should not be viewed as mutually exclusive; instead, they are interdependent. For example, *beneficence* and *nonmaleficence* are complementary concepts. Thus, to act in the best interest of an individual typically entails minimizing potential risks. Similarly, *compliance* presupposes a degree of respect for governing bodies, whereas the construct identified here as *respect* emphasizes the rights of individuals (which, of course, may be protected by rules or regulations). The relationship among the proposed principles is depicted in Figure 2.1.

Ethical guidelines share certain characteristics with laws (i.e. both define standards of behavior to protect society); however, they differ significantly in other ways (Horner, 2003). Whereas laws are enacted and enforced by governments and apply to all citizens, codes of ethics typically are enacted by associations or institutions and may lack a formal means of enforcement (Irwin *et al.*, 2007). Ethical guidelines tend to be less coercive than laws, encouraging individuals to monitor their own performance. But the line differentiating ethics and laws is not always clearly drawn.

For example, many nations have codified ethical constructs into law, such as those that target conflicts of interest. As discussed in Section 2.3.3, history has documented recurrent ethical transgressions that have motivated the enactment of laws to govern research endeavors.

This chapter is organized around three stages of the research process: planning, implementation, and dissemination. Key ethical considerations are identified relative to each of these three stages. Finally, several trends impacting research ethics are examined at the conclusion of this chapter.

Section Summary

- The term *ethics* is inclusive of principles such as beneficence, nonmaleficence, competence, integrity, compliance, and respect. Investigators are bound to these ethical principles and must anticipate and address potential ethical challenges throughout the research process.

2.3 Planning for Ethical Research

Good research is painstakingly designed. Investigators develop research questions that are motivated by the literature – as well as clinical challenges – to address theoretical and applied problems. Competing methodologies should be considered and a pilot study may be undertaken to test procedures to ensure their appropriateness. At the same time, participant recruitment procedures must be developed, necessitating the identification of inclusion, as well as exclusion, criteria. As the researcher plans the study, a number of ethical issues must be considered (Irwin, Pannbacker, and Lass, 2008).

2.3.1 Rationale and Methodologies

The breadth of potential ethical issues can be daunting for both novice and experienced investigators. Therefore, the model of ethics that is depicted in Figure 2.1 may provide a useful structure for identifying major areas of ethical challenges in a systematic manner. This section begins by demonstrating such an application.

- *Beneficence.* Early in the planning stages, it is worthwhile for investigators to consider potential benefits for the participants, as well as other individuals with communication disorders. This suggestion does not imply that basic research programs without obvious clinical applications are somehow unethical; such research certainly may benefit society by increasing our understanding of the nature of our world. However, if there are potential benefits (or therapeutic implications) that may proceed from a study, then the ethically sensitive researcher will consider those benefits while developing the research protocol.

- *Nonmaleficence.* Some research programs may require the use of invasive procedures, such as certain imaging techniques. In such cases, the researcher is ethically bound to consider alternative methodologies to minimize the potential for harm to the participant. If invasive techniques are necessary and justified, then the researcher should take steps to minimize exposure and discomfort to the participant, and to maximize safety. When applicable, infection control procedures must be developed and documented. The purview of nonmaleficence is not limited to physical risks, as research procedures may involve some degree of psychological risk (e.g. frustration, distress, fatigue). Potential risks – whether physical or psychological – need to be identified and steps should be taken to ensure a favorable ratio of benefits to risks.

- *Competence.* Research may involve the use of complex equipment or procedures. The investigator must have the appropriate knowledge and skills to undertake the project. Further, one must be competent in the research design, whether qualitative or quantitative in nature. Often, investigators collaborate with individuals whose knowledge and skills complement their own abilities. Primary investigators also may delegate certain tasks to others, but they shoulder the ultimate responsibility for addressing competence by providing sufficient and appropriate education and training.

- *Integrity.* Existing (and potential) conflicts of interest must be identified as early in the project as possible so that steps can be taken to control for investigator bias. For example, a researcher may derive benefit if certain types of results are obtained. Such benefits may be fiscal in nature, such as when the investigator has a financial interest in a product whose value may be enhanced by certain research outcomes. In other cases, the benefit may be intangible, as in enhanced status (e.g. special treatment, recognition, tenure). When conflicts of interest are identified, it is critical for the researcher to declare the nature of the conflicts and to take whatever steps may be necessary to objectify data collection and analysis.

- *Compliance.* As mentioned previously, investigators may delegate duties to others as long as steps are taken to monitor competence. Student assistants warrant special consideration to ensure that their experience is consistent with educational accreditation standards and institutional regulations, as well as applicable laws. For example, some studies involve a program of speech or language treatment that is provided by a student in training. In this type of research, the individual supervising the treatment should possess the appropriate credentials to be compliant with professional, accreditation, and legal requirements.

- *Respect.* Early in the planning stages, the research team should address issues related to participant recruitment. In some cases, speech and language professionals who work in educational or medico-rehabilitation settings may identify potential participants. As outlined above, the construct of *respect* charges us with the responsibility to empower individuals by enabling them to participate – or not to participate – freely and without prejudice. When a trusted professional refers an individual to the research program, it is possible that the person will feel some degree of pressure to participate. Such coercion is likely to be flagged by ethics review committees (see Section 2.3.3). To minimize coercive effects, it may be preferable for a representative of the research team to describe the project to potential participants, rather than the familiar clinician. This procedure may help reduce clients' perceptions of pressure to participate in order to please the clinical specialist.

Additionally, clinical records are protected communication and are subject to confidentiality requirements. In research settings, procedures will be necessary to code participant data to protect the confidentiality and privacy of those who participate in the study. Traditionally, research records were stored under lock and key, identified only by participant codes. Access to the actual names has been restricted to the principal investigator and research associates who are directly involved with data collection. Today, many research records are digital, and therefore vigilance is necessary to ensure the safety and confidentiality of the records. Password protection should be routine, especially when files are saved to portable drives or removable media. The level of security or encryption should be sufficient to protect the files from access in case of loss or theft.

2.3.2   *Informed Consent*

An important tenet of research ethics is that human participants must be apprised of the goals, methods, and duration of the research program. Potential benefits and risks must be identified and explained honestly and clearly. Participants must understand that their decision to participate in the project is voluntary, and that they may withdraw from the study at any point without prejudice. Although some institutions have standard procedures for obtaining informed consent, their use is likely to be inappropriate for young children and individuals with clinical conditions that impact language or cognitive abilities (e.g. aphasia, dementia, head injury, intellectual and developmental disabilities). Such groups often are referred to as 'vulnerable populations' (Penn *et al.*, 2009).

As participant selection criteria are established, the researcher should anticipate conditions that may limit auditory and reading comprehension (e.g. aphasia, limited English proficiency). Such cases necessitate the development of special procedures for obtaining informed consent. These procedures may entail modifications to the consent form (reduced reading level, pictographic forms, and multimedia presentations), as well as the assent process (advocacy by proxy or adviser).

For participants with mildly reduced literacy skills, minor modification of the informed consent form may be sufficient to accommodate reading level. Typically, this process involves simplification of vocabulary and sentence structure (avoiding the passive voice and complex clausal structures, for example). Word processing software may provide a rough estimate of readability, typically using the Flesch–Kincaid procedure (Kincaid *et al.*, 1975).

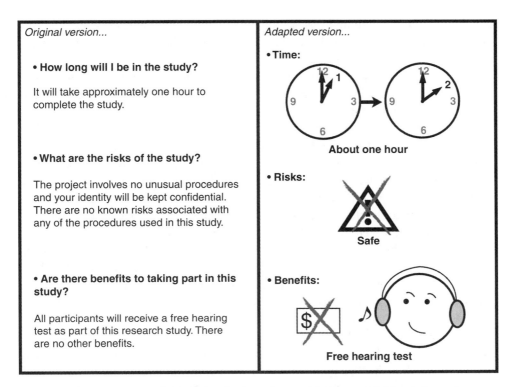

Figure 2.2 A comparison of original and adapted materials for establishing informed consent.

For participants with more severe cognitive-communicative constraints, the use of adapted materials may be appropriate. For example, Kagan and Kimelman (1995) describe procedures for use with individuals with aphasia. Their approach presents concepts such as risks/benefits and right to withdraw using pictographic symbols and a limited amount of large-print text. These adapted materials are in sharp contrast with the language used in traditional informed consent forms and will require review and approval by the relevant ethics review committees (see Figure 2.2).

A potential confound with such procedures is the issue of whether the iconic symbols communicate to the participant the specific concepts that the researcher intended. For example, some have used 'smiley faces' or a 'thumbs up' icon to signify assent (e.g. Braunack-Mayer and Hersh, 2001). It is not clear, however, that such symbols communicate 'agreement to participate' to the person with aphasia. For this reason, Kagan and Kimelman (1995) argue that the researcher must evaluate and document comprehension to validate the participant's response using, for example, a series of immediate comprehension checks consisting of simple yes/no questions.

The use of proxies or advisers has been discussed in the literature, especially in regard to patients with neurological conditions that may compromise understanding (e.g. aphasia, dementia). Individuals with aphasia may be loath to allow a proxy (typically their spouse or another member of the family) to make decisions on their behalf. Instead, research suggests that they prefer the use of an adviser who asks questions on their behalf and discusses the pros and cons of participation, but who allows the individual to make the final decision independently (Kagan and Kimelman, 1995; Stein and Brady Wagner, 2006).

Penn *et al.* (2009) noted that participants with aphasia – especially those with severe language disabilities – challenge the researcher to develop appropriate procedures for establishing informed consent. Many variables must be considered, including severity and subtype of disorder, literacy, cultural diversity, as well as personality variables (trust, scepticism, etc.). Penn *et al.* argue against the use of generic informed consent forms and procedures; instead, they provide a model that includes procedures that are tailored to the specific needs of the participants and advocates, as well as informational materials for home use. A waiting period is recommended to allow the participant time to weigh the advantages and disadvantages of participation. Penn and colleagues reiterate the importance of assessing the effectiveness of the informed consent procedures. Comprehension and decision-making capacity must be assessed carefully (Ferguson, Duffield, and Worrall, 2010).

The challenges of establishing informed consent also extend to research with other populations with cognitive-communicative disorders, including individuals with dementia or autism spectrum disorder. The use of multimedia presentations has been successful with some higher-functioning individuals on the autism spectrum (e.g. Irwin, Glabus, and Massey, 2006). One advantage of this methodology is that it may be used to simulate the type of activity to be used in the research. Such practices may reduce the likelihood of attrition because participants have a clearer understanding of the nature of the study when assent is obtained.

Finally, the use of minors in research poses additional challenges relative to informed consent. A parent or guardian must provide informed consent on behalf of the child; however, researchers are now providing even very young children with an age-appropriate description of the research, including the voluntary nature of participation and the option of withdrawing from the study at any time. This practice may help establish rapport between the researcher and the child; it also exhorts the research team to develop engaging and age-appropriate tasks. Because children are viewed as an especially vulnerable group, special care has been given to policies governing their participation and informed consent (see, for example, Schwartz, 2006).

2.3.3   Ethics Review Procedures

History documents many abuses involving human and animal experimentation. Following World War II, the discovery of forced human experimentation by Mengele and other Nazi experimenters led to the development of the Nuremberg Code, which established many of the principles that define modern approaches to research ethics (Weindling, 2005). These principles include: voluntary participation, informed consent, minimizing of harm, and evaluating risk-to-benefit ratios. Later, the Declaration of Helsinki (World Medical Association, 1964) expanded and updated the principles of the Nuremberg Code. Nevertheless, ethical transgressions continued. A classic paper by Beecher (1966), which described 22 published research studies with serious ethical problems, helped to heighten awareness of this ongoing issue and suggested that ethical lapses were, indeed, quite common.

Much has been written about the Tuskegee study, which began in 1932. This longitudinal study documented the effects of syphilis among African American prisoners, who were unaware of their diagnosis and denied treatment. The study continued until 1972. Soon thereafter, the US Congress passed the National Research Act (PL93-348), leading to the establishment of a commission on biomedical and behavioral research. The findings of the commission were released as the Belmont Report (1979), which reaffirmed and expanded ethical guidelines for researchers.

Many countries have established formal procedures for reviewing research proposals to identify potential ethical challenges prior to the initiation of the research project. In the United States, institutions that conduct research must establish an Institutional Review Board (IRB), which is charged with implementing formal procedures for review, evaluating proposals on a regular basis, and monitoring approved research programs for compliance. Although federal guidelines specify the basic procedures that are to be used by the IRBs, there may be some variation in the implementation of those procedures by individual institutions. For this reason, researchers are advised to establish contact with the local IRB early in the development of a research protocol to ensure that all required training and proper assurances are obtained before the study can be initiated. Other nations have similar bureaucracies, although the structure, terminology, and procedures may vary.

The US model recognizes three levels of review: exempt, expedited, and full. To qualify for *exempt* review, a study must meet specified criteria related to the type of data (e.g. educational test data, interview, observation of public behavior, anonymous surveys) as well as the level of analysis (e.g. analysis of group trends that preclude identification of individual participants). For example, a researcher proposed the use of a Likert-type scale to measure speech and language clinicians' confidence in their ability to transcribe the speech of individuals with severe communicative disorders. The proposal specified that respondents would be anonymous and only group trends were to be reported. This study would likely qualify for exempt review, allowing the IRB chair or designee to approve the proposal. It is important to note that the term 'exempt' does *not* imply that the investigator is exempt from IRB procedures or paperwork; rather, the appropriate forms must be submitted with a detailed description of the study's methodology, ratio of potential risks and benefits, and materials for eliciting and documenting informed consent.

Studies that involve minimal risks (defined as the level of risk encountered in daily life) may qualify for *expedited* review in which the study may be approved by a subgroup of the IRB. It is the responsibility of the researcher to document the methodologies and associated risks carefully. For example, Epstein (2005) provided recommended wording for IRB proposals for speech research involving ultrasound. Studies that involve data collection from 'vulnerable' individuals (e.g. children, people with speech, language, or cognitive impairments) are usually subject to expedited review, even when the data collection and analysis procedures preclude identification of individual participants.

If the study does not clearly meet criteria for exempt or expedited review, then it will require consideration by the entire IRB (i.e. *full* review). Studies that employ invasive techniques, for example transnasal endoscopy, usually require full review. Because ethics review boards must consider proposals from a wide range of disciplines using a multitude of methodologies, there may be no member of the board with expertise in the communication sciences and disorders. Therefore, it is important that the application materials are written as clearly as possible so as to be interpretable by individuals who are not familiar with discipline-specific terminology.

The ethics review process can be time-consuming; therefore, it may be a good investment of time to request an appointment with the IRB chair (or designee) to discuss the project before submitting paperwork. A brief meeting of this type can help identify potential areas of concern that could delay approval of the proposal. Research-intensive departments may find it helpful to have a designated IRB delegate who can read and provide feedback on proposals prior to their submission.

Although discussions of research ethics tend to focus on the medical sciences, it is unfortunately true that many studies in the social and behavioral sciences may be criticized on ethical grounds. Of special interest to clinical linguists is a master's thesis written by Mary Tudor at the University of Iowa in 1939 (see Reynolds, 2006). Under the direction of Wendell Johnson, Tudor evaluated the effects of differential feedback on the speech fluency of 22 children who were living in an orphanage. Ten of the children were identified as stutterers; the remaining participants were randomly selected from children believed to have normal speech patterns. The sample was subdivided into four groups: two groups of children who stuttered and two groups of typically speaking children. Each group received feedback that was either positive (e.g. "your speech is fine") or negative ("you have a great deal of trouble with your speech"). Of greatest interest here is group IIA, which consisted of six children with apparently normal speech who were told that they were developing stuttering. The hypothesized relationship between certain environmental conditions (e.g. calling a child's attention to nonfluencies, labeling stuttering) and the onset of fluency disorders was later developed into the diagnosogenic theory, for which Johnson was well known (Ambrose and Yairi, 2002).

Like many a thesis, Tudor's study was shelved in the university library and was largely ignored for many years until Silverman (1988) published a paper about it entitled "The Monster Study." Some years later, a series of rather sensationalized newspaper articles were published in the *San Jose Mercury News* (Dyer, 2001). The stories generated much publicity – and much criticism. Ethical concerns were raised regarding the use of orphaned children and providing an experimental condition that some believed could cause typically developing children to become stutterers. Following the publication of Dyer's articles, several of the surviving participants sued the University of Iowa and received a settlement from the state in the amount of $925,000 for "lifelong emotional stress" (Keen, 2007).

The ethics of the Tudor case have been widely debated from several vantage points (see Goldfarb, 2006). A re-analysis of the original data raised questions about the adequacy of the study's design, as well as Tudor's interpretation of the results (Ambrose and Yairi, 2002; Yairi, 2006). It has been argued, too, that the ethical ramifications of the study must be judged relative to the timeframe in which the study was conducted (Ambrose and Yairi, 2002; Johnson, 2006).

The Tudor study reminds us that the field of clinical linguistics and phonetics is not without ethical challenges. Investigators sometimes express frustration with the requirements of ethics review boards, but compliance is essential. Although most studies within the field are well intentioned and relatively innocuous, it is also true that investigators are sometimes unable or unwilling to review their own work objectively. The ethics review process is important because it helps to ensure protection of the human participants. Less obvious, perhaps, is its role in protecting the investigators themselves. The review board, with members representing a variety of viewpoints, helps to identify potential issues before they become real problems.

Section Summary

- Researchers need to consider a variety of issues before they initiate data collection. Care should be taken to identify potential ethical implications of the study's rationale and methodologies. Procedures for establishing informed consent are critical for studies that involve clinical samples or other vulnerable groups. There has been a history of ethics abuse by researchers studying human participants; however, procedures for ethics review have been established to help ensure the responsible conduct of research. Investigators in clinical linguistics and phonetics must comply with applicable review procedures.

2.4 Conducting Research Ethically

Clearly, many ethical issues need to be considered prior to the implementation of a research study. Careful planning is especially important to clinical linguists and phoneticians because their work is likely to involve low-incidence conditions and vulnerable populations. Steps must be taken to ensure respect for autonomy, which often necessitates special methods for the process of establishing informed consent (Penn *et al.*, 2009). Once the project has been approved by the ethics review board, recruitment of participants and data collection can begin. A sample of associated ethical issues is considered next.

2.4.1 Data Collection and Analysis

As noted previously, recruitment of participants and the informed consent process requires careful planning to ensure procedures are clear, fair, and non-coercive. If participants are to be compensated for their time, then that process needs to be established and monitored in accordance with institutional requirements. For example, some facilities may allow a petty cash fund to reimburse participants – subject to careful record-keeping and auditing. Other facilities may require the use of vouchers, which are exchanged for payment at a specified location. Some facilities also require tax papers to be completed, especially if the participants are otherwise employed by the facility.

As participants are identified, it is important to monitor the informed consent process to enable adaptation to accommodate the needs of the individual. It is important that evidence of informed consent is documented and stored securely. Compliance is to be monitored on an ongoing basis by the principal investigator; on-site visits to review compliance may be initiated by the ethics review board.

It is important, too, for investigators to monitor the demographic composition of the sample in compliance with the ethical concept of *justice*. In this context, 'justice' refers to the shared responsibility of all members of society to be represented in research for the good of all. In other words, one segment of society (such as individuals from lower socioeconomic strata) should not be unduly burdened with the responsibility of participating in the research. This is not to imply that equal representation among groups is always necessary (or even possible), as conditions may be more pervasive among certain demographic groups than others, making equal representation across groups unlikely. However, skewed recruitment patterns *may* be suggestive of systematic bias in the recruitment methods, and that possibility should be considered accordingly.

Finally, equipment must be inspected on a regular basis and universal precautions should be adopted to ensure infection control. When applicable, calibration checks should be completed and documented. As data are collected, a plan should be implemented to ensure compliance with the coding, analysis, and archiving methods that were specified in the research plan.

2.4.2   Management Issues

Data collection is time-consuming and the principal investigator may recruit others – often students – to assist in the collection and analysis of data. The relationship between the investigator and research associates is subject to ethical concerns. Special care needs to be taken when one recruits student workers, as there is unevenness in the power between parties. The investigator should avoid statements that may be misconstrued as pressuring the student to participate in the project. Associates, subordinates, and participants are entitled to respect; harassment or prejudicial statements cannot be tolerated.

It is critical that all individuals are well trained in working with participants and significant others, as well as knowledgeable of the research protocol. Delegation of tasks should be done with care to ensure data collection is performed competently. Students who are working to earn clinical credentials in speech and language therapy must be supervised in accordance with educational guidelines and relevant laws.

Accordingly, principal investigators must recognize the limits of their own competence. Certain procedures require a high level of expertise and should not be attempted by those without the appropriate qualifications. Some procedures may be legally restricted to individuals who have completed specific educational requirements. Legal restrictions are especially likely for invasive procedures that have the potential to cause harm if misapplied.

> **Section Summary**
>
> • Once a research plan has been approved by the relevant ethics review committees, data collection can begin. Participant recruitment should be non-discriminatory and non-coercive. Procedures should be monitored to ensure compliance with the approved research plan. Investigators have a responsibility for ensuring all associates working on the project have appropriate expertise and are supervised in accordance with pertinent guidelines.

2.5   Disseminating Results Ethically

Once data collection and analysis have been completed, the investigator's attention turns to dissemination of results, usually through presentations at professional and scientific meetings and through publication. Integrity is a guiding ethical principle during this stage of the research process. Results should be reported honestly and objectively. Funding sources should be identified, as well as any potential conflicts of interest. Indeed, most publishers explicitly require the author to disclose this type of information when manuscripts are submitted for editorial consideration.

2.5.1   *Manuscript Preparation*

Authorship should be reserved for individuals who made significant contributions to the research process. Typically, the order of authorship reflects the amount of effort devoted to the project and/or the responsibility assumed in the interpretation of the results and development of the manuscript. In cases where authors contributed equally to the process, the order of authorship may be alphabetical or decided by a coin toss; such decisions are usually disclosed in a footnote. Individuals whose contributions were valuable but not worthy of authorship, may be identified in the *acknowledgements* section of the manuscript. At times, the contributions and roles played by individuals on the research team may be subject to dispute. Such disputes may involve gift authorship (i.e. authorship is credited, although the individual's contributions were not significant) or ghost authorship (whereby an individual making a significant contribution was not recognized as an author). Albert and Wager (2003) provide useful recommendations regarding resolution of authorship disputes.

A large-scale study is likely to yield too many findings for a single manuscript. There are, however, no clear guidelines to determine the number of manuscripts that may be published from a single project. The general expectation is that each manuscript must make a unique and significant contribution to the literature. Manuscripts with considerable overlap may be viewed as multiple submissions – an ethical transgression according to the Committee on Publication Ethics (COPE; http://publicationethics.org).

The fields of clinical linguistics and clinical phonetics make frequent use of naturalistic language transcripts. When selecting examples from a linguistic corpus, the author should consider not only the form of the utterances, but also the content. In some cases, the topics under discussion may inadvertently disclose the identity of the participant or have the potential to cause embarrassment. Today's electronic search engines make the retrieval of scientific articles a simple process. It is more likely than ever for a participant (or a relative, or a friend) to retrieve the published article and to read excerpts that may contain embarrassing – or even libellous – revelations.

2.5.2   The Peer-Review Process

Scientific journals employ a peer-review process to evaluate the suitability of submissions for publication. Upon receipt of a submission, journal editors invite two or more individuals with relevant expertise to read the manuscript and to provide a candid appraisal of its suitability for publication in the journal, as well as areas of strength and weakness. Reviewers may identify theoretical, methodological, and interpretive shortcomings. In some cases, these shortcomings may be successfully addressed in a revision; in other cases, a flaw may be sufficiently serious that no amount of revision will produce a manuscript of publishable quality (Nippold, 2011). Reviewers also identify shortcomings related to the efficiency or effectiveness of communication. Spelling, grammar, and typographical errors may be identified, as well as portions of the manuscript in which writing is awkward, unclear, or redundant.

Several ethical issues may arise during the peer-review process. Editors have a responsibility to identify potential peer reviewers who are qualified and impartial. Further, editorial decisions should be as objective, opaque, and fair as possible. Peer reviewers have a responsibility for reporting conflicts of interest, as well as situations when their own knowledge is insufficient to render a valid review of the submission. It is important, too, that peer reviewers maintain confidentiality throughout the review process. By accepting a peer review assignment, individuals enter into a commitment to read and evaluate the submission within a specified time frame. If it becomes apparent that the review cannot be completed in a timely manner due to extenuating circumstances, then the peer reviewer should notify the editor as quickly as possible.

Authors, too, have ethical responsibilities related to the peer-review process. It can be a very humbling experience to read critical reviews of one's work, but it is important for authors to retain a professional demeanor when responding to criticism. Personal attacks and accusations are not a productive means of responding to critiques. A more positive reaction is to weigh the criticisms, revise the manuscript accordingly, and document the changes in a cover letter to the editor. At times, it may be possible that the reviewer misinterpreted a part of the original manuscript. The author should take this observation as an opportunity to reword that portion of the manuscript to clarify the intent. Chances are, if the peer reviewer misunderstood what was written, then casual readers are likely to misunderstand it as well.

Finally, the topic of data archiving deserves a few words. It is customary to keep all raw data for at least seven years to allow verification of findings. Increasingly, language data may be archived online (e.g. CHILDES; MacWhinney, 1995) to allow other researchers access to the raw data (see also Chapter 15 in this volume). Because web-based archives are widely accessible, informed consent must be obtained prior to posting (Powell, Müller, and Ball, 2003). Further, participants should be given the opportunity to restrict access to their data. If the data are posted publicly, then it is imperative that steps are taken to ensure anonymity.

Section Summary

- Once data are collected and analyzed, ethical issues related to the dissemination of findings are highlighted. Results must be presented clearly and honestly with sufficient detail so as to enable evaluation of procedures and replication. The privacy of participants must be protected and linguistic examples should be examined to ensure the content does not compromise the speaker's anonymity. The peer-review process is intended to provide authors with a candid evaluation of their work and to help editors decide whether publication is warranted. Although critical reviews of one's work may be distressing, the investigator should maintain a professional demeanor when responding.

2.6   Emerging Trends

Postal (2004) lamented, "in more than forty years in linguistics, not only have I never heard of the existence of a professional ethics course in linguistics but I also have never heard anyone even mention the possibility" (p. 341). In recent years, however, the field of linguistics has made strides in the area of ethical issues. The Linguistic Society of America (LSA) has published an Ethics Statement (2009) that identifies responsibilities to individual research participants, communities, students and colleagues, scholarship, and the public. The LSA Ethics Discussion Blog (http://lsaethics.wordpress.com/) provides a forum for linguists to discuss ethical issues. Also, ethical issues are highlighted in textbooks, especially those that deal with field linguistics (e.g. Bowern, 2008; Ladefoged, 2003).

Ethical issues have been prominent in the clinical field of speech and language therapy for many years; however, the emphasis has been on professional ethics rather than on research ethics (Body and McAllister, 2009; Irwin *et al.*, 2007). Although professional codes of ethics provide some guidelines that are relevant for research, there are many issues that impact scientific investigations that are not addressed (Costello Ingham, 2003). To address this shortcoming, the American

Speech-Language-Hearing Association (2009) published a separate document entitled *Guidelines for the Responsible Conduct of Research: Ethics and the Publication Process*. Many of the issues addressed in this document have clear relevance for clinical linguists and phoneticians. In 2011, a series of papers on research integrity was published (Moss, 2011). Papers in this series are cited in the Further Reading section at the end of this chapter.

The publishing industry, too, has responded to ethical challenges. The Committee on Publication Ethics (http://publicationethics.org) is an association that addresses the integrity of peer-reviewed publications and the challenges that are faced by editorial teams. Included on their website are discussions of redundant publication, plagiarism, fabricated data, authorship disputes, and so on. Also addressed are issues related to the peer-review process (breaches of confidentiality, bias, disregard of timelines, etc.). Likewise, the International Committee of Medical Journal Editors (http://www.icmje.org) has developed procedures for biomedical journals to increase consistency of manuscript requirements, peer-review, and conflict resolution.

These developments clearly document the importance of research ethics and the increasing emphasis placed on the ethical and responsible conduct of research.

> **Section Summary**
>
> - Increasingly, ethical issues are being highlighted in the field of linguistics. In speech and language therapy, recent work has expanded coverage of research and publication ethics, building upon a strong foundation of professional ethics. Publishers, too, have taken a strong stand on ethical procedures for publications. These trends and resources help investigators to meet standards of excellence in research ethics.

2.7 Conclusion

Research is a complex process with many ethical challenges. Most of these ethical challenges can be minimized through careful planning, formal ethics reviews, and continuous monitoring throughout the research process. Sensitivity to the needs and perceptions of participants, colleagues, and assistants can help prevent many ethical problems.

2.8 Resources

Committee on Publication Ethics (COPE); http://publicationethics.org.
LSA Ethics Discussion Blog: Linguistic Ethics Discussion and Commentary; http://lsaethics.wordpress.com/.

NIH Office of Human Subjects Research: Regulations and Ethical Guidelines; http://ohsr. od.nih.gov/guidelines/index.html.

2.8.1 Further Reading

Horner, J. and Minifie, F. D. (2011a). Research ethics I: responsible conduct of research (RCR). Historical and contemporary issues pertaining to human and animal experimentation. *Journal of Speech-Language-Hearing Research*, 54, S303–S329.

Horner, J. and Minifie, F. D. (2011b). Research ethics II: Mentoring, collaboration, peer review, data management and ownership. *Journal of Speech-Language-Hearing Research*, 54, S330–S345.

Horner, J. and Minifie, F. D. (2011c). Research ethics III: Publication practices and authorship, conflicts of interest, and research misconduct. *Journal of Speech-Language-Hearing Research*, 54, S346–S362.

Ingham, J. C., Minifie, F. D., Horner, J. *et al.* (2011). Ethical principles associated with the publication of research in ASHA's scholarly journals: importance and adequacy of coverage. *Journal of Speech-Language-Hearing Research*, 54, S394–S416.

Minifie, F. D., Robey, R. R., Horner, J. *et al.* (2011). Responsible conduct of research in communication sciences and disorders: faculty and student perceptions. *Journal of Speech-Language-Hearing Research*, 54, S363–S393.

Sales, B. D. and Folkman, S. (eds) (2000). *Ethics in Research with Human Participants*. Washington, DC: American Psychological Association.

References

Albert, T. and Wager, E. (2003). How to handle authorship disputes: a guide for new researchers. *The COPE Report*. http://www.publicationethics.org/files/2003pdf12.pdf, accessed March 27, 2012.

Ambrose, N. J. and Yairi, E. (2002). The Tudor study: data and ethics. *American Journal of Speech, Language, and Hearing Research*, 42, 895–909.

American Speech-Language-Hearing Association (2009). *Guidelines for the Responsible Conduct of Research: Ethics and the Publication Process*. www.asha.org/docs/pdf/ GL2009-00308.pdf, accessed March 27, 2012.

Beauchamp, T. L. and Childress, J. F. (1979). *Principles of Biomedical Ethics*. New York: Oxford University Press.

Beecher, H. K. (1966). Ethics and clinical research. *New England Journal of Medicine*, 274, 1354–1360.

Belmont Report (1979). *Federal Register*, 44(76), April 18, 23192–23197.

Body, R. and McAllister, L. (2009). *Ethics in Speech and Language Therapy*. Oxford: Wiley-Blackwell.

Bowern, C. (2008). *Linguistic Fieldwork: A Practical Guide*. Basingstoke: Palgrave Macmillan.

Braunack-Mayer, A. and Hersh, D. (2001). An ethical voice in the silence of aphasia: judging understanding and consent in people with aphasia. *Journal of Clinical Ethics*, 12, 388–396.

Costello Ingham, J. (2003). Research ethics 101: the responsible conduct of research. *Seminars in Speech and Language*, 24, 323–337.

Dyer, J. (2001). Ethics and orphans: the monster study. Part one of a Mercury News Special Report. *San Jose Mercury News*, June 10, p. 1A.

Elliott, D. and Stern, J. E. (eds) (1997). *Research Ethics: A Reader*. Lebanon, NH: University Press of New England.

Epstein, M. A. (2005). Ultrasound and the IRB. *Clinical Linguistics and Phonetics*, 19, 567–572.

Ferguson, A., Duffield, G., and Worrall, L. (2010). Legal decision-making by people with aphasia: critical incidents for speech pathologists. *International Journal of Language and Communication Disorders*, 45, 244–258.

Goldfarb, R. (ed.) (2006). *Ethics: A Case Study from Fluency*. San Diego, CA: Plural Publishing.

Horner, J. (2003). Morality, ethics, and law: introductory concepts. *Seminars in Speech and Language*, 24, 263–274.

Irwin, D. L., Glabus, M. F., and Massey, N. (2006). The influence of language delay/disorder upon neuroimaging studies for individuals with Autism Spectrum Disorder. *Diagnostico Journal*, 22(5), 8–11.

Irwin, D., Pannbacker, M. and Lass, N. J. (2008). *Clinical Research Methods in Speech-Language Pathology and Audiology*. San Diego, CA: Plural Publishing.

Irwin, D., Pannbacker, M., Powell, T. W., and Vekovius, G. T. (2007). *Ethics for Speech-Language Pathologists: An Illustrative Casebook*. Clifton Park, NY: Thomson Delmar Learning.

Johnson, N. (2006). Retroactive ethical judgments and human subjects research: the 1939 Tudor study in context. In R. Goldfarb (ed.), *Ethics: A Case Study from Fluency*. San Diego, CA: Plural Publishing, pp. 139–199.

Kagan, A. and Kimelman, M. D. Z. (1995). Informed consent in aphasia research: myth or reality? *Clinical Aphasiology*, 23, 65–75.

Keen, J. (2007). Legal battle ends over stuttering experiment. *USA Today*, August 27. http://www.usatoday.com/news/nation/2007-08-26-stuttering_N.htm.

Kincaid, J. P., Fishburne, R. P., Rogers, R. L., and Chissom, B. S. (1975). Derivation of new readability formulas (Automated Readability Index, Fog Count and Flesch Reading Ease Formula) for Navy Enlisted Personnel. *Research Branch Report,* 8–75. Memphis, TN: Naval Air Station.

Ladefoged, P. (2003). *Phonetic Data Analysis: An Introduction to Fieldwork and Instrumental Techniques*. Malden, MA: Blackwell.

Linguistic Society of America (2009). Ethics Statement. www.lsadc.org/info/pdf_files/Ethics_Statement.pdf, accessed March 27, 2012.

MacWhinney, B. (1995). *The CHILDES Project: Tools for Analyzing Talk*, 2nd edn. Hillsdale, NJ: Lawrence Erlbaum Associates.

Moss, S. E. (2011). Research integrity in communication sciences and disorders. *Journal of Speech-Language-Hearing Research*, 54, S300–S302.

Nippold, M. A. (2011). The fatal flaw: what it is and how to avoid it. *Language, Speech, and Hearing Services in Schools*, 42, 1–2.

Penn, C., Frankel, T., Watermeyer, J., and Müller, M. (2009). Informed consent and aphasia: evidence of pitfalls in the process. *Aphasiology*, 23, 3–32.

Postal, P. M. (2004). *Skeptical Linguistic Essays*. Oxford: Oxford University Press.

Powell, T. W. (2007). A model for ethical practices in clinical phonetics and linguistics. *Clinical Linguistics and Phonetics*, 21, 849–857.

Powell, T. W., Müller, N., and Ball, M. J. (2003). Electronic publishing: opportunities and challenges for clinical linguistics and phonetics. *Clinical Linguistics and Phonetics*, 17, 421–426.

Reynolds, G. (2006). The stuttering doctor's "Monster Study." In R. Goldfarb (ed.), *Ethics: A Case Study from Fluency*. San Diego, CA: Plural Publishing, pp. 1–12.

Ross, W. D. (1930). *The Right and the Good*. Oxford: Clarendon Press.

Schwartz, R. G. (2006). Would today's IRB approve the Tudor study? Ethical considerations in conducting research involving children with communication disorders. In R. Goldfarb (ed.), *Ethics: A Case Study from Fluency*. San Diego, CA: Plural Publishing, pp. 83–96.

Silverman, F. (1988). The monster study. *Journal of Fluency Disorders*, 13, 225–231.

Stein, J. and Brady Wagner, L. C. (2006). Is informed consent a "'yes or no" response? Enhancing the shared decision-making process for persons with aphasia. *Topics in Stroke Rehabilitation*, 13(4), 42–46.

Weindling, P. J. (2005). *Nazi Medicine and the Nuremberg Trials: From Medical War Crimes to Informed Consent*. Basingstoke: Palgrave Macmillan.

World Medical Association (1964). Human experimentation: code of ethics of the World Medical Association (Declaration of Helsinki). *British Medical Journal*, 2, 177–183.

Yairi, E. (2006). The Tudor study and Wendell Johnson. In R. Goldfarb (ed.), *Ethics: A Case Study from Fluency*. San Diego, CA: Plural Publishing, pp. 35–62.

3 Experimental and Quasi-experimental Research in Clinical Linguistics and Phonetics

Vesna Mildner

3.1 Introduction

Research is a process of studying a phenomenon or behavior through a series of steps that include data collection, analysis, and interpretation. It starts with a research question, a problem that the investigator sets out to explore in hopes of reaching a satisfactory answer. Research design is a plan to gather, analyze, and interpret data in order to answer research questions. The type of research will depend on subjects, instruments, data collection and analysis, expected outcome, and these will, of course depend on the research question that the investigator asked to begin with. Any good experiment must be designed to test a hypothesis while at the same time meeting the requirements of reliability, validity, and replicability.

3.2 Research Design

There are several steps that need to be taken in any research. First of all, when preparing a study, the researcher must *survey the available literature*. The simplest way to tell that you have covered most relevant sources is when they start referring to one another – that may mean 10 or 200 sources, depending on the problem. Consulting review articles and meta-analyses may be useful and save time, but beware of too much indirect quoting, as results have a way of being distorted and/or lost in interpretations.

Research Methods in Clinical Linguistics and Phonetics: A Practical Guide,
First Edition. Edited by Nicole Müller and Martin J. Ball.
© 2013 Blackwell Publishing Ltd. Published 2013 by Blackwell Publishing Ltd.

The second step is to *identify and define the problem*. Of course, these steps are an interactive process. The initial survey serves as a starting point, to decide on the topic, to discover possible flaws in earlier work, etc. Helpful hints may be found in discussion sections of published sources, where the authors discuss what questions they left unanswered or speculate on possible consequences of different approaches, etc. Once the problem has been identified, consulting additional sources targeted specifically to the problem at hand is necessary.

The result should be a clear definition of the problem that enables the researcher to *formulate the hypothesis*. This step must include the prediction of outcomes and relationships among variables. A hypothesis is a statement about the expected relationship between two or more variables that can be formulated on the basis of existing knowledge, previous research, and review. It is an estimate of values that hold for a population and can be inferred on the basis of the data obtained for the sample. A so-called null hypothesis would be in the form: There is no significant difference/relationship between the studied groups (control vs. experimental, or two comparison groups) with respect to a parameter measured (dependent variable). An alternative hypothesis can be in the form: There is a difference between the two studied groups on the dependent variable (non-directional), or in the form: Group 1 will have a higher score than Group 2 on the measured (dependent) variable (directional hypothesis). Any combination of these is possible, but ultimately the hypothesis will depend on what can be expected on the basis of literature and/ or previous work.

This step includes the decision on what *variables* to use. Except independent (those that can be selected, measured, and manipulated by the experimenter) and dependent (those that are the object of study and measurement) variables, there are extraneous (confounding, spurious), control, intervening (mediator), and moderator variables (www.experiment-resources.com). In clinical linguistics and phonetics research, the independent variables most commonly used are onset and course of pathology, type and duration of treatment (therapy and rehabilitation), to name just a few. In more specific contexts the independent variables are selected depending on the problem studied. Obviously, not all of the independent variables can be manipulated. In such cases comparison groups are used that differ only in the selected independent variable. Typical dependent variables are voice quality, speech production and perception (e.g. intelligibility, comprehension, mean length of utterance), language status (e.g. vocabulary size, emergence of phonological systems), communication abilities, and many others, but independent variables in one study may become dependent variables in another or in a later segment of the same study. It is important to detect all extraneous variables and implement control mechanisms.

When it is clear what problem the study is supposed to address and what the expected outcomes and relations are, it is time to *construct the experimental design* that will enable the researcher to answer the research questions and test hypotheses in the best possible way.

There is no such thing as the perfect design: designing a research study is a series of trade-offs. Therefore, keeping in mind that it must address your research problem(s), carefully evaluate your design, the data you expect to collect, and the data after you have collected them.

Be aware of potential sources of threats to validity and establish control techniques that will lead to an unambiguous answer. When it is impossible to have a control group, consider using control mechanisms instead. Address ethical issues, as they may render even the best-planned research unfeasible. Last, but not least, be realistic with respect to the time and money it will take to complete.

Obviously, there are a number of considerations in selecting research design and the final choice will depend on how they all come together. This decision-making process is a very important part of the entire study, because an inappropriate design may fail to ensure collection of all relevant data, neglect important segments of the population or the problem it is supposed to study, or apply unsuitable statistical analyses, and as a consequence render results that are unreliable and invalid, and therefore useless.

Section Summary

Steps in research design:

- survey the available literature
- identify and define the problem
- formulate the hypothesis
- define variables
- construct the experimental design.

3.2.1   Concerns in Experimental Design: Reliability and Validity

3.2.1.1   Reliability

Reliability measures the consistency of a test, an instrument, a method, a set of measures or evaluation scores.

Inter-rater reliability (agreement, concordance) measures variation in scores across different raters (judges) on the same test and same subjects. High consensus among judges makes the researcher confident that the score reflects what the test was designed to measure. Low inter-rater agreement suggests that the scale provided is inappropriate, the instructions need to be clearer, or that the judges need to be retrained, replaced, or treated differently (e.g. trained vs. untrained).

Test–retest reliability refers to variation in measurement (e.g. responses) of the same person at different times but under identical conditions. A correlation between two measurements of 0.70 or higher is considered good. If the results obtained on two measurements of constructs that are not expected to change exhibit low or no correlation, it is possible that one or both of the measurements were not accurate, that the instrument is inappropriate, or that there are some uncontrolled variables.

Test–retest reliability may refer to variation in evaluation of the same task by the same rater/judge on different occasions but under identical conditions (*intra-rater reliability*). In tests designed to have several occurrences of the same stimulus, intra-rater reliability will be manifested as identical (or sufficiently correlated) responses to the stimulus, regardless of its position in the test or the number of its occurrences.

Inter-method reliability refers to the variation in the results obtained by testing the same construct in the same subject(s) by different methods and/or instruments.

Parallel forms reliability is based on designing two tests that draw on the same pool of items of similar difficulty and checking for the correlation between the results.

Internal consistency depends on the degree to which all test items measure the same thing (i.e. correlate with each other). Reliability is acceptable if this correlation ranges between 0.60 and 0.70, and good if it is between 0.80 and 0.90. Higher correlations are not necessary (or desirable) as they would indicate items' redundancy.

3.2.1.2   Validity

In general terms, the notion of validity may be regarded as synonymous with truthfulness or appropriateness. In scientific research it refers to whether a study or a test provides the answers to issues it has been designed to address and whether the results and interpretations are applicable to similar samples or populations.

Basic requirements of *test validity* are *construct validity* (does a test actually measure what we expect it to measure), *content validity* (does a test cover the entire, or a representative, sample of the behavior it is intended to measure), and *criterion validity* (are the test results related to the value of the predefined criterion variable). For example, a valid language test will measure patients' linguistic performance and cover various aspects of language functioning, exhibiting high correlation between test results and presented symptoms.

Whereas test validity aspects are focused on test design and its consequences, *experimental validity* is more concerned with procedures and interpretations.

Internal validity refers to the existence of a causal relation between two variables that has to satisfy three criteria: (1) temporal precedence ('cause' precedes 'effect'); (2) covariation ('cause' and 'effect' are related); and (3) non-spuriousness (there are no plausible other explanations for the covariation, or rival hypotheses). Internal validity is more a quantitative than a qualitative feature, because apart from controlled variations in the independent variable, characteristics of the instruments, and statistical methods, there are a number of uncontrolled/uncontrollable sources of variation that may produce additional or alternative explanations. Direct manipulation of the independent variable will lead to greater internal validity than simple inferences based on observed correlations or associations. Some of the so-called threats to internal validity are briefly described in Table 3.1 (Campbell and Stanley, 1963; Creswell, 2009; Rich, 2010; Trochim, 2006).

Confounding (most closely related to the requirement of non-spuriousness) – changes observed in the dependent variable – may be attributed to some uncontrolled/uncontrollable variation that justifies rival hypotheses. In that respect all threats to validity are said to have confounding or extraneous effects.

Table 3.1   Threats to internal validity.

Threat	Description
Selection bias	Caused by pretest differences between study groups that are unknown to or neglected by the researcher.
History	Events that occurred between pre- and posttest situations, unrelated to treatment, may affect the outcome of the study (especially relevant in repeated-measures design).
Maturation	Participants change over time due to normal developmental and maturational factors. If these changes occur between measurements it may not be clear to what extent they (rather than treatment) contribute to the outcome.
Testing situation	Particularly on tests of ability and achievement, practice effects may occur. Also, regular and frequent participation in testing may lead to some subjects being more "test wise."
Regression to the mean (statistical regression)	Participants' performance may be affected by chance factors: those who have performed extremely well or extremely poorly on the pretest tend to perform more in line with the average on the posttest.
Ceiling/floor effect	Performance has reached maximum or minimum that the test allows.
Attrition (mortality)	Some subjects fail to complete the study. Not accounting for drop-out rate may lead to erroneous inferences about the effects of treatment.
Selection-maturation interaction	Members of experimental/treatment group develop/ change over time differently from those in the comparison/control group.
Diffusion	Treatment effects spread from the experimental group to the control group (possible disappearance of between-group differences).
Compensatory rivalry/ resentful demoralization	Subjects in one group make additional efforts to match up to subjects in the other group, reaching performance levels they would not have achieved in a natural setting or the subjects may be overcome by the feeling that "it's just not worth trying."
Experimenter bias, lack of implementation integrity and instrument change	Investigators behave inconsistently in different testing conditions (e.g. toward the members of the experimental group and control); treatment is not delivered as planned; there are changes in instruments, procedures, programs for analysis, and/or observers (e.g. concentration, fatigue).
Post-hoc bias	The investigator is not objectively interpreting the data.

Table 3.2   Threats to external validity.

Threat	Description
Situation	The testing situation in general and its specific details (e.g. time, place, distractions).
Aptitude–treatment/ selection–treatment interaction	A particular sample of subjects may not be representative of the population, having features that interact with the independent variable in idiosyncratic ways.
Interaction between treatment and testing	In the broadest sense refers to the subjects being affected by the knowledge that they are being tested.
Pretest and posttest effects	The subjects are affected by pretesting in ways that reflect on their posttest scores (pretest sensitization).
Reactivity	Causal relationships occur only as a consequence of studying them and would not occur in different situations or outside the research context.
Multiple treatment interference	Several treatments are applied simultaneously or within short periods of time to the same subjects, producing results that cannot exclude interaction and/or cumulative effects.

External validity refers to generalizability of the obtained results and conclusions. It too is a matter of degree. A study with high external validity is the one whose results and conclusions are applicable to other individuals, places, and times. This is only possible if the subjects in the study and/or constructs measured are representative of the population from which the sample was taken. Some threats to external validity are briefly described in Table 3.2 (Campbell and Stanley, 1963; Creswell, 2009; Rich, 2010; Trochim, 2006).

The safest way to strengthen external validity is to replicate one's own study in different conditions, with different people. Replicability is an important scientific requirement of any research. A study is replicable (or reproducible) if other (independent) researchers in different laboratories get similar results following the same methodology.

The best way to increase internal and external validity is to use control groups and randomly select and assign participants. Working with reasonably large samples also contributes to research quality. It is important to collect all available subject-related information (interviews and standardized tests, such as intelligence and achievement tests, appropriate tests pertaining to specific disorders and conditions). Whenever possible, it is good research practice to use pretests.

Ecological validity refers to the extent to which the results are applicable outside the laboratory. An ecologically valid study mimics real-life situations while preserving the characteristics of scientifically sound research. Some trade-off is unavoidable: good experimental studies have satisfactory internal validity, but while the high degree of control and manipulation allows inferences about causality, it makes the study unnatural. Observational research does not provide such controlled conditions (and consequently has low(er) internal validity) but its high ecological validity is achieved by carrying out the study in a natural environment.

External and ecological validity are independent. Also, an experiment cannot be externally valid if it is not internally valid, but the opposite does not necessarily apply. Additional types of experimental validity include intentional validity (does the method measure what the study was designed to assess) and conclusion validity (to what extent are the studied variables related).

Section Summary

Concerns in experimental design: reliability and validity

Reliability

- inter-rater reliability
- test–retest reliability
- intra-rater reliability
- inter-method reliability
- parallel forms reliability
- internal consistency.

Validity

- test validity
- experimental validity
  - ○ *internal validity* – causal relation between two variables
    - – *threats to internal validity*: selection bias; history; maturation; testing situation; regression to the mean (statistical regression); ceiling/floor effect; attrition (mortality); selection–maturation interaction; diffusion; compensatory rivalry/resentful demoralization; experimenter bias; lack of implementation integrity and instrument change; post hoc bias
  - ○ *external validity* – generalizability
    - – *threats to external validity*: threat; situation; aptitude–treatment/selection–treatment interaction; interaction between treatment and testing; pretest and posttest effects; reactivity; multiple treatment interference
- ecological validity.

3.2.2   Choosing Appropriate Experimental Design

Research can be carried out on individuals (single-case studies) or groups (single- and multiple-group studies). Multiple-group studies involve at least two groups – an experimental/treatment and a control/comparison group. Typically, a control group is the one to which no treatment is applied as opposed to the experimental/treatment group. The term 'treatment' does not necessarily mean active intervention – it may refer to any change in the independent variable, natural or caused by experimental manipulation (e.g. in a study of age-dependent changes in voice characteristics, the process of aging will be the independent variable (selected) and measures of voice will be the dependent variable). Many studies are designed to compare treatments or conditions, in which case we do not speak of control and experimental groups, but of comparison groups. Furthermore, studies may have single-variable design (one independent variable) or factorial design (at least two independent variables, and at least one of them can be manipulated); they can be between-subjects or within-subjects (repeated measures) studies. Depending on the amount of control over other variables, studies based on single-variable design are further classified (increasing in the degree of control) into: non-experimental/pre-experimental designs, quasi-experimental designs, and true experimental designs (Campbell and Stanley, 1963; Creswell, 2009; Rich, 2010; Trochim, 2006). All of these types belong to the larger class of quantitative methods, but some of them, especially in the non-experimental and pre-experimental category, may be considered mixed or qualitative (e.g. observational studies), since the classification is not a rigid one and each method is positioned on the continuum between quantitative and qualitative ends. The type of data to be collected determines whether the method of conducting research will be quantitative (numerical data), qualitative (textual), or mixed and whether the scales used are nominal, ordinal, interval, or some other. In the case of developmental studies the decision has to be made between longitudinal and cross-sectional studies. Quantitative methods are best if we wish to identify predictors and factors that produce/affect an outcome and if we want to test the (relative) success of a treatment. On the other hand, qualitative methods, which are exploratory in their nature, are preferred when the topic has never been studied before or it has not been studied in specific conditions, or if the investigator cannot single out the important variable(s). Mixed methods, of course, rely on strengths of both approaches (www.cps.nova.edu; www.experiment-resources.com).

3.2.2.1   Non-experimental and pre-experimental design

Although in some sources (e.g. Creswell, 2009) pre-experimental designs are discussed as synonymous to non-experimental, there is a subtle difference, with pre-experimental design moving a notch closer to the quasi-experimental types.

In *non-experimental design* a behavior or phenomenon is observed as it occurs in a natural environment (independent variables have already occurred, beyond the experimenter's control). The greatest problem is its inherent lack of control and lack of any possibility of manipulating independent variables, which may lead to difficulties in distinguishing between cause and effect, failure to detect significant factors and recognize the complexity of causation, to name just a few. Although non-experimental studies do not represent the strongest research design, they are useful for a number of reasons: some variables cannot be manipulated due to their characteristics, ethical or practical considerations, or the researcher wants to observe certain types of behavior and phenomena in natural environments. Furthermore, non-experimental research may be used as an exploratory tool to get an idea of possible causal relationships in order to formulate hypotheses for a future study (Campbell and Stanley, 1963; Creswell, 2009; Rich, 2010; Trochim, 2006).

In *descriptive/exploratory surveys* the researcher assesses existing conditions and practice through observations, descriptions, and available documentation. Variables include opinions, attitudes, or facts, and data are collected by means of question-naires, surveys, interviews, or self-reports. Univariate studies describe the frequency of occurrence of a phenomenon or behavior. The aim of descriptive/exploratory studies is not to determine causal relations, but possible correlations among varia-bles, prevalence (e.g. number of children diagnosed with dyslexia out of at-risk can-didates), incidence (frequency of newly developing cases over a given period out of at-risk population), and distribution.

Interrelationship/difference studies include correlational studies, *ex post facto* studies, and developmental studies.

Observational/correlational research measures two or more variables and tries to establish correlation (not causal relations) between them. There is no manipulation of independent variables, subjects are not randomly selected or assigned but observed in their existing conditions. This lack of control is a disadvantage, but the results may be applicable in clinical contexts as this method enables collecting large amounts of data and observing relationships in naturally occurring phenomena and behavior.

Ex post facto studies are also correlational. Research is carried out post-treatment: the groups differ in some respect and the researcher tries to determine how.

Developmental studies are designed to include the element of time. They can be longitudinal (pooled time series) or cross-sectional.

A typical longitudinal study follows a single person (case study) or a group of subjects over time, taking samples of the dependent variable at regular intervals. Obviously, sampling periods must be carefully determined, depending on the depend-ent variable, and may change over the course of the study. The nature of these studies makes them expensive, time-consuming and labor-intensive, and subject to most threats to internal validity (e.g. maturation, history, attrition). Causality can be inferred, but details about the true causes of the observed effects are usually missing or incomplete. Generalizability is not the strongest feature of these studies, mostly due to small sample size.

Cross-sectional studies eliminate some disadvantages of longitudinal ones by using a cross-section of the population. For example, rather than basing our conclu-sions about the emergence of children's phonological systems on a longitudinal study that will take years to complete we can use several groups of children of different ages and analyze their phonological systems. Obviously, groups need to be equal in all other respects (e.g. IQ, sex, health). In a clinical setting, additional variables may need to be considered (e.g. onset and severity of a condition, comorbidity, duration and method of rehabilitation). This is not always possible and may lead to results being influenced by individual differences. Although this type of design takes care of some of the threats to internal validity inherent in longitudinal studies, it is still weak in determining causality. However, its power of generalizability is satisfactory.

Developmental studies may be classified as quasi-experimental studies, depending on the amount of manipulation and control added to the normal course of development.

Characteristics of *pre-experimental design* include absence of control or comparison groups, little or no manipulation of independent variables, and little or no control over extraneous factors that influence the outcome, hence low degrees of validity and reliability (Campbell and Stanley, 1963; Creswell, 2009; Rich, 2010; Trochim, 2006).

Single-case (subject) (N = 1) studies are based on repeated, systematic measurement of the dependent variable before, during, and after manipulation of the independent variable. These may involve an individual or a small group of (often in some way related) people monitored over time for possible patterns of responses to treatment. Apart from direct observation these studies may involve interviews, archival records, physical artifacts, and audiovisual materials. They improve understanding of cause and effect, but are not generalizable.

There are three types of single-case (subject) designs. In the A-B-A withdrawal design and its variants (A-B, A-B-A-B) the subject is exposed to conditions without treatment (A) and with it (B) and the differences in behavior are analyzed. This design is frequently applied in clinical settings to check for treatment effects. Multiple baseline designs are used when the effects of treatment in the A-B design are irreversible. Alternating treatments design is used to study relative effects of more than one treatment. The problem with this design is possible carry-over of effects among treatments.

In *one-group after (one-shot case study; one-group posttest only) design* there is one group of subjects and one measure: after applying the treatment (posttest). This means that we are attributing the measured value to treatment without knowing what the patient's status before the treatment was. This is a very weak design riddled with many threats to internal and external validity (e.g. history, maturation, selection, attrition, interaction between selection and treatment) and should be avoided, or any inferences must be carefully evaluated.

In *one-group pretest–posttest design (one-group before–after)* there is one group of subjects and two measures – one taken before the application of treatment (pretest), and the other after treatment (posttest). The two measures are compared and the difference attributed to treatment. This type is subject to most threats to internal validity and offers little room for causal inferences. Threats to external validity include interaction between testing and treatment as well as interaction between selection and treatment.

In *non-equivalent posttest only (static-group) design* there are two groups, two different treatments are applied, and the differences in the measures (posttest) are attributed to the difference between treatments, but there are no data on the status before treatment (pretest/pre-treatment) in either group. This also includes cases when treatment was applied to one group but not to the other. This design is similar to posttest-only control group design (which belongs to the category of true experimental designs) but lacks random subject selection and group assignment. Threats to internal validity include selection, attrition, and selection–maturation interaction. Selection–treatment interaction is a threat to external validity.

3.2.2.2 Quasi-experimental design

Quasi-experimental design resembles true experimental design but lacks random subject selection (and frequently assignment) and has less control over extraneous (confounding) variables. It enables comparison of groups and manipulation of independent variables. It is mainly used in applied research, particularly in cases when it is impossible to control for potentially confounding variables and/or when subjects cannot be randomly selected and assigned to groups for ethical, practical, or other reasons. Such studies are called 'natural experiments' because subjects already belong to specific populations due to conditions beyond the experimenter's control and groups are formed by matching rather than randomization (Campbell and Stanley, 1963; Creswell, 2009; Rich, 2010; Trochim, 2006). They are easier and more frequently used than true experiments. In clinical linguistics and phonetics, much published work is quasi-experimental, because random subject selection and large sample studies are often not possible, due to the small number of available participants.

In this type of study the results are more likely to be interpreted as correlations than causality, although it is possible to have quasi-experimental designs exhibiting causal relationships (in which case rival hypotheses have to be clearly excluded). A well-designed quasi-experiment should render rival hypotheses unlikely, if not impossible. In order to do that it is best to consider potential rival hypotheses in the planning phase so that sampling and data collection may control for these factors.

The *non-equivalent groups design (NEGD)* is one of the most frequent types of quasi-experimental research. Such studies have the form of a pretest–posttest experiment but share with other types the common lack of random subject selection and assignment. Sample groups are selected (by matching) from two populations. In the selection process, care has to be taken that groups be as similar as possible: the only difference between them should be the difference in treatment, i.e. in the dependent variable that the study is intended to measure. No matter how careful the selection it is unlikely that the two groups do not differ in some unknown and uncontrollable details (e.g. motivation, family support), which makes them not equivalent, hence the name non-equivalent groups design. Obviously, this presents a threat to internal validity (especially selection threats) because there is no way of ensuring that the results of the study are unaffected by these differences. On the other hand, this design is a good alternative when it is impossible to conduct a true experimental study with random group assignment. It controls reasonably well some of the threats to internal validity, such as history, maturation, testing, instruments, and attrition.

(Interrupted) time series design involves multiple pretesting (baseline) and post-testing on a single group. Its main advantage is the ability to reveal trends, because the effect of treatment is revealed in the differences between the pattern of pre- and posttest responses. This type of research design takes care of many confounding variables because they exist in pre-treatment as well as in post-treatment responses,

with the exception of history and possibly interaction between testing and treatment. It may be used to assess the impact of some naturally occurring event or of some broad treatment within a group.

Interrupted time series design with (non-equivalent) control group is basically the same type of design as above and involves existing groups but tries to match the treatment group with a control group. Potential threats to internal validity can be found with respect to history, maturation, and instrument changes.

In *equivalent time series design* there is one group of subjects and treatment is applied or withheld according to a predetermined protocol. Measures are taken in with- and without-treatment conditions and possible differences are attributed to the treatment. This type of study may be used when no control group is available and when treatment effects are short term. History is a potential threat to internal validity; interaction between testing and treatment, and multiple-treatment effects may be threats to external validity.

In *counterbalanced design* there is no pretesting, but all groups eventually receive all treatments. The so-called Latin square is a type of this design. For example, if there are three treatments that we want to apply to all subjects, the non-random sample will be divided into three equal groups and each group will receive treatment in a different order. Obviously, the number of groups should equal the number of different treatments. Related to that is the *switching replications design*. It starts as a typical two-group pre–post study: both groups are pretested, treatment is implemented to one group, both are posttested. Then the groups' roles are reversed: the one that was originally control is given treatment and the originally treated group serves as control. This design has improved internal and external validity and resolves ethical issues of selectively giving treatment to some patients.

In *regression discontinuity design* the subjects are assigned to treatment or control groups on the basis of a cut-off score on a pretest. Obviously, this type of design is susceptible to selection threats.

In *proxy pretest design*, the subjects are asked to recollect what their status had been at a certain time before the study started. Although imprecise for many research purposes, this type of design is useful in measuring perceived change. Another type of study belonging to this group relies on data collected before the study began.

In a *retrospective study*, existing data are used to evaluate the effects of some past treatment.

Separate pre–post samples design involves different groups of subjects in the pretest and posttest stages. This type is typically applied when the fluctuation of subjects is such that it is impossible to include the same individuals at two different times. One group is taken as the pretest group and the other as the posttest group. The strength of this design may be improved by choosing groups that are equal in all respects except in the treatment, but the researcher must be aware of its limitations and pitfalls (no information about how the individuals in the first group would react to treatment or what the status of the individuals in the second group was prior to treatment). A control condition may be added: there may be two different separate groups, one being pretested and the other posttested, but without treatment.

Double pretest design takes care of some of the threats to internal validity that are characteristic of quasi-experimental designs in general (e.g. selection–maturation).

Two measurements are taken at different times before applying the variable to be measured. Possible changes due to factors other than the dependent variable are expected to emerge in this kind of design.

Recurrent institutional cycle (patched-up) design is often used in field work (e.g. clinical settings) and it typically involves a combination of longitudinal and cross-sectional measures. A group of patients may be administered one type of treatment and tested (posttest only), another group may be introduced at the same time and tested later, treatment may be discontinued or improved, better diagnostic tools may be developed which will cause different assignment to groups, etc. Thus, the same patients may be at one point subjects of a cross-sectional study, while at the same time being followed over longer periods of time (longitudinal design). It starts as a less than adequate design, but as the study progresses the researcher adds on control mechanisms to minimize rival hypotheses, improve validity, and refine research.

3.2.2.3   True experimental design

True experimental design may be defined as a hypothesis-testing research design that allows inferences about cause and effect. There are several essential elements of true experiments that help test the hypothesis: (1) random selection and group assignment of subjects; (2) two groups that function as a source of comparison and as control for rival hypotheses: one that receives treatment (experimental/treatment group) and one that does not (control); (3) generalizability and replicability of results (Campbell and Stanley, 1963; Creswell, 2009; Rich, 2010; Trochim, 2006). The basic logic of experimental design is this: two groups were the same to start with (pretest); treatment was applied to one (experimental) group; as a consequence, this group is now (posttest) different from the group that did not receive treatment (control); the difference can be attributed to treatment (causal relationship) because any other effects (extraneous/confounding variables) or alternative explanations (rival hypotheses) were controlled for and ruled out; the same would happen in identical conditions elsewhere (replicability, generalizability). In other words, experimental research can prove that manipulation of the independent variable affects the dependent variable, as opposed to correlational type of studies where the researcher can only predict or describe a relationship (correlation) between variables. Among disadvantages of true experimental studies are their unnaturalness, ethical considerations, and feasibility (Campbell and Stanley, 1963; Creswell, 2009; Rich, 2010; Trochim, 2006).

Posttest-only (after-only) control group/two groups posttest only design is similar to non-equivalent posttest only design, but with random subject selection. It is the simplest of experimental designs, easy to use, and good for assessing causal relationships. It involves a treatment/experimental group and a control group. The key question is whether the two groups are different after treatment. The groups' means on one or more measures are compared by statistical analysis (e.g. t-test, one-way analysis of variance (ANOVA)). Random assignment supposedly takes care of internal and external validity threats, but if used in institutional settings (e.g. school, clinic) it may be subject to internal validity threats stemming from social interaction (e.g. compensatory rivalry/resentful demoralization). This design may be used when pretesting is impossible and the sample of subjects is large enough (>30 per group). Research may be conducted *within groups* or *between groups*. It may be randomized (randomized groups design) or matched (matched groups design).

In *pretest–posttest control group (pretest–posttest two-group) design* there are two groups formed by random selection and assignment of subjects, two measurements (pretest and posttest) administered to each group, and treatment applied to one group (treatment/experimental group) and not the other (control). In terms of internal validity this is a powerful design, but it may not be generalizable because the subjects may be affected by the knowledge that they are being pretested (threats to external validity).

Solomon four-group design is another design that works well at protecting internal and external validity. It combines the pretest–posttest control group design and posttest-only group design.

Experimental design does not necessarily have to be conducted on two independent groups (*between groups/subjects design*). Instead, a single group of subjects may be measured under different conditions (*within group/subject design*). This is called *repeated measures design*, reflecting the fact that the same group of subjects is repeatedly measured for different dependent variables. Some of the advantages of this variation are that it requires fewer subjects and eliminates the issue of nonequivalent groups. Apart from the fact that it is not always applicable as an alternative to between-subjects design, it involves some methodological concerns, such as practice, fatigue, and carry-over effects. Some of the problems stemming from order effects inherent in this type of study may be resolved by counterbalancing (e.g. Latin squares, randomized blocks) (Creswell, 2009; Trochim, 2006; www.cps.nova.edu; www.experiment-resources.com) and increasing the time interval between treatments. One of the considerations in deciding whether to use between- or within-subjects designs is external validity (Campbell and Stanley, 1963; Creswell, 2009; Rich, 2010; Trochim, 2006).

In *within- and between-subject pre- and posttest type of study* a pool of subjects is selected and all subjects are submitted to pretesting, followed by random assignment into treatment (experimental) and control groups. The post-treatment measures may then be taken as a within-subject repeated measures design in the control group and group membership may be taken as a between-subject factor.

Factorial design is a complex research design where two or more independent variables are studied in order to determine their independent and interactive effects on the dependent variable. This design allows testing of more than one hypothesis, building potentially confounding variables into the design as factors, and testing interaction effects. The experiment may be in the form of posttest-only control group design or pretest–posttest control group design with or without random assignment.

The two kinds of effects to look for are *main effects* (reflected in the deviation of two or more treatment means from the grand mean) and *interactions* (the degree to which the effect of one independent variable (factor) depends on the level of the other independent variable (factor) in affecting the dependent variable). The variables that the independent variable interacts with are called moderator variables. They may be treatment- or subject-related. For example, in a study designed to evaluate the quality of speech of cochlear implant users the researcher may want to determine how age at implantation and preoperative rehabilitation (independent variables) affect the score (dependent variable), each on its own (main effects) and when taken together (interaction). The results may show a main effect on only one variable (either age at implantation or rehabilitation affects the score) or on both variables simultaneously. An interaction effect exists when differences on one factor depend on the other.

Apart from being the best way to study interaction effects, this type of design replaces a series of independent studies.

Section Summary

Choosing appropriate experimental design

- qualitative, quantitative, mixed
- case-studies vs. group studies
- between-subjects vs. within-subjects (repeated measures) design
- single-variable design vs. factorial design.

Non-experimental and pre-experimental design

Non-experimental design

- descriptive/exploratory surveys
- interrelationship/difference studies
  - observational/correlational
  - *ex post facto*
  - developmental studies
    - longitudinal
    - cross-sectional.

Pre-experimental design

- single-case (subject) (N = 1) studies
- one-group after (one-shot case study; one-group posttest only) design
- one-group pretest–posttest design (one-group before–after)
- non-equivalent posttest only (static group).

Quasi-experimental design

- the non-equivalent groups design (NEGD)
- (interrupted) time series design
- interrupted time series design with (non-equivalent) control group
- equivalent time series design
- counterbalanced design and the switching replications design
- regression discontinuity design
- proxy pretest design

- retrospective study
- separate pre–post samples design
- double pretest design
- recurrent institutional cycle (patched-up) design.

True experimental design

Basic characteristics

- random selection and group assignment of subjects
- two groups that function as a source of comparison and as control for rival hypotheses
- generalizability and replicability of results.

Single variable design

- posttest-only (after-only) control group/two groups posttest-only design
- pretest–posttest control group (pretest–posttest two-group) design
- Solomon four-group design.

Factorial design – two or more independent variables

- main effects
- interactions.

3.2.3 Subject Selection, Data Collection, and Data Interpretation

The next step in research design is *subject selection*. Since it is impossible to study all individuals who share some characteristics, behavior, or are subjected to the treatment that we want to examine (population), we need to engage a smaller group that is representative of the larger group (sample). *Probability sampling* involves random selection – any individual can be selected from a population with equal probability. *Non-probability sampling* does not involve random selection. It can be *convenience sampling* (also called accidental or haphazard), in which the subjects are recruited from the individuals who are "at hand" (healthy volunteers or patients who happen to be available), or *purposive sampling*, which is carried out in order to find subjects with predefined characteristics that we want to study (e.g. hearing impairment) (Campbell and Stanley, 1963; Creswell, 2009; Rich, 2010; Trochim, 2006).

Random selection is not synonymous with random assignment (random allocation of the selected subjects to treatment, or experimental vs. control groups). Non-random selection may be combined with random assignment, for example we may select a group of hearing-impaired subjects by means of purposive sampling, but randomly assign them to two treatment groups for the purposes of the study.

Whenever possible, random sampling should be preferred, but in clinical linguistics and phonetics research, it is frequently not feasible or desirable. Since research questions that are typically asked in clinical settings are determined in part by the nature of the field of study, subject selection is more often purposive than random. When randomization is impossible, other steps include *matching*, which ensures that the subjects in one group (e.g. experimental) match those in the other (e.g. control) with respect to characteristics that are related to the dependent variable (e.g. age, sex), *randomized block designs* or using *analysis of covariance* (ANCOVA) that will equalize any initial differences between groups or on a covariate.

The number of necessary subjects is influenced by the aim of the study, and the population to which the results are expected to be generalized, but at this stage the minimum sample size should be calculated, taking into consideration all subject-related threats to internal validity (e.g. attrition, history, maturation). Standardized tests should be used to equalize the subjects on variables that are not part of the study. All relevant background information on the subjects should be collected and taken into consideration before making the final selection (Campbell and Stanley, 1963; Creswell, 2009; Rich, 2010; Trochim, 2006; www.experiment-resources.com; www.cps.nova.edu).

Next, the *instruments and data collection* procedures need to be defined (e.g. testing, recording, interview, etc.), all the time keeping in mind internal and external validity. Data collection needs to include information on the place and manner of conducting the experiments (individually or in groups, laboratory or school/clinic).

Once the design has been decided upon, in the process of *conducting the experiment* it is very important that the experimenters be consistent in their instructions, attitudes toward subjects, interaction with them, timing, etc. All experiments need to be carried out under identical conditions. Whenever possible it is advisable to use pilot studies. It may seem like a waste of time, but in the long run they may save the study because they will tell us what our misconceptions might be, whether the instructions are clear, timing right and material appropriate, how typical subjects behave. They may reveal possible floor and ceiling effects and confounding variables, and point to some necessary design modifications. If possible, it is advisable to get some introspective feedback from the subjects after testing. Also, when appropriate, a training session should be included before the test. It will familiarize subjects with the test and control for any learning effects and initial differences between subjects or groups.

When we finally have the raw data they need to be organized and prepared for statistical analysis. At the same time, *well-organized data* will enable a clearer look at the effects that the research was intended to study and make inferences and interpretations more systematic.

Experimental design should also include *statistical methods* that will be used and the significance level against which the results will be checked. Statistical methods should be suitable for the type of data collected and generally have two purposes: descriptive (summarize and describe the collected data) and inferential (enable inferences from the collected data, including generalization to the population). Choice of statistical method(s) will also influence the procedure of data collection and organization.

Regardless of design, sampling procedures, hypotheses, and statistical methods, *interpretation and presentation* of research results should be grounded on theory and previous work, it should logically follow from the study and clearly address the originally defined problem/question.

Section Summary

Subject selection, data collection, and data interpretation

Subject selection

- probability sampling (random selection)
- non-probability sampling (non-random selection)
  - convenience sampling
  - purposive sampling
  - matching.

Instruments and data collection
Conducting the experiment:

- pilot studies
- training/practice sessions.

Data organization
Statistical methods:

- descriptive
- inferential.

Interpretation and presentation

3.3   General Discussion

Although true experimental design may seem appealing due to its highly controlled conditions and the apparently foolproof causal inferences that can be drawn from the results obtained, it must have become clear by now that a good experiment is very difficult to plan and conduct. Moreover, in the context of humanities and social sciences true experimental design is appropriate in a very small proportion of research: according to some authors not more than 10% (Trochim, 2006). For example, in studying child language, true experimental design may ensure greater control of the variable studied (e.g. speech comprehension, level of phonological development), but dealing with some threats to internal validity may give rise to others, especially in matching procedures. In addition, generalizability of results obtained in such studies applied to small children may be questionable.

Obviously, in a clinical setting one of the key issues in preventing more frequent use of true experimental designs is an ethical one, because random group assignment would mean that some patients would be denied treatment for purely experimental reasons.

Observational studies have the advantage of 'naturalness' (hence their nickname: naturalistic), and absence of possibly harmful treatments, to name just two most obvious ones. They are, therefore, suitable for studies dealing, for example, with small children or patients with difficulties in communication. Field experiments may be considered a subtype of naturalistic research, because data collection happens in the natural environment of the subjects or some other data source. Naturalistic studies should not be confused with natural experiments. These are situations when there has been a substantial change in some characteristic of the population (e.g. epidemic studies) or individuals (e.g. feral children).

Clearly, in observational studies, the experimenter has limited control over collected material. The very presence of the experimenter decreases the naturalness of the situation, and there may be technical limitations (e.g. noisy background in a school). Some of the problems may be solved by engaging children in structured play and directed rather than fully spontaneous activities, using rooms with two-way mirrors, preconditioning the subjects by making contact and familiarizing them with the experimenter and the setting in advance, etc. An observational study can be valid only if the experimenter is aware of the confounding factors and accounts for them. Some of the biases inherent in observational studies may be reduced by sophisticated statistical methods. Whenever possible, results should be quantified, rather than relying on subjects' responses or experimenters' interpretations (Campbell and Stanley, 1963; Creswell, 2009; Rich, 2010; Trochim, 2006).

To conclude, the best research design is the one that is well grounded in theory, adequately addresses the well-defined research question, using appropriate sampling and testing procedures, maximally satisfying the requirements of validity, reliability, and replicability.

3.4 Resources

The research page on the website of the American Speech-Language Hearing Association (www.asha.org/research/) provides links to a variety of resources for students and researchers, including databases, evidence-based practice, and grant funding.

The privately owned site www.experiment-resources.com contains information about many topics related to experimental research, including methods, study designs, key concepts in statistics, and ethics.

References

Campbell, D. T. and J. C. Stanley (1963). *Experimental and Quasi-Experimental Designs for Research*. Chicago: Rand McNally College Publishing Company.

Creswell, John W. (2009). *Research Design: Qualitative, Quantitative and Mixed Methods Approaches*, 3rd edn. California: Sage.

Rich, J. (2010). *Psychological Testing: A Guide to Psychological Testing and Assessment*. http://www.psychologicaltesting.com (accessed September 10, 2010).

Trochim, William M. (2006). *The Research Methods Knowledge Base*, 2nd edn. www.socialresearchmethods.net/kb/ (version current as of October 20, 2006).

4   The Investigation of Speech Production: Experimental and Quasi-experimental Approaches

B. May Bernhardt, Penelope Bacsfalvi, Marcy Adler-Bock, Geetanjalee Modha, and Barbara Purves

In its description of human attributes in terms of "Body and Function" on the one hand, and "Activity and Participation" on the other, the International Classification for Function (ICF; WHO, 2007) provides a framework for research on speech production. Body and Function refer to anatomy and physiology of speech production and perception. Activity and Participation relate to people's everyday communication. Communication difficulties may result from body or function impairments, and/or from restrictions on activity and participation. Thus, research on communication has a wide range of possibilities. This chapter discusses topics ranging from data collection and analysis at the micro-level (body/function) to the macro-level (comprehensibility studies), although only briefly touches on topics that are discussed in depth in other chapters (experimental and quasi-experimental research methods, data recording, transcription, qualitative research). Our focus in this chapter is on speech production and its (re)habilitation. Methods may apply to all types of studies (experimental/quasi-experimental; intervention) or more uniquely to one type. The theoretical underpinnings of the chapter follow below.

4.1   Overview of Speech Difficulties: Theoretical Underpinnings

The chapter takes a broad view of speech difficulties, and is based on an interactive model of speech production (Stemberger, 1985), one that does not espouse a strict separation of phonetics and phonology. Breakdown can occur at single or multiple

Research Methods in Clinical Linguistics and Phonetics: A Practical Guide, First Edition. Edited by Nicole Müller and Martin J. Ball.

levels during speech production, with interactions between many components of the language system (Bernhardt, Stemberger, and Charest, 2010). Although research tends to focus on one "domain" of the language system, the researcher needs to at least reflect on potential interactions with other domains in setting up stimuli for elicitation, and in interpretation of the data later.

Although we assume that representations are based primarily on input (auditory-perceptual), motoric and structural articulatory constraints may also impact the representation and access of speech sounds and structures, through within-speaker memory traces for speech production. In current models of the lexicon, a "word" is assumed to have both auditory-acoustic and articulatory-motor information or "representations" (Bernhardt and Stemberger, 1998), which generally are considered to be aligned with each other. However, the perception–production match can misalign given, for example, noisy environments, reduced hearing or articulatory disturbances, i.e. dental retainers, tooth loss, or structural/functional impairments. The longer a person's hearing or oral mechanisms remain atypical, the wider the range of *acceptability* may become for the alignment of perception and production. For example, a speaker with a history of cleft palate may continue with long-standing atypical speech patterns, even after surgery significantly improves the oral mechanism structures (Gibbon and Hardcastle, 1989). The phonetic (articulatory) output constraints can create a phonological system that diverges from the typical system in the perception–production alignment. Listeners familiar with the "atypical" speech may also develop a wider tolerance for the perception–production alignment. The line between "typical" and "atypical/disordered" thus is not fixed. Similarly, degree of experience with accented speech or different dialects may affect a listener's judgments. Any research evaluating or requiring naturalness or typicality of speech thus needs to consider speaker/listener experience and bias.

By phonological system, the chapter assumes the entire phonological hierarchy from the phrase to the feature (Bernhardt and Stemberger, 1998). Research may focus on one or various levels of the phonological hierarchy, depending on the goals of the study. Well-designed experimental studies in the phonological domain will include (a) large, randomly selected cohorts balanced for demographic characteristics, (b) theoretically grounded speech elicitation probes (see below), and (c) comprehensive data analysis, with reliable evaluations. Generally, speech production research utilizes quasi-experimental small *n* or single subject designs (e.g. Bacsfalvi, 2007; Bernhardt *et al.*, 2003; Bernhardt *et al.*, 2010; Gibbons and Hardcastle, 1989), due to the labor-intensive aspects of such investigations and the lack of sufficient funding for larger studies. While quasi-experimental studies cannot provide population-level statistical patterns, they can be conducted with rigor in terms of design, data collection, and analysis, and can often provide more detailed analyses of individual performance than is possible in large-scale studies. Human communication is complex and such detailed analysis of individuals (case studies and small *n* studies) can help unravel this complexity at least for one or a few individuals. This chapter provides an overview of possibilities and limits concerning speech production research using experimental and quasi-experimental designs, focusing on the following:

- Data collection considerations (participants; elicitation methods).
- Evaluation methods (perceptual, technological, comprehensibility).
- Triangulation of data.

Section Summary

- This chapter assumes no strict separation of domains of language. Researchers need to consider the potential interactions of language domains even when focusing on one "small" aspect of phonetics.
- The phonological system has many levels from the phrase to the feature. Research can be focused at one or many levels assuming the caveat above.
- Perception-production representational systems are generally aligned, but may misalign. This misalignment may affect the speaker's output and/or a listener's perception. The researcher needs to consider possible influences of speaker and listener experience and bias with typical or disordered speech, language background and dialect.
- Speech research tends to focus on individuals or small groups of individuals, which provides a wealth of detail about speech patterns. Large trials remain to be done.

4.2   Data Collection Considerations

4.2.1   *Participants*

Ideally, research will provide information across ages, genders, cultural, language and dialect backgrounds for both typical and atypical speech production. The reality is that even with larger-scale inter-agency/university collaborations, researchers are able to collect data only in a limited number of languages/dialects, and from a limited number of participants who do not necessarily represent a homogeneous group. However, this does not mean that information gathered from these participants is not important or interesting. As noted above, case studies and controlled single subject designs can provide details on individual patterns that may challenge or support theories and models and advance knowledge about human communication. While controlling for some participant variables, the researcher needs (a) to identify those variables that have not been controlled, and (b) to describe the participant demographic characteristics in detail.

4.2.2   *Speech Elicitation*

4.2.2.1   *Recordings*

Recording methods are discussed in Chapter 10. One guiding principle is crucial – to maintain a high signal-to-noise ratio during recording.

4.2.2.2   *Stimuli for elicitation*

Connected speech and/or word/phrase lists and/or singleton segments (consonants, vowels) may be the target of elicitation. Natural conversational speech best represents everyday communication. However, the conversation needs to be set up to maximize the speaker's comfort and speaking naturalness, for example, by using familiar conversational partners. A number of aspects of conversational speech are also challenging for research focusing on specific speech targets. Between-participant comparisons may be difficult, because speakers may say very different things. In addition, certain speech targets are naturally lower in frequency and may not appear in the samples. It can also be difficult to transcribe indistinct conversational speech (when orthographic targets are unknown) or to segment phones for acoustic analysis. The preceding challenges can be partially overcome through use of predictable stimuli material, for example, picture books, oral reading materials, or delayed sentence repetition tasks. The Assessment of Intelligibility of Dysarthric Speech (Yorkston and Beukelman, 1981), for example, includes both word-level and sentence-level stimuli. The Rainbow Passage (Fairbanks, 1940/1960) is also well known, but has the disadvantage of including infrequent words, for example, "grasp," "prism" and "horizon," making it less useful for individuals with limited English vocabulary. In general, oral reading is subject to reading proficiency (either as an advantage or disadvantage) and thus for some people, pictures may be better stimuli. Whatever material is used, however, it is important to consider its appropriateness and relevance for the age, culture, language knowledge, and interests of the participant.

If the researcher decides to use systematically organized word lists for elicitation, a wide variety of phonological contexts need to be considered because of their impact on speech output. Considering phonetic contexts can help control for co-articulation and prosodic effects on segment production and can also provide information on co-articulation. Some examples for English follow, but note that other languages or a bilingual context may require attention to different or additional variables (e.g. tonal differences in tone languages). However, the general principles hold for the following categories:

a   word length, for example, /s/ in "sell" vs. "cellar" vs. "celery" (same vowel and consonant contexts in increasingly longer words);

b   stressed vs. unstressed syllables, for example, /g/ of "guitar" (onset to a weak initial unstressed syllable) vs. /g/ of "garden" (onset to a stressed initial syllable);

c   word position, that is, word-initial (WI), word-final (WF), and word-medial (WM) (which can also be subdivided in terms of coda of the first syllable, onset of the second, or both, i.e. ambisyllabic). In "tractor," for example, the /k/ is a word-medial coda, and the second /t/ is an onset. In "cozy," the /z/ might be considered as onset to the second syllable or as ambisyllabic;

d   singleton (C) or cluster CC(C) (e.g. /s/ of "sing" vs. /s/ of "sting" or "string," that is, with the same vowel but differing onsets);

e   type of clusters (contiguous sequences), for example, /k/ in /kl/ vs. /kɹ/ vs. /kw/ vs. /sk/;

f   type of consonants across vowels by place, manner, and laryngeal features, for
     example, "sip" (Alveolar-Labial) vs. "sick" (Alveolar-Velar) and "sit" (Alveolar-
     Alveolar). (Similar contrasts can be made for manner and laryngeal features.);
g   vowel contexts for consonants, for example, /s/ in "see" vs. "say" (front, high vs.
     mid vowel) versus "sew" (back, mid).

Similar within-word context considerations can be made for vowels. If the research
concerns a particular word position or word shape (e.g. CVC), a variety of segments
will need to be elicited in that context or shape.

Words may be elicited as single items with a naming or sentence cloze technique
or in phrases/sentences. Having more than one token of a target is necessary for later
analysis, but it is not clear what the maximum number of a given target should be
(given learning or fatigue effects within trials). For studies of phonological systems,
single word elicitation is relatively common and ensures clarity of referent and coverage of the phonological system (Masterson, Bernhardt, and Hofheinz, 2005). For
studies focusing on particular segments or co-articulation, carrier phrases are often
used in speech research. Carrier phrases allow consistent parameters for segmentation
for acoustic analyses and provide relatively constant measures of duration, energy,
and pitch (Jurafsky and Martin, 2009). A carrier phrase needs to be constructed,
however, to maximize the naturalness of the articulation, to provide a clear distinction between the target and the surrounding phones (Baken and Orlikoff, 2000), and
to avoid phrase-initial or phrase-final effects. Embedding the target within the utterance avoids the latter effects. For example, the phrase "say _ again" is relatively
common. Adler-Bock *et al.* (2007) elicited /ɹ/ in this phrase except for word-final
(WF) /ɹ/, where the context was "say _ day". The carrier phrase was altered for word
final /ɹ/ because, if the participants used a vowel substitution for /ɹ/, segmentation of
the vowel substitution and the initial vowel of "again" was challenging for acoustic
analysis. Naturalness will sometimes be sacrificed to enhance acoustic analysis but,
ideally, both factors will be considered in stimuli creation.

Section Summary

- Participants: ideally, we would like to have information on people of different ages, genders, cultures, languages, dialects, socioeconomic groups, and
  typicality backgrounds. The individual researcher may only be able to control or consider some of these variables, but at least needs to describe his or
  her participants' demographic characteristics.
- Speech elicitation: a good signal-to-noise ratio and high-fidelity recording
  equipment is essential for data collection.
- Stimuli: conversational speech has higher naturalness than word or sentence lists, but can be more difficult to analyze phonetically. If word lists are
  created, they need to reflect a variety of phonetic contexts. If elicited in carrier phrases, it is important to consider the phonetic context of that phrase.

4.3   Perceptual Evaluation Methods

A variety of methods are available to evaluate speech production. The following section outlines considerations for perceptual (listener) methods, which range from phonetic and/or orthographic transcription to listener judgments of various types.

Phonetic transcription provides detailed information about speech articulation and remains an evaluation method of choice for many studies concerning speech production. See Chapter 11 of the present volume for a detailed account of transcription issues. Guiding principles include considerations of transcriber reliability and decisions on level of narrowness. Bernhardt and Stemberger (2012) describe a methodology for transcription training which involves determination of most important and least important aspects of transcription for a given parameter for a given language, using a team of researchers with knowledge of the language and the domain of interest.

Another perceptually based method involves judgments, for example, rating scales or on/off target judgments (on-, near-, or off-target). The listener hears attempted targets (randomly presented) and makes a decision about the quality of each attempt compared to a pre-described target or "auditory anchor" (Awan and Lawson, 2009; Bacsfalvi, 2007, 2010). Alternatively, the researcher might choose a paired comparison task in which listeners decide which of two tokens presented is more like the target (Radanov, 2007).

Judgment tasks require clear instructions for the listeners, because factors such as rate of speech, fluency, or hesitation may affect the listener's judgments. For example, in Bernhardt *et al.* (2005), everyday listeners disagreed as to which sentence productions were "better," those that sounded more "natural" (but which had misarticulations) or those that were accurate but in slower, careful speech. Researchers must decide whether they want to measure subtle changes or the naturalness or "goodness" of the sound or both, and construct their stimuli and experiment accordingly.

Everyday listeners do have a vital role to play in studies of speech production (and see the section on Comprehensibility below). Their "untrained" ears can provide information on whether the stimuli are socially acceptable or intelligible, that is, whether production is functional for everyday communication (the Activity/Participation aspect of the ICF).

Auditory perception is a reasonably robust aspect of human behavior, but subject to many variables, such as the quality of the signal (signal-to-noise ratio), the headphones used, the training, experience, interest and fatigue of the listener, etc. The researcher has some control over variables of training and experience, stimuli creation, and task appeal. The more personal variables are harder to control, and only overcome by larger listener sample sizes (perhaps 20 to 30 listeners, for statistical power). Due to the potential confounds associated with perceptual evaluations, it is important that research evaluations include other measures of data analysis, for example, acoustic information and articulatory recordings as discussed below.

> **Section Summary**
>
> - Transcription reliability is a key consideration, as is degree of narrowness of transcription required.
> - Non-transcription judgments can be made about speech stimuli, that is, as matching some internal or external anchor or target, or in comparison of paired stimuli.
> - Both "expert" and everyday listeners have something unique to contribute in evaluating speech production.

4.4   Technology and Speech Production Studies

A number of instruments have contributed to our greater understanding of speech production. Articulatory information is obtained for example, with electropalatography (EPG), ultrasound (U/S), electromagnetic articulography (EMA), or magnetic resonance imaging (MRI). Information about palate function and nasality in speech is available through nasoendoscopy, pharyngoscopy, or nasometry. Vocal functioning is interpretable through the use of laryngoscopy or glottography. Acoustic analysis also provides information about speech production, albeit indirectly.

4.4.1   Acoustic Analysis

Acoustic analysis of speech is a relatively common procedure (Hillenbrand *et al.*, 1995; Houde, 1980) and continues to be informative (see Chapter 12 of the present volume). We would add a caveat that acoustic analysis has the semblance of greater accuracy than auditory perception but is itself subject to human judgment and speaker differences. For example, the acoustic speech displays of people with speech difficulties may have indistinct formants (Bacsfalvi, 2007); segmentation of an utterance for purposes of analysis of individual phonemes can thus be even more challenging than for spectrograms from typical speakers. Thus, the researcher must check any automatized displays for accuracy, consider the parameters of measurement carefully, and work towards high intra- and inter-rater reliability.

4.4.2   Articulatory Records

A variety of articulatory measures of speech production have become more widespread in recent research, e.g. electropalatography (EPG; Fletcher, 1992; Gibbon, 1999; Hardcastle, Gibbon, and Jones, 1991), ultrasound (Bacsfalvi, 2007; Bernhardt *et al.*, 2003; Davidson, 2005; Stone, 2005), and electromagnetic articulography (EMA; Katz, Bharadwaj, and Carstens, 1999). These tools (described in turn below) provide information on speech production that is not available from perceptual or acoustic analyses.

4.4.2.1 Electropalatography

For electropalatography (EPG), the speaker wears a (usually) custom-fit artificial palate that fits over the teeth. On a computer screen, EPG provides tongue–palate contact information that can be stored for further analysis (Gibbon, 1999). Some EPG models provide tongue–palate contact synchronization with acoustic signals (Wrench, 2007) or with acoustic signals and ultrasound images (Zharkova, Hewlett, and Hardcastle, 2008). EPG does not, however, offer information on proximity of the tongue to the palate, or on the part of the tongue that is contacting the palate, or whether there is continuous lingual contact (Hardcastle, Gibbon, and Jones, 1991). EPG also does not offer information on tongue shape or clear information on co-articulation. There is probably a lower limit on age of potential use for EPG (perhaps age 4 or 5), and not all speakers can comfortably wear a palate (especially if they have few teeth, or discomfort with acrylic or dental retainers). Repeated measurements over time are difficult with children, because they require continuing adjustment of the palate size. Furthermore, even some typical adult speakers do not accommodate easily to the palate during studies (McAuliffe *et al.*, 2008). It is generally recommended that the speaker wear the palate for a given amount of time on the day of data collection, before data are collected.

4.4.2.2 Ultrasound

An ultrasound display can reveal information about tongue shape and movement (Stone, 2005) from the tongue tip and blade to the tongue root, as well as mid-line tongue grooving. Ultrasound can provide information on static and dynamic tongue shapes and movements for typical and atypical speakers (e.g. Bressmann *et al.*, 2010; Gick, 2002; Lundberg and Stone, 1999; Munhall and Ostry, 1985; Shawker and Sonies, 1985; Stone *et al.*, 1987, 1988, 1992; Stone and Lundberg, 1996) and has been used in intervention case or small *n* studies (e.g. Adler-Bock *et al.*, 2007; Bacsfalvi, 2007, 2010; Bernhardt *et al.*, 2003, 2005; Modha *et al.*, 2008; Shawker and Sonies, 1985).

Depending on the purpose of the study, the researcher may wish to obtain coronal and/or sagittal views of the tongue. The sagittal view provides a measure of tongue root activity, the timing of articulatory events, and overall tongue shape (Gick, Campbell, and Oh, 2001; Gick and Wilson, 2001). Mid-line tongue grooving or elevation/depression of the sides of the tongue can be evaluated with the coronal view. It is important to be aware of the limitations of ultrasound imaging; for example, the jaw and the hyoid bones refract soundwaves before they reach the tongue's surface. Thus, in a sagittal view, shadows may appear at both edges of the image, obscuring parts of the tongue tip and root (Stone, 2005). In a coronal image the lateral edges of the tongue may not be visible due to the shadow created by the air under the tongue (Stone, 2005).

The researcher may choose to employ quantitative or descriptive measures in evaluation of speech characteristics. Quantitative measures can be made using a grid superimposed on the ultrasound image (Stone, 2005; Wrench and Scobbie, 2008). Curvature of the tongue can also be used as a method of analysis, the benefit being that such a measure is not influenced greatly by transducer and head positioning (Stone, 2005). Assuming a study requires reliable tongue shape measurements, relative head stability and orientation is generally considered crucial. Stone (2005) suggests using a bite mold for the speaker across data collection points. Helmets and various other head-stabilizing equipment may be used (Bressmann *et al.*, 2005; McLeod and Wrench, 2008).

Descriptive judgments about speech production (perceptual analyses) and tongue displays may be used in conjunction with or instead of quantitative measures. Judges can be asked to identify presence or absence of particular components of the target phone. Studies which have a descriptive rather than a quantitative purpose may choose less rigid head stabilization for reasons of equipment limitations, participant comfort, or speech naturalness (see Gick, 2002).

In comparison with EPG, ultrasound is less invasive, and does not rely on the presence of intact palates or full sets of teeth. The size of the transducer relative to chin size and tolerance of the head-stabilizing equipment or even the gel may be limiting factors for some speakers.

4.4.2.3   *Palatal function views*

For direct visualization of palatal function, nasoendoscopy (tube inserted through nose to look down on palate) and videofluoroscopy (various radiographic views of the vocal tract, after barium is inserted into the nasal cavity) can assist in detecting structural abnormalities of the palate not visible with other technologies or perceptually. Imaging may demonstrate a phone-specific pattern, compensatory misarticulations, and presence or absence of certain closure mechanisms (Peterson-Falzone *et al.*, 2006). A disadvantage of such tools is the invasive nature (and low radiation exposure for videofluoroscopy). Other tools such as nasometers can provide information on oral–nasal balance although without identifying areas of palatal insufficiency.

4.4.2.4   *Magnetic resonance imaging (MRI) and EMA*

MRI and EMA, powerful investigative tools, allow the collection of images over the entire vocal tract in detail. Until recently MRI was used only to investigate static images of the tongue (Masaki *et al.*, 1999) (and may be best suited to sustained sounds: Aron, Berger, and Kerrien, 2008). MRI can, however, offer information on tongue movement, soft palate, lip opening, and jaw movement. For example, Shinagawa *et al.* (2005) reported clear observation of bilabial, alveolar, and velar consonants, tongue and pharyngeal wall movement in an MRI study comparing an individual with cleft lip and palate and a speaker with a normal oral mechanism. Although noninvasive, the cost of both MRI and EMA is currently prohibitive. Furthermore, the effects of the supine position for MRI and the head stabilization mechanisms for EMA on speech production are unknown. Children and probably many adults are less likely to find these technologies appealing in research or treatment. But they are there for the speech researchers and adults with tolerance for such equipment.

> **Section Summary**
>
> - Technological study of the acoustics or articulatory aspects of speech provides information on speech sounds in context or individually.
> - All technologies (EPG, ultrasound, acoustic analysis, EMA, nasoendoscopy, etc.) have strengths and weaknesses, and the researcher needs to read the literature carefully and work with the technology in order to understand its utility and its limitations.

4.5   Beyond Speech

Technological evaluations often focus on very specific aspects of speech production (and sometimes perception). But a discussion of speech production is limited without consideration of speech in context. Thus, we discuss comprehensibility briefly below, and direct the reader to the chapters elsewhere in this volume on qualitative research methodology.

4.5.1   *Comprehensibility*

Comprehensibility is a concept related to the Activities and Participation descriptors of the ICF. Related to intelligibility, comprehensibility has been defined as listener processing of an acoustic signal, but with inclusion of, in addition, information such as gestures, visual information, context, etc. (Yorkston, Strand, and Kennedy, 1996). An even broader conceptualization of comprehensibility incorporates characteristics of the listener (e.g. familiarity), as well as the speaker–listener dyad's use of breakdown–repair strategies in arriving at comprehension of a spoken message (Visser, 2004).

   Research regarding comprehensibility of speech necessitates attention to somewhat different variables from those for other aspects of speech production. First, the dyadic nature of comprehensibility means the necessary inclusion of both speakers and listeners as participants, especially given research findings pointing to the impact of familiarity, that is, both experimental familiarization with a given speaker's production (e.g. D'Innocenzo, Tjaden, and Greenman, 2006) and personal familiarity, which appears to influence both intelligibility of the speech signal (Flipsen, 1995; Johnston, 2009) and strategy use (Johnston, 2009; King and Gallegos-Santillan, 1999). Second, measures of comprehensibility need to capture how a given speaker–listener dyad negotiates the listener's understanding of the speaker's production. To date, the majority of research in this area has focused on measures of intelligibility, where a listener is asked to transcribe either video- or audio-recorded speech, often based on oral reading or repetition of words or sentences such as those provided in the Assessment of Intelligibility of Dysarthric Speech (AIDS; Yorkston and Beukelman, 1981). However, a small but growing body of research also demonstrates the value of studies of speaker–listener interactions (e.g. King and Gallegos-Santillan, 1999), with two relatively recent studies describing a protocol for a systematic evaluation of comprehensibility during speaker–listener interactions (Johnston, 2009; Visser, 2004). Depending on the goal of the study, it may be useful to consider the interactions between the speaker participant and one or more listeners, as one way of evaluating outcomes in intervention study, or for characterization of speech characteristics in context.

4.5.2   *Qualitative Research*

The chapter would not be complete without allusion to qualitative research, which is uniquely oriented toward uncovering the details of the social phenomenon of communication (Bacsfalvi, 2007; Damico and Simmons-Mackie, 2003). This research tradition is discussed in Chapters 6, 7, and 8 of this volume and thus here we only underline the importance and relevance of such research for evaluating real-life effects in communication impairments.

4.5.3   *Triangulation of Data*

As implied in the last two sections, studies can benefit from taking a number of different approaches to reveal aspects of a phenomenon. Triangulation of data may utilize within- or cross-domain evaluations. An example of within-domain triangulation is Wrench and Scobbie (2003), where EPG, EMA, and U/S were used in an investigation of English /l/. An example of cross-domain triangulation is Bacsfalvi (2007): data from EPG contact palates, ultrasound images, phonetic transcriptions, listener evaluations, and qualitative methods offered a comprehensive evaluation of speech production in an intervention study with ultrasound and EPG. The researcher can choose from a number of options for learning more about a phenomenon than can be learned with one method only.

Section Summary

- Speech takes place in a context, and the researcher may want to use the context of a dyadic pair to assess comprehensibility and intelligibility.
- Qualitative methods may also provide information relevant to speech production variations and disorders.
- All methods have their limitations, and thus triangulation of data from a variety of sources may provide a better profile of speech performance.

4.6 Conclusion

This chapter has provided an overview of key elements in experimental and quasi-experimental studies in clinical speech research, particularly as it concerns speech production. Many aspects that are considered crucial are discussed in depth in other chapters (as has been noted). The state of the art is quasi-experimental and descriptive. However, description has reached new levels of sophistication due to recent advances in technology and research methods (both quantitative and qualitative). Whichever methods are used, the appropriateness of methods for participants remains a key consideration. For example, the immobilization required of technologies such as ultrasound, EMA, or MRI may not be suitable for speakers of all cultures and ages. Not all children or speakers will be comfortable with technology. Thus, perceptual analyses and qualitative research will continue to have a key role to play in evaluation of speech production. Whatever the research approach, the need for rigor in participant or evaluator selection, stimuli creation, and data collection and analysis remains vital.

4.7 Resources

Bacsfalvi, P. and Radanov, B. (2005). Ultrasound in speech training. Video files retrievable through http://www.audiospeech.ubc.ca/research/child-phonology-phonetics-and-language-acquisiton-lab/ultrasound-in-speech-training.

Bernhardt, B. H. and Stemberger, J. P. (2001). *Workbook in Nonlinear Phonology for Clinical Application*. Austin, TX: Pro-Ed.

Clinical Linguistics and Phonetics (2005). Volume 19(6/7) on ultrasound.

Sonies, B. C., Shawker, T. H., Hall, T. E. *et al.* (1981). Ultrasonic visualization of tongue motion during speech. *Journal of the Acoustical Society of America*, 70, 683–686.

Stone, M. (1997). Laboratory techniques for investigating speech articulation. In W. J. Hardcastle and J. Laver (eds), *Handbook of Phonetic Sciences*. Blackwell Handbooks in Linguistics. Oxford: Blackwell, pp. 11–32.

References

Adler-Bock, M., Bernhardt, B. M., Gick, B., and Bacsfalvi, P. (2007). The use of ultrasound in remediation of /r/ in adolescents. *American Journal of Speech-Language Pathology*, 16(2), 128–139.

Aron, M., Berger, M.-O., and Kerrien, E. (2008). Multimodal fusion of electromagnetic, ultrasound and MRI data for building an articulatory model. In R. Sock, S. Fuchs, and Y. Laprie (eds), *Proceedings of the 8th International Seminar on Speech Production 2008, Strasbourg, France, 8–12 December 2008*. Strasbourg: INRIA, pp. 349–352.

Awan, S. N. and Lawson, L. L. (2009). The effect of anchor modality on the reliability of vocal severity ratings. *Journal of Voice*, 23(3), 341–352.

Bacsfalvi, P. (2007). Visual feedback technology with a focus on ultrasound: the effects of speech habilitation for adolescents with sensorineural hearing loss. Unpublished doctoral dissertation, University of British Columbia, Vancouver, British Columbia, Canada.

Bacsfalvi, P. (2010). Attaining the lingual components of /r/ with ultrasound for three adolescents with cochlear implants. *Canadian Journal of Speech-Language Pathology and Audiology*, 34(3), 206–216.

Baken, R. and Orlikoff, R. (2000). *Clinical Measurement of Speech and Voice*, 2nd edn. San Diego, CA: Singular Publishing.

Bernhardt, B. M., Bacsfalvi, P., Gick, B. *et al.* (2005). Exploring electropalatography and ultrasound in speech habilitation. *Journal of Speech-Language Pathology and Audiology*, 29, 169–182.

Bernhardt, B. M., Bopp-Matthews, K., Daudlin, B. *et al.* (2010). Nonlinear phonological intervention. In L. Williams, S. MacLeod, and R. MacAuley (eds), *Treatment of Speech Sound Disorders*. Baltimore, MD: Brookes Publishing, pp. 315–331.

Bernhardt, B., Gick, B., Bacsfalvi, P., and Ashdown, J. (2003). Speech habituation of hard of hearing adolescents using electropalatography and ultrasound as evaluated by trained listeners. *Clinical Linguistics and Phonetics*, 173, 199–216.

Bernhardt, B. H. and Stemberger, J. P. (1998). *Handbook of Phonological Development: From a Nonlinear Constraints-Based Perspective*. San Diego, CA: Academic Press.

Bernhardt, B. M., Stemberger, J. P., and Charest, M. (2010). Intervention for speech production in children and adolescents: models of speech production and therapy approaches. Introduction to the issue. *Canadian Journal of Speech-Language Pathology and Audiology*, 34(3), 157–167.

Bernhardt, B. M. and Stemberger, J. P. (2012). Transcription of the speech of multilingual children. In. B. Goldstein and S. McLeod (eds), *Multilingual Aspects of Speech Sound Disorders in Children*. Bristol, UK: Multilingual Matters, pp. 182–190.

Bressmann, T., Flowers, H., Wong, W., and Irish, J. C. (2010). Coronal view ultrasound imaging of movement in different segments of the tongue during paced recital: findings from four normal speakers and a speaker with partial glossectomy. *Clinical Linguistics and Phonetics*, 24(8), 589–601.

Bressmann, T., Thind, P., Bollig, C. M. *et al.* (2005). Quantitative three-dimensional ultrasound analysis of tongue protrusion, grooving and symmetry: data from twelve normal speakers and a partial glossectomee. *Clinical Linguistics and Phonetics*, 19, 573–588.

Damico, J. S. and Simmons-Mackie, N. N. (2003). Qualitative research and speech-language pathology: a tutorial for the clinical realm. *American Journal of Speech-Language Pathology*, 12, 131–143.

Davidson, L. (2005). Addressing phonological questions with ultrasound. *Clinical Linguistics and Phonetics*, 19(6/7), 619–633.

D'Innocenzo, J., Tjaden, K., and Greenman, G. (2006). Intelligibility in dysarthria: effects of listener familiarity and speaking condition. *Clinical Linguistics and Phonetics*, 20(9), 659–675.

Fairbanks, G. (1940, 1960). *Voice and Articulation Drillbook*. New York: Harper.

Fletcher, S. (1992). *Articulation: A Physiological Approach*. San Diego, CA: Singular Publishing.

Flipsen, P. (1995). Speaker–listener familiarity: parents as judges of delayed speech intelligibility. *Journal of Communication Disorders*, 28, 3–19.

Gibbon, F. E. (1999). Undifferentiated lingual gestures in children with articulation/phonological disorders. *Journal of Speech, Language, and Hearing Research*, 42(2), 382–397.

Gibbon, F. E. and Hardcastle, W. J. (1989). Deviant articulation in a cleft palate child following later repair of the hard palate: a description and remediation procedure using electropalatography (EPG). *Clinical Linguistics and Phonetics*, 3(1), 93–110.

Gick, B. (2002). The use of ultrasound for linguistic phonetic fieldwork. *Journal of the International Phonetic Association*, 32, 113–121.

Gick, B., Campbell, F., and Oh, S. (2001). A cross-linguistic study of articulatory timing in liquids. *Journal of the Acoustical Society of America*, 110(5), 2, 2656.

Gick, B. and Wilson, I. (2001). Pre-liquid excrescent schwa: what happens when vocalic targets conflict. In P. Dalsgaard, B. Lindberg, and H. Benner (eds), *Proceedings of the 7th European Conference on Speech Communication and Technology (Eurospeech 2001)*. Aalborg, Denmark: Center for Personkommunikation (CPK), pp. 273–276.

Hardcastle, W. J., Gibbon, F. E., and Jones, W. (1991). Visual display of tongue–palate contact: electropalatography in the assessment and remediation of speech disorders. *British Journal of Disorders of Communication*, 26, 41–74.

Hillenbrand, J., Getty, L., Clark, M., and Wheeler, K. (1995). Acoustic characteristics of American English vowels. *Journal of the Acoustical Society of America*, 97(5), 3099–3111.

Houde, R. A. (1980). Evaluation of drill with visual aids for speech training. In J. Subtelny (ed.), *Speech Assessment and Speech Improvement for the Hearing Impaired*. Washington, DC: Alexander Graham Bell Association for the Deaf, pp. 150–166.

Johnston, J. K. (2009). Comprehensibility assessment: the influence of familiar and unfamiliar communication partners. Unpublished master's thesis, University of British Columbia, Canada.

Jurafsky, D. and Martin, J. (2009). *Speech and Language Processing*, 2nd edn. Upper Saddle River, NJ: Pearson Prentice Hall.

Katz, W., Bharadwaj, S., and Carstens, B. (1999). Electromagnetic articulography treatment for an adult with Broca's aphasia and apraxia of speech. *Journal of Speech, Language, and Hearing Research*, 42, 1355–1366.

King, J. M. and Gallegos-Santillan, P. (1999). Strategy use by speakers with dysarthria and both familiar and unfamiliar conversational partners. *Journal of Medical Speech-Language Pathology*, 7(2), 113–116.

Lundberg, A. and Stone, M. (1999). Three-dimensional tongue surface reconstruction: practical considerations for ultrasound data. *Journal of the Acoustical Society of America*, 106, 2858–2867.

McAuliffe, M. J., Lin, E., Robb, M. P., and Murdoch, B. E. (2008). Influence of a standard electropalatography artificial palate upon articulation. *Folia Phoniatrica et Logopaedica*, 60(1), 45–53.

McLeod, S. and Wrench, A. (2008). Protocol for restricting head movement when recording ultrasound images of speech. *Asia Pacific Journal of Speech, Language, and Hearing*, 11(1), 23–29.

Masaki, S., Tiede, M. K., Honda, K. *et al.* (1999). MRI-based speech production study using a synchronized sampling method. *Journal of the Acoustical Society of Japan (E)*, 20, 375–379.

Masterson, J., Bernhardt, B., and Hofheinz, M. (2005). A comparison of single words and conversational speech in phonological evaluation. *American Journal of Speech-Language Pathology*, 14, 229–241.

Modha, G., Bernhardt, M., Church, R., and Bacsfalvi, P. (2008). Case study using ultrasound to treat /r/. *International Journal of Communication Disorders*, 43(3), 323–329.

Munhall, K. G. and Ostry, D. J. (1985). Ultrasonic measurement of laryngeal kinematics. In I. R. Titze and R. C. Scherer (eds), *Vocal Fold Physiology: Biomechanics, aAcoustics and Phonatory Control*. Denver, CO: Denver Center for the Performing Arts, pp. 145–162.

Peterson-Falzone, S. J., Trost-Cardamone, J. E., Karnell, M. P., and Hardin-Jones, M. A. (2006). *The Clinician's Guide to Treating Cleft Palate Speech*. St. Louis: Mosby, Inc.

Radanov, B. (2007). Evaluations of /r/ attempts of children in speech therapy by speech-language pathologists and child educators. Unpublished master's thesis, University of British Columbia, Canada.

Shawker, T. H. and Sonies, B. C. (1985). Ultrasound biofeedback for speech training. instrumentation and preliminary results. *Investigative Radiology*, 20, 90–93.

Shinagawa, H., Ono, T., Honda, E. *et al.* (2005) Dynamic analysis of articulatory movement using Magnetic Resonance Imaging movies: methods and implications in cleft lip and palate. *Cleft Palate-Craniofacial Journal*, 42(3), 225–230.

Stemberger, J. P. (1985). An interactive activation model of language production. In A. Ellis (ed.), *Progress in the Psychology of Language*, vol. 1. London: Lawrence Erlbaum Associates, pp. 143–186.

Stone, M. (2005). A guide to analysing tongue motion from ultrasound images. *Clinical Linguistics and Phonetics*, 19, 455–501.

Stone, M., Faber, A., Raphael, L. J., and Shawker, T. H. (1992). Cross-sectional tongue shape and linguopalatal contact patterns in [s], [ʃ], and [l]. *Journal of Phonetics*, 20, 253–270.

Stone, M. and Lundberg, A. (1996). Three-dimensional tongue surface shapes of English consonants and vowels. *Journal of the Acoustical Society of America*, 99, 3728–3737.

Stone, M., Morrish, K., Sonies, B. C., and Shawker, T. H. (1987). Tongue curvature: a model of shape during vowel production. *Folia Phoniatrica*, 39, 302–315.

Stone, M., Shawker, T. H., Talbot, T. L., and Rich, A. H. (1988). Cross-sectional tongue shape during the production of vowels. *Journal of the Acoustical Society of America*, 83, 1586–1596.

Visser, T. (2004). Comprehensibility: a potential measure for improvement in communication. Unpublished master's thesis, University of British Columbia, Canada.

World Health Organization (WHO) (2007). International Classification of Functioning, Disability and Health. Retrieved December 5, 2010 from www.who.int/classifications/icf/en/.

Wrench, A. A. (2007). Advances in EPG palate design. *Advances in Speech-Language Pathology*, 9(1), 3–12.

Wrench, A. A. and Scobbie, J. M. (2003). Categorising vocalisation of English /l/ using EPG, EMA and ultrasound. In S. Palethorpe and M. Tabain (eds), *Proceedings of the 6th International Seminar on Speech Production*. Sydney: Macquarie University, pp. 314–319.

Wrench, A. A. and Scobbie, J. M. (2008). High-speed cineloop ultrasound tongue imaging: comparison of front and back lingual gesture location and relative timing. In R. Sock, S. Fuchs, and Y. Laprie (eds), *Proceedings of the 8th International Seminar on Speech Production 2008, Strasbourg, France, 8–12 December 2008*. Strasbourg: INRIA, pp. 57–60.

Yorkston, K. M. and Beukelman, D. R. (1981). *Assessment of Intelligibility of Dysarthric Speech*. Tigard, OR: CC Publications.

Yorkston, K. M., Strand, E. A., and Kennedy, M. R. T. (1996). Comprehensibility of dysarthric speech: implications for assessment and treatment planning. *American Journal of Speech-Language Pathology*, 5, 55–66.

Zharkova, N., Hewlett, N., and Hardcastle, W. (2008). An ultrasound study of lingual coarticulation in children and adults. In R. Sock, S. Fuchs, and Y. Laprie (eds), *Proceedings of the 8th International Seminar on Speech Production 2008, Strasbourg, France, 8–12 December 2008*. Strasbourg: INRIA, pp. 161–64.

5 Investigating Disordered Language: Experimental and Quasi-experimental Approaches

Judith D. Oxley

5.1 Overview of Territory

The scope of clinical linguistic interest in language disorders is broad and encompasses diverse perspectives on assessment and treatment, ranging from nosological issues through fine-tuning of treatment protocols (Chapter 1, this volume). Mildner (see Chapter 3, this volume) presented a comprehensive overview of specific experimental and quasi experimental research models available to investigators; however, the interaction between the rationalist underpinning of experimental research and the diverse constructs of "language disorders" poses some idiosyncratic challenges to investigators. Good research is anchored in theory concerning the nature of language and its disordered manifestations. Language disorders manifest themselves in characteristically idiosyncratic ways, and consequently, effective interventions typically demand customization; and the more severe the disorder is, the greater the need to individualize treatment. This reality results in problems with research design, including: matching participants, finding sufficient numbers of similar participants, adhering to a rigid protocol, and so forth. Although the issues covered here have relevance to the broader domain of disordered language, this chapter focuses mainly on childhood language disorders

5.2 Focusing the Research Question

From the expansive research agenda menu suggested in this volume's Introduction, the researcher's first planning step is to narrow the question of interest by posing some general questions (e.g. Creswell, 2009):

Research Methods in Clinical Linguistics and Phonetics: A Practical Guide,
First Edition. Edited by Nicole Müller and Martin J. Ball.
© 2013 Blackwell Publishing Ltd. Published 2013 by Blackwell Publishing Ltd.

- What am I *really* interested in: what is my *agenda*?
  - what is already known?
  - what are known concerns about existing findings?
  - how does my topic fill a gap or expand the body of knowledge?
- How should I set about framing my question?
- Does my question lend itself wholly or partially to a quantitative approach?

With answers in hand, investigators can then work toward specifying a working hypothesis that can be put to the test. Because research is costly in terms of time and resources, it is important to optimize the possibility of obtaining a result. Time spent in first fine-tuning one's hypothesis and methodology is beneficial and can include several techniques.

5.2.1   Focusing the Question via Attention to an Agenda

Nosology: experimental research may be used to test the accuracy of nosological features of a disorder. Preliminary research might include surveys to investigate the nature of working constructs used by speech-language pathologists to diagnose/treat a particular condition (e.g. word-finding problems), followed by carefully planned experimental research designed to establish which "symptoms" are core or optional to the construct.

a   *Nature of phenomenon: difference or disorder*: surface problems may reflect a different, but adequate developmental path, or they may indicate the presence of an underlying disorder. Such issues arise in bi/multilingual development, in language development via alternative modalities (manual sign language, visual graphic signs), and language development in the presence of blindness or severe visual impairment.
b   *Course of a disorder*: longitudinal studies track participants over an extended period of time and actively test hypotheses concerning relative contributions of different variables to the disorder, such as contributions of syntactic and pragmatic processing to children's use of reference (Schelletter and Leinonen, 2003).
c   *Course of a step in progress*: microgenetic methods can track the course of a developing phenomenon, including linguistic and related development. This methodology yields profiles of microdevelopment from a period when some type of learning is not evident within an individual to when it is fully mastered and functional. Thus, the researcher learns about the nature and predictability of developmental errors. Experimental approaches can then incorporate this knowledge into active testing of specific agents of change (e.g. materials or therapeutic interventions).
d   *Particular treatment approaches*: appropriateness of relying on the ability of certain populations (e.g. autism spectrum disorder) to engage in particular learning strategies observed in typical peers (e.g. spontaneous imitation of communication forms and functions (Vivanti *et al.*, 2008).
e   *Mechanism of change studies*: discovering how a particular therapeutic strategy works; for example, how does "following the child's lead" facilitate certain improvements in social engagement in terms of number and quality of participations turns by caregiver and child?
f   *Mechanics studies*: what specific activities by partners are implied by a facilitating strategy, such as "following the child's lead"? Interesting use of experimental

design has revealed important characteristics of these phenomena as they arise in parent–child dyads comprising, for example, children with Down syndrome and mothers (Mahoney *et al.*, 2011); blind toddlers of blind vs. sighted parents; or deaf/hard-of-hearing children of deaf vs. hearing parents (Harris *et al.*, 1989); and aided communicators (those using communication displays) and speaking parents (Cress, Moskal, and Hoffmann, 2008).

g *Intensity/duration studies*: just how much treatment is necessary for treatment to have an effect: blocked treatment, interspersed treatment, and so forth?

5.2.2 Focusing the Question via Pilot Experimental Studies

Pilot studies relax some of the constraints of experimental research, including number of participants, length of study, and so forth. Experimental research taxes time and money resources and so prior to jumping into a study, the researcher needs to consider numerous factors. A selection is listed below:

- suitability of materials, procedures, and time demands for tasks
- availability of suitable locations for conducting research
- identification and recruitment of suitable participants
- obtaining necessary approval for ethics panels
- identification and training of those who will carry out the research
- practicality of chosen recording instruments
- overall coordination of logistics such that participation is facilitated.

External funding may hinge on successful demonstration of the feasibility of research proposals. When experimental research for field studies is planned, these details must be worked out in advance if treatment fidelity is to be maintained (see below). Completion of adequate pilot work increases overall reliability of the research. Findings from pilot studies can help the researcher choose between experimental and quasi-experimental methods, or they may point to a need for supplemental methods to capture the data, including use of qualitative components.

5.2.3 Focusing the Question via Preliminary Use of Microgenetic Research Methods

Unlike the experimental models specified in Chapter 3, which look at beginning/end states of behavior, or else snapshots of change over extended windows of time, microgenetic research looks at mechanisms and trajectories of change on behavior over much shorter time frames. Both styles, however, share the feature of using controlled conditions as backdrops to research. Important benefits of the microgenetic approach are "that it allows profiles of performance to be: (i) recorded, to provide an indication of what the change looks like as it is happening, and (ii) analysed, to explain how the changes are being brought about" (Flynn and Siegler, 2007: 135). So, a pilot study using this methodology may enable the researcher to focus questions along the lines of agendas d, f, and g, listed above. Microgenetic methodology will be addressed further in Section 5.7.

> **Section Summary**
>
> - An early step in conducting experimental and quasi-experimental research is identifying an agenda within which to focus.
> - Pilot studies can help narrow the focus, but also fine tune procedures and details.
> - Preliminary studies can use diverse methodologies.
> - Microgenetic methods are useful for identifying specific agendas pertaining to language learning strategies, including therapeutic techniques.

5.3   Overview of Language Disorders: Theoretical Underpinnings and the Nature of Data

Researchers approach language disorders from many angles and philosophical backgrounds. Together, these influences powerfully shape critical matters:

- the questions asked in the first place
- the tasks and contexts of investigation
- the data selected for analysis
- the final use to which data are put (e.g. validating a treatment, testing a hypothesis, and so forth)
- how the data are *framed* for interpretation.

Contemporary investigation of language disorders draws on numerous theoretical models/constructs of language and language disorder. In turn, diverse modes of investigation have emerged, each drawing on the tools of a particular tradition. Within the scope of clinical linguistics, language disorders research may be approached from micro- to macro-analysis of text, and from brief through extended "snapshots" of change, or series of snapshots. Language disorders can be construed as problems thought to lie in:

- a specific linguistic domain (i.e. phonology, morphology, syntax)
- integration of linguistic domains with non-linguistic cognitive ones
- sociolinguistic domains (semantic-pragmatic).

5.3.1   *Relationship between Demand of Experimental Control and Language Construct*

Issues explored through experimental and quasi-experimental methods are theory-driven and their starting point is necessarily highly focused. A hypothesis is stated and experiments are designed to maximize the focus on a phenomenon or behavior of interest, by eliminating or minimizing sources of extraneous influence on the target; at the very least, rich description of context, participants, and materials can help account for extraneous influences. An essential component therefore is the researcher's *control* of the experimental setting. Researchers seek to identify specific associations and differences between single or multiple groups of a target population and additional populations. When difficulties arise in terms of forming sufficiently large groups, use can be made of single-subject designs (see Mildner, Chapter 3, this volume). Clusters of experiments may be conducted to establish the relative contribution of individual factors on a target. Underlying these approaches are some important constructs about the nature of language and language disorders. Some of these are listed below. Traditions can be viewed on a continuum of breadth of inclusion of critical variables: so at the narrow end lies structuralism, and at the broadest end is constructivist and emergent theory. The continuum fits nicely with the spectrum of research methods (strictly experimental through qualitative). Creswell (2009) provides a more detailed account of the influence of "worldview" on selection of research methods and strategies of enquiry. Contrasting beliefs about the nature of language and language disorders are reflected in the following:

- Language is decomposable into components (with some degree of modularity) for the purpose of the research (theoretical, applied): semantics, syntax, morphology, phonology, and pragmatics.

  vs.

- Decomposition is difficult if not impossible, and all domains exert mutual influence on one another.
- We can isolate core linguistic aspects of communication from their broader social and meaning-making contexts.

  vs.

- Linguistic and non-linguistic aspects of communication are inextricable and attempts to separate them will limit, if not invalidate results.
- We can form groups of participants based upon nosological constructs of language disorders, many of which were borrowed from the medical field.

  vs.

- Presence of specific diagnosis does not guaranty a sufficiently similar profile for a claim to uniformity of a group so-formed (i.e. 'medical' does not necessarily determine performance).

Theories accounting for language growth and change that drive research include behaviorism (particularly the growing field of Applied Behavior Analysis), structuralism, constructivism, emergent theory (from dynamic systems theory), to mention just a few. These accounts of language itself, and consequently language disorders, differ vastly and the differences can be seen in research in terms of questions formulated, designs chosen, data analyzed, and conclusions drawn.

5.3.2   *Behaviorism and Applied Behavior Analysis*

Behavioral approaches for remediating expressive and receptive language deficits are particularly prominent in research addressing the language needs of individuals with autism spectrum disorder (ASD) and individuals with intellectual disability (ID). On this view, language is seen as a behavior (structural phenomenon) that, like other behaviors, is subject to the principles of learning theory (Greer, 2002). Expressive and receptive language are seen as decomposable into discrete units that can be trained in systematic, controlled ways, and subsequently generalized into everyday use. The learner's role can be relatively passive, or more active, but always carefully controlled. No claims draw on "mentalistic" constructs that potentially have bearing on the language situation. So, for example, no assumptions about a person's "semantic network" or level of symbolic development would be considered relevant to the matter of training a child to name things. Instead, the focus would be upon contingency shaping. Context is construed as part of a complex array of potential setting events that may facilitate or inhibit correct production of trained responses, which could range from simple to complex. Language production and reception are treated as responses subject to control by consequences. Thus, research models favored are generally strictly experimental in nature and characterized by careful attention to matters of experimental control. Variants of single-subject designs feature prominently because of the idiosyncratic nature of the communication difficulties of individuals with ASD and II (intellectual impairment). There is an extensive terminology associated with the popular applied behavior analysis (ABA) approaches (see Greer, 2002). A cursory literature search indicates diverse research agendas in language disorders:

- Training functional language forms (asking questions, answering questions, requesting, protesting, etc.).
- Differentiating subpopulations with a larger group (e.g. different subtypes of autism spectrum disorder).
- Identifying contextual variables that support or interfere with functional use of trained language behaviours.
- Differentiating aspects of independent variables (e.g. nature, context, rigor, duration of a particular method of training).

5.3.3   *Structuralism and Generative Theories*

Structural linguistic theory and generative theories of language have considered rule learning as a mechanism of change, and deficits in rule learning as the subject of training. The historical coincidence of behavioral modes of service delivery and the dominance of linguistic structuralism created a curious mixture of operant learning as a means of training linguistic "rules." A key characteristic of such methods is decontextualization of training (Evans, 2001). Activities include practice to criterion of accuracy of target forms in response to pictures, for example (Fischer *et al.*, 2010). Fischer *et al.* used a multiple baseline design with changing criterion features to evaluate "the effectiveness of training with pictorial prompts to increase the syntactical complexity and length of novel utterances by 4 preschoolers with autism" (p. 76). Examples can also be found in aphasia research. Thompson, in a series of papers, has examined training and generalization of syntactic forms by participants with agrammatism (Thompson and Shapiro, 2005). According to the authors, "the underlying, abstract, properties of language are seriously considered, with the assumption that training such properties will allow for effective generalisation to untrained structures that share similar linguistic properties" (p. 1021). Thompson and colleagues used single-subject designs to address not just training, but also generalization of training to other grammatical forms.

5.3.4   Constructivism

Constructivism assumes an active role by the learner, and expects language to develop within natural contexts with guidance and mediation from more experienced language users. Experimental research driven by this construct uses group comparisons to examine the relative contribution of different types of mediators and mediation on language change within disordered populations. For example, conversational setting and partner can influence numerous measures of typical language production (Hoff, 2010). The same group can be assessed repeatedly, across varied contexts, or with various partners as independent variables. Early intervention for at-risk children frequently draws on group designs and single-subject designs to evaluate the effects of particular types of therapeutic scaffolding, or on dynamic assessment procedures (e.g. Kapantzoglou, Restrepo, and Thompson, 2012).

5.3.5   Emergent Theory, Neuroconstructivist Theory, Neoconstructivism

The broader impact on language, normal and disordered, of interactions among multiple systems is shared by researchers within these theories, whereas specific research tools differ. What has come to be viewed as an emergent view draws from Dynamic Systems Theory and characterizes the process of learning as "the unique interaction between the intrinsic properties of the child's processing system and the distributional properties of the language input that results in language disorders in these children" (Evans, 2001: 50). Assessment and training follow accordingly, based on the belief that "frequency and intensity of exposure to weakly represented linguistic features will increase a child's ability to discover the regularities in those language patterns" (p. 51).

It is increasingly accepted that some glitch in the system (however defined) is likely to produce cascading (negative) effects on a developing language system that have repercussions over time as the individual interacts with others. From a disorders perspective, emergent theory has much to offer because it ascribes a much broader domain to the construct of language, and provides the necessary scope for analyzing a highly complex human ability (see O'Grady, 2010, for review). Specific language impairment, unlike the genetic disorders Williams syndrome or Down syndrome, is a behaviorally defined disorder. Language profiles manifested across these three populations may share particular features, or not, but certainly multidimensional factors account for islands of strength or weakness. Neuroconstructivists (e.g. Karmiloff-Smith, 2009) raise particular questions for future research, and some of these have been identified by Thomas, Purser, and Richardson (in press):

- Are uneven cognitive profiles in behaviorally defined disorders on a continuum with the strengths and weaknesses found in typically developing children?
- What are the genetic effects on early brain development that contribute to uneven cognitive profiles?
- To what extent does the subsequent process of cognitive development change the nature of the even profile, by spreading deficits via interactions or attenuating them via compensation?
- To what extent can exposure to particular environments (such as interventions) remove weaknesses in uneven profiles or build on strengths?

Section Summary

- Language disorders are investigated from diverse professional perspectives and theories, and these, in turn inform agendas and methodologies.
- Applied behavior analysis as a theory and clinical approach features prominently in clinical literature about autism, and adheres strictly to experimental and quasi-experimental methods.
- Constructivist, neoconstructivist, neuroconstructivist, and emergent theory share recognition of the need to account for "context" in experimental research.
- ABA, in contrast to other theories, does not ascribe an active role to a child learning language, but identifies contingencies as guiding forces.

5.4   Experimental (and Quasi-experimental) Methods: Examples of Contributions to Nosology

5.4.1   *Specific Language Impairment*

The diagnostic entity specific language impairment (SLI) has been established through numerous and different lines of investigation. Recent reviewers surveyed historical findings that have collectively built and refined this construct (Gillam and

Kamhi, 2010; Oetting and Hadley, 2009). Their surveys also help to situate contributions of experimental methodology, relative to other approaches used for exploring this area. Experimental methods have been applied to tease out important findings concerning treatment approaches and strategies; however, a wide array of research tools has been used and will continue to contribute to our understanding of SLI. See Gillam and Kamhi for answers to these questions:

1   How has this construct emerged from the data?
2   How does it manifest itself?
3   What is the core set of determining features?
4   What are exclusion criteria?
5   In which populations is it found?

See Oetting and Hadley for methodologies used to address the following questions:

6   Is it treatable?
7   How should it be treated?
8   Are some treatments better than others?
9   Can particular components of treatment by customized to optimize improvement?
10   How does SLI impact other aspects of the child/adult who has this condition?

5.4.2   *Pragmatic Impairment*

Questions 1–10 (above) are applicable to pragmatic impairment. The history of the emergence of this construct illustrates how ongoing research in one domain of language disorder drives better understanding of the existence and nature of problems in another domain. Unlike SLI, pragmatic impairment is not a unitary disorder, but rather an umbrella term covering many different phenomena and multiple causalities (Perkins, 2010). Methodologies for answering the question listed above differ considerably from those used to explore SLI. This construct helps to illustrate the vital importance of recognizing how the nature of an object of investigation influences the validity and reliability potential research methodologies. The metaphor of photography is relevant here: do we need a wide-angle lens or a narrow focus?

Section Summary

- The main point is that within language disorders, some impairments lend themselves more readily to experimental paradigms.
- Current understanding of SLI has greatly benefitted from experimental research.
- By contrast, Pragmatic Impairment lends itself less to experimental and quasi-experimental methods, than to those at the qualitative end of the spectrum.

5.5   Experimental Research and Language Intervention

Experimental and quasi-experimental research methods require careful attention to control of every aspect of the project: selection or design of independent variables, data collection (participants, elicitation methods, data recording methods, stimuli for elicitation), data coding, and data triangulation. The focus in this section is mainly on intervention within the scope of clinical linguistics.

5.5.1   Dealing with Independent Variables: Treatment Fidelity/Integrity

Central to the issue of reliability in research design is adherence to a protocol; however, experimental and quasi-experimental research addressing human behavior is inherently constrained by specific factors that are, to some degree, out of the researcher's control. In clinical research, the extent to which a treatment is implemented as planned is reflected in a measure known as *treatment integrity*, or *treatment fidelity*, which has been evolving in terms of nature, scope, and importance (Lane *et al.*, 2004). In addition, the need to document it explicitly in research publications has also been addressed (Kaderavek and Justice, 2010). In an excellent tutorial on the treatment fidelity specific to best practices in speech-language pathology, Kaderavek and Justice identify two of the many critical clinical questions demanded when the clinical researcher considers the *independent* variable (i.e. the intervention itself), (1) "Have I administered the intervention exactly as described?" and (2) "What are the active ingredients of the intervention?"

5.5.2   Administering a Protocol: The People and Their Actions

To the extent that therapists and others fail to fit treatment to the ideal model, fidelity is reduced. The researcher must therefore address two types of fidelity: intended fidelity, which reflects an optimal condition, and achieved fidelity, which reflects actual implementation (Kaderavek and Justice, 2010). Significant differences between these two measures have far-reaching implications for clinical decision making, and research conclusions. Relevant concepts include *interventionist adherence* (to protocol) and *competence*; *participant adherence and responsiveness*. It may be that certain types of interventions are potentially more susceptible problems arising from failure of key participants to follow a protocol. For example, parent training programs (e.g. Eames *et al.*, 2009), and training dependent on consultation models (Wesley *et al.*, 2010). Eames *et al.* (2009) concluded that "delivering an intervention with a high level of treatment fidelity not only preserves the behaviour change mechanisms of the intervention, but can also predict parental behaviour change, which itself predicts child behaviour change as a result of treatment." Team collaboration is a core component of treatment in educational and medical settings and service provision often includes consultation services that supplement or replace direct service provision. Research conducted within this consultation framework requires careful planning that takes into account threats to treatment fidelity. Results from a large-scale study of consultation services provided within early intervention programs revealed numerous challenges to assessment and documentation of issues of treatment fidelity (Wesley *et al.*, 2010). Fixsen *et al.* (2005) used the terms *source, destination, communication link,* and *feedback* to specify a model comprising, respectively, some "best practice" model chosen for implementation, the practitioner (individual or agency) implementing it, consultants responsible for monitoring the program as implemented on site, and the flow of information about onsite performance. This conceptual model of characterizing a means of assuring treatment fidelity has obvious relevance to clinical linguistic service delivery and preprofessional training. This model must then be set against a broader context labeled *influence*, which takes in broader societal factors that can affect a treatment/service program. In clinical research, dominant and competing theoretical paradigms fall under this component.

5.5.3　*Identifying the Active Ingredients*

Any clinical treatment is likely to have core and optional components. The optional components may be preplanned, in the sense their use is at the discretion of the interventionist, or they may be incidental and pass under the radar as having potential impact on treatment. The term *active ingredients* refers to the essential parts, described by Kaderavek and Justice as the "hows and whys" of a treatment:

> These active ingredients may be based largely on theory, or they may be based on empirical evidence. Active ingredients most typically include specific treatment targets (e.g. specific grammatical forms), the therapeutic techniques (e.g. modelling these forms during interactive play), and the requirements for dosage (e.g. highly concentrated exposures several times per week). In combination, the active ingredients describe how and why the intervention brings about predicted outcomes.
>
> (Kaderavek and Justice, 2010: 371)

As a corollary to the medical metaphor of "active ingredients," which contrasts with "inactive ingredients", there is also the possibility of investigating the supposedly "inactive" counterparts (e.g. the "incidental/optional" components mentioned above) with a view to discovering helpful or unhelpful contributions to a particular treatment (Müller, personal communication). Relevant terminology used to cover these notions includes *exposure, dosage received, unique and essential behaviors, essential but not unique behaviors, acceptable but not necessary behaviors,* and *proscribed behaviors.*

These terms were selected from the literature (see review by Sanetti and Kratochwill, 2009). Additional information by ways of checklists of suggestions for strategies for assessing and enhancing treatment fidelity specific to communication disorders is readily available (Kaderavek and Justice, 2010; NIH website, see Resources section below).

> **Section Summary**
>
> - Treatment fidelity or integrity is the extent to which an intervention is administered as planned.
> - One must check how closely one adheres to the project protocol.
> - Whether the core or *active ingredients* of a project are implemented must also be established.

5.6   Data Collection Considerations

5.6.1   *Participants and Groupings*

Choice of participants is based upon the relevance of the topic to specific age groups, gender, cultural, language and dialect backgrounds for both typical and atypical language production and comprehension. Experimental control involves grouping and matching participants according to predetermined criteria, which frequently include use of norm-referenced data. A broad differentiation within the field of language disorders is made between problems arising during the developmental period, and those occurring subsequently. Performance may be compared across groups. Norms can be used to establish comparisons. Norms for many populations have been published for numerous aspects of language development and disorder (see Resources below). Norms are available for vocabulary, syntactic structure, morphological development, text structure (e.g. narratives, conversations), literacy tasks, auditory perception, and much more. Norms can be used to inform experimental task development (materials, activities, duration of tasks, etc.). Any reference to norms, however, must be tempered with caution, particularly for young children, because of the extent of normal variability, and for individuals with Intellectual Disability because of the potential for positive and negative effects of life experience on language (e.g. vocabulary).

Another limitation of reliance of norm-referenced findings is the impact of context on performance. Natural contexts for language sample elicitation are conditioned by partners, tasks, and a host of other variables. Similarly, experimentally "contrived" contexts have the potential to skew performance positively and negatively. Then there is the issue of usefulness of comparisons; for example, knowing the comparative status of a particular structural linguistic phenomenon (e.g. syntactic adequacy of conversational turns taken by an adult with aphasia) may have little bearing on assessment of communication success.

Attention to participant selection will help render findings valid and reliable.

- We can group people so as to minimize differences that might invalidate our study (simple demographics, such as age, gender, ethnicity, SES, etc.)

- We can group people according nosological constructs of language disorders.
- We can provide equal opportunities during the experiment (materials, time of day, partners, time limits, checks on physical/mental state of participants, etc.).

Experimental designs may include two control groups, comprising typical peers matched on chronological age and language age, respectively. Control groups may also be created based on known characteristics of disorder types: individuals with Down syndrome are known to have acceptable social-communication skill, but relatively poorer syntactic skill. By contrast, individuals with Williams syndrome appear to have islands of ability in terms of use of unusual and low frequency words. Thus, researchers may include a variety of control groups to establish relative contributions of cognition, social skill, vision, hearing, and language skill to some target skill (e.g. referential adequacy of language).

The ability to group participants meaningfully based on constructs of language disorders can present difficulties due to heterogeneity of individuals with the same diagnostic label, and to the potential for co-occurring difficulties. For example, communication breakdowns secondary to an insult to the neurological system are likely to stem from diverse causes: primary linguistic problems (aphasia), cognitive-linguistic problems (head injury), motor problems affecting speech, gesture and affect. Blindness, deafness, dual-sensory impairment, and the presence of multiple challenges exemplify situations in which grouping and matching participants can be tricky (Rosel *et al.*, 2005). Crystal (1987, 2001) described the growing recognition that performance across domains is interdependent, and that, for example, growth in one domain may be accompanied by regression or difficulty in another. Dynamic Systems Theory uses the metaphor of "cascade effects" to encapsulate the idea that small and large changes occurring at a particular moment can have far-reaching effects later in development.

5.6.2 *Age Appropriateness in Experiments with Children*

Language disorders typically manifest themselves before children are 3 or 4 years of age. Experimental research implies the use of control across a range of issues, including procedures used by the researcher to elicit language samples, to embed treatment, and to assess outcomes. The need for experimental control can, but need not, lead to unfavorable circumstances from the child's perspective. For example, young children are particularly susceptible to situations, tasks, or participant roles that seem "artificial" in some way. A litany of variables (specially designed materials, inflexible activities, contrived tasks, time constraints, and sincerity violations by adults) individually and collectively can themselves exert unwanted influence on the children's language, participation style, and spontaneity. Relative to older age groups, preschoolers and toddlers are more quixotic in their responses and are vulnerable to fatigue, lack of interest, fleeting attention to tasks, sensitivity to frustration, and so forth. Developmental norms for language span rather broad age ranges: the younger the child, the broader the range for what is considered "typical" development. Efforts to control an experimental situation can work against researchers by destroying the validity and reliability of children's contributions. Thus, researchers are potentially caught in a double bind: tasks must be simple enough to maintain the children's interest and willingness to participate as dictated by the experimental design, while at the same time providing sufficient challenge to allow for measurement of upper boundaries of ability or improvement. Thus, opportunities for floor and ceiling effects arise and avoiding them can be notoriously tricky. A similar array of problems also arises in connection with experimental designs for chronologically older children with language disorders, particularly when there are additional developmental problems.

5.6.3   Cultural and Language Appropriateness of Tasks for Participants

It is well known that researchers and research participants may "relate" to one another to a greater or lesser degree, and that this connection (or lack thereof) exerts a powerful influence in research. Language is social phenomenon, and as such bears cultural identity markers. Scientific objectivity is a central tenet of experimental research; thus, the researcher seeks to minimize confounding effects from numerous sources, including age, gender, physical characteristics, education level, and SES status. Positive and negative biases can arise as a result of goodness of fit, which can be difficult to achieve. Work-arounds include allocation of adequate time for participants to settle into the experimental situation, to familiarize themselves with materials, and to establish some level of rapport with investigators. Culture is hard to define, but violations of cultural norms can jeopardize the validity and reliability of research findings. Planning experimental research related to language must include attention to such matters as: choice of materials and communication partners; appreciation of what is considered an appropriate communication role for a participant; expectations of "respect" accorded on the basis of age, gender, and so forth; and scheduling criteria, to name just a few variables.

5.6.4   Issues of "Matching" Participants

When a research design involves group comparisons for some purpose, issues of matching participants becomes relevant: who will serve as the comparison group(s)? In the case children with a diagnosis of SLI, typical comparison groups include chronologically same-age peers (CA) without SLI, and younger non-SLI peers matched on the basis of language level (LA). A variant of this model made possible by the presence of a longitudinal data set comprised a fourth-grade SLI group, and a single group of typically developing children assessed at second and fourth grades (Guo, Tomblin, and Samelson, 2008). The study was designed to investigate speech disruptions in the narratives of English-speaking children with SLI. The authors argued that inclusion of the CA group permits comparisons between the SLI and CA groups, with a goal of determining the relationship between language impairment and speech disruptions. Inclusion of the LA group provides a means of determining the extent to which speech disruptions are related to differences in linguistic processing by children with SLI, rather than an overall syntactic delay. Matching is based on children's performance on a battery of standardized language tests and a composite score of nonverbal IQ.

When different clinical populations are to be compared with one another in terms of performance of a linguistic task, special attention must be paid to the specific language characteristics of each population. In their classic review, Bates, Dale, and Thal (1995) considered the role of individual differences in language development. Their main contention was stated thus: "Far from simply reflecting noise in our measuring instruments or variability in low-level aspects of physiological maturation, the variations that we will document here are substantial, stable, and have their own developmental course" (p. 96). These known developmental courses have particular relevance to the issue of matching and to investigations of assessment procedures in clinical studies. Two populations used to illustrate the issue are children with Down syndrome and children with Williams syndrome. Children with DS were identified as the only group they had seen in which there was "a clear dissociation between grammar and vocabulary during this stage of language learning. For these children, early grammar falls far behind vocabulary growth, suggesting that lexical size is a necessary but not sufficient condition for the extraction of grammatical regularities" (p. 150). They found a strong association between lexical and grammatical development in the period from 16 to 30 months of age (and its developmental equivalent in clinical populations, including late talkers, early talkers, children with focal brain injury, and children with Williams syndrome). The existence of associations or disassociations of this type appear at different stages of development and must be considered as independent variables in their own right, and not merely "noise."

5.6.5 Recording

Recording methods are covered in Chapter 10 of this volume. Special considerations for language disorders research may include the need for video/audio editing software that allows for integration of video and audio signals for calibration of sources, ability to annotate files, and more (e.g. Noldus products; see Resources below).

5.6.6 Tasks and Stimuli

5.6.6.1 Experimental approaches to production and comprehension of discourse

Discourse encompasses extended texts (i.e. written/spoken exposition and narratives; conversations. Experimental manipulations may involve comparisons within and/or between clinical and nonclinical populations; within/across age groups; within/across genres, and much more. Experiments seek to establish possible factors in breakdowns, to evaluate the effects of hypothesized "supports" in the face of a language disorder, to identify specific trouble spots, and so forth. Manipulation of supports hypothesized to facilitate/confound successful engagement in discourse may be:

- visual support (e.g. play materials, books, video recordings)
- auditory support (use of FM systems for amplification and reduction of background noise; modulation and type of background noise)
- use of trained/untrained confederates as communication partners to control specific discourse characteristics including:
  - chronemic demands (e.g. strategic use of pauses vs. rapid flow of conversation)
  - attention demands (e.g. interruptions/distracters)
  - strategic use of discourse supporting strategies for:
    - at risk children (e.g. recasts, models, expansions, extensions, open questions, redirects)
    - individuals with neurologically based language disorders (e.g. reduced utterance length, use of accompanying gesture, etc.)
- room arrangement (continuum of natural to highly structured, distraction-free)
- discourse materials themselves (e.g. familiarity, interest, modality, inherent properties in terms of cultural style of narrative or conversation, accessibility in terms of print size, loudness, and rate of presentation
- choice of partners:
  - matched (or not) for age, disorder, gender, racial/ethnic/cultural identity)
  - control of participants in terms of number during a conversation.

Psycholinguistic and neurolinguistic approaches are exemplified by the works of researchers with Haskins Labs, such as Van Dyke (Van Dyke and McElree, 2006). On her website (see Resources), Van Dyke provides a discussion of one particular methodology and its rationale:

> The critical dependent measure for distinguishing different types of retrieval mechanisms and evaluating how particular disabilities may affect the time-course of accessing information is retrieval speed. Measures of reaction or reading times are insufficient for this purpose, however, because they may be influenced both by the speed of accessing information and the quality of memory representations. The Speed-Accuracy Tradeoff (SAT) method avoids this problem by tracking changes in the accuracy of a response as information accrues over time.

This methodology has been applied to the study of interference in memory and language, text comprehension, and various types of computer-assisted instruction.

The Haskins researchers also use eye-tracking technology to provide a non-invasive online method for investigating eye movements while participants are reading. "We also employ the method to study oral comprehension, either via the 'visual worlds' paradigm, which involves measuring looks to pictures that represent the content of an utterance, or in sentence–picture matching tasks, where participants judge whether a sentence they hear matches a picture they see."

5.6.6.2   *Experimental approaches to language output at sentence level and below (lexis, morphology, syntax)*

Resources for these tasks include customized software for computerized stimulus delivery, specialized recording tools that can provide fine-tuned synchronization of stimulus delivery and response according to selected modalities. It is always advisable to use "standard" materials whenever possible to facilitate cross-study comparisons. Resources for word frequency, neighborhood measures and so forth are readily available (see Resources). Stimuli vary in terms of length of unit, presentation modality (visual or auditory; orthographic vs. pictured in some way), response modality (speech, gesture with or without selection tools such as a mouse, keyboard, or customized switch), response timing, manipulation of foils (number, size, and type-match/mismatched, perceptual salience, semantic salience, etc.).

Semantics. Exploration of the semantic system may be accomplished via diverse methodologies and tasks, including (1) semantic fluency, (2) elicited word associations and definitions, (3) semantic priming, (4) short-term memory and (5) naming (Thomas *et al.*, 2006). These psycholinguistic tasks incorporate elements of lexical retrieval and lexical choice and can be combined with lexical frequency norms for a given language. Difficulties in learning vocabulary and retrieving it constitute primary characteristics of language learning disorders and literacy, and acquired language disorders. Experimental research is useful for examining "how much" training is enough, after a particular training strategy has proved efficacious.

Syntax/morphology. Experimental designs can be used to test hypotheses concerning conditions that influence obligatory use of specific language forms for clinical vs. typical populations. For example, in the case of agrammatism questions arise concerning the nature of the deficit: modular accounts of language may predict specific deficits in syntactic processing, whereas other accounts suggest memory deficits. To test the hypothesis that underlying syntactic competence is potentially masked by deficits in short-term memory, researchers have used computer software, such as SentenceShaper (see Resources). The computer software allows the individual with agrammatism to use visual supports to construct ideas onscreen, and revise them offline through repeated listening to the sentences read aloud by the computer. This methodology enables researchers to tease out the relative contribution of working memory and syntactic/morphological processing to the grammatical deficits observed during online performance (Linebarger *et al.*, 2008).

5.6.7   *Experimental Contexts and Settings*

Possibly one of the thorniest issues for language researchers is the matter of context. Cultural context is clearly important, but other contexts are also relevant. Working from a Dynamic Systems Theory ("emergent") background, Nelson (2000) concluded that "all significant learning depends on tricky mixes of learning conditions, with rapid learning occurring only when the tricky and partly chaotic mix of conditions converges strongly" (p. 135). He advocated for a new role for empirical research; specifically an "exploration of how the broader range of social, emotional, motivational, and cognitive/linguistic factors interact to create the strong individual differences so evident in each of the communicative domains" (p. 135). An example provided described ways in which summary scores of enjoyment/engagement could be developed for videotaped sessions of learners with teacher/therapist partners participating in sessions addressing syntactic skills. Nelson (2001) elaborated on the specifics for "how to mix a learning cocktail" (pp. 142–143) via a rubric comprising five elements: *Launches* of challenges, *Enhancers*, *Adjustment*, *Readiness*, and *Networks*. This rubric could be a useful reference point for designing and evaluating treatments. These data were found to predict subsequent syntactic gain across various typical and clinical populations. Thus, the interventionist is considered as an independent variable! In general, experimental designs typically attempt to control for this type of individual variability through provision of adequate training to those conducting a training or experiment, and through strict specification of acceptable types of extraneous interactions, and so forth (see above, in the discussion of treatment fidelity). So, a move from strict rationalist to an emergent (dynamic system theory) stance is accompanied by a shift in how context is characterized and addressed: is it simply "noise" to be reduced, or a critical variable in its own right? To put it another way, is it to be treated as an independent variable?

5.6.8 Data Set

Once collected, data must be scrutinized for the presence of systematic error that might compromise interpretation of findings. Examination of attrition rates can reveal something about goodness of fit of experimental tasks and age of participants. Investigators researching factors conjectured to contribute to difficulties associated with SLI have considered several cognitive (executive function) skills, including working memory (Leonard, 2007; Montgomery, 2005) and attention (see Redmond, 2005, for review). Children develop the ability to sustain attention to age-appropriate tasks for longer duration; this skill is largely due to increasing ability to inhibit irrelevant responses. A 2009 study (Finneran, Francis, and Leonard) provides rich information about the nature of attrition, which may be extraneous to the task or systematically related to it. Through a series of experiments, the researchers discovered that by adapting existing experimental tasks for use by younger children, they introduced an extraneous variable: need for instructor feedback (e.g. encouragement, reminders to attend to task, etc.), which in turn could have influenced task performance (and attrition). The authors next purposefully manipulated task interest value to more clearly distinguish children with SLI from their TD peers. It is clear that these young children in the 4–7-year range posed dilemmas for the researchers: by limiting the appeal of the task so as to reveal hypothesized differences in attention, they altered the disposition of the children to participate!

Section Summary

- Attention must be given to avoiding numerous confounding issues surrounding matching and grouping participants.
- Task demand in relation to age and impairment should be considered.
- Tasks should be culturally appropriate: actual wording of protocols, topics introduced, artifacts used, and gender/age/status of participants in relation to experimenters, and so forth.
- Methods of recording can alter the situation and so care should be taken to reduce interference from video recording cameras.
- Stimuli, settings, and experimental tasks are chosen with reference to the object of investigation, language, which is highly influenced by these factors.
- Data sets can provide evidence of systematic error in methodology.

5.7   Microgenetic Research: An Underused Research Tool

Crystal (1986) mentioned the importance of characterizing language handicap as a diachronic phenomenon, the result of failure of language to change over time in the normal way. Thus, there is a need for research that addresses the nature of change, the kinds of clinical insights that guide programmatic decisions and formulation of continuing treatment plans, and so forth. Individual, process-oriented approaches (dynamic systems theory and the microgenetic perspective) can help.

Within the microgenetic research framework, change is examined in terms of five features: path, rate, breadth, variability, and source (Siegler, 2006). The method is said to yield evidence not available through cross-sectional or long-term longitudinal approaches. To understand how change actually occurs, one needs to consider it in terms of the five features. This methodology has yielded valuable information in numerous developmental domains, including mathematical insight and use of cognitive strategies. In terms of where it lies on the methodological spectrum, microgenetic methods vary according to how they have been use. They certainly can be incorporated into the most rigorous experimental designs and into studies at the qualitative end.

The microgenetic approach to investigating change has yet to be adopted widely in the field of language disorders (e.g. van Dijka and van Geert 2007). In light of the critical need to obtain insight into the actual *mechanics of change* (see Section 5.1) in language ability in the presence of some intervention, it is surprising that more studies have not incorporated it. Apart from intervention, other applications include investigation of helpful and non-helpful compensations for a disorder by populations of interest over time.

In terms of intervention, many important questions concern such matters as generalization (or lack thereof), and identification of critical facilitators or inhibitors to the systematic adoption of new learning or skills. Many interventions for language disorders rely upon the client learning to use specific strategies, either as bridges to better receptive or expressive language, or as means of compensation.

For example, a clinical dilemma in the field of augmentative and alternative communication concerns balancing the needs of listeners and speakers in the presence of challenges presented by the length of time needed to construct and communicate complex ideas. The listener/speaker roles are reflexive, in that each partner may need to attend to the other person while simultaneously gathering thoughts and composing or receiving messages via alternative modalities (speech-generating device, spelling board, etc.). Augmentative and alternative communication strategies are diverse, and successful and competent integration of multimodal means of communication into one's communication toolbox emerges over time and with experience. Clinicians commonly observe that trained compensations (e.g. use of conscious strategies for enhancing conversation skill within multiple communication modalities) and trained "forms" (e.g. richer morphological and syntactical structuring of ideas) proceed in seemingly *unpredictable* ways. One of the observations drawn from numerous microgenetic studies is that there is predictability even within the apparent unpredictability of change: "Change does occur, but it appears as a gradual shift in the distribution of use of multiple strategies of varying adequacy – a considerably more complex picture of developmental change than the traditional one of a singular transition from *a* to *b*" (Kuhn, 1995: 133).

Section Summary

- Change is measured in terms of five features: path, rate, breadth, variability, and source.
- Microgenetic research reveals patterns of change more complex than a simple state a to state b (e.g. pre–post).
- It lends itself to study of mechanisms and mechanics of change ("hows and whys") and has relevance to specific treatment protocols, whether for clients being treated, or the clinicians administering treatments.

5.8   Conclusion

The tradition of experimental and quasi-experimental research has enriched current understanding of language disorders. The trend toward theoretical models that ascribe great importance to factors outside the linguistic system calls for better ways to account for and potentially integrate these variables into experimental research. Quasi-experimental methods dominate the field of language disorders research, and microgenetic methods promise to promote greater understanding of patterns of change. The dialectical tension within language disorders research reflects the need for experimental control versus the need to include context, which can introduce complexity and messiness to the data. The nature of language disorders invites valid research designs comprising both quantitative and qualitative data ("mixed methods"), evidenced by the growing number of stipulations by funding agencies for combined approaches.

5.9   Resources

5.9.1   *General Research*

http://linguistics.byu.edu/faculty/henrichsenl/researchmethods/RM_2_06.html: books, databases with/without norms, analytical tools, metalinks.

Crystal, D., Fletcher, P., and Garman, G. (1989). *The Grammatical Analysis of Language Disability*, 2nd edn. London: Cole and Whurr. Developmental norms for English syntax. (See also Ball, M. J., Crystal, D., and Fletcher, P. (eds) (2012). *Assessing Grammar: The Languages of LARSP*. Bristol, UK: Multilingual Matters.

Francis, W. N. and Kucera, H. (1982). *Frequency Analysis of English Usage: Lexicon and Grammar*. Boston: Houghton Mifflin.

For American English, an extensive review of norm-referenced tests can be found in:

Paul, R. (2007). *Language Disorders from Infancy through Adolescence: Assessment and Intervention*, 3rd edn. St. Louis: Mosby Elsevier.

For British English some frequently used tools with norms include:

Bishop, D. (2003). *The Children's Communication Checklist-2 (CCC-2)*.

Bishop, D. (2003). *Test for Reception of Grammar (TROG-2)*. Both available at http://www.psychcorp.co.uk/.

Dunn, L. M., Dunn, D. M., Styles, B., and Sewell, J. *British Picture Vocabulary Scale*, 3rd edn. http://www.gl-assessment.co.uk/.

Renfrew, C. (2010). *Bus Story Test. Revised Edition*. Abingdon, UK: Speechmark.

Databases, metalinks, analytical tools include:

http://childes.psy.cmu.edu/.

http://www.saltsoftware.com/.

http://www.clips.ua.ac.be/ CLiPS (Computational Linguistics and Psycholinguistics) is a research center associated with the Linguistics Department of the Faculty of Arts of the University of Antwerp.

http://www.essex.ac.uk/psyling/links.html is a treasure trove of resources of all kinds: Links to experimental and statistics software; online databases; numerous resources specific to language research.

http://www.haskins.yale.edu/staff/vandyke.html#methodology: eye tracking methodology for analysis of reading.

http://www.noldus.com: lab system for collecting, coding, and analyzing observational data, such as interactions between children and caregivers, and so forth.

http://www.sentenceshaper.com/: software for use by people with aphasia.

5.9.2   Treatment Fidelity Resources

A good starting point for terminology and concepts:
Bellg, A. J., Borrelli B., Resnick, B. *et al.* (2004). Enhancing treatment fidelity in health behavior change studies: best practices and recommendations from the NIH Behavior Change Consortium. *Health Psychology*, 23(5), 443–451. www.ncbi.nlm.nih.gov/pubmed/15367063.
National Institutes for Health, Office of Behavioral Social Sciences Research, http://obssr. od.nih.gov/publications/archives/archives.aspx: source data for ongoing projects and issues pertaining to treatment fidelity.

5.9.3   Microgenetic Research Resources

Additional sources of ideas for how microgenetic methodology can be used to investigate clinical linguistic issues can be found in:
Flynn, E., Pine, K., and Lewis, C. (2007). *Infant and Child Development*, 16(1), Special Issue: Using the microgenetic method to investigate cognitive development, 1–149.
Lavelli, M., Pantoja, A. P. F., Hsu, H.-C. *et al.* (2004). Using microgenetic designs to study change processes. In D. M. Teti (ed.), *Handbook of Research Methods in Developmental Science*. Oxford: Blackwell, pp. 40–65.
Miles, S. and Chapman R. (2002). Narrative content as described by individuals with DS and typically-developing children. *Journal of Speech, Language, and Hearing Research*, 45, 175–189.

References

Bates, E., Dale, P. S., and Thal, D. (1995). Individual differences and their implications for theories of language development. In P. Fletcher and B. MacWhinney (eds), *The Handbook of Child Language*. Oxford: Blackwell, pp. 96–51.
Cress, C. J., Moskal, L., and Hoffmann, A. (2008). Parent directiveness in free play with young children with physical impairments. *Communication Disorders Quarterly*, 29, 99–108.
Creswell, J. W. (2009). *Research Design*, 3rd edn. Thousand Oaks, CA: Sage.
Crystal, D. (1986) Pasado, presente y futuro de la lingüística clinica. (The past, present and future of clinical linguistics.) In M. Montfort (ed.), *Investigaccion y logopedia. III Logopedics Congress*, Madrid. Madrid: Ciencias de la Educacion Preescolar y Especial, pp. 34–42. Retrieved December 15, 2011 from http://www.davidcrystal.com/.
Crystal, D. (1987). Towards a "bucket" theory of language disability: taking account of interaction between linguistic levels. *Clinical Linguistics and Phonetics*, 1, 7–22.
Crystal, D. (2001). Clinical linguistics. In M. Aronoff and J. Rees-Miller (eds), *The Blackwell Handbook of Linguistics*. Oxford: Blackwell, pp. 673–82. Retrieved December 15, 2011 from http://www.davidcrystal.com/.
Eames, C., Daley, D., Hutchings, J. *et al.* (2009). Treatment fidelity as a predictor of behaviour change in parents attending group-based parent training. *Child: Care, Health and Development*, 35, 5, 603–612.
Evans, J. L. (2001). An emergent account of language impairments in children with SLI: implications for assessment and intervention. *Journal of Communication Disorders*, 34, 39–54.

Finneran, D. A., Francis, A. L., and Leonard, L. B. (2009). Sustained attention in children with Specific Language Impairment (SLI). *Journal of Speech, Language, and Hearing Research*, 52, 915–929.

Fischer, J. L., Howard, J. S., Sparkman, C. R., and Moore, A. G. (2010). Establishing generalized syntactical responding in young children with autism. *Research in Autism Spectrum Disorders*, 4(1), 76–88.

Fixsen, D. L., Naoom, S. F., Blasé, K. A. *et al.* (2005). *Implementation Research: A Synthesis of the Literature*. FMHI Publication no. 231. Tampa: University of Florida, Louis de la Parte Florida Mental Health Institute, National Implementation Research Network.

Flynn, E. and Siegler, R. (2007). Measuring change: current trends and future directions in microgenetic research. *Infant and Child Development*, 16, 135–149.

Gillam, S. and Kamhi, A. (2010). Specific language impairment. In M. Ball., J. Damico, and N. Mueller (eds), *Blackwell Handbooks in Linguistics: The Handbook of Language and Speech Disorders*. Oxford: Wiley-Blackwell, pp. 210–226.

Greer, R. D. (2002). *Designing Teaching Strategies: An Applied Behavior Analysis System Approach*. San Diego, CA: Academic Press.

Guo, L., Tomblin, J. B., and Samelson, V. (2008). Pauses in the narratives of English-speaking children with specific language impairment. *Journal of Speech, Language, and Hearing Research*, 51, 722–738.

Harris, M., Clibbens, J., Chasin, J., and Tibbitts, R. (1989).The social context of early sign language development. *First Language*, 9(25), 81–97.

Hoff, E. (2010). Context effects on young children's language use: the influence of conversational setting and partner. *First Language*, 30(3/4), 461–472.

Kaderavek, J. N. and Justice, L. M. (2010). Fidelity: an essential component of evidence-based practice in speech-language pathology. *American Journal of Speech-Language Pathology*, 19, 369–379.

Kapantzoglou, M., Restrepo, M. A., and Thompson, M. S. (2012). Dynamic assessment of word learning skills: identifying language impairment in bilingual children. *Language, Speech, and Hearing Services in Schools*, 43, 81–96.

Karmiloff-Smith, A. (2009). Nativism versus neuroconstructivism: rethinking the study of developmental disorders. *Developmental Psychology*, 45(1), 56–63. http://www.psyc.bbk.ac.uk/research/DNL/personalpages/annette.html (accessed February 23, 2012).

Kuhn, D. (1995). Microgenetic study of change: what has it told us? *Psychological Science*, 6, 133–139.

Lane, K. L., Bocian, K. M., MacMillan, D. L., and Gresham, F. M. (2004). Treatment integrity: an essential – but often forgotten – component of school-based interventions. *Preventing School Failure*, 48, 36–43.

Leonard, L. B., Ellis Weismer, S., Miller, C. A. *et al.* (2007). Speed of processing, working memory, and language impairment in children. *Journal of Speech, Language, and Hearing Research*, 50, 408–428.

Linebarger, M. C., Romania, J. R., Fink, R. B. *et al.* (2008) Building on residual speech: a portable processing prosthesis for aphasia. *Journal of Rehabilitation Research and Development*, 45(9), 1401–1414.

Mahoney, G., Perales, F., Wiggers, B., and Herman, B. (2011).Responsive teaching: early intervention for children with Down syndrome and other disabilities. *Down Syndrome Research and Practice*, 11(1), 18–28.

Montgomery, J. W. (2005). Effects of input rate and age on the real-time language processing of children with specific language impairment. *International Journal of Language and Communication Disorders*, 40, 171–188.

Nelson, K. E. (2000). Methods for stimulating and measuring lexical and syntactic advances: why Fiffins and lobsters can tag along with other recast friends. In L. Menn and N. B. Ratner (eds), *Methods for Studying Language Production*. Hillsdale, NJ: Erlbaum, pp. 115–148.

Nelson, K. E. (2001). Dynamic tricky mix theory suggests multiple analyzed pathways (MAPS) as an intervention approach for children with autism and other language delays. In S. von Tetzchner and J. Clibbens (eds), *Understanding the Theoretical and Methodological Bases of Augmentative and Alternative Communication*. Toronto: International Society for Augmentative and Alternative Communication, pp. 141–159.

O'Grady, W. (2010). Emergentism. In P. Hogan (ed.), *The Cambridge Encyclopedia of the Language Sciences*. Cambridge: Cambridge University Press, pp. 274–276.

Oetting, J. B. and Hadley, P. A. (2009). Morphosyntax in child language development. In R. G. Schwartz (ed.), *Handbook of Language Disorders*. New York: Psychology Press, pp. 341–364.

Perkins, M. R. (2010). Pragmatic Impairment. In J. S. Damico, N. Müller, and M. J. Ball (eds), *Blackwell Handbooks in Linguistics: The Handbook of Language and Speech Disorders*. Oxford: Wiley-Blackwell, pp. 227–246.

Redmond, S. M. (2005). Differentiating SLI from ADHD using children's sentence recall and production of past tense morphology. *Clinical Linguistics and Phonetics*, 19, 109–127.

Rosel, J., Caballer, A., Jara, P., and Oliver, J. C. (2005). Verbalism in the narrative language of children who are blind and sighted. *Journal of Visual Impairment and Blindness*, July, 413–425.

Sanetti, L. M. H. and Kratochwill, T. R. (2009). Toward developing a science of treatment integrity: introduction to the special series. *School Psychology Review*, 38, 445–459.

Schelletter, C. and Leinonen, E. (2003). Normal and language-impaired children's use of reference: syntactic versus pragmatic processing. *Clinical Linguistics and Phonetics*, 17, 335–443.

Siegler, R. S. (2006). Microgenetic analyses of learning. In W. Damon and R. M. Lerner (series eds) and D. Kuhn and R. S. Siegler (vol. eds), *Handbook of Child Psychology*, vol. 2, *Cognition, Perception, and Language*, 6th edn. Hoboken, NJ: John Wiley & Sons, Inc., pp. 464–510. http://www.psy.cmu.edu/~siegler/siegler06hnbk.pdf (accessed February 23, 2012).

Thomas, M. S. C., Dockrell, J. E., Messer, D. *et al.* (2006). Speeded naming, frequency and the development of the lexicon in Williams syndrome. *Language and Cognitive Processes*, 21(6), 721–759.

Thomas, M. S. C., Purser, H. R. M., and Richardson, F. M. (in press). Modularity and developmental disorders. In: P. D. Zelazo (ed.), *Oxford Handbook of Developmental Psychology*. Oxford: Oxford University Press. http://www.bbk.ac.uk/its/psyc/staff/academic/mthomas (accessed February 23, 2012).

Thompson, C. and Shapiro, (2005). Treating agrammatic aphasia within a linguistic framework: treatment of underlying forms. *Aphasiology*, 19(10/11), 1021–1036.

van Dijka, M. and van Geert, P. (2007). Wobbles, humps and sudden jumps: a case study of continuity, discontinuity and variability in early language development. *Infant and Child Development*, 16, 7–33.

Van Dyke, J. A. and McElree, B. (2006) Retrieval interference in sentence processing. *Journal of Memory and Language*, 55(2), 157–166.

Vivanti, G., Nadig, A., Ozonoff, S., and Rogers, S. J. (2008). What do children with autism attend to during imitation tasks? *Journal of Experimental Child Psychology*, 101(3), 186–205.

Wesley, P. W., Bryant, D., Fenson, C. *et al.* (2010). Treatment fidelity challenges in a five-state consultation study. *Journal of Educational and Psychological Consultation*, 20, 209–227.

6 Qualitative Research in Clinical Linguistics and Phonetics

Nicole Müller

6.1 Definitions

This chapter will introduce basic principles and tools of qualitative research as they apply to clinical linguistics,[1] with the role of the researcher as a focal point. Many introductions to research methods make a basic distinction between quantitative and qualitative methodologies (see e.g. Creswell, 2003), and I shall therefore adopt this contrast, with an important caveat: A key concept in research design is that of control. An experiment tests a preformulated hypothesis by specifically addressing the variables of interest to the researcher and controlling for variables that are not of interest. In order to be able to do that, researchers need to unambiguously define variables and conditions. Experiments can be regarded as 'static' entities, in that for the duration of the study, conditions are kept identical across subjects in any one group (experimental or control), and variables are predefined. In an experimental study, flexibility and adapting to the context or the responses of participants are to be avoided. Therefore, the defining parameter of 'quantitative' (i.e. experimental research) studies is the degree of control (the same is true for quantificational survey research), rather than the quantification of results.

Thus, reductionist, decontextualized experiments that are designed to permit generalization of findings from a study sample to a population can be regarded as being at one end of a continuum with control as the operative principle. At the other end, there are maximally emergent and methodologically flexible qualitative studies that furnish detailed investigations of complex, contextually embedded (and context-dependent) phenomena. Definitions of what constitutes qualitative research vary, and as Creswell (2007) notes, have evolved over time. The multiple editions of one of the key resources in this field in the anglophone literature serves as an illustration.

Research Methods in Clinical Linguistics and Phonetics: A Practical Guide,
First Edition. Edited by Nicole Müller and Martin J. Ball.
© 2013 Blackwell Publishing Ltd. Published 2013 by Blackwell Publishing Ltd.

The at the time of chapter preparation most recent edition of Denzin and Lincoln's (*Sage*) *Handbook of Qualitative Research* (Denzin and Lincoln, 2011b) defines the enterprise as follows:

> Qualitative research is a situated activity that locates the observer in the world. Qualitative research consists of a set of interpretive, material practices that make the world visible. These practices transform the world. They turn the world into a series of representations, including fieldnotes, interviews, conversations, photographs, recordings and memos to the self. At this level, qualitative research involves an interpretive, naturalistic approach to the world. This means that qualitative researchers study things in their natural settings, attempting to make sense of, or interpret, phenomena in terms of the meanings people bring to them.
>
> (Denzin and Lincoln, 2011a: 3)

This definition stresses a transformative quality of qualitative research; in other words, the researcher does not stand apart from the objects studied, but rather attempts to discover meaning with a view towards improvement of a status quo (a concept central to action research). This, as Creswell points out, "conveys the ever-changing nature of qualitative inquiry from social construction, to interpretivist, and on to social justice" (2007: 36). A more value-neutral definition is offered by Damico and Simmons-Mackie (2003: 132): "Qualitative research refers to a variety of analytic procedures designed to systematically collect and describe authentic, contextualized social phenomena with the goal of interpretive adequacy."

Different authors foreground different characteristics of qualitative research (see e.g. Creswell, 2007; Taylor and Bogdan, 1998). The principles in the following paragraphs (based in part on Guendouzi and Müller, 2006: 8–10) have guided my own qualitative work, and collaboration with colleagues:

1   The researcher is a learner, rather than the a priori expert on the situation under investigation. The researcher may thus "ask the questions," but will listen to what individuals have to say, and thus let the voices of the participants be heard. This in turn implies that our approach to our participants is one of partnership, which may extend to, for instance, involvement of participants in research study design.

2   Researchers need to enter into real-life contexts, they need to "go to the people" (Taylor and Bogdan, 1998), and keep an open mind as to what might be encountered in these contexts, and, importantly, about what might become relevant for the investigation at hand. Context is crucial, and rather than attempting to control and eliminate contextual factors and make the research essentially context-free (and thereby replicable, a hallmark of a well-designed experiment), the researcher needs to account for the role(s) of context. Qualitative research is often immersive, with the researcher spending extended time in the field.

3   Qualitative research typically starts with a fairly general, open-ended research question, and avoids research hypotheses that predefine the variables to be investigated and those to be controlled for. Data-gathering and analysis often proceed

in multiple cycles, during which narrower foci of analysis emerge, and which often involve multiple data sources and types of data.

4 Qualitative research is inductive: researchers examine patterns emerging from their data to come to an understanding of, and develop theories about, the objects of research. As Taylor and Bogdan point out, "[p]ure induction is impossible" (1998: 8), in that one cannot escape one's assumptions, training, preferences, values, and indeed interests (which prompt research in the first place).

5 Therefore, rather than attempt to remove the influence of the researcher from the investigation, the qualitative researcher is the most important data-gathering instrument. This means that the subjectivities that the researcher brings to the research enterprise need to be acknowledged and made explicit.

Section Summary

Among the characteristics of qualitative research are the following:

- Researchers adopt the role of learner, and enter into the life contexts of their participants; much of qualitative research requires extensive immersive fieldwork.
- Research questions are formulated initially from a wide-angle perspective; data-gathering and analysis often proceed in cyclical fashion.
- Qualitative research is inductive: patterns are allowed to emerge from the data.
- The researcher is the key instrument of data-gathering, and needs to acknowledge the subjectivities he or she brings to the research.

6.2 Traditions of Inquiry

Researchers make philosophical assumptions, and bring to their inquiries beliefs or worldviews that guide their choices in approach and methodology (see also Chapter 1 of this volume). Within the scope of qualitative research, practitioners may choose between various traditions of inquiry. The multiplicity of philosophical underpinnings, traditions, and methods is often a source of bewilderment for researchers who have come of age in an applied field (such as clinical linguistics or speech pathology), and are looking for a handy method to investigate, for instance, how people make sense of their experience in speech therapy, or what bilingual nursing home residents' language preferences are, or how people use language to construct and negotiate their personal identities and relationships with others. A thorough treatment of the history of approaches in qualitative research and their underlying philosophical assumptions would go far beyond the scope of this chapter, and readers are referred to Denzin and Lincoln's Handbook (2011, and earlier editions), and to Creswell (2007; the following very brief summary of the first four approaches below draws heavily on this latter source).

Biographical study (a subtype of *narrative inquiry*) draws chiefly on traditions in the humanities, including anthropology and literature. The focus of inquiry is the life of an individual, and that individual's experiences, who may have been approached by the researcher in hopes of understanding, through that individual's stories a certain life context or phenomenon. Researchers analyze their data (interview transcripts, participant journals, or other documents) by looking for stories, and 'restorying' them, which Creswell (2007: 56) defines as "the process of reorganizing the stories into some general type of framework." The goal is to develop a coherent narrative about the stories of the participant's life. While most clinical linguists will likely agree that biographical studies are somewhat peripheral to a focus on language or speech as the object of inquiry, they can furnish invaluable perspectives on relevant contexts. For instance, I would recommend Kidder's book *Old Friends* (to which Jack Damico drew my attention) to anyone who contemplates working with nursing home residents (Kidder, 1994).

Phenomenology is grounded in philosophy, specifically in the work of Edmund Husserl (1859–1938), a German mathematician. The focus of investigation is a human experience (or phenomenon), and data are collected from individuals who have experienced this phenomenon. The goal is to discover the meaning of the phenomenon for the individuals, and to filter out the "description of the universal essence" (Creswell, 2007: 58) of the phenomenon from the individual participants' experiences. A recent phenomenological study in the arena of speech-language pathology was conducted by Kardosh (2011), in which the author investigated the phenomenon of recovery from aphasia from the perspective of persons with aphasia, and their significant others.

Grounded theory was developed by sociologists Barney Glaser and Anselm Strauss (Glaser and Strauss, 1967) as a framework to allow for the generation of theory of social processes (for instance, interactions between individuals) based on, or grounded in, data collected from individuals. There are now several distinct variants of grounded theory; a recent development in this tradition is Charmaz's *constructivist grounded theory*, which emphasizes the co-construction of data with participants, detailed description, and the participants' perspectives and subjectivities, while de-emphasizing the identification of core categories and providing abstract accounts (see Charmaz, 2006). Skeat and Perry (2008) provide an overview of the evolution of grounded theory and its application in speech-language therapy.

Ethnography aims to describe and interpret the patterns of behaviors, values, beliefs, language use, and other shared cultural patterns and their meanings, from the perspective of the cultural group sharing them. Originating in cultural anthropology, methods used in ethnographic research have been adopted by many researchers in speech-language pathology and clinical linguistics. A specific development within ethnography, the ethnography of communication, is discussed in detail and illustrated in Chapter 7 of this book.

Conversation analysis, a method designed to investigate how individuals achieve social interaction through conversation, was developed in the context of sociology, and has become probably the most popular approach to analyzing conversational interaction in the context of communication disorders, where the emphasis is on the processes of interaction. This approach, its background, and application to clinical data are the topics of Chapter 8 of this volume.

Systemic Functional Linguistics (SFL; see Halliday and Matthiessen, 2004) is a theory of language use, and therefore would probably not be considered a tradition of qualitative inquiry by many theorists and research design scholars in the field (and, indeed, it is possible to do predictive, statistical research using the analytical tools of SFL). However, since SFL explicitly foregrounds the investigation of real-life, contextualized language use, it is proving to be an increasingly popular toolkit for clinical linguists doing qualitative work.

Section Summary

- Qualitative researchers choose from a number of approaches, grounded in different philosophical assumptions and worldviews.
- The choice of an approach will be guided by the object of investigation, as well as by the researcher's methodological and philosophical preferences, be it for instance the life of an individual (biographical study), or the investigation of a social process for which there are no adequate theories explaining it (grounded theory), or the study of a cultural group's practices, values and beliefs from their perspective (ethnography).

6.3 Case-Based Research and Qualitative Case Studies

The investigation of individual cases has always been a cornerstone of the clinical communication sciences. Case-based research in our field is heavily influenced by the medical sciences and psychology (especially neuropsychology), and therefore often employs quasi-experimental designs, which involves the collection of predetermined, closed sets of data. For instance, researchers use language or speech data generated by the repeated administration of norm-referenced assessments, separated by a period of intervention (the effect of which is the object of investigation), or by an extended time period, in order to measure deterioration of functioning in a progressive condition (see e.g. Code *et al.*, 2006). However, the investigation of individual cases employing qualitative methods has developed a strong following in clinical linguistics and speech-language pathology in recent decades.

Case studies are treated as a separate tradition of inquiry by Creswell (2007), whereas Stake (2000: 435) describes case study research as "not a methodological choice but a choice of what is to be studied," and defines a "case" as a "specific, unique, bounded system" (p. 436). In clinical linguistics, a case can thus be, for instance, a person displaying systematic behaviors related to a given speech or language disorder, or a therapy program (for instance a specific application of a type of aphasia intervention), or an institution (e.g. a nursing home). While case study researchers may ultimately seek to generalize from a single case to a wider population, and may indeed select cases with a view towards that end, an important characteristic of a case study is that it is "a concentrated inquiry into a single case" (Stake, 2000: 436), and the researcher's goal is to develop an in-depth understanding of that particular case. Qualitative case studies typically use multiple sources of information, and several methods of data-gathering, such as participant observation, interviews, recorded conversations, or narratives, but also the analysis of documents and other artifacts, while clinical linguists doing case studies use primarily language data (recordings, transcripts). As with all qualitative research, the analysis of data foregrounds description of patterns arising out of the data.

6.3.1   *Categories of Qualitative Case Studies*

Case selection can be guided by different motivations. An *instrumental case* study is undertaken because a researcher is interested in investigating a particular issue or question and selects one or several cases on the basis of which he or she hopes to gain insight into the issue at hand (when several cases are selected, we typically speak of a *collective case study*) (Creswell, 2007; Stake, 2000). For example, Mok (2011) purposefully approached residents in an assisted living facility as potential 'cases' in her investigation of how people with dementia use language to build and sustain relationships.

In contrast to an instrumental case study, an *intrinsic* case study is one where the case itself is the researcher's focus of interest, rather than a question or issue exemplified by the case(s). The researcher wishes to gain an understanding of a particular child with speech-output impairment, or a specific speech-intervention program situated at a particular school. Thus Kroll (see Kroll and Müller, 2011) elected to investigate the speech output of a child with a diagnosis of moderate to severe speech-output impairment on his clinical case load, because the child's speech production showed unusual fluctuations in intelligibility. In this particular study, identification and subsequent investigation was incidental to another role of the researcher, namely Kroll's role as the child's speech-language pathologist. While all participant and case selection should of course be purposeful, an interesting case appearing incidentally to a primarily non-research activity is not an uncommon scenario for researchers who are also speech-language pathologists, or linguists embedded with speech-language pathology departments. Such cases can trigger an investigation that may then at a later stage be repeated as an instrumental case study with one or more other participants (or indeed develop into a testable hypothesis and be investigated using an experimental paradigm). While the distinction between instrumental and intrinsic case studies is widely recognized, there is no strict dividing line between the two categories; rather, Stake (2000: 437) describes them as being separated by "a zone of combined purpose"; that is, researchers simultaneously have multiple interests, in the specific case and in gaining more general insights.

> **Section Summary**
>
> - A qualitative case study represents the intensive study of a specific, bounded system, and the researcher's goal is to develop an in-depth understanding of that case.
> - A case can be a person, or a place, or an activity.
> - An *instrumental* case study is motivated by a researcher's interest in a specific issue or problem, and the case is selected as an illustration of the issue; in an *intrinsic* case study, the case itself is the primary interest.

6.4 Preparing the Ground: Finding a Question, Preparing a Study, and Finding Participants

Given the characteristics of qualitative research discussed above, it follows that in the context of clinical linguistics, and communication impairments, qualitative methods are particularly suited for the investigation of complex, context-embedded phenomena that involve the discovery of meanings from the perspective of the participants, and of behavior patterns (for instance, language use patterns) that cannot sensibly be teased apart from the outset into discrete (testable) variables. In other words, the flexible, context-embedded, and emergent nature of qualitative methods makes them especially suitable for contexts where we know that "something (worth investigating) is going on," but we don't quite know what, yet.

6.4.1 Identifying a Problem and Situating a Study Methodologically

Given the flexible and responsive nature of qualitative research, it may seem counterintuitive to distinguish discrete phases in a research project, along the lines of planning, data-gathering, analysis, and interpretation. However, it would be fatal to any research project for a researcher to just "go in and see what happens," and hope to come up with usable results. Qualitative research in the clinical realm is typically applied research, in that a problem is identified, and one's research is intended to contribute to the understanding and eventual amelioration of said problem. A problem can be a 'real-life' problem, identified in a specific setting, or a gap in the available literature. The researcher's assumptions, background, and experience will have a significant impact on how a problem or issue is translated into a broad research question. For example, clinical linguists may investigate how people with, for instance, dysarthria and their non-impaired peers manage conversational interactions, and what is treated as a conversational breakdown and what is not (see e.g. Rutter, 2008). They may be interested in the cultures of dementia from the perspective of those affected by it (people with dementia and their caregivers), and how cultural notions, norms, and expectations are constructed through language use (see e.g. Guendouzi and Müller, 2006).

At the planning stage, a researcher also needs to methodologically situate her- or himself and the study to be undertaken. While it has long been acknowledged that clinical linguistics is a somewhat eclectic field in terms of available methods, one needs to keep in mind that methods arise out of philosophical and theoretical traditions, and will constrain the available perspectives on the data. In addition, different methods and approaches of course require different types of data and data-collection methods. With contextualized use of language and speech as research priorities, qualitative researchers in clinical linguistics often use methods grounded in ethnography (for instance, participant observation, ethnographic interviewing; see e.g. Simmons-Mackie and Damico, 1999). Where the moment-by-moment negotiation of conversational interaction is the object of inquiry, conversation analysis (see Chapter 8 of this volume) is often the method of choice. In addition, an increasing number of clinical linguists use analytic tools from Systemic Functional Linguistics combined with immersive field research (see e.g. Müller and Mok, 2012; Müller, Mok, and Keegan, in press).

Question formulation may initially be based on a review of the relevant literature, combined with an exploration and acknowledgment of the researcher's values and assumptions, along with exploratory fieldwork. To illustrate, Mok (2011; see also Müller, Mok, and Keegan, in press) started with background knowledge regarding the communicative impairments consequent to dementia of the Alzheimer's type, and the assumption, supported by published literature, that social isolation is a common experience for elders with dementia living in residential care. A review of the literature on communication in dementia revealed a gap leading to a broad question, namely, "how do people with dementia interact with each other?", led by the assumption that in residential care, interactants available to residents are most likely other residents. Further assumptions, also supported by published literature, led this research, namely that "it's good to talk"; in other words, social interaction is important for an individual's well-being, and further, that an important part of interacting with others is the construction of interpersonal processes, that is, establishing and projecting how we relate to others. In addition, it was assumed that face-to-face conversations are the prime 'site' for the construction of interpersonal processes. This resulted in a narrowing down of the research question to "how to people with dementia in residential care use language to enact their roles and relations in their talk with each other?"

6.4.2   *Sampling, and Getting Access to Sites and Participants*

Sampling, that is, the selection of participants in qualitative research, is purposeful: participants and sites are selected because they can contribute to the researcher's understanding of the issue or problem to be investigated. Sample sizes are typically small (as few as a single participant), but extensive corpora of data are collected, often involving multiple types of data. Researchers working with people who have communication disorders often need to obtain access to institutions such as schools, special education units, rehabilitation centers, or nursing homes. Several years ago

I conducted observations in a nursing home in South Louisiana; my broad research question was, "what are language practices and preferences of bilingual elders in residential care?" (see Müller, 2009). Getting access took several weeks, required making the rounds of several facilities, and then multiple levels of permission (from the facility owner, manager, and the activities director, as well as of course IRB clearance; see Chapter 2 of this volume). Individuals that may control access to a facility are often referred to as 'gatekeepers'. In dealing with gatekeepers, I have found it helpful to be maximally open and explicit about what I was trying to learn – though researchers of topics involving, for instance, questionable interventions may beg to differ (see e.g. Taylor and Bogdan, 1998, for further discussion). What all researchers aiming to get access to vulnerable populations and institutions or individuals caring for them, should keep in mind is that a researcher is rather more likely to be welcomed into the participants' lives if these participants perceive that the researcher's presence is not a threat or disruption, but, on the contrary, that they benefit in some way, for instance, because she is good company, or volunteers to help out (see also DeClercq, 2000, on participant observation in nursing homes for persons with dementia). Benefits for an institution can include that the researcher shares insights from the study with gatekeepers, for example activities directors or case managers, or initiatives such as a researcher offering an in-service course for care staff education.

There are numerous strategies for the selection of research sites and participants, and Creswell (2007) provides a very useful summary. Researchers need to make decisions at the planning stage as to what approximate sample size they will need, as well as on sampling strategies. For instance, grounded theory research employs the notion of theoretical sampling, where researchers select participants in order to discover more about categories and properties emerging from the data, and sampling and data analysis are an iterative process, rather than two discrete phases (see Skeat and Perry, 2008, for a detailed discussion). In a collective case study, a researcher may aim for maximum variation among the individual cases, in order to gain access to different perspectives; a single case may be selected because it presents an unusual perspective on the issue at hand, or conversely, because a researcher may perceive it to represent a 'typical' case.

Section Summary

- At the planning stage, qualitative researchers identify a broad research question or problem.
- A review of the literature, an examination of one's own pre-existing knowledge and assumptions, and exploratory fieldwork (as well as other factors) can contribute to the narrowing down of a broad problem to a question that can be investigated.
- A researcher needs to choose an approach and methods suited to the question, as these will impact data-gathering.
- Sampling in qualitative research is purposeful, rather than random.
- Getting access to participants and institutions needs careful planning, and often involves multiple layers of permission.

6.5   Data Types and Data Sources: A Brief Selection

As qualitative research continues to establish itself in the mainstream of applied clinical research, the types of data collection, sites, and methods, as well as the types of data under scrutiny, continues to expand. In addition, it is now much easier for researchers to record, archive, and integrate multiple types of data, owing to the rapid development of relevant technologies (see also Chapter 10 of this volume, on data recording). What follows is a brief selection of data types and sources, with specific reference to the 'raw data' generated, and the role of the researcher.

6.5.1   Field Notes and Participant Observation

Detailed *field notes* are the product of *participant observation*, a mainstay of immersive ethnographic research; the researcher's goal is to gain an 'insider' perspective on daily life in the setting or community observed, while, of necessity, also remaining an outsider. The 'rawest' form of data generated here are the observations themselves; however the first layer of tangible data are field notes generated by the researcher (typically, participant observers do not audio- or video-record). Thus the researcher's perceptions (in turn informed by assumptions, values, expectations, and indeed observation and memory skills) are the lens through which 'what happened' is filtered. There are many possible variations to the participant observation enterprise; what follows is a brief discussion of some relevant factors (many detailed introductions are available, see e.g. Patton, 1987; Spradley, 1980; Taylor and Bogdan, 1998). Different scholars prefer different methods of note taking. Some recommend taking very brief notes 'on the job' that are later expanded; however, this can raise suspicions among the observed community, unless the observation site is such that everyone takes notes (such as a classroom). During observations in a nursing home some years ago (see Müller, 2009), a resident who had clearly been observing me very closely came up to me when he saw me writing down some brief notes, and asked me whether I was working for the state – as it turned out from our subsequent conversation, 'working for the state' was not a good thing in his eyes, and roughly equated with 'spy'.

The form of field notes will vary from researcher to researcher; the bottom line is that the product field notes is supposed to serve as a tangible record of the process of observation, in as much relevant detail as can be recalled (see e.g. Spradley, 1980; Taylor and Bogdan, 1998, for detailed practical advice). There are some general guidelines that most researchers doing participant observation and field notes would agree with. (a) The sooner the better: notes should be written up as soon as possible after the observation session. (b) Lots of detail is better than trying to summarize: an hour in the field usually requires several hours of note-writing. (c) The focus of observation will (usually) grow narrower, and redefine itself, as a series of observations progresses. When new to a setting, a wide-angle perspective is most helpful, and observers need to overcome the selective inattention that is the normal human mode of functioning in a busy environment: Our attention focuses on what we perceive as important; however, this is counterproductive for a participant observer who essentially does not know yet what may or may not become important. (d) Notes should include 'factual' detail as well as detail about the observer's perceptions, emotional reactions, hunches, etc. The observer's reactions are part of 'what happened', and therefore need to be recorded. It is important that observers don't try to make notes more 'objective' by leaving their reactions out of the picture: these reactions will color perceptions and interpretations. Having said that, it is important to clearly distinguish between factual descriptive information, and description of the observer's reactions. Some researchers separate observer comments graphically by using parentheses and 'O.C.' for 'observer comment' (Taylor and Bogdan, 1998); I like to use italics in parentheses for observer comments, evaluations, hunches and the like.

6.5.2 *Interviews*

Interviews play a central role in many qualitative traditions and approaches. For clinical linguists, interviews (like conversations; see below) can furnish two broad levels of information: *content*, and *form*, or *expression*. In other words, interview data are of interest not only for the content-based interpretations of the phenomenon under investigation, but they can also give valuable information on how impairment impacts interactional language use a functional, natural context. Face-to-face interviews are typically considered the most useful form of data for clinical linguists, especially if they can be video- as well as audio-recorded. The development of technologies such as Skype™ has also made it easier to conduct interviews with participants in far-flung locations, as long as they have access to computers, and are willing to use them.

Interviews in the qualitative tradition are not pre-scripted (along the lines of clinical diagnostic interviews), but rather open-ended and flexible in nature. The most commonly used model, with some variations, in speech-language therapy and clinical linguistics is probably the ethnographic interview (Spradley, 1979), widely disseminated in the clinical context by Westby and colleagues (e.g. Westby, 1990). Interviews can be individual or group interviews; if the latter, it is desirable that groups be small in order to give everyone ample opportunity to talk and voice their 'take' on the topics at hand. For the purposes of the clinical linguist, interviews always need to be recorded and transcribed (see Chapters 10 and 11 of this volume). The role that the researcher projects in a qualitative interview should be that of an interested listener, of a learner who values what the respondent has to say, rather than an interviewer (worst possible scenario: interrogator) who is looking for information specified a priori. Thus, while the researcher guides the interaction and chooses the overall topic (the rationale for the interview), the directions that the interview may take should be flexible, and the researcher needs to guard against insistence on predetermined questions at the expense of cutting off a potential promising flow of information. Ethnographic interviews employ open-ended, descriptive questions that ask about broad experiences (sometimes referred to as 'grand tour' questions); on the basis of the interviewee's responses, more narrowly focused questions follow up on the specifics. Throughout, the researcher has to guard against imposing her or his perspective or evaluation of what the participant has to say on the course of the interview – rather, the aim is to keep the informant talking, and to thereby access their perspective. There is a place for the researcher's 'take' on the development of an interview and on what is said: It is useful to keep an interview journal, or field journal, where not only logistical data are kept for future reference (date, time, place, duration of interview, setting) as well as a record of other factors that may have an impact (such as the presence of others within earshot or visual range), but where the researcher also notes her or his own reactions and reflections on what has happened.

6.5.3   *Conversations*

There is not always a strict dividing line between qualitative research interviews and casual conversations; in fact, an atmosphere of having a casual conversation with an interested stranger is one of the desirable characteristics of an ethnographic interview. Casual conversation, however, does not typically have a specific transactional agenda: In other words, there are no predetermined topics that need to be discussed, rather, as Eggins and Slade (1997: 6) put it, casual conversation happens when we "talk for the sake of talking." Casual conversations are extremely useful data sources for qualitative clinical linguists, in that (as do interviews) they can provide different levels of information: they give insight into how a person perceives and relates to their environment and their conversation partner(s), in that much of what casual conversations are about is the "joint construction of social reality" (Eggins and Slade, 1997: 6); that is, they are an important tool people use to establish social identities and their relationships with others. We can also learn from investigations of casual conversations how people manage to achieve interaction, which is a question that Conversation Analysts are centrally interested in (see Chapter 8 of this volume). A more linguistically focused question, rather than "how do these two people do conversation?" is "how does language make it possible to do conversation?" and in the clinical context, one of many variations on this question would be "what are the linguistic tools at the disposal of this person with aphasia, and his conversation partner without aphasia, that enable them to have a conversation?"

Researchers planning to use casual conversation data have to decide whether it is desirable for the researcher her- or himself to take part in the conversations. This can have logistical advantages (no need to hand over one's precious recording equipment to others, knowing that data collection happens, rather than relying on others, for example), but it can also have drawbacks. The main point to consider is that in order to have an extended casual conversation, one needs to establish sufficient rapport with one's participants that they are willing to sit down (typically) and "just talk": they have to be interested enough and sufficiently well disposed towards the researcher to find having a conversation with her or him an attractive notion. In addition, the presence of recording equipment, especially cameras, can remove much of the "casualness" from the conversation. There are ways to overcome this dilemma (see also Chapter 10), and I consider the most important piece of advice here, "give it time." This refers both to any one individual conversation, and to the extended data collection period: When working with people with dementia (see e.g. Guendouzi and Müller, 2006), I found that, often, conversations were slow to start; participants required a certain "warm-up" period, as it were, in order for a conversation to gain momentum. As well as that, I would invest time in multiple visits with my participants before attempting to record our conversations, and therefore build a relationship of trust in which the presence of a microphone was not perceived as a threat. It is important that when researchers act as conversation partners as well as data collectors, they learn to find a balance of participation. It is easy to dominate a conversation and crowd out one's conversation partners, but on the other hand, a researcher should facilitate where necessary and keep a conversation going.

If a researcher wishes to remain out of the picture, there is the option of providing recording equipment to participants and to agree in advance on a recording schedule. This strategy can be very useful if repeated recordings are targeted with multiple conversational dyads in their own homes. Alternatively, a researcher can set up recording equipment for participants, and then remove her- or himself from the scene (see Rutter, 2008).

6.5.4   *Multiple Data Sources*

Many qualitative studies make use of several different data sources and data types; in fact, this is the norm in ethnographic studies. In theory, there is no limit to what can become useful data. For example, remote communication such as e-mails, text messages, or social networking is becoming more and more relevant for many people, and therefore also deserves increased attention in the clinical enterprise. Therapy interactions are a good example of a situation where multiple potential data types and collection methods converge: video recordings of therapy sessions, artifacts generated as part of the therapy, diagnostic data pre- and post-intervention, interviews with therapists, clients, and significant others, "off-therapy" e-mail interactions between client and therapist, are some of the data types that become potentially relevant (see e.g. Simmons-Mackie and Damico, 1999, for a discussion of an ethnographic study of aphasia therapy). The researcher's role here is not only that of a collector, but rather a 'generator': Objects become data when they are treated as such. Thus, whether any given document or potential source is activated as data, that is, gets funneled into the descriptive and interpretive process, is up to the researcher's judgment.

Section Summary

- Many qualitative studies involve multiple data sources and data types, and in theory there is no data source that *cannot* be included.
- Field notes are the researcher's record of field observations. While the researcher needs to acknowledge and record her or his feelings, impressions, hunches, and tentative interpretations in the field notes, it is important to

clearly separate them from factual content. The focus of observation typically starts broad, and narrows and redefines itself as observations progress.

- Qualitative research interviews are not pre-scripted; rather, the researcher has an overall topic and a broad outline that is implemented by means of open-ended, descriptive questions, but has to be prepared to follow the interviewee's lead. The aim is to keep the interviewee talking, and to access their perspective on the topic under investigation.
- Casual conversation is particularly useful in the investigation of how participants relate to their environment and others, and how a specific speech or language impairment impacts linguistic interaction.

6.6   Working with Data: Analysis and Interpretation

Qualitative researchers typically generate enormous amounts of data, and the question arises, what to do with a pile of transcripts? Different qualitative traditions approach the minutiae of descriptive analysis and interpretation differently (see e.g. Creswell, 2007, and Taylor and Bogdan, 1998, for more detailed discussion and further references), but there are certain principles and aspects that are common to most. In a qualitative *linguistic* study, researchers focus on a finite number of resources (e.g. lexical choices, collocations, interactional choices such as clause structure) that, however, in combination can produce a potentially unlimited number of meanings. An important aspect of qualitative analysis is its *iterative* nature, as illustrated below.

In investigations of how people with dementia use language to build and sustain relationships (see e.g. Mok, 2011; Müller and Wilson, 2008), useful data sources include casual conversations, more interview-oriented, researcher-led conversations specifically targeting social relationships, as well as participant observation field notes. The process of making sense of the data should start while a researcher is still in the field and before data collection is completed. Researchers should read and reread their field notes and transcripts as they compile them, and thoroughly familiarize themselves with them; at this stage, it is very useful to make notes that record initial thoughts, hunches, ideas, or keywords that occur to one. In a study specifically targeting language use, a useful next step is the investigation of lexical choices, and the company they keep: what are people talking about, and how? Lexical analyses can usefully be accomplished using concordance programs, depending on the amount of data to be processed. What is interesting or relevant to the research question will largely emerge from the researcher's reading of the data; however, in the example I am using here, namely linguistic construction of identities, some types of word choices can be assumed to be inherently relationship-relevant, such as address terms, or terms of endearment, or negative epithets and swearwords.

Other word choices may emerge as relevant after multiple passes through the data: For instance, in interactions between a man with dementia in his nineties and a young fieldworker/visitor, the topic of 'money' was initiated regularly by the old man. Thus an initial theme, or category, is identified. Is this relevant to the question (how does he use language to establish his relationship with the young man)? A further pass through the data reveals that 'money' occurs in certain contexts, namely earning and saving it, getting credit and paying one's debt. A shift in perspective from lexical to interactional language choices reveals that the old man uses the theme of 'money' when he positions himself as the information-giver (using statements expressing sound financial practice, as in "I pay my debt"), accompanied by exhortations (e.g. "let me tell you"), and inviting confirmation (e.g. by asking "that not true?") from his interlocutor. Thus, the theme 'money' was identified as contributing (along with other themes) to a projected identity of the wise and knowledgeable old man who on the basis of his life experience is in a position to give valuable advice to the young man.

Importantly, a researcher needs to *verify* findings as they are made, and essentially 'plug' a finding from one pass through the data ('money' is a recurring topic and could be a relevant theme) into the next analytic round. This process of verification, which is also part of an increasingly detailed interpretation, should involve multiple instances and different occasions (repeated conversations or conversations with different interlocutors, for example). It may also usefully involve more than one researcher to verify the identification of what is a relevant theme and its interpretation, or checking by non-researcher participants (this can be difficult with people with dementia, but can be accomplished with non-impaired interlocutors).

Section Summary

- Qualitative data collection, analysis, and interpretation are iterative processes, and researchers need to begin the process of analysis and interpretation while still "in the field."
- Researchers need to verify their findings as data analysis progresses: A finding from one round of data analysis becomes the starting point for the next cycle.

6.7   Conclusion and Outlook

At the time of chapter preparation, there is no question that qualitative methods in clinical linguistics are here to stay, and are well established in the clinical context overall. The aim of this chapter was to introduce and discuss some basic concepts of qualitative research, specifically with reference to the role of the researcher in the qualitative enterprise. As stated above, the researcher is the key element throughout all stages of a qualitative study, from the conception of a research question through participant selection, data collection and interpretation, to the write-up and eventual dissemination of a study (see Chapter 16 of this volume on the latter aspect). Given this, how does one ensure that the findings of a qualitative study are not "just the researcher's opinion"; in other words, what makes for a good qualitative study in clinical linguistics? The following points reflect my own priorities and preferences, and are strongly motivated by the circumstance that by definition, clinical linguists work with vulnerable populations. Readers may find detailed discussions on the quality of qualitative research for example in Taylor and Bogdan (1998), Lincoln and Guba (2000), or Creswell (2007).

A good qualitative study is an *ethical* study. This does not only mean that a researcher has secured all necessary permissions (including IRB approval, for studies originating in university settings), but more fundamentally that the study has the interests and benefit of the participants at heart, that there is an element of giving back to the participants (reciprocity), that we respect our participants (even if at times we may fundamentally disagree with their values and opinions), and make an active effort to contribute to the dismantling of existing stereotypes about the populations we work with in the clinical context.

The requirement that a study be *well motivated* in essence follows on from, and overlaps with, ethical concerns. A study should address a genuine problem, that is, something that genuinely affects the lives of our participants. While a gap in the available literature may serve as a starting point for question formulation, researchers need to ask themselves whether what they intend to investigate is an issue that genuinely affects the lives of the participants they intend to recruit (and by implication, inconvenience). This is not to say that every qualitative study should be able to be translated into a practical application and improvement of the immediate participants' lives; however, it should be a genuine effort to construct a building block in a growing knowledge base in an applied field of research.

A study needs to be *carefully situated methodologically*, using methods appropriate to the question at hand, and give evidence of the researcher examining and documenting the usefulness of the method(s) chosen. I do not necessarily advocate methodologically 'pure' research as the ideal scenario, and as a clinical linguist I prefer methods of analysis that directly address the linguistic resources used by participants. However, when a researcher combines data collection methods originating in ethnography (e.g. ethnographic interviewing) with an analytic framework that is firmly grounded in linguistics (Systemic Functional Linguistics), she or he needs to make the rationale for these choices explicit.

A qualitative researcher needs to situate the investigation squarely in the real-life contexts of the participants. For a clinical linguist, this of course includes the use of therapy data, since speech-language therapy is part of our client's 'real life', and how to make therapy meaningful and therefore efficacious is a constant concern. However, researchers should go beyond the immediate data collection tasks and contexts to learn about the participants' lives, histories, and cultures, and integrate this learning into their studies.

Data collection has to be *rigorous in method and detail, and carefully documented*. This does not necessarily mean that multiple disparate types of data need to be collected for every good qualitative study in clinical linguistics (although adding, for example, a participant observation component to the investigation of casual conversations not only contextualizes the primary data source further but is a useful validation strategy; see below). However, a qualitative clinical linguist needs to commit to extended time in the field, and to multiple instances of data collection with any one participant.

Researchers need to employ (and document) *validation strategies* to document that their readings of the data and their meanings are defensible and well grounded in the data. There have been numerous debates on the usefulness or otherwise of applying the terms 'validity' and 'reliability', as they are used in experimental science to qualitative research (Creswell, 2007, provides a very useful summary; see also Gergen and Gergen, 2000, and Lincoln, Lynham, and Guba, 2011). *Triangulation* is a technique whereby researchers use multiple methods and data sources in a study to corroborate conclusions drawn. Thus, a participant observer may also use interview data, or existing documentation, or involve other observers. A researcher may recruit a *peer reviewer*, defined by Lincoln and Guba (1985, quoted in Creswell, 2007: 208) as a "devil's advocate who keeps the researcher honest; asks hard questions about methods, meanings, and interpretations," but who is also a sympathetic listener. *Member checking* is a process whereby a researcher shares data, interpretations, and conclusions with the study participants and asks them to contribute their judgment about credibility and accuracy (this is, of course, problematic with some participants, such as people with dementia or other cognitive impairments). *'Thick' description* is an additional validation strategy, in that a detailed description of participants, data collection settings, techniques, and so forth not only make these details explicit, but they allow readers to judge whether findings from a study can be transferred to other settings (Creswell, 2007: 209).

Last but not least, a good qualitative study is a *'good read'*: It draws the reader with a wealth of detail, both descriptive and interpretive, and brings the research participants, the problem investigated, and the researcher's process of investigation and interpretation to life.

Section Summary

- Good qualitative research is conducted ethically; it is well motivated, carefully situated methodologically, and firmly anchored in the lives of the participants.
- Good qualitative data collection is rigorous in method and detail and carefully documented.
- Researchers employ and document validation strategies such as triangulation, peer review, member checking, and 'thick' description.
- In addition, a good qualitative study should be well written.

6.8   Resources

The CAQDAS Networking project, hosted at the University of Surrey, UK (www.surrey.ac.uk/sociology/research/researchcentres/caqdas/index.htm) provides advice, training, and support to researchers using computer applications for data analysis in qualitative research. The site offers guidance in the choice of computer software, reviews of available software packages, as well as other resources, such as links to working papers, e-mail discussion lists, and an online bibliography on computer-assisted qualitative data analysis.

The Centre for Qualitative Research at Bournemouth University, UK, hosts a website on qualitative research in health and social care (www.bournemouth.ac.uk/cqr/index.html).

The Forum: Qualitative Social Research (for German speakers: Forum Qualitative Sozialforschung) is an open-access, peer-reviewed journal and archive with contributions covering a wide range of methods and topics in qualitative research. It can be accessed at: www.qualitative-research.net.

The International Institute for Qualitative Methodology at the University of Alberta, Canada, publishes an online journal, the *International Journal of Qualitative Methods* (ejournals.library.ualberta.ca/index.php/IJQM/index), which is available free of charge.

The Online Q(ualitative) D(ata) A(analysis) site hosted by the University of Huddersfield, UK, offers online tutorials and resources on qualitative methods, and can be accessed at: onlineqda.hud.ac.uk/index.php.

The Qual Page: Resources for Qualitative Research (www.qualitativeresearch.uga.edu/QualPage/methods.html) links to a wealth of resources on, among others, qualitative methods and their philosophical foundations, journals and other publications, and data analysis software.

Note

1   In this chapter, for reasons of economy of space, the term 'clinical linguistics' is to be read as 'clinical linguistics and phonetics'; likewise 'clinical linguist', etc.

References

Code, C. F. S., Müller, N., Tree, J. T., and Ball, M. J. (2006). Syntactic impairments can emerge later: progressive agrammatic aphasia and syntactic comprehension impairment. *Aphasiology*, 20, 1035–1058.

Creswell, J. W. (2003). *Research Design: Qualitative, Quantitative and Mixed Methods Approaches*, 2nd edn. Thousand Oaks, CA: Sage.

Creswell, J. W. (2007). *Qualitative Inquiry and Research Design: Choosing among Five approaches*, 2nd edn. Thousand Oak, CAs: Sage.

Charmaz, K. (2006). *Constructing Grounded Theory*. Thousand Oaks, CA: Sage.

Damico, J. S. and Simmons-Mackie, N. (2003). Qualitative research and speech-language pathology: a tutorial for the clinical realm. *American Journal of Speech-Language Pathology*, 12, 131–143.

DeClercq, A. (2000). (Participant) observation in nursing home wards for people suffering from dementia: the problems of trust and emotional involvement. *Forum Qualitative Sozialforschung / Forum: Qualitative Social Research* [online journal], 1(1). Retrieved August 8, 2004 from: http://www. qualitative-research. net/fqs-texte/1-00/100declercq-e. htm.

Denzin, N. K. and Lincoln, Y. S. (2011a). Introduction: the discipline and practice of qualitative research. In N. K. Denzin and Y. S. Lincoln (eds), *The Sage Handbook of Qualitative Research*, 4th edn. Thousand Oaks, CA: Sage, pp. 1–20.

Denzin, N. K. and Lincoln, Y. S. (eds) (2011b). *The Sage Handbook of Qualitative Research*, 4th edn. Thousand Oaks, CA: Sage.

Gergen, M. M. and Gergen, K. J. (2000). Qualitative inquiry: tensions and transformations. In N. K. Denzin and Y. S. Lincoln (eds), *Handbook of Qualitative Research*. Thousand Oaks, CA: Sage, pp 1025–1046.

Eggins, S. and Slade, D. (1997). *Analysing Casual Conversation*. London: Cassell.

Guendouzi, J. A. and Müller, N. (2006). *Approaches to Discourse in Dementia*. Mahwah, NJ: Erlbaum.

Glaser, B. G. and Strauss, A. L. (1967). *The Discovery of Grounded Theory*. Chicago: Aldine.

Halliday, M. A. K. and Matthiessen, C. M. I. M. (2004). *An Introduction to Functional Grammar*, 3rd edn. London: Edward Arnold.

Kardosh, B. M. (2011). The nature of recovery in aphasia from two perspectives: a phenomenological study. Unpublished PhD dissertation, University of Louisiana at Lafayette.

Kidder, T. (1994). *Old Friends*. New York: Mariner Books.

Kroll, T. and Müller, N. (2011). The impact of contextual, conversational, and affective factors on a child's speech intelligibility. *Journal of Interactional Research in Communication Disorders*, 2, 309–335.

Lincoln, Y. S. and Guba, E. G. (1985). *Naturalistic Inquiry*. Newbury Park, CA: Sage.

Lincoln, Y. S. and Guba, E. G. (2000). Paradigmatic controversies, contradictions, and emerging influences. In N. K. Denzin and Y. S. Lincoln (eds), *The Sage Handbook of Qualitative Research*, 3rd edn. Thousand Oaks, CA: Sage, pp. 191–215.

Lincoln, Y. S., Lynham, S. A., and Guba, E. G. (2011). Paradigmatic controversies, contradictions and emerging confluences, revisited. In N. K. Denzin and Y. S. Lincoln, (eds.), *The Sage Handbook of Qualitative Research*, 4th edn. Thousand Oaks, CA: Sage, pp. 97–128.

Mok, Z. (2011). The linguistic construction of interpersonal processes among people with dementia: an application of Systemic Functional Linguistics. Unpublished PhD dissertation, University of Louisiana at Lafayette.

Müller, N. (2009). Aging with French: observations from South Louisiana. *Journal of Cross-Cultural Gerontology*, 24, 143–155.

Müller, N. and Mok, Z. (2012). Applying Systemic Functional Linguistics to conversations with dementia: the linguistic construction of relationships between participants. *Seminars in Speech and Language*, 33, 5–15.

Müller, N., Mok, Z., and Keegan, L. (in press). The application of Systemic Functional Linguistics to qualitative research in communication disorders. In M. J. Ball, N. Müller, and Nelson, R. (eds), *The Handbook of Qualitative Research in Communication Disorders*. New York: Psychology Press.

Müller, N. and Wilson, B. T. (2008). Collaborative role construction in a conversation with dementia: an application of Systemic Functional Linguistics. *Clinical Linguistics and Phonetics*, 22, 767–774.

Patton, M. Q. (1987). *How to Use Qualitative Methods in Evaluation*. New York: Sage.

Rutter, B. (2008). Acoustic properties of repair sequences in dysarthric conversational speech: An interactional phonetic study. PhD dissertation, University of Louisiana at Lafayette.

Simmons-Mackie, N. and Damico, J. S. (1999). Qualitative methods in aphasia research: ethnography. *Aphasiology*, 13, 681–687.

Skeat, J. and Perry, A. (2008). Grounded theory as a method for research in speech and language therapy. *International Journal of Language and Communication Disorders*, 43, 95–109.

Spradley, J. P. (1979). *The Ethnographic Interview*. New York: Holt, Rinehart and Winston.

Spradley, J. P. (1980). *Participant Observation*. New York: Holt, Rinehart and Winston.

Stake, R. E. (2000). Case studies. In In N. K. Denzin and Y. S. Lincoln (eds), *Handbook of Qualitative Research*, 2nd edn. Thousand Oaks, CA: Sage, pp. 435–454.

Taylor, S. J. and Bogdan, R. (1998). *Introduction to Qualitative Research Methods*, 3rd edn. New York: John Wiley and Sons, Inc.

Westby, C. E. (1990). Ethnographic interviewing: asking the right questions to the right people in the right way. *Communication Disorders Quarterly*, 13, 101–111.

7 An Ethnographic Approach to Assessing Communication Success in Interactions Involving Adults with Developmental Delay

Jacqueline Guendouzi and Paula S. Currie

7.1 Introduction

Ethnographic methods are a key part of qualitative research in clinical linguistics. The ethnographic interview (Patton and Westby, 1992) is frequently used to elicit data that will either reveal the interactional or grammatical constructions under scrutiny, or provide background information about how a disorder affects the life of a particular client (e.g. Daniels and Gabel, 2004; Klompas and Ross, 2004). Despite the fact that ethnography is part of both research and clinical practice, it is not typically taught as an independent subject area within the field of communication disorders. For example, it is our experience that students undertaking research projects often state they are taking an ethnographic approach when analyzing their data; statements that typically mean they are giving background information on the participants and context involved in the interaction being examined. Ethnographic approaches, however, can be used in more systematic ways to analyze data (Guendouzi and Müller, 2006), that is, they can be used as an *active* part of the research process rather than simply providing a backdrop for the context.

It is important to note that ethnography encompasses more than one approach to gathering and analyzing data, and is used across a range of disciplines and research contexts. For the purposes of this chapter we will focus the discussion on one particular ethnographic method, the *ethnography of communication* (EC) (Hymes, 1972a). We will then set out the principal steps followed by EC in order to illustrate how EC can be used as a research tool to explore the specific question of why a

Research Methods in Clinical Linguistics and Phonetics: A Practical Guide,
First Edition. Edited by Nicole Müller and Martin J. Ball.
© 2013 Blackwell Publishing Ltd. Published 2013 by Blackwell Publishing Ltd.

training program involving student clinicians and non-professional care assistants working with adults with severe developmental delay (AWDD) was not successful.

7.1.1   What Is Ethnography?

Ethnography is a method of research that emerged from the social sciences, and in particular from anthropology (e.g. Malinowski, 1923/1972; Mead, 1928). In the early twentieth century, ethnographic methods were increasingly used to gather *empirical* data on human social groups through both observation of and interaction with a particular group. Thus ethnography was the field work carried out by anthropologists when recording the day-to-day habits and behaviors of a social group from the perspective of those under scrutiny. Ethnography encompasses several methods of investigation including, but not limited to, ethnographic interviewing, longitudinal studies, immersive research (e.g. Cheshire 1982), and ethnography of communication. The key element that underpins all ethnographic methods is that they are embedded within the cultural context under investigation; "thus context frames, or constrains, the research being undertaken, as well as being an object of research" (Müller and Guendouzi, 2009: 200).

Traditionally, an ethnographic approach is an attempt to provide a *holistic* description of a culture or social group. Typically it will include aspects of the historical and cultural background of the social group or individual being investiga-ted. For example, this might include information about the physical geography (or location, e.g. a clinic), the customs, behaviors (e.g. rites, rituals, etc.), relationships and hierarchies (e.g. kinship, leadership dynamics, clans, etc.), social structure and details of the group members (e.g. age, gender, etc.). However, we might ask whether the process of the research method (in this case ethnography) leads to a holistic view of a phenomenon that is actually based on a researcher-generated explanation; an explanation that results from the need to account for many separate and (perhaps) non-related details of an interaction that has been described in "the ethnography." We should note that in using a determiner to refer to "the ethnography" we run the risk of appearing to create a "product" that may be construed by students as something akin to a result in experimental research. The ethnographic narrative is not only an outcome of an ethnographic study but also a part of the research process that aids the researcher in positing an interpretation of the data.

Ethnography, like all qualitative research, is often accused of providing descriptions rather than explanations. Hermeneutic approaches (Packer, 2011) have described this process in terms of *erklären* (explaining) and *verstehen* (understanding). Thus the researcher interprets or explains (*erklären*) his or her data in order to account for what he or she finds, which leads to understanding (*verstehen*). The researcher's interpretation is part of the hermeneutic process that "constructs" an understanding of the object or phenomenon under study. However, critics might point out that the interpretive space between explanation and understanding is dependent on the researcher's perspective and the methodology they select to analyze their data (e.g. conversation analysis or ethnography). Therefore it could be claimed that ethnography like all qualitative methods is a highly subjective process and the resulting *understanding* depends on what the ethnographer includes in his or her ethnography, and indeed how he or she describes the information they include in their description.

Ethnography attempts to *describe* a particular group, culture, or linguistic practice in order to better *understand* the object under study but, as noted above, there is still a pervading opinion that qualitative methods such as ethnography can provide only a description and never an explanation. However, as Packer (2011) points out such methods can provide explanations because if we understand something (from the ethnography) we can in turn explain it to a third party (our readers or audience). Explanation (through the ethnography) is making something transparent (or less opaque) about a culture or interaction. "Explanation is an articulated reading that is both transparent and warranted", that is, it (the ethnography) is "transparent when it spells out the details, warranted when it lays out the evidence" (Packer, 2011: 113). Thus, an ethnographic approach lays out the details (evidence) which in turn creates "the ethnography" (the understanding) allowing us to attempt to provide an explanation of the interaction.

> **Section Summary**
>
> - Ethnography is a descriptive tradition of research that examines human social groups in order to uncover and interpret patterns of behaviors, and cultural practices from the perspective of the group under scrutiny.
> - Ethnography aims to be holistic in its approach.

7.2   Culture and Context: Situating Interactions

Holstein and Gubrium (1995) suggest that ethnographic research requires sensitivity to *context* or, at least, a minimal awareness on the part of the researcher of the cultural background in which the data to be collected are embedded. Furthermore, understanding the impact that contextual factors, such as social, historical, and cultural background, have on an interaction is a very important consideration when undertaking any ethnographic research.

As with the term *ethnography*, the terms *culture* and *context* are often used vicariously with the assumption they are implicitly understood by the general reader. Culture has many definitions (Geertz, 1977; Guendouzi and Müller, 2006) but is generally understood to be a social construct (although see Pinker, 2002, for a more evolution-driven explanation) that reflects a society's belief systems and ways of life. Likewise, context can be a complex phenomenon to define. Often context is taken to be a description of the physical environment (i.e. location, time of day, etc.) and participants involved in the interaction being examined. However, context should not be approached as a scene-setting device, that is, context is not something that is outside of or contains the interaction, but rather a dynamic interactive element of that interaction (see Duranti and Goodwin, 1992, for a comprehensive discussion of this topic).

Heller notes that "ethnographies allow us to get at things" (2008: 250) we might not otherwise discover. They provide the researcher with analytical tools that illuminate the complexities of communicative practices, allowing access to how communication acts are embedded within the everyday lives and histories of the people who use them. However, as Heller (2008) rightly points out, ethnographies are not simply a matter of giving a "voice" to the participants; interpretations of the information reported are the responsibility of the researcher. Nor do ethnographies necessarily give a complete and accurate picture of the culture or group being studied. Drawing on Giddens (1984), Heller discusses the issue of whether we can consider ethnographies to be a "bounded whole" and she suggests we consider them as socially constructed processes that "link across space and time" (2008: 251). In her discussion of ethnography in the context of bilingualism, Heller posits the idea of a "critical ethnographic study" (2008: 253), which encompasses ideologies, institutional discourses, and dynamics of power within its scope.

It has been suggested that ethnography in contrast to *action research* is a method that seeks to reveal and sustain a culture. Action research is a method "that explicitly targets change in the object under investigation" (Müller and Guendouzi, 2009: 200). However, in line with Heller's notion of a critical ethnography, the researcher needs to remember that it is not always an easy task to remain a neutral observer when describing cultural and social norms. In any ethnographic research, at some point the researcher is translating their data through the lens of their own perceptions and invariably must add to the cultural *meanings* that are generated through the reports that s/he eventually writes. Furthermore, once the research findings enter the public domain the researcher cannot be responsible for how they are then reinterpreted or used to support other viewpoints. It is important therefore to remember that research does not have to be overtly action-based in order to change the object under investigation.

Section Summary

- Ethnographic approaches incorporate both context and culture as dynamic subsystems of the interaction.
- Features of the ethnography can be seen as integral units of analysis rather than simply background information.

7.3   The Role of Ethnography in Investigating Speech and Language Disorders

Typically, ethnographic research is seen as data-driven rather than hypothesis-driven; it can, however, also support experimental research. The researcher has two options when using ethnographic information. The first is an emergent approach, where a broad interest (e.g. communication skills in children with Asperger syndrome) is identified. This in turn might lead to observations of children with Asperger syndrome (AS) in a classroom setting. Areas for analysis emerge as part of a cyclical approach to reviewing (and re-examining) the data collected. For example, after reviewing video footage it might be noted that boys with AS frequently interrupt others in class activities and that particular topic (i.e. interruptions) then becomes the focus of the research. Thus the questions or issues that are ultimately analyzed emerge from the process of collecting, reviewing, and analyzing the data.

The second option may be based on the researcher's prior knowledge of certain aspects of a topic area. A specific question is generated, but the researcher may need to employ ethnographic methods to support his/her claims regarding which communication behaviors are being singled out for analysis. For example, after reading the literature on formulaic language (van Lancker-Sidtis, 2011; Wray, 2002) we might note that people who have a communication disorder such as aphasia or dementia are more likely to use formulaic language. This knowledge would lend itself to, eventually, being investigated experimentally. However, in order to establish that the linguistic units we are counting can be legitimately labeled as formulaic expressions we would need several conversational samples from each of the participants. We might also need to interview the participants' regular communication partners to identify their use of formulaic expressions and attempt to establish whether the use of such expressions had changed over time. This type of research would involve using a range of ethnographic methods, for example, open-ended questions, participant-driven interviews, or participant observation. By using an ethnographic approach we might be better able to clarify and determine a definition of what comprises a formulaic expression for each individual participant. Thus contextualized methods of investigation can inform the formation of research questions and hypotheses that underlie experimental and quantificational studies.

7.3.1 *Participant Observation and the Role of Immersion*

Ethnographic methods are *immersive*; that is, the researcher may not only describe the society or group s/he is studying but also become an active *participant observer* within that society over time. Ward Schofield (2006) noted that immersion implies an "intensive, on-going involvement with individuals in their everyday settings" (2006: 81) and stressed that ethnography is not simply a matter of visiting a site on one or two occasions to record background information, but rather might involve multiple levels of involvement. These different levels of participation can be thought of as a continuum ranging from observer-participant (minimal involvement with the activities at hand) at one end to full participant at the other end.

The immersive aspect of ethnographic research does make it vulnerable to the observer's paradox (Labov, 1966) or Hawthorne effect. That is, by participating in or observing a social group or individual, the researcher invariably changes the dynamics of the interaction and may affect the interactional behaviors of partici-pants. When using ethnographic methods, the researcher needs to be aware that contextual factors introduced by the interviewer/observer (e.g. age, gender, cultural differences, types of questions asked, etc.) might affect the situational outcomes and, indeed, the researcher's interpretation of the meaning attributed to those interactions (Cukor-Avila, 2000).

Section Summary

- Ethnography is immersive, in that the researcher becomes a "participant" of the culture under scrutiny.
- Ethnography can be at risk of the "observer's paradox."
- Ethnography is often seen as an exploratory or emergent qualitative research method.
- Ethnography can also play a role in hypothesis-driven quantitative research, and can be used in studies that employ mixed-method research designs.

7.4   Ethnography of Communication

Hymes (1972b), drawing on traditional ethnographic studies (e.g. Malinowski, 1923/1972) and functional approaches to language (Firth, 1957) developed a method known as ethnography of communication (EC). Malinowski's work, in particular, highlighted the importance of language as a context-dependent phenomenon. He maintained that a language evolves in response to the demands of the society that uses it, and that language and context are co-dependent; in other words, we cannot understand an utterance without considering the situation in which it occurs (see also Guendouzi and Müller, 2006; Müller and Guendouzi, 2009; Saville-Troike, 1982; Schiffrin, 1994). EC is an approach to studying language that attempts to systematically include features of the situation within analysis of the data. EC concerns itself with holistic explanations of meanings that emerge from speech events. Speech events are a focal element of EC methodologies and can be defined as a socially and culturally recognized activity where language (including non-verbal and paralinguistic features) plays a specific role in the interaction (Levinson, 1983). Thus, EC is a method that interprets the meaning(s) generated from utterances in relation to both the global situation (e.g. social context) and the local situation (i.e. the interactional framework).

As Hymes (1981) suggested EC is both *etic* in that it attempts to formulate a typology of universal observations from a perspective outside of the system (Guendouzi and Müller, 2006) and *emic* in that it attempts to interpret the data under analysis in relation to the interactional and cultural context. *Emic* and *etic* are terms used by social scientists to refer to the kinds of fieldwork done and viewpoints obtained in constructing their accounts. An emic account is a description of a behavior or a belief in terms of its meaningfulness (consciously or unconsciously) to the actor, that is, an emic account comes from a person within the culture. An etic account is a description of a behavior or belief by an observer, in terms that can be applied to other cultures, that is, an etic account attempts to be culturally neutral observation from an "impartial" observer.

In carrying out EC the researcher provides a typology of observations, and attempts to uncover shared habits or behaviors within a particular population. In the case of people with communication disorders this becomes highly salient to, for instance, (a) understanding features that might be common diagnostic markers or manifestations of the disorder, and (b) helping to establish the extent to which the disorder impacts an individual's interactions with others.

7.4.1 Speech Situations, Events, and Acts

A *speech situation* can be defined as a situation in which speech (and non-verbal communication) occurs. Such situations might be described by their overall function, for example, a birthday party, a wedding, and the like. In contrast a *speech event* takes place in a speech situation and comprises of one or more speech acts, for example, telling a story at a birthday party, or giving a speech at a wedding. Hymes (1972b) suggested that speech events are bounded spaces within the interaction; that is, a speech event has a beginning and end. Therefore, a speech event could be a lengthy communication exchange, as in the case of a diagnostic interview, or a shorter exchange, as in the telling of a joke. Hymes suggested that speech events are communicative interactions governed by the rules or norms of language and also the expectations of the social context.

A *speech act* is generally coterminous with a single interactional function, such as a referential statement (declarative), a request, or a command, and may be either verbal or nonverbal (Saville-Troike, 1982: 29). They represent a level distinct from sentences, and cannot be identified with any single portion of other levels of grammar, and can consist of a single word or gesture (e.g. beckoning). Speech acts or communicative acts are smaller units of speech, an utterance or gesture that serves a function in communication. Speech acts describe what action is getting done when a particular utterance is used.

7.4.2 EC: Creating a Typology

Hymes utilized the acronym SPEAKING to produce a classification of features that are integral to a speech event (1972a). SPEAKING stands for Setting, Participants, Ends (goals), Act Sequence (speech acts used), Key (tone or manner), Instrumentalities (mode of communication, e.g. verbal, gesture, etc.), Norms (social or cultural), and Genre (e.g. formal, casual, etc.). Hyme's acronym reflects a wide range of factors that the researcher should consider when analyzing the data (see Table 7.1).

Table 7.1   Factors that may impact speech events.

Factors impacting speech events

1   Speech community, the group under scrutiny, and who is included within that group.
2   Setting, the location where the interaction takes place (e.g. speech clinic, school, etc.).
3   Speech situation, the occasions when the speech event is considered appropriate in the particular speech community and setting (e.g. an exploratory interview would be expected at the commencement of a diagnostic session).
4   Speech event, or episodes, the communicative frames for a particular setting (e.g. an interview, a lecture, or a conversation).
5   Speech act, the type of utterances one would expect in a speech event (e.g. questions and answers would be expected in an interview).
6   The ideal speaker or an individual who is communicatively competent within a speech community.
7   The speaker's status or participant roles (Goffman, 1981). For example, a clinician or client, their relationship to each other, and their functional role in the speech event.
8   Speaker goals, the interactional goals of the speakers (e.g. a speech-language pathologist's goal might be to diagnose a condition or to counsel a client).
9   The rules or norms of communicating within a particular speech event.
10 Ways of speaking, patterns of communication that would familiar to members of a speech community (e.g. giving advice in a counseling session or gossiping when having coffee with friends).
11 The functions of speech in the speech community, that is, the participants' beliefs about what should be accomplished within a particular speech event (e.g. that a diagnostic session might yield a specific diagnosis that will lead to treatment or intervention).
12 Historical/cultural background, the larger global history/culture which might affect or impact on any of the participants of a speech event (e.g. historical context of slavery of African Americans in relation to workplace hierarchies).

Source: adapted from Guendouzi and Müller, 2006: 50.

Section Summary

- EC provides a means to create a typology of observations.
- EC attempts to uncover shared habits or behaviors within a particular population.
- EC considers speech situations, speech events and speech acts.

7.5 Applying the Typology

In this section we will apply the EC typology to the context of two speech events, a clinical research interview and a training session that took place in an institution for adults with developmental delay.

7.5.1 *EC and the Research Interview*

Schiffrin (1994) noted that the *interview* is a highly recognizable speech event in many societies, not only in formal settings such as a job interview, police interview, or diagnostic interview but also because of its ubiquitous use in the media (e.g. news interviews, celebrity talk shows, etc.). Interviews represent *talk-in-action* and there are expectations about specific discursive activities that occur within this speech event, for example, the finding out of information in the case of formal interviews, or entertainment in the case of celebrity interviews (Guendouzi and Müller, 2006). For a more detailed discussion of the role of ethnography in the clinical research interview see Guendouzi and Müller (2006).

Research interviews are often thought to involve clearly defined participant roles and agendas (Goffman, 1974, 1981). In the case of fluency disorders, for example, the participant who stutters is expected to answer questions and provide descriptions of his/her experiences of stuttering, while the interviewer is expected to ask questions and "lead" the interaction. The interviewee typically will be expected to take longer turns and provide more information and the interviewer takes the role of facilitator. If we apply Hymes's SPEAKING units to this situation we might suggest a description of the situation as detailed in Table 7.2. It is important to note that the list isn't exhaustive. SPEAKING provides the researcher with a framework for filling in the details but could be extended depending on the context of the speech event.

A common mistake when using EC to create a typology is to simply provide a list of the SPEAKING units without considering how the subsystems interact with each other. For example, one of the goals (ENDS) for the researcher/interviewer is to find out information to inform his/her research study (see Table 7.2). But a secondary goal of wanting to establish a good relationship with the participant may override the goal of trying to directly find out information. So the KEY or tone of the interaction may become less formal than we would expect. Thus, the GENRE of the interaction may at times resemble a structured interview but at other times be more like an everyday conversation between friends or acquaintances (Guendouzi and Müller, 2006). Indeed, if we consider that a speaker's contributions are often influenced by their desire to be liked or approved of by others (i.e. *positive face*; see Brown and Levinson, 1987), a researcher's style may tend more towards *face* goals than professional instrumental goals. That is, in order to maintain the participant's positive self-image the researcher may choose not to pursue a sensitive line of questioning (e.g. the effects of stuttering on romantic relationships) that would be useful to extend their research. Therefore it is important to remain aware that

Table 7.2 Typology of a fluency interview.

EC unit	Features of analysis
SETTING	Clinic room, or interviewee's home.
Speech event	Research interview.
PARTICIPANTS	Researcher, person who stutters (PWS).
ENDS	*Researcher goals:*
	Instrumental goals: to find out information about the extent of the stuttering; to find out how it impacts the PWS's everyday life; to establish the PWS's temperament, to collect a language sample.
	Interpersonal goals: to establish interactional rapport with the client and be perceived in a positive way (in clinical situations this could also be seen as an instrumental goal).
	Participant goals:
	Instrumental: to give information about stuttering; to obtain advice/information about stuttering from expert.
	Interpersonal: to maintain good rapport with interviewer.
ACTS	Information-seeking questions and answers from both participants; narrative segments (participant's description of symptoms, impact on life events, etc.); elaborations; phatic (small-talk) to initiate interview.
KEY	Shifting between formal (delivering information) and informal (establishing interactional rapport and reassuring client).
INSTRUMENTALITIES	Primarily verbal with accompanying non-verbal gestures.
NORMS	Typical norms associated with this type of situation might be that the clinician fulfills the role of facilitator/expert and leads the interaction.
GENRE	Mixed domain – formal and technical language mixed with more casual talk to establish interactional relationship and encourage client to talk about potentially sensitive topics.

speakers have multiple goals and, as such, are continually adjusting their talk to address both their own and their interlocutor's *face* needs. The interviewer may also shift from one discursive alignment (e.g. his/her identity as a researcher) to an alternative discursive position (e.g. the identity of a friend or empathetic listener), and this too will affect the way the interaction unfolds.

Data taken from interviews can be a problematic issue in research (e.g. Briggs, 1986; Cicourel, 1974; Guendouzi and Williams, 2011). Interviewers are not neutral participants; their actions (or presence) may influence the outcomes of an interaction. However, as Holstein and Gubrium (1995) note, this is a *necessary* constraint of the process. To counter this effect, they suggest researchers should be more transparent about both their agenda and their own role in the interaction (e.g. how they might affect the KEY or ACTs used in a speech event). Thus, the ethnographic researcher should be aware that the interviewees' responses may be constrained (1) by the researcher's agenda (overt and covert), (2) the interviewer's presence and interactional style, (3) the context (both social and historical), and (4) the local dynamics of the interaction. That is, the data may not reflect genuine characterizations of how participants enact their lives on a daily basis and therefore cannot be generalized beyond the context of the specific interaction at hand.

A way to counteract this weakness is to apply the SPEAKING units not only as descriptive scene-setting devices but also as analytical tools. That is, we can use these units (e.g. ENDS) to cross-reference with other units (e.g. NORMS) in order to ask the types of questions necessary for a more comprehensive analysis; an analysis that captures the dynamic nature of communication. For example, if in reviewing the data the researcher/analyst notes that the interviewer's PARTICIPANT role as investigative expert shifts during the course of the interaction towards a discursive identity of friendly acquaintance, s/he should ask whether this fits within the NORMS of the speech event. Thus the researcher can ask what these discursive shifts in alignment tell us about the participants' perception and implementation of the interactional norms, allowing for a more fine-grained distinction between speech events (e.g. different types of interviews). For example, is the change from a more formal interrogative questioner to an empathetic peer a common phenomenon within the SETTING of the particular speech event under investigation (e.g. research interview)? Does this interactional shift match our expectations of this GENRE? Does the manner the interviewer projects at any given point reflect a change in the KEY of the interaction, and do the ACTs used by either PARTICIPANT seem appropriate for the particular speech event? If the answer to any of these questions is *no*, then the researcher/analyst can begin to consider what effect these phenomena have on the interaction, the participants, the outcomes, and last but not least the analytical conclusions of the researcher. Thus the researcher needs to consider that s/he may need to revise expectations of the features of the speech event under investigation.

7.5.2   EC and Adult Daycare Interactions

For the purposes of this chapter we intend to discuss the PARTICIPANT roles and NORMS of a particular speech event pertaining to a research study investigating how to improve care assistants' communication with adults with developmental delay (AWDD) that took place in a daycare center in a southern state of the USA (Table 7.3). The study involved clinical training sessions between "unqualified" care assistants who were African American, and Caucasian pre-professionals (graduate

Table 7.3   Ethnographic typology of a training interaction.

EC unit	Descriptions
SETTING	Table in activities area of daycare center (with picture cards and blocks); daytime; southern state of the USA; regular place of work (care assistants); temporary workplace environment (student clinician).
Speech event	Communications training event and clinical experience (students); compulsory work-related training experience (care assistants).
Socio-historical context	Issues of low socio-economic status for African Americans in this region, historical issues of slavery, and more recently institutionalized segregation. In this town there was still noticeable segregation and mistrust between the two groups, and lack of representation of African Americans in well-paid jobs requiring education (particularly within speech pathology).
PARTICIPANTS	1. Female white speech pathology student-clinician (multiple roles, e.g. communications trainer/ graduate student, research observer). 2. Care assistant, female African American (employee of daycare center), who was older than the student clinician acting as "teacher." 3. Adult with developmental delay (AWDD).
ENDS	*Care assistant goals* **Instrumental** – carry out work responsibilities (e.g. assist AWDD with acts of daily living, etc.); follow the administrator's requests as a means to an end. **Interpersonal** – as this was mandatory training, the care assistants' interpersonal goals are harder to assess but we might suggest that they would include being cooperative and to get through the interaction with the least amount of friction. *Student clinician goals* **Instrumental** – to help educate care assistants; gain clinical experience; gather research data; improve client's communication skills; prove competence to clinical supervisor; gain an acceptable grade for clinical class. **Interpersonal** – student clinician is also taking part in mandatory training and therefore her interpersonal goals are also instrumental goals in that she has been "trained" to establish a good rapport with clients, in this instance the care assistant and AWDD.

Table 7.3   (cont'd).

EC unit	Descriptions
	Potential goals for AWDD *(these are speculative) *Compliance; to utilize free time more constructively; to gain human interaction; to gain attention; to have needs met.
ACTS/act sequence	*Verbal* – explanations, instructions, evaluations, questions. *Non-verbal* – gestures (e.g. pointing), body posture, proxemics, facial expressions including eye movement/contact, facial expressions.
KEY	Formal professional/didactic. Some informal (AWDD – pragmatic boundaries not recognized).
INSTRUMENTALITIES	Verbal with accompanying gestures. AWDD: primarily non-verbal, non-linguistic vocalizations.
NORMS	Student clinicians taking on the role of clinical educator, expecting to take lead in the interaction. Care assistants – typically in their daily work setting they would expect to lead interactions with AWDD and give commands but in this situation they are the recipients of information (and lower in the hierarchy than they would normally expect). AWDD – typically PARTICIPANT with least power in this situation.
GENRE	Mixed domain – *talk-in-action* instrumental, goal-oriented rather than interpersonal. Expectations of formal, technical language interspersed with some casual conversation.

students in a communication sciences and disorders program) of non-African American descent. Background information noting the historical positions of both these groups is, therefore, an important part of not only the ethnographic background, but also the analysis of the interactions. However, the researcher needs to be aware of potential circularity in the conclusions drawn by using historical background as both a source of information and as a frame of interpretation.

The study was multi-faceted and involved several contexts of data collection including video-taped sessions of (a) the student clinicians working with the AWDD; (b) the student clinicians giving advice to the care assistants on how to facilitate communication with AWDD; (c) the care assistants working with the AWDD; and (d) ethnographic interviews with administrators of the care facility. One aspect of the study involved training the non-professional care assistants in how to use augmentative communication devices (AAC) in interactions with the AWDD in order to improve their functional communication skills. The care assistants were not CNAs (certified nursing assistants) and were at the bottom of the institutional hierarchy; they received the least amount of training but spent the most interactional time with the residents. Training sessions were delivered by graduate student clinicians and a clinical educator (certified speech-language pathologist). Following the training period, video cameras were set up to record whether, and to what extent, the care assistants generalized the skills they were shown by the student clinicians. Overall the outcome of this intervention was not very successful. Once the clinical educators were no longer in the daycare center, the care assistants were less likely to use the methods or AAC support that had been demonstrated, if indeed they were used at all. At the time of data collection and analysis several reasons were given for this outcome; in particular, it was noted that without a clinical educator present to reinforce and monitor the use of these techniques, the care assistants were less likely to use the skills they had been shown. However, reviewing the data from an ethnographic perspective allows us to suggest some further factors that may have contributed to this outcome.

Given the limitations of space, we can examine only one interaction from this corpus and thus we will describe one particular training session and then present a typology of some of the ethnographic factors involved. The session involved a graduate student clinician (SC) working with non-professional care assistant (CA) who was African American (the care assistants in this facility were predominantly African American females). The purpose of the session was to allow the student clinician to model the intervention with a female AWDD and then observe and advise when the care assistant undertook the same task. It should be noted that for the student clinicians this was not only an information-giving speech event, but also an occasion for practicing their clinical skills. Furthermore the student clinicians were likely to be assessed on their performance by a clinical educator who was supervising them.

For the purpose of this chapter, we will present a five-minute segment taken from a twenty-minute training session. In the original analyses of the data the verbal content of this training session was reviewed and did not appear to reveal any evidence to explain why the training sessions were not successful. The AWDD was non-verbal throughout the interaction and the care assistant's contributions were minimal, she simply uttered the commands the student clinician modeled for her. The student clinicians' utterances consisted of explanations of the AAC techniques being used and were delivered in an appropriate manner for the context. However, the original analyses did not examine non-verbal behaviors, and it is this aspect of the interactions we will focus on for the purposes of this case example. We will consider how the non-verbal behaviors in the ACTs sequence (hereafter NV Com Acts) interact with the participants' goals (ENDS) and the socio-historical culture of the setting. In analyzing the non-verbal communication acts, we will describe the sequence of events in terms of body posture (e.g. stance, body positioning), gestures (e.g. hand movements, finger tapping), and eye movement.

The three participants are seated around a table which is placed flush against a wall in the activities area of the daycare center. SC is in the center of the group but seated slightly back, while the CA was seated to the left of SC and the AWDD (hereafter Flo) was seated to right side of SC. Three large boxes with blocks of varying sizes are towards the back of the table and picture cards and a board with holes for placing the blocks are at the front of the table. The speech event is an intervention exercise in which SC is teaching CA how to better communicate with Flo in an attempt to get her to follow instructions relating to the blocks activity and the picture cards.

Extract 1

NV Com Act 1:
SC is sitting upright in her chair with her shoulders pulled back. Her face is directed towards the center of the table but her eyes are slightly lowered and gazing left towards CA. Her mouth is shut and lips slightly pursed. The overall impression is one of disdain but equally she may be somewhat tense because she is being videotaped and may be evaluated by her supervisor. CA is leaning left with her arm on the table, the forearm is lifted upwards towards the ceiling and her hand is loosely clenched in a fist. She is looking across at Flo, who is looking towards SC. Flo occasionally glances towards CA and she has a slightly confused expression on her face. It is likely she doesn't normally encounter CA in the context of this type of activity.

NV Com Act 2:
CA continues to lean back with her arm on the table but passes something (possibly a block) towards Flo and then points towards one of the picture cards but she does not touch the card. CA is looking at Flo but then glances very quickly towards SC who is still sitting in an upright position her head pointing directly towards the picture cards in the center of the table, her eyes are still tilted slightly down and are following CA's actions. CA's action of pointing towards the cards has not resulted in a reaction from Flo, who is still looking toward SC. CA now moves her arm towards her head, places fingers on side of head and leans her head towards the left. Her facial expression and body stance appear to project an air of being slightly agitated, perhaps fed up that she has been asked to carry out this activity.

NV Com Act 3:
SC leans in towards the table and points out to CA that she should "Touch the card when you are pointing." SC repeats this statement accompanying it with a rapid tapping of her finger on the card. SC then turns towards Flo and asks "What piece do you want now?" After SC models this action CA attempts to repeat the exercise. CA is looking towards SC when pointing to the card and asking Flo which block she wants. SC then leans back, lowers her eyes and gazes towards CA whilst gesturing toward Flo with her finger and thumb in a quick movement. Again her mouth is shut and lips pursed then she comments to CA, "Tell <u>her</u> not <u>me</u>." She stresses the two pronouns and the pitch moves down on the pronoun me. Although she is not speaking loudly, the intonation suggests she is reprimanding CA. SC then turns to demonstrate again and asks Flo which picture she wants. Flo points to a picture without looking at it and starts tapping her finger in the same manner that SC did when modeling the behavior for CA. Flo keeps her eyes directed toward SC.

NV Com Act 4:

CA then takes a block and shows Flo how to place it in the board. CA also asks Flo if she wants "a short piece." Flo watches but doesn't make eye contact with CA, rather she looks directly at SC. CA then throws the block across the table into one of the boxes and leans her head further down towards the left. CA's body posture becomes more closed. There is a distinct tightening of muscular tension in her shoulders. SC pulls herself further upright and leans back while CA is carrying out this action. Flo shifts her gaze back and forth from CA to SC.

NV Com Act 5:

SC then demonstrates the activity again for CA. She uses a verbal style that is associated with child-directed language, that is, her vowels are elongated, the pitch slightly higher and louder than normal conversation, and she speaks at a slower rate. SC's facial expression is more relaxed with lips slightly open and smiling. She then turns to her left and looks to make sure CA is following her actions. At this point her face muscles tighten and she again purses her lips slightly, her face is directed downwards but her eyes are uplifted and directed towards CA. CA pulls her arms into her chest and adopts a closed position; she appears annoyed.

This particular segment of the interaction was representative of both CA and SC's behaviors throughout the twenty-minute session. It appears, based on the non-verbal behaviors of the participants, that it was not a very successful interaction. CA does not appear to engage in this task from the outset of the session; she increasingly leans to her left and at times places her hand on her temple. CA uses only her right hand when carrying out and demonstrating the activity, suggesting she is not engaging thoroughly with the task at hand. As the session progresses her body posture becomes more closed: She draws her arms inwards and leans further away from SC suggesting she is either not impressed with what she has been asked to do, is feeling patronized by SC's manner, or feels this is a waste of her work time. Certainly, her non-verbal behaviors suggest she is reluctant and at times (when throwing the block) hostile to participating in this session. SC's verbal and non-verbal behaviors appear to be slightly patronizing. She does not appear to make an effort to adjust her verbal behaviors when talking to CA, rather she maintains the same style as when talking to Flo, a style associated with child-directed language. SC's body posture and eye contact with CA do not suggest someone who is treating her interlocutor as an equal. It is also interesting that although Flo is more familiar with CA she continually directs her actions and looks towards SC when undertaking her part in the activity, suggesting she is aware who holds the interactional power.

What then can EC add to this discussion? By examining the ENDS of the participants we can see there is a potential mismatch of goals that could be causing a barrier to an effective teaching session. We might suggest there is a mismatch in both CA's and SC's instrumental goals. As noted above SC has three salient instrumental goals; to educate CA, to present competency as a clinician (given she may be assessed on her performance), and to accomplish the task at hand (facilitate Flo's communication skills). CA on the other hand is possibly motivated by her overall goal of working at the daycare center, that is, to maintain a job where she can earn a living in a town that doesn't offer a large range of employment opportunities. CA, as part of her employment conditions, was required to participate in this activity, so doesn't have an overt *stakehold* in the outcomes of this session, that is, she views it as just another employment duty rather than an opportunity to further the communication skills of Flo. This view would appear to be supported by the fact that many of the care assistants appeared to make no effort to continue using the methods the clinical educators modeled when the project came to an end.

If we then situate this speech event within the larger historical context we might also note that there are cultural and contextual barriers operating within this interaction. SC is a younger, Caucasian college graduate whereas CA is a non-professional, older, African American woman who did not complete as much formal education (she did not graduate senior high school) as the graduate student clinician. Furthermore, this speech event is taking place in a geographical location (a small town in the south of the United States) where race and segregation are still social issues. If we consider some of the above contextual factors, in addition to the varying participant goals, we can begin to suggest reasons why this particular session was not a success and why the program being implemented did not achieve its overall goals. There are many factors at play in the dynamic of this interaction (e.g. education, economic class, race, and job responsibilities, etc.) that could act as barriers to successful communication. In other words a thorough ethnographic study of the context prior to designing and implementing the research project might have improved the outcomes. In particular, it might have been useful to establish through in-depth interviews *what* the care assistants thought their role and job responsibilities were, and what they thought of the training program itself. For the CA it might be that she was simply there to earn a living. She may also see her major role as assisting AWDD go about their acts of daily living (e.g. eating, taking walks, etc.) and therefore may consider the communications training program as outside the scope of her employment, particularly her initial employment conditions. Thus, in this case, the larger socio-historical context may have framed the speech situation adding an extra communicative barrier to the speech event (a training session).

7.6 Summary and Conclusion

In summary, ethnography is not a static descriptive device but an "active" method of analysis that aids the researcher to uncover many of the complex variables within interactions. EC can be used to create typologies of speech events that the researcher can use to systematically examine his/her data and, in particular, consider such typologies from the perspective of units of analysis that interact with each other. This enables the researcher to situate the speech event both within its larger socio-cultural context and locally within the interactional context of the talk itself. In doing ethnography we are asking the question "what can we learn from the people we interact with, interview or observe"? These people may participate in a world that is very different from our own, and their worldview may encompass different perspectives and experiences. The conclusions we present here should not be thought of as a definitive interpretation of the training session – carrying out ethnographic research does not give us a direct route into the participants' intentions or thoughts. Rather it allows us to make transparent the complex range of variables that underpin a speech event. As Packer (2011) has suggested, by making the details transparent we can begin to understand the speech event and thereby offer an explanation for why, in this case, a communications training program was not successful.

7.7   Recommended Reading and Resources

Fetterman (2009); Guendouzi and Müller (2006); Heller (2008); Holstein and Gubrium (1995); Hymes (1972a); Kozinets (2009); LeCompte and Schensul (2010); Packer (2011); Patton and Westby (1992); Saville-Troike (1982); and Schiffrin (1994).

7.7.1   Listservs and Online Sources

ETHNOG-L National Communication Association's Listserv; http://ncaethnographydivision. wordpress.com/listserv/.
Autoethnography listserv (post message): autoethnography@yahoogroups.com; (subscribe): autoethnography-subscribe@yahoogroups.com.
Ethno@cios.org; ethnomethodology/conversation analysis; to subscribe, send this message to comserve@cios.org.

References

Briggs, C. (1986). *Learning How to Ask: A Sociological Appraisal of the Role of the Interviewer in Social Science Research*. Cambridge: Cambridge University Press.

Brown, P. and Levinson, S. (1987). *Politeness: Some Universals in Language Usage*. Cambridge: Cambridge University Press.

Cheshire, J. (1982). Dialect features and linguistic conflict in schools. *Educational Review*, 34, 53–67.

Cicourel, A. V. (1974). *Theory and Method in a Study of Argentine Fertility*. New York: John Wiley and Sons, Inc.

Cukor-Avila, P. (2000). Revisiting the observer's paradox. *American Speech*, 75(3), 253–254.

Daniels, D. E. and Gabel, R. M. (2004). The impact of stuttering on identity construction. *Topics in Language Disorders*, 24, 200–215.

Duranti, A. and Goodwin, C. (1992). *Rethinking Context: Language as an Interactive Phenomenon*. Cambridge: Cambridge University Press.

Fetterman, D. M. (2009). *Ethnography: Step-by-Step*, 3rd edn. Thousand Oaks, CA: Sage.

Firth, J. R. (1957). A synopsis of linguistic theory, 1930–1955. In Firth *et al.* (eds), *Studies in Linguistic Analysis*. Special volume of the Philological Society. Oxford: Blackwell, pp. 1–32.

Geertz, C. (1977). "From the native's point of view": on the nature of anthropological under-standing, In J. L. Dolgin, D. S. Kemnitzer, and D. M. Schneider (eds), *Symbolic Anthropology: A Reader in the Study of Symbols and Meanings*. New York: Columbia University Press, pp. 221–237.

Giddens, A. (1984). *The Constitution of Society: Outline of the Theory of Structuration.* Cambridge: Polity Press.

Goffman, E. (1974). *Frame Analysis.* New York: Harper and Row.

Goffman, E. (1981). *Forms of Talk.* Philadelphia, PA: University of Pennsylvania Press.

Guendouzi, J. and Müller, N. (2006). *Approaches to Discourse in Dementia.* Mahwah, NJ: Lawrence Erlbaum.

Guendouzi, J. and Williams, M. J. (2011). Discursive resources in clinical interviews with people who stutter. *Communication and Medicine*, 7(2), 119–129.

Heller, M. (2008). Doing ethnography. In L. Wei and M. G. Moyer (eds), *The Blackwell Guide to Research Methods in Bilingualism and Multilingualism.* Oxford: Wiley-Blackwell, pp 249–262.

Holstein, J. A. and Gubrium, J. F. (1995). *The Active Interview.* Thousand Oaks, CA: Sage.

Hymes D. (1972a). Towards ethnographies of communication: the analysis of communicative events. In P. Giglioli (ed.), *Language and Social Context.* London: Penguin Books, pp. 21–44.

Hymes, D. (1972b). Models of the interaction of language and social life. In J. Gumperz and D. Hymes (eds), *Directions in Sociolinguistics: The Ethnography of Communication.* New York: Holt, Rhinehart and Winston, pp. 35–71.

Hymes, D. (1981). *In Vain I Tried to Tell You: Essays in Native American Ethnopoetics.* Philadelphia, PA: University of Pennsylvania Press.

Klompas, M. and Ross, E. (2004). Life experiences of people who stutter, and the perceived impact of stuttering on quality of life: personal accounts of South African individuals. *Journal of Fluency Disorders*, 29, 275–305.

Kozinets, R. V. (2009). *Netnography: Doing Ethnographic Research Online.* London: Sage.

Labov, W. (1966). *The Social Stratification of English in New York City.* Washington, DC: Center for Applied Linguistics.

LeCompte, M. D. and Schensul, J. J. (2010). *Designing and Conducting Ethnographic Research*, 2nd edn. Lanham, MD: AltaMira.

Levinson, S. (1983). *Pragmatics.* Cambridge: Cambridge University Press.

Malinowski, B. (1923/1972). The problem of meaning in primitive languages. In C. K. Ogden and I. A. Richards (eds), *The Meaning of Meaning.* London: Routledge and Kegan Paul, pp. 146–152.

Mead, M. (1928). *Coming of Age in Samoa.* New York: William Morrrow and Company.

Müller, N. and Guendouzi, J. (2009). Discourses of dementia: a call for ethnographic, action research approach to care. *Seminars in Speech and Language*, 30(3), 198–206.

Packer, M. (2011). *The Science of Qualitative Research.* Cambridge: Cambridge University Press.

Patton, M. and Westby, C. (1992). Ethnography and research: a qualitative view. *Topics in Language Disorders*, 12(3), 1–14.

Pinker, S. (2002). *The Blank Slate: The Modern Denial of Human Nature.* New York: Viking.

Saville-Troike, M. (1982). *The Ethnography of Communication.* Oxford: Blackwell.

Schiffrin, D. (1994). *Approaches to Discourse.* Oxford: Blackwell.

van Lancker-Sidtis, D. (2011). Formulaic expressions in mind and brain: Empirical studies and a dual process model of language competence. In J. Guendouzi, F. Loncke, and M. J. Williams (eds), *The Handbook of Psycholinguistic and Cognitive Processing: Perspectives in Communication Disorders.* New York: Psychology Press, pp. 247–272.

Ward Schofield, J. (2006). Increasing the generalizability of qualitative research. In R. Gomm, M. Hammersley, and P. Foster (eds), *Case Study Method.* London: Sage, pp. 69–97.

Wray, A. (2002). *Formulaic Language and the Lexicon.* Cambridge: Cambridge University Press.

8 Conversation Analysis Applied to Disordered Speech and Language

Scott Barnes and Alison Ferguson

8.1 Introduction

Conversation analysis (CA) has enjoyed an increasingly prominent profile in research and clinical practice with communication disorders. Researchers have used conversation-analytic principles to examine interactions involving people with autism spectrum disorders, cerebral palsy, developmental language disorder, dementia, dysarthria, traumatic brain injury, and, especially, aphasia. CA takes as its primary object of study real-time instances of interaction between people conducting the activities of their everyday lives; be it ordinary, everyday talk (e.g. a family discussion over dinner), or talk in institutional contexts (e.g. a medical consultation). The activities of human societies are, by and large, conducted in and through "talk-in-interaction." This term encompasses talk across contexts, and is also inclusive of non-vocal phenomena such as gaze, hand gestures, facial expressions, etc. (e.g. Schegloff, 2006).

In this chapter we aim to provide the reader with an introduction to the main characteristics and methods of CA, and briefly outline how CA has been applied to communication disorders. Throughout this chapter, an extract from an interaction involving a woman with aphasia and dysarthria (V) and one of her friends (E) will be used to support our discussion of conversation-analytic practices and features of talk-in-interaction. Transcription conventions and the complete extract can be found in Appendices 8.A and 8.B respectively.

Research Methods in Clinical Linguistics and Phonetics: A Practical Guide,
First Edition. Edited by Nicole Müller and Martin J. Ball.
© 2013 Blackwell Publishing Ltd. Published 2013 by Blackwell Publishing Ltd.

8.2 Development and Principles

CA was developed as a method for doing sociology. Two significant influences in its formulation were Harold Garfinkel's ethnomethodology (e.g. Heritage, 1984) and Erving Goffman's work on the interaction order (e.g. Goffman, 1983). The founder of CA, Harvey Sacks, drew on their ideas and interests and, with his colleagues (in particular, Emanuel Schegloff) and students (e.g. Gail Jefferson, Gene Lerner, Anita Pomerantz), began investigating social interaction in novel ways.

8.2.1 *Approaching Analysis*

First and foremost, CA is concerned with how talk-in-interaction is organized for the accomplishment of social action. Sacks hypothesized that talk is highly orderly, and the research generated over the intervening half-century has strongly supported this position. Methodologically, CA is data-driven in a number of respects. First, CA does not use idealized, researcher-generated data as the basis for its claims. Instead, its analyses are grounded in authentic instances of talk-in-interaction, and the observable phenomena therein (i.e. it is empirical). Second, the focus and findings of investigation are guided by the data, rather than prior hypotheses of the researcher (i.e. it is inductive). The rationale here is that, because the orderly features of talk cannot be conclusively established a priori, researchers should not reject phenomena as irrelevant without serious empirical investigation. These principles are reflected in CA's detailed approach to transcription. However, it should be noted that transcripts are necessarily selective, and that the actual recordings of talk-in-interaction are the materials from which analytic findings are ultimately derived (ten Have, 2007). Third, CA uses the sense making practices of interactants (i.e. people involved in the interaction) to guide analytic interpretation. It is, therefore, not up to the researcher to decide whether (and how) some interactional phenomena (e.g. pauses, mid-turn in-breaths) are meaningful. Instead, the researcher's task is to establish whether interactants treat their occurrence and non-occurrence as meaningful.

Extract 1

```
004  V  n:o- aw yes, uh .hh b't all of the CASTLE on t'night¿
```

Taken in isolation and intuitively analyzed, one might conclude that V was asking whether (the film) *The Castle* was on TV that night, likely because of the rising terminal intonation. Although plausible, the expanded extract below easily defeats this intuition.

Extract 2

```
        002  E   >so e'< you been watching anyth:ing on telly?
        003      (.)
   ->   004  V   n:o- aw yes, uh .hh b't all of the CASTLE on t'night¿
        005      (0.9)
        006  V   [dreadful ( ).
                 [((smiling & shaking her head))
        007  E   you don't like the castle¿
        008      (.)
        009  V   ↑o:hw y'know,
        010      (0.5)
        011  E   hm?
        012  V   terrible.
```

With the inclusion of the surrounding turns, we can see that E did not provide a response like "it's on at 8:30 on Channel 7, I think," nor did V reformulate this turn when such a response was absent. As such, it seems that neither E nor V oriented to V's turn at 4 as performing the action of "a question," and it indeed emerged as something else in the turns that followed. It is in these surrounding turns that interactants display to each other how they have made sense of a particular turn-at-talk. By virtue of these displays, scientific observers can align their sense-making practices with interactants' (Schegloff and Sacks, 1973). This analytic practice is central to CA's methodology because it provides access to how people formulate observable and accountable social action on a moment-to-moment basis.

The commitments and procedures described so far are also reflected in CA's approach to macro-sociological issues (e.g. race, gender, class). Rather than beginning investigation with a categorical label like "woman" or "autistic" in mind, and assuming its relevance to the interaction at hand, CA instead focuses on how (and if) interactants work to make these categories relevant during interaction.

8.2.2 CA and Language

The objective of Sacks and Schegloff was to create a methodology for doing sociology, rather than linguistics, or anthropology, or psychology, etc. While language is, therefore, not a 'privileged' object of study (Schegloff, 1996: 52), the general investigative orientation of CA does have consequences for how it is viewed analytically. CA treats language as a system with essentially social-interactional origins and motivations (Couper-Kuhlen and Selting, 2001; Ochs, Schegloff, and Thompson, 1996). With regard to origins, Schegloff (1996) argued that language evolution and language development are both processes that are enacted through interaction. He therefore suggested that aspects of the language system must be 'adapted' to the structural 'environment' provided by interaction (e.g. turn-constructional units, turns, sequences, etc.; see Section 8.3). With regard to motivations, conversation-analytic researchers view the phonetic, prosodic, lexical, and grammatical structures used during interaction as resources for dynamically enacting praxis (i.e. action) between interactants.

Extract 3

```
  ->   058  V   °°(2 syll)°°  .hh aw [(did) you see: (.)
                                     [((gazes to E))
  ->   059       [sixty minutes?  .hh
                 [((points up to television))
  ->   060       (0.5)
  ->   061  V   on sunday?
       062       (0.7)
       063  E   °ah: what w's on sixty mi[nutes.°
       064  V                            [liz hay:es, .hh where she put
       065       .hh like a cap on (h:o-) on head,
       066       (0.2)
       067  E   mm:?
```

In light of its interrogative grammatical format and rising terminal intonation, V's turn at 58–59 appears to have been pursuing a response from E. The lack of response at 60 suggests that this turn was problematic for E in some way and, at 61, V added an 'increment' (Ford, Fox, and Thompson, 2002) to her initial talk. Although more could be said about this extract, we can note that the linguistic structure of V's turn at 58–59 was fashioned to implement a particular action, but that this action was unsuccessful. Consequently, the interaction stalled. To remedy this situation, V used her initial turn as a basis – a practical structure – upon which further linguistic elements could be added (at 61) in aid of the action she began at 58. Hence, we can only fully understand talk used at 61 with reference to the linguistic format, and course of action initiated by V, at 58.

Section Summary

- CA was developed as a method for doing sociology. It uses interactants' own orientations towards micro- and macro-phenomena to shape both the focus and the findings of analysis.
- CA treats language as an essentially social-interactional system. Linguistic structure supports the dynamic implementation of social action.

8.3   Organizing Talk-in-Interaction

Schegloff (2006) argued that there are a number of generic problems that interactants must solve in order to successfully conduct social interaction. Three central (and interrelated) organizations of practice that interactants employ in the production of

talk-in-interaction are turn-taking (Sacks, Schegloff, and Jefferson, 1974; SSJ hereafter), sequence organization (Schegloff, 2007; Schegloff and Sacks, 1973), and repair
(Schegloff, Jefferson, and Sacks, 1977).

8.3.1   Turn-Taking

Schegloff (2006: 72) argued that "[w]hat is at stake in 'turn taking' is not politeness
or civility, but the very possibility of coordinated courses of action between the participants." SSJ (pp. 700–701) highlighted a number of recurring patterns in turn-
taking during everyday conversation. They noted that speaker change occurs;
overwhelmingly, one party speaks at a time; overlapping talk is common, but typically brief; and that transition between speakers most often occurs with no gap, a
slight gap (e.g. between 0.1 and 0.3 seconds), or slight overlap in talk. Taken together,
these patterns make the achievement of speaker transition seem somewhat unreal,
but interactants actually, consistently, and precisely determine who should speak,
and when.

The turn-taking system proposed by SSJ includes two components, with an accompanying set of rules. The components provide methods for allocating turns, and
methods for constructing turns. The "turn-allocational component" is divided into
two sets of practices: those that allow for a current speaker to select the next speaker,
and those that allow a potential next speaker to self-select. The rule set addresses
how interactants ensure one party is selected (thereby ensuring one-speaker-at-a-
time), and how gap and overlap are minimized. See SSJ (pp. 704–706) for further
details on the rule set.

Extract 4

```
 ->    028   E   you've been watching that¿
        029   V   m[m:.          ]
 ->    030   E    [you- >(uh)<] have you been watching packed t' the
        031       rafters?
        032   V   °ye:s.°
 ->    033   E   d'ye like that?
        034       (0.5)
        035   V   yes. (°°m[m:°°)
        036   E             [it's very popular.
        037       (0.6)
        038   V   that's rig[ht. mm,        ]
 ->    039   E             [yeah. >why dy'e] think it's< such a good
        040       show¿
```

The arrowed turns in Extract 4 were built by E to explicitly choose V as the next
speaker. By contrast, E's turn at 36, and V's turns at 29, 32, 35, and 38 did not determine who should speak next as strongly, and allowed for speaker self-selection instead.
Given that neither the content nor the length of interactants turns were "specified in

advance" (SSJ, p. 701), one might query how E and V knew precisely when to speak. The answer can be found in the attributes of the "turn-constructional component."

Interactants build turns-at-talk from turn-constructional units (TCUs). Upon beginning a turn, the turn-taking system entitles speakers to at least one TCU, and speakers can utilize different unit-types when building it (e.g. lexical, phrasal, clausal, sentential, etc.). As a TCU approaches its first point of possible completion, speaker transition becomes achievable, that is, a "transition-relevance place" is generated (SSJ, p. 703). Possible completion is typically negotiated by interactants with reference to grammar, intonation, and action, with the coordination of all three features commonly occurring (Ford and Thompson, 1996). All unit-types project the kinds of next-parts that will be required to bring a TCU to possible completion (SSJ; Schegloff, 1996). As can be seen below in Extract 5, the possible next-parts that TCUs project can vary.

Extract 5

```
      014  V   .hh he's [keep repeating, .hh himself.
                        [((circular gesture with index finger))
      015      (0.5)
      016  E   >right so it's< not the movie you don't like, you get
      017      [sick of (.)] uh: the fact that they're repeating=
      018  V   [ye:s,      ]
  ->  019  E   =all these [old stuf]f. yeah. [I thou]ght that- the=
  ->  020  V              [yes.   ]          [mm,   ]
  ->  021  E   =same thing. hh [>when i looked<] at the program,=
  ->  022  V                   [that's °right,°]
  ->  023  V   =m[m:,
      024  E    [.hh °ahm°
```

V's (minimal) turns at 20, 22, and 23 occurred in very close proximity to points at which E's TCUs were potentially complete grammatically, intonationally, and actionally. For example, V uttered *that's right* at 22 after the TCU beginning *I thought* had reached possible completion (i.e. after ... *the same thing*). This was also the case with V's *mm* at 23. But, one might ask, how was it that the *mm* in 20 came to be placed so closely to the preceding *yes*? One answer is that, unlike the TCUs beginning *right so* and *I thought*, the *yeah* in 20 could stand alone as a TCU that is "projectedly one word long" (SSJ, p. 701). By contrast, the former TCUs projected further grammatical elaboration in order to bring them to their first points of possible completion. In the case of the TCU beginning *right so*, the elaboration required was quite substantial because it was a "compound TCU." For further details, see Lerner (1996).

Taking a turn, however, is not just a matter of finding the right place and starting. One cannot just say anything, in any place, in any way. Turn production is constrained by what has come directly before it and, as such, any current turn has been shaped by the context provided by preceding turns. At the same time, any current turn will transform the context in which it is occurring; renewing it for the turns to come.

Turns are, therefore, designed to address prior, current, and future talk (SSJ, pp. 710, 722).

8.3.2 Sequence Organization

Turns-at-talk are arranged by interactants into distinct and coherent patterns of action, or sequences. By arranging series of consecutive turns in particular ways, interactants work to create observable and identifiable courses of action together. For example, there are sequential practices for making invitations (e.g. Schegloff, 2007), initiating new topics (e.g. Button and Casey, 1985), telling stories (e.g. Jefferson, 1978), and closing conversations (e.g. Schegloff and Sacks, 1973). Importantly, sequence organization also creates a framework for the interpretation of talk. This means that, unless otherwise marked, turns will be understood as fitted to and furthering the current sequence-in-progress (Schegloff, 2007; Schegloff and Sacks, 1973).

A basic organizational unit for sequences is the "adjacency pair" (Schegloff, 2007; Schegloff and Sacks, 1973). Adjacency pairs minimally consist of two component actions: a "first-pair part" (FPP) coupled with a "second-pair part" (SPP) (Schegloff, 2007). Upon the production of a particular type of FPP (e.g. a question, an invitation, a complaint), the production of a particular type of SPP (e.g. an answer, an acceptance, an apology) from another speaker becomes relevant, that is, normatively expected (Schegloff, 2007). If the projected SPP is not forthcoming, or a non-conforming type of SPP is used, the normative expectation will have been violated, and a particular interactant may be held accountable.

Extract 6

```
        038  V  that's rig[ht. mm,          ]
    ->  039  E             [yeah. >why dy'e] think it's< such a good
        040     show¿
        041     (0.4)
        042  V  °eheh (.hhh) i dunno?° (0.3) °(b't)° (0.5) .hh see, (.)
        043     w- (the:). .hh GOLD (LOGIES), and um- (0.5) .hh [(w:-)
        044  E                                                 [yeah,
    ->  045     who's up for a gold logie;
        046  V  ye:s,
    ->  047  E  who is,
        048     (0.4)
    ->  049  E  dy'know?
        050  V  .hh °eh-° (.) [mm hm:¿          ]
                              [((slight nods))]
        051     (1.4)
```

E produced FPPs at the arrowed lines, but the production of a SPP by V was somewhat problematic in each instance. V responded to the FPP at 39–40 with a delayed, quiet, and unelaborated claim not to know. V then attempted to initiate a new, but perhaps unclear, line of talk. In response, E launched another FPP at 45 (seemingly emerging from V's talk), to which V responded (more emphatically and immediately than before) with *yes*. The trouble here, though, was that E's FPP had projected that the responsive SPP should properly include a person reference. Hence, the lone *yes* produced by V did not constitute an appropriate type of SPP in this instance. E attempted to address this – to hold V accountable – by pursuing a response at 47 and 49.

8.3.3   *Repair*

Repair refers to the practices that interactants use to address difficulties with speaking, hearing, and understanding (Schegloff, Jefferson, and Sacks, 1977), that is, occurrences that may threaten mutual understanding. What constitutes a difficulty (i.e. the trouble source) is not defined by what an analyst thinks is correct or incorrect but by what the interactants themselves attend to as problematic. The course and distribution of repair manifests in a number of characteristic ways (see Schegloff, Jefferson, and Sacks, 1977). First, repair (usually temporarily) displaces all other interactional projects, and is commenced as close to a trouble source as possible. Second, there are two distinct phases that repair typically moves through: initiating repair and carrying out repair. Participation in these phases, however, is not symmetrically available to all interactants. There is a strong preference for the speaker of the trouble source (i.e. the "self") to initiate and undertake repair, rather than its recipient(s) (i.e. the "other") (Schegloff, Jefferson, and Sacks, 1977). Note that the term "preference" is used technically in CA. In essence, it refers to the practices involved with the production of alternative types of actions. See Schegloff (2007: 58–96) for an introduction.

Extract 7

```
  ->  019  E  =all these [old stuf]f. yeah. [I thou]ght that- the=
      020  V             [yes.    ]            [mm,  ]
  ->  021  E  =same thing. hh [>when i looked<] at the program,=
      022  V                  [that's °right,°]
```

Here, E self-initiated repair via a cut-off of *that*, and carried out repair by immediately recasting the grammar of her turn. Other-initiated repair trajectories are also preferably self-repaired. A canonical example of other-initiated self-repair would be the production of a "huh?", "what?", "who?", etc. in the turn after a trouble source, followed by repair from the first speaker. Third, there is a preference for repair to be resolved as quickly as possible, so as (amongst other things) displaced activities may be resumed. Finally, it is important to note that repair is an optional resource (Schegloff, Jefferson, and Sacks, 1977). Interactants can initiate or withhold repair on virtually any turn no matter how problematic or unproblematic it might seem. This highlights the distinctly local and discretional nature of these practices.

Section Summary

- The turn-taking system coordinates the participation of interactants. It has practices for allocating and constructing turns, which interactants closely attend to.
- Sequence organization concerns the systematic patterning of action across turns, while repair organization concerns practices available to interactants to deal with "trouble" in talk.

8.4   Communication Disorders and CA

We will now turn our attention to research that has applied CA to communication disorders. Four studies in particular topic areas will be described in detail, with some further studies (across diagnostic categories) highlighted in summary boxes for interested readers to independently pursue. The aim here is to demonstrate how the organizations of practice described above have informed research with communication disorders, and to sketch the kinds of findings that have been generated through the application of CA.

8.4.1   *Turn Construction*

Wilkinson, Beeke, and Maxim (2003) examined the turn construction practices of two people with fluent aphasia, and identified a number of recurrent patterns. First, when these people with aphasia attempted to produce turns with a conventional subject-verb-object (SVO) structure and/or rich lexical items, the ongoing progression of their turns was often significantly inhibited, resulting in the initiation of repair and meta-interactional displays of orientation toward these difficulties. In these instances, "being aphasic" became the "business" of interaction, and displaced whatever was happening before. Second, these speakers regularly constructed turns in which a noun or noun phrase was produced as the initial (or near-initial) element in the turn (i.e. it was "fronted," Wilkinson, Beeke, and Maxim, 2003: 62), and then followed by a proposition about the noun phrase (e.g. "that thing ... it's a good one"). Third, and often in combination with fronted noun phrase turns, the speakers commonly used "general meaning lexical items," such as "thing," "do," and pronouns like "one." Wilkinson and colleagues argued that these latter turn-construction practices offered a number of interactional advantages. For example, they suggested that fronting can help an aphasic speaker bid for the floor by introducing a particular focus for the coming turn, but also making clear that the there is more to come in it. Further, by beginning a turn in this way, an aphasic speaker has a wider range of grammatical options as to the next parts that can be added to the turn than if they committed to producing an

SVO construction. In addition, the use of general meaning lexical items likely avoided problematic word retrieval, and could indexically invoke semantically rich lexical items in the surrounding talk. Wilkinson and colleagues (2003) therefore argued that these practices were adaptations to the pressures of constructing turns in the face of real interactional consequences if/when their production was problematic.

8.4.2 Sequence Organization

Tarplee and Barrow (1999) focused on the use of delayed echolalia during spontaneous interactions between a 3-year-old with autism spectrum disorder ("Kenneth") and his mother at home. This study offered an innovative view of the functions and distribution of delayed echoes because, unlike previous work, it provided empirical examples of their occurrence in specific sequential contexts. Tarplee and Barrow demonstrated that Kenneth's use of delayed echoes (from a favorite cartoon) set off a particular sequential trajectory, in which his mother repeated each echo as Kenneth moved through a consistent series of different echoes. It was not the case, however, that Kenneth produced each echo irrespective of his mother's responses. For example, when Kenneth's mother produced a response that did not fit with the typical sequence (i.e. her response was not the expected type of SPP), Kenneth pursued an appropriate response (e.g. through a repeat of his previous turn). If his mother's turn was a later occurring echo, Kenneth produced the echo that would be expected after his mother's problematically placed turn, which allowed him to maintain his position as the initiator in the echo sequences. In sum, Kenneth displayed a distinct locus of social competence, using echoes as a means of eliciting particular responses from his mother, and creating a sequential context in which he and his mother could talk on terms they both understood.

8.4.3 Repair

Bloch and Wilkinson (2009) investigated the nature of trouble sources in dyadic interactions between two women with dysarthria (as a result of motor-neuron disease) and their husbands. In particular, they focused on instances of other-initiated repair in response to turns produced by the speakers with dysarthria. In some cases, the turn that initiated repair provided some clues as to the nature of the trouble source, for example, it included partial repetition of the turn, and/or a relevant "wh" word (e.g. *you saw who?*). One would intuitively expect trouble sources like this involving speech intelligibility, but Bloch and Wilkinson noted the occurrence of another kind as well: those in which the intended action of the turn was unclear, that is, the turn was intelligible, but the fit with the talk so far was problematic (e.g. Wilkinson, 1999a). Bloch and Wilkinson also observed that the speakers with dysarthria did not self-initiate repair after (potential) trouble sources turns, despite long pauses in which they might be expected to do so. The authors suggested that self-initiated repair after problematic turns may have been absent because the speakers with dysarthria were not able to ascertain the kind of trouble that was implicated until the recipient of the turn initiated repair. The upshot of these observations is that the "understandability" of dysarthric speech is not a simple function of intelligibility, and that the repair practices used by speakers with and without dysarthria are implicated in its moment-to-moment maintenance.

8.4.4   Co-Construction and Multimodality

Goodwin (2003) explored how "Chil," a man with severe non-fluent aphasia and a vocabulary of three words – "yes," "no," and "and" – was able to formulate social action in concert with his familiar communication partners (see also the Introduction to this volume). The talk examined by Goodwin involved the planning of a dinner reservation between Chil and some family members, with analysis focusing on Chil's configuration and placement of gesture in the ongoing talk. In the course of these arrangements, two other people were mentioned, and Chil began an attempt to suggest that they also be invited. In large part, this was accomplished through Chil's use of a hand shape (with his left, unparalyzed hand) shifting between the form prototypically associated with the number five, to one in which only his thumb and index finger were extended.

Retrospectively, it is evident that Chil was attempting to show the number "seven" to signify that seven people should attend the dinner. One challenge was, therefore, that his consecutive hand shapes be identified as the correct number. When incorrect guesses were made at the target number, Chil subtly altered the configuration of his hand so as the "two" gesture was titled laterally (i.e. so his thumb was level or above the highest point of his index finger), which eventually resulted in the correct number being guessed. However, Chil also needed to ensure that the correct "thing" was being counted. Throughout the sequence, the other interactants alternated between counting time and counting people, with Chil's wife finally suggesting "seven people". Chil guided their interpretation by resetting his gesture when the incorrect object (or object–number combination) was adopted by momentarily dropping his hand, and then quickly raising it back into the same space as before. Although the semiotic resources used in this interaction may seem clear in retrospect, in real time Chil and his interlocutors needed to attend to one another's conduct in a fine-grained manner in order to co-construct this course of action successfully.

Section Summary

- Researchers have used CA to demonstrate how the organization of interaction can shape the conduct of people with communication disorders and their conversation partners. This work has revealed unique problems faced by people with communication disorders in conversation, and resources used to address them.

8.5 Motivations and Future Research

There are common-sense reasons to study communication disorders in talk-in-interaction (Wilkinson, 1999b: 251). Most simply, people live their lives through conversation, and for many people with communication disorders this is where the (social) consequences of disorder will be most acutely experienced. As we have discussed, CA provides a unique, empirically grounded, and systematic approach to understanding the structure of social interaction. In particular, the social-interactional conceptualization of language that CA carries with it offers an interesting contrast to the cognitive-representational view that has (often implicitly) prevailed in much communication disorders research.

Although we have framed CA's approach to language as a theoretical shift, there are also some more concrete corollaries. For example, as Wilkinson and colleagues (2003) argued, language impairment and its social consequences have often been segregated from each another, particularly in clinical practice. But, by examining how talk is structured to implement social action, CA offers a systematic means of bringing impairment and its consequences into simultaneous focus (Wilkinson, Beeke, and Maxim, 2003: 80). This has clear (and significant) import for assessment and intervention, and CA's contribution to clinical practice has been steadily developing (see Beeke, Maxim, and Wilkinson, 2007, on CA, therapy, and aphasia). Future avenues for research here include examining how the linguistic and interactional competencies identified in previous work might be exploited or enhanced by intervention, how amenable these practices are to therapeutic manipulation, and how they vary between individuals (and dyads).

CA's focus on observable action may appear somewhat restrictive for a field like communication disorders, where so much work has been directed to understanding the mechanisms underlying pathological behavior. In fact, the principles and practices of conversation-analytic research set the scene for new, challenging, and innovative ways of thinking about communication pathology. For example, as the four studies discussed above have demonstrated, conversation-analytic investigation casts communication disorders as the dynamic, and ongoing, achievement of multiple parties. Put another way, communication disorders are constructed as phenomena that people *do together*, rather than just deficits that one *has alone*. The challenge for researchers is to continue unpicking the ways that that *dis*order emerges from, and articulates with, the deeply orderly practices people use for talking-in-interaction.

8.6 Resources

8.6.1 *Textbooks*

Have, Paul ten (2007). *Doing Conversation Analysis: A Practical Guide*, 2nd edn. London: Sage Publications.

Schegloff, Emanuel A. (2007). *Sequence Organization in Interaction: A Primer in Conversation Analysis*. Cambridge: Cambridge University Press.

8.6.2 Further Reading

8.6.2.1 Turn construction

Beeke, Wilkinson, and Maxim (2003); Beeke, Wilkinson, and Maxim (2007); Ferguson (1998); Heeschen and Schegloff (2003); Mahon (2009); Stribling, Rae, and Dickerson (2007); Wilkinson (2009); Wilkinson, Gower, Beeke, and Maxim (2007).

8.6.2.2 Sequence organization

Body and Parker (2005); Clarke and Wilkinson (2008); Collins (1996); Frankel and Penn (2007); Mikesell (2009); Muskett, Perkins, Clegg, and Body (2010); Radford and Tarplee (2000); Schegloff (2003); Stribling, Rae, and Dickerson (2009); Wilkinson (1999a).

8.6.2.3 Repair

Bloch and Wilkinson (2004); Ferguson (1994); Helasvuo, Laakso, and Sorjonen (2004); Laakso (2003); Laakso and Klippi (1999); Lindsay and Wilkinson (1999); Oelschlaeger and Damico (2003); Perkins (2003); Radford (2009); Watson, Chenery, and Carter (1999).

8.6.2.4 Co-construction and multimodality

Bloch (2005); Bloch and Beeke (2008); Clarke and Wilkinson (2009); Dickerson, Stribling, and Rae (2007); Goodwin (1995); Lind (2005); Oelschlaeger and Damico (1998); Rhys (2005); Wilkinson, Beeke, and Maxim (2010).

8.6.3 Useful Websites

Charles Antaki's introduction to CA, with tutorial materials: http://www-staff.lboro.ac.uk/~ssca1/sitemenu.htm.

Paul ten Have's Ethnomethodology and CA resources: http://www.paultenhave.nl/EMCA.htm

Emanuel Schegloff's publication archive and transcription tutorials: http://www.sscnet.ucla.edu/soc/faculty/schegloff/pubs/; http://www.sscnet.ucla.edu/soc/faculty/schegloff/TranscriptionProject/.

Publication archive for Gail Jefferson: http://www.liso.ucsb.edu/Jefferson/.

8.6.3.1 Transcription and related software

CABank

Data and transcript archives, as well as the CLAN transcription software; http://talkbank.org/CABank/.

ELAN
A program for the annotation of linked audio and video data; http://www.lat-mpi.eu/tools/elan.

Transana
A program which simultaneously presents audio, video, and a transcription window; http://www.transana.org/.

References

Beeke, S., Maxim, J., and Wilkinson, R. (2007). Using conversation analysis to assess and treat people with aphasia. *Seminars in Speech and Language*, 28, 136–147.

Beeke, S., Wilkinson, R., and Maxim, J. (2003). Exploring aphasic grammar 1: a single case analysis of conversation. *Clinical Linguistics and Phonetics*, 17(2), 81–107.

Beeke, S., Wilkinson, R., and Maxim, J. (2007). Grammar without sentence structure: a conversation analytic investigation of agrammatism. *Aphasiology*, 21(3/4), 256–282.

Bloch, S. (2005). Co-constructing meaning in acquired speech disorders: word and letter repetition in the construction of turns. In K. Richards and P. Seedhouse (eds), *Applying Conversation Analysis*. Basingstoke: Palgrave Macmillan, pp. 38–55.

Bloch, S. and Beeke, S. (2008). Co-constructed talk in the conversation of people with dysarthria and aphasia. *Clinical Linguistics and Phonetics*, 22(12), 974–990.

Bloch, S. and Wilkinson, R. (2004). The understandability of AAC: a conversation analysis study of acquired dysarthria. *Augmentative and Alternative Communication*, 20(4), 272–282.

Bloch, S. and Wilkinson, R. (2009). Acquired dysarthria in conversation: identifying sources of understandability problems. *International Journal of Language and Communication Disorders*, 44(5), 769–783.

Body, R. and Parker, M. (2005). Topic repetitiveness after traumatic brain injury: an emergent, jointly managed behaviour. *Clinical Linguistics and Phonetics*, 19(5), 379–392.

Button, G. and Casey, N. (1985). Topic nomination and topic pursuit. *Human Studies*, 8(1), 3–55.

Clarke, M. and Wilkinson, R. (2008). Interaction between children with cerebral palsy and their peers 2: understanding initiated VOCA-mediated turns. *Augmentative and Alternative Communication*, 24(1), 3–15.

Clarke, M. and Wilkinson, R. (2009). The collaborative construction of non-serious episodes of interaction by non-speaking children with cerebral palsy and their peers. *Clinical Linguistics and Phonetics*, 23(8), 583–597.

Collins, S. (1996). Referring expressions in conversations between aided and natural speakers. In S. von Tetzchner and M. H. Jensen (eds), *Augmentative and Alternative Communication: European Perspectives*. London: Whurr, pp. 89–100.

Couper-Kuhlen, E. and Selting, M. (2001). Introducing interactional linguistics. In M. Selting and E. Couper-Kuhlen (eds), *Studies in Interactional Linguistics*. Amsterdam: John Benjamins, pp. 1–22.

Dickerson, P., Stribling, P., and Rae, J. (2007). Tapping into interaction: how children with autistic spectrum disorders design and place tapping in relation to activities in progress. *Gesture*, 7(3), 271–303.

Ferguson, A. (1994). The influence of aphasia, familiarity and activity on conversational repair. *Aphasiology*, 8(2), 143–157.

Ferguson, A. (1998). Conversational turn-taking and repair in fluent aphasia. *Aphasiology*, 12(11), 1007–1031.

Ford, C. E., Fox, B. A., and Thompson, S. A. (2002). Constituency and the grammar of turn increments. In C. E. Ford, B. A. Fox, and S. A. Thompson (eds), *The Language of Turn and Sequence*. Oxford: Oxford University Press, pp. 14–38.

Ford, C. E. and Thompson, S. A. (1996) Interactional units in conversation: syntactic, intonational, and pragmatic resources for the management of turns. In E. Ochs, E. A. Schegloff, and S. A. Thompson (eds), *Interaction and Grammar*. Cambridge: Cambridge University Press, pp. 134–184.

Frankel, T. and Penn, C. (2007). Perseveration and conversation in TBI: response to pharmacological intervention. *Aphasiology*, 21(10/11), 1039–1078.

Goffman, E. (1983). The interaction order. *American Sociological Review*, 48, 1–17.

Goodwin, C. (1995). Co-constructing meaning in conversations with an aphasic man. *Research on Language and Social Interaction*, 28(3), 233–260.

Goodwin, C. (2003). Conversational frameworks for the accomplishment of meaning in aphasia. In C. Goodwin (ed.), *Conversation and Brain Damage*. New York: Oxford University Press, pp. 90–116.

Have, P. ten (2007). *Doing Conversation Analysis: A Practical Guide*, 2nd edn. London: Sage.

Heeschen, C. and Schegloff, E. A. (2003). Aphasic agrammatism as interactional artifact and achievement. In C. Goodwin (ed.), *Conversation and Brain Damage*. New York: Oxford University Press, pp. 231–282.

Helasvuo, M. L., Laakso, M., and Sorjonen, M. L. (2004). Searching for words: syntactic and sequential construction of word search in conversations of Finnish speakers with aphasia. *Research on Language and Social Interaction*, 37(1), 1–37.

Heritage, J. (1984). *Garfinkel and Ethnomethodology*. Cambridge: Polity Press.

Jefferson, G. (1978). Sequential aspects of storytelling in conversation. In J. Schenkein (ed.), *Studies in the Organization of Conversational Interaction*. New York: Academic Press, pp. 219–248.

Laakso, M. (2003). Collaborative construction of repair in aphasic conversation: an interactive view on the extended speaking turns of persons with Wernicke's aphasia. In C. Goodwin (ed.), *Conversation and Brain Damage*. New York: Oxford University Press, pp. 163–188.

Laakso, M. and Klippi, A. (1999). A closer look at the "hint and guess" sequences in aphasic conversation. *Aphasiology*, 13(4/5), 345–363.

Lerner, G. H. (1996). On the "semi-permeable" character of grammatical units in conversation: conditional entry into the turn space of another speaker. In E. Ochs, E. A. Schegloff, and S. A. Thompson (eds), *Interaction and Grammar*. Cambridge: Cambridge University Press, pp. 238–276.

Lind, M. (2005). Conversation – more than words. A Norwegian case study of the establishment of a contribution in aphasic interaction. *International Journal of Applied Linguistics*, 15(2), 213–239.

Lindsay, J. and Wilkinson, R. (1999). Repair sequences in aphasic talk: a comparison of aphasic–speech and language therapist and aphasic–spouse conversations. *Aphasiology*, 13(4/5), 305–325.

Mahon, M. (2009). Interactions between a deaf child for whom English is an additional language and his specialist teacher in the first year at school: combining words and gestures. *Clinical Linguistics and Phonetics*, 23(8), 611–629.

Mikesell, L. (2009). Conversational practices of a frontotemporal dementia patient and his interlocutors. *Research on Language and Social Interaction*, 42(2), 135–162.

Muskett, T., Perkins, M., Clegg, J., and Body, R. (2010). Inflexibility as an interactional phenomenon: using conversation analysis to re-examine a symptom of autism. *Clinical Linguistics and Phonetics*, 24(1), 1–16.

Ochs, E., Schegloff, E. A., and Thompson, S. A. (eds) (1996). *Interaction and Grammar*. Cambridge: Cambridge University Press.

Oelschlaeger, M. L. and Damico, J. S. (1998). Joint productions as a conversation strategy in aphasia. *Clinical Linguistics and Phonetics*, 12(6), 459–480.

Oelschlaeger, M. L. and Damico, J. S. (2003). Word searches in aphasia: a study of the collaborative responses of communication partners. In C. Goodwin (ed.), *Conversation and Brain Damage*. New York: Oxford University Press, pp. 211–227.

Perkins, L. (2003). Negotiating repair in aphasic conversation. In C. Goodwin (ed.), *Conversation and Brain Damage*. New York: Oxford University Press, pp. 147–162.

Radford, J. (2009). Word searches: on the use of verbal and non-verbal resources during classroom talk. *Clinical Linguistics and Phonetics*, 23(8), 598–610.

Radford, J. and Tarplee, C. (2000). The management of conversational topic by a ten-year-old child with pragmatic difficulties. *Clinical Linguistics and Phonetics*, 14(5), 387–403.

Rhys, C. S. (2005). Gaze and the turn: a non-verbal solution to an interactive problem. *Clinical Linguistics and Phonetics*, 19(5), 419–431.

Sacks, H., Schegloff, E. A., and Jefferson, G. (1974). A simplest systematics for the organization of turn-taking for conversation. *Language*, 50(4), 696–735.

Schegloff, E. A. (1996). Turn organization: one intersection of grammar and interaction. In E. Ochs, E. A. Schegloff, and S. A. Thompson (eds), *Interaction and Grammar*. Cambridge: Cambridge University Press, pp. 52–133.

Schegloff, E. A. (2003). Conversation analysis and communication disorders. In C. Goodwin (ed.), *Conversation and Brain Damage*. New York: Oxford University Press, pp. 21–55.

Schegloff, E. A. (2006). Interaction: the infrastructure for social institutions, the natural ecological niche for language, and the arena in which culture is enacted. In S. C. Levinson and N. J. Enfield (eds), *Roots of Human Sociality: Culture, Cognition and Interaction*. Oxford: Berg, pp. 70–96.

Schegloff, E. A. (2007). *Sequence Organization in Interaction: A Primer in Conversation Analysis*. Cambridge: Cambridge University Press.

Schegloff, E. A., Jefferson, G., and Sacks, H. (1977). The preference for self-correction in the organization of repair in conversation. *Language*, 53(2), 361–382.

Schegloff, E. A. and Sacks, H. (1973). Opening up closings. *Semiotica*, 30, 298–327.

Stribling, P., Rae, J., and Dickerson, P. (2007). Two forms of spoken repetition in a girl with autism. *International Journal of Language and Communication Disorders*, 42(4), 427–444.

Stribling, P., Rae, J., and Dickerson, P. (2009). Using conversation analysis to explore the recurrence of a topic in the talk of a boy with an autism spectrum disorder. *Clinical Linguistics and Phonetics*, 23(8), 555–582.

Tarplee, C. and Barrow, E. (1999). Delayed echoing as an interactional resource: a case study of a 3-year-old child on the autistic spectrum. *Clinical Linguistics and Phonetics*, 13(6), 449–482.

Watson, C. M., Chenery, H. J., and Carter, M. S. (1999). An analysis of trouble and repair in the natural conversations of people with dementia of the Alzheimer's type. *Aphasiology*, 13(3), 195–218.

Wilkinson, R. (1999a). Sequentiality as a problem and resource for intersubjectivity in aphasic conversation: analysis and implications for therapy. *Aphasiology*, 13(4/5), 327–343.

Wilkinson, R. (1999b). Introduction. *Aphasiology*, 13(4/5), 251–258.

Wilkinson, R. (2009). Projecting a reference in aphasic talk and normal talk. *Discourse Processes*, 46(2), 206–225.

Wilkinson, R., Beeke, S., and Maxim, J. (2003). Adapting to conversation: on the use of linguistic resources by speakers with fluent aphasia in the construction of turns at talk. In C. Goodwin (ed.), *Conversation and Brain Damage*. New York: Oxford University Press, pp. 59–89.

Wilkinson, R., Beeke, S., and Maxim, J. (2010). Formulating actions and events with limited linguistic resources: enactment and iconicity in agrammatic aphasic talk. *Research on Language and Social Interaction*, 43(1), 57–84.

Wilkinson, R., Gower, M., Beeke, S., and Maxim, J. (2007). Adapting to conversation as a language impaired speaker: changes in aphasic turn construction over time. *Communication and Medicine*, 4(1), 79–97.

Appendix 8.A   Transcription Conventions

Sequence and timing

[hey,]	Brackets signify overlap between speakers' talk and actions.
[yeah.]	Left-hand brackets indicate where overlap begins, and right-hand brackets where overlap concludes.
=	Equal signs come in a pairs. If they link talk from the same speaker, it is usually signifying that a speaker's talk smoothly continues, although a transcription line is ending. If they link talk from different speakers, it signifies that the second speaker's talk has been "latched" to the end of the first's with no recognizable gap.
(0.5)	Numbers in parentheses signify pauses, timed in tenths of seconds. Parentheses enclosing a single period signify a "micro pause"; typically, less than two-tenths of a second.

Speech delivery

,	A comma signifies non-final, "continuing" intonation.
?	A question mark signifies rising intonation.
¿	An inverted question mark signifies less strongly rising intonation.
;	A semi-colon signifies falling intonation, but not as low as a period.
.	A period signifies falling, final intonation.
ː _ː	An underlined colon signifies a rising pitch contour. If the letter preceding a colon is underlined, the pitch contour is falling.
↑↓	Up and down arrows mark sharper shifts in pitch, or resetting of the pitch register of the talk.
he:y	A colon signifies that the preceding sound has been elongated. The more colons, the greater the elongation.

–	A hyphen signifies that the preceding sound has been cut-off abruptly, typically with a glottal or dental stop.
<u>hey</u>	Underlining signifies emphasis, typically carried by pitch or loudness. The more underlining, the greater the emphasis.
HEY	Upper-case script signifies talk that is much louder than the surrounding talk.
°hey°	Degrees signs signify talk that is much quieter than the surrounding talk. Double degrees signs signify talk that is even quieter.
hey	Asterisks signify talk delivered in a creaky voice.
>hey<	Inward-pointing "more than" and "less than" symbols signify talk that is faster than the surrounding talk.
<hey>	Outward-pointing "more than" and "less than" symbols signify talk that is slower than the surrounding talk.
b't	Talk is typically transcribed to represent features of its delivery. Here, the word "but" has been produced with a short, unstressed vowel, as is common in talk.
.hh hh	Signifies hearable aspiration, such as a breath or laughter. If preceded by a full stop (or a degrees sign), this signifies inhalation. The more "h"s, the longer the aspiration.
h(h)ey	Signifies hearable aspiration, such as a breath or laughter, within a word.
Transcriptionist comments	
((smiles))	Notes in double parentheses are a description of events.
(hey)	Words in parentheses signify a transcriptionist's "best guess."
( )	Empty parentheses signify that that talk is unable to be identified sufficiently.
(2 syll)	Signifies the number of syllables in an otherwise unidentifiable stretch of talk.
->	Signifies phenomena of interest in the transcript

Based on Ochs *et al.*, 1996: 461–465.

Appendix 8.B

V and E's discussion largely concerned Australian television programming. *The Castle* is a film, while *Find My Family* (produced by V as *Where Is My Family*), *Packed to the Rafters*, and *Sixty Minutes* are all television shows. The "Logies" are annual television awards, with the "Gold Logie" being the highest honor.

```
BARNES [023103] (00:49 - 02:18)
001  V   [(and uh)      ]
002  E   [>so e'< you be]en watching anyth:ing on telly?
003      (.)
004  V   n:o- aw yes, uh .hh b't all of the CASTLE on t'night¿
005      (0.9)
006  V   [dreadful ( ).
         [((smiling & shaking her head))
007  E   you don't like the castle¿
008      (.)
009  V   ↑o:hw y'know,
010      (0.5)
011  E   hm?
012  V   terrible.
013      [(0.6)
         [((V gazes down while E gazes at V))
014  V   .hh he's [keep repeating, .hh himself.
                  [((circular gesture with index finger))
015      (0.5)
016  E   >right so it's< not the movie you don't like, you get
017      [sick of (.)] uh: the fact that they're repeating=
018  V   [ye:s,      ]
019  E   =all these [old stuf]f. yeah. [I thou]ght that- the=
020  V             [yes.    ]          [mm,   ]
021  E   =same thing. hh [>when i looked<] at the program,=
022  V                   [that's °right,°]
023  V   =m[m:,
024  E     [.hh °ahm°
025  V   and *uh- you:* ((short cough)) (1.4) .tk ohw >(w- there
026      w'z)< WHEre is my fam[l'y hh (lu-) that's- (0.4)
                             [((E nods))
027      °very.° (0.5) that's good,
028  E   you've been watching that¿
029  V   m[m:.          ]
030  E    [you- >(uh)<] have you been watching packed t' the
031      rafters?
032  V   °ye:s.°
033  E   d'ye like that?
034      (0.5)
035  V   yes. (°°m[m:°°)
036  E            [it's very popular.
037      (0.6)
038  V   that's rig[ht. mm,            ]
039  E            [yeah. >why dy'e] think it's< such a good
```

```
040       show¿
041       (0.4)
042   V   °eheh (.hhh) i dunno?° (0.3) °(b't)° (0.5) .hh see, (.)
043       w- (the:). .hh GOLD (LOGIES), and um- (0.5) .hh [(w:-)
044   E                                                     [yeah,
045       who's up for a gold logie;
046   V   ye:s,
047   E   who is,
048       (0.4)
049   E   dy'know?
050   V   .hh °eh-° (.)  [mm hm:¿               ]
                         [((slight nods))]
051       (1.4)
052   E   °(d-)° dy'know who's up for the gold logie?
053   V   (°°e- e-°°) °hh° (0.3) i don' know
054   E   it's the mother.
055       (0.3)
056   E   ↑dy'e remember her name?
057       [(0.4)            [(1.6)
          [((V gazes at E [then shifts & holds gaze to E's left))
058   V   °°(2 syll)°° .hh aw [(did) you see: (.)
                              [((gazes to E))
059       [sixty minutes? .hh
          [((points up to television))
060       (0.5)
061   V   on sunday?
062       (0.7)
063   E   °ah: what w's on sixty mi[nutes.°
064   V                            [liz hay:es, .hh where she put
065       .hh like a cap on (h:o-) on head,
066       (0.2)
067   E   mm:?
          ((V tells E about a segment that was on Sixty Minutes))
```

9 Clinical Sociolinguistics

Martin J. Ball and Louise Keegan

9.1 Introduction

In his seminal work on clinical linguistics, Crystal (1981) discussed the possibility of the creation of a 'clinical sociolinguistics' to complement the advances in other areas of clinical linguistics (a point he returned to in Crystal, 1984). In this discussion, Crystal gave the example of a clinical linguistic interaction between a clinician and a patient that illustrates the difference between discourse in clinical settings, and 'natural' conversation. In this chapter we discuss the methods used in sociolinguistics and see in what ways they can be applied to the clinical situation, and how sociolinguists investigate variation in natural language and how clinical linguists may have to adapt these approaches when dealing with speech- and language-disordered clients.

Sociolinguistics traces its roots to dialectology work in the middle of the twentieth century that began to integrate social variables into the analysis of geographical variation in language use. The explosive rise of this area of study, however, is generally dated to William Labov's seminal studies of English in Martha's Vineyard (1963) and of New York (Labov, 1966; see further Ball, 2010), leading to a range of variationist studies from the 1960s onwards.

Sociolinguistics has developed greatly from the early emphasis on linguistic variation and its correlation to social variation, and now may be found as a cover term for a wide variety of research, including that into bilingualism, together with code-switching and diglossia, language planning, language and culture, language change, and even discourse management (see, for example, Wardhaugh, 1998).

However, when it comes to the application of the insights from sociolinguistic research to disordered speech and language, the micro-sociolinguistic variationist approach has been dominant, although the study of language and power, and multi-

Research Methods in Clinical Linguistics and Phonetics: A Practical Guide,
First Edition. Edited by Nicole Müller and Martin J. Ball.
© 2013 Blackwell Publishing Ltd. Published 2013 by Blackwell Publishing Ltd.

lingualism have also been important concerns (see Ball, 2005: preface). Indeed, it is the variationist approach that has been responsible for the development of novel research methods, in both data collection and analysis, and it is thus this approach that we concentrate on in this chapter. We will first look at some basic concepts used in sociolinguistics, then turn attention to data collection techniques, data analysis, and finally some of the main studies in clinical sociolinguistics.

9.2   Basic Concepts

9.2.1   *Speech Community*

The nature of the group of speakers that sociolinguists should investigate has been the topic of some debate within the field. Labov (1972: 120–121) stated that "the speech community is not defined by any marked agreement in the use of language elements, so much as by the participation in a set of shared norms." Britain and Matsumoto (2005) note that this approach has been criticized in that it excludes speakers in an area (who may be leaders in sound change) who do not fall within the definition. They discuss alternative approaches, such as social networks (discussed further below), and communities of practice.

Within clinical sociolinguistics, of course, the speech community being investigated will be defined by a shared speech or language disorder, transcending the debate just noted and, indeed, may consist of a single speaker (we return to this point later).

9.2.2   *Vernacular*

Another concern of sociolinguists is to access the vernacular speech form of their participants, rather than simply the careful speech that many use when taking part in any kind of interview (though the collection of varying degrees of formal speech will also be useful in order to examine stylistic shifts in participants' speech). Labov (1972: 208) describes it as the variety adopted by speakers when they are monitoring their speech least closely. Early sociolinguistic studies adopted varying methods to overcome the observer's paradox (in order to discover how people speak in normal interactions one has to establish a non-normal interaction to observe this) and obtain vernacular speech, and some of these are described below. Interestingly, Ball (1988) found that a technique from speech-language pathology (the Reporter's Test; DeRenzi and Ferrari, 1978) was efficacious in producing casual, unmonitored speech styles. However, the usual context of data collection in the speech pathology clinic militates against the successful collection of vernacular speech and this is therefore an area to consider when attempting clinical sociolinguistic studies.

9.2.3   *Variables*

The main analysis unit of the variationist approach to sociolinguistic research is the *variable*. The variable consists of two or more *variants*; further, they are divided into linguistic variables and non-linguistic (or social) variables (Labov, 1972; Wardhaugh, 1998). One of the main aims of the analysis of the data is to chart any correlations between the linguistic variables, on the one hand, and the social variables, on the other.

What kind of things can be variables? For linguistic variables, one can investigate any linguistic form that has variant realizations within a specific speech community.[1] In some instances, the variation may be solely due to phonetic or linguistic context (e.g. lip-rounding of consonants before rounded vowels in English), but in many cases there will be some non-linguistic factors to take into account. Among linguistic variables that have been studied are phonological ones, including vowels (Labov, 1966, included (æh) and (oh)), consonants (Trudgill, 1974, investigated h-dropping in his study of Norwich, England); morphonological ones (Ball, 1993, looked at the realization of initial consonant mutation in Welsh); morphology (Cheshire, 1980, examined the use of the third-person singular present ending in the English of Reading, Berkshire); and syntactic ones (Wolfram, 1969, examined the use of double negatives in the speech of Detroit).

Social variables that have been included in sociolinguistic research have included social class, age, sex, regional background, ethnicity or cultural background, dominant language in multilingual situations, power relations and in-group or social network membership status, along with the context of utterance (i.e. style) (see Labov, 1966, 1972; Trudgill, 1974; Wardhaugh, 1998; and contributions to Ball, 2005).

Section Summary

- Different ideas exist in sociolinguistics concerning how to define the groups of speakers to be investigated; clinical populations cut through these distinctions.
- Sociolinguists are mainly concerned with accessing the vernacular: the style produced by speakers who are not monitoring their speech; this is also important in clinical applications.
- Variable are the main unit of analysis in variationist sociolinguistics. Variables can be linguistic or social, and their different instantiations are termed variants.

9.3   Collecting Data

9.3.1   *Sampling*

As Milroy and Gordon (2003) note, in sociolinguistic research speaker selection or sampling is extremely important. The researcher must be careful to avoid bias and ensure that the sample really represents the population being studied and is not merely a subgroup of this population. Unfortunately bias is not always predictable or evident and obtaining a representative sample when studying diverse populations in urban settings is extremely challenging. A random sample is a selection process that allows anyone within the sample frame or population under investigation an equal chance of being selected (Milroy and Gordon, 2003).

Milroy and Gordon (2003) mention how it is important to define a sampling universe by defining the rough boundaries of the group or community under investigation, assess the dimensions of variation within this community and determine the sample size. Usually it is not difficult to define the sampling universe, the boundaries of the group under investigation, such as residents of a particular area, members of a particular social group, and so on.

Researchers must also decide on the size and structure of the sample to be taken. Samples for linguistic studies are often much smaller than for other types of surveys. It has been suggested that large samples are not necessary for linguistic surveys as the linguistic usage is more homogenous than other phenomena due to the fact that it is not subject to conscious manipulation (Milroy and Gordon, 2003). Additionally, practical considerations play a role in sample-size selection. As the method of data handling becomes more demanding the subjects that can be included become more limited (Milroy and Gordon, 2003). Similarly the social variation affects the sample size for, if the researcher plans to make any assumptions about subgroups such as males, females, unemployed individuals, the sample size must be large enough to ensure these subgroups are representative of their population. The more subgroups or variables included, the more participants are needed. With the introduction of such variables, obtaining a balanced stratified sample becomes more difficult, if the sample is a random sample of the greater population (Milory and Gordon, 2003). It is for this reason that many sociolinguistic researchers look to methods other than random sampling (Wardhaugh, 1998). In quota sampling the researcher identifies the types of speakers to be studied and seeks out, based on their own judgment, a quota of speakers who fit the desired categories (Milroy and Gordon, 2003). It is important that the researcher keeps their goal or research question in mind when selecting the sample. Variables that need to be considered during sampling include age, which demonstrates evidence of language change over time, as well as social class, which is less vague a concept when defined in terms of income, housing, and employment (Chambers and Trudgill, 1980).

9.3.2 Eliciting Different Styles of Speech

The style of speech known as the vernacular is most recently thought of as the language of locally based communities, and sociolinguists argue that the vernacular offers the best database for examining the processes and mechanisms of linguistic change or the structural characteristics of a variety (Milroy and Gordon, 2003). Labov in several studies employed a variety of techniques to elicit a variety of different speech styles (see, for example, Labov, 1972).

Researchers believe that even when being interviewed by a stranger a participant will settle into a pattern approximating their everyday language use after the first hour, and hence Labov advocates long interviews (Milroy and Gordon, 2003). A single speech style may not be maintained for the entire interview (Labov, 1972). In Labov's study of the speech of the neighborhoods in Philadelphia, he utilized structured interviews with prepared modules or sets of questions, organized around specific topics (Milroy and Gordon, 2003). He stressed the importance of formulating questions in advance to ensure they are short, clear, and colloquial and elicit the most natural responses.

For phonological variation Labov suggested the reading of texts rather than word lists, and in an interview situation, in order to elicit most casual speech, he supported the use of the "danger of death" question in order to observe the emotional, unmonitored speech that would become evident in replies (Milroy and Gordon, 2003). Labov also used a technique of outnumbering the interviewer by interviewing several people at once and hence eliciting more natural conversations and so obtaining rich and natural samples of the vernacular under investigation (Milroy and Gordon, 2003).

9.3.3   Milroy's Social Network Approach

Participant observation is one of the more appropriate methods of obtaining a natural sample of the vernacular of the participants under investigation (Wardhaugh, 1998). James and Lesley Milroy carried out research in Belfast in Northern Ireland and included a variety of data collection methods including participant observation (Milroy, 1980; Milroy and Gordon, 2003). Communities were approached through persons encountered directly or indirectly in the course of everyday activities; persons, who although members of the community, had no institutional status (Milroy and Gordon, 2003). This situation allowed for such successful observation that it was followed as closely as possible in other communities, and the other fieldworkers, although not local residents, adopted the role of a "friend of a friend." This status and the mention of an insider's name had the effect of guaranteeing the fieldworker's good faith and assigning the fieldworker a status in the community, creating for the residents a social obligation to help them (Milroy and Gordon, 2003). The fieldworkers recorded conversations between groups of two to five people and participated minimally in such conversations. Such methods have been found to be very effective in close-knit communities at evading the observer's paradox and eliciting speech that is representative of the vernacular (Milroy and Gordon, 2003).

In the Milroy (1980) study the researchers also used a door-step survey to complement the participant observation. For this survey the researcher was familiar with the linguistic characteristics of the area and the purpose of the survey and was therefore able to obtain specific and limited linguistic information (Milroy and Gordon, 2003). A random sample of households was drawn from the Northern Ireland Housing Executive and in total surveys of 60 speakers were analyzed. The main emphasis was on recording word lists that were carefully designed, although some spontaneous speech and demographic information was also recorded. This instrument, although not suitable for exploratory research, enhanced the results of the participant observation (Milroy and Gordon, 2003). A study of the rural hinterland was also carried using similar participant observation techniques, indicating how the use of multiple methods and projects to supplement the participant

> **Section Summary**
>
> - Sociolinguistics adopted the notions of random sampling and quasi-random sampling.
> - More recently the notion of the social network has been employed to gain access to groups of speakers so that the investigator is not considered an outsider.
> - Various means have been used to obtain vernacular speech: danger of death question, humorous anecdotes, and becoming part of a social network.

observation study allowed language variation to be analyzed in many dimensions and demonstrating how this social network approach adopted proves to be a powerful analytic construct (Milroy and Gordon, 2003).

9.4   Data Analysis

9.4.1   Correlational Analysis

Correlations between linguistic and non-linguistic variables are usually portrayed in table and graph form. For example, Ball (1984) contrasts his male and female subjects' use of the aspirate mutation (see Ball and Müller, 1992) following the conjunction *a* 'and' in a study of southwestern Welsh. Table 9.1 shows the results, listing both percentages and numbers of occurrences (published studies often only give percentages, e.g. Trudgill, 1974).

Wardhaugh (1998) has criticized over-simplistic reliance on means in such tables, which may hide considerable overlap in linguistic usage between members of different social groups. We can illustrate this in Table 9.2, which gives the percentage usage of aspirate mutation for each of the 11 male and 11 female subjects reported on by Ball (1984). The table shows that there is considerable overlap between these two groups of speakers that the overall percentages masked. Indeed, further analyses undertaken in Ball (1984) demonstrated that groupings of speakers by their main language affiliation (Welsh versus English) and by age produced more insightful analyses with less overlap.

9.4.2   Variable Rules

In efforts to move beyond the simple presentation of percentages to demonstrate correlations between linguistic and social variables sociolinguists have developed the notion of the "variable rule." Rules of this sort were first suggested by Labov (1969), and were clearly an attempt to adapt generative linguistics to enable it to deal with

Table 9.1   Use of aspirate mutation following *a* 'and' in
southwest Welsh by gender.

	Male subjects		Female subjects	
	%	*n*	%	*n*
+ aspirate	33	33	28	29
No aspirate	67	68	72	76

Table 9.2   Percentage use of aspirate mutation for each subject following
a 'and' in southwest Welsh.

Male subjects	% no aspirate	Female subjects	% no aspirate
M1	17	F1	100
M2	100	F2	100
M3	66	F3	76
M4	27	F4	80
M5	78	F5	73
M6	100	F6	100
M7	100	F7	94
M8	100	F8	100
M9	27	F9	17
M10	64	F10	100
M11	83	F11	0

the data on language variation that was being collected in increasing amounts at that time. Labov's topic was the contraction and deletion of the copula in non-standard African American English, and the problem of accounting for this within generative phonology. He proposed to do this as follows: "the notion 'rule of grammar' is enlarged to include the formal treatment of inherent variation as part of linguistic structure" (Labov, 1969: 715). If variable rules are incorporated into a generative approach, "it will be possible to enlarge our current notion of the 'linguistic competence' of a native speaker" (p. 736), and thus variation need no longer be classed with other types of performance "errors."

The way such rules would work is explained by Labov in relation to the copula contraction and deletion processes:

> First is an input variable which sets the overall frequency with which the rule is selected. Second, there are variable constraints which differentiate the frequencies with which the rule applies according to the syntactic and phonological features of the environment … and third, of course, there are extra-linguistic features such as age, sex, ethnic group, social class, and contextual style.

(Labov, 1969: 733)

Labov's ideas about variable rules were further developed in Labov (1970) and (1972), though the latter considered also the work of Cedergren and Sankoff (written in 1972, though published in 1974). These researchers suggested several modifications to Labov's original variable rule format. Most important of these was the provision that constraints on rule operation should be independent of each other. Labov (1972) felt that "this hypothesis is of the greatest importance to linguistic theory, for it provides the first strong justification for the linguist's assembly of individual rules into rule schema" (p. 231). Cedergren and Sankoff were also the first to bring numerical and statistical data into the format of the variable rule, and Labov (1972) followed this by attempting to characterize the effect of some of the non-linguistic variables.

Space does not permit a detailed account of how the variable rule program works, and readers are directed to a detailed account of the program, how to use it, and the analyses provided (e.g. distributional and multivariate analyses), and how to interpret results in Tagliamonte (2006).

Section Summary

- Many variationist studies in sociolinguistics present results in percentages and attempt to demonstrate correlations between linguistic and sociolinguistic variables without use of statistics.
- This approach can disguise overlap between individual scores in different groups.
- The development of the variable rule and computer programs to calculate these rules represent an advance in data analysis in sociolinguistics.

9.5   Clinical Sociolinguistics

9.5.1   *Applying Sociolinguistics to the Clinic*

A specific clinical application for sociolinguistics was first discussed in the work of Walt Wolfram (e.g. 1993). Wolfram asks:

> How does the variation model developed originally in sociolinguistics apply to communication disorders? … One way relates to the interpretation of normative variable behavior and the other to an understanding of change in the remediation process.
>
> (Wolfram, 1993: 3)

Ball (1992) was an early attempt to provide a means of noting possible sociolinguistic variation in a clinical assessment of speech or language. This paper was written within the tradition of linguistic profiling (as described in Crystal, 1982), and suggested adding to profiling charts an extra layer allowing a fairly detailed description of the target variety of the language, including variables that correlated with style, and other non-linguistic factors.

Clearly, a more manageable solution is to provide assessments that cover ranges of sociolinguistically acceptable target forms for specific dialects or groups of dialects; and in this regard, we can note the work of Oetting (e.g. 2005), where she describes one step along this path: the Diagnostic Evaluation of Language Variation (DELV), devised by Seymour, Roeper, and de Villiers (2003). This was designed to assess children from a range of American English dialects, and test items cover phonology, syntax, semantics, and pragmatics, and its goal is to allow clinicians to note which variety of American English the client is a speaker of, and to allow classification of the client as impaired or not impaired in speech and/or language.

Both variationist sociolinguistic approaches (as concentrated on in this chapter) and broader macro-level studies (covering, for example, features such as societal bilingualism) have been applied to clinical data, and several such studies are available in Ball (2005).

One problem in applying sociolinguistic methodology to the speech and language clinic (especially variationist methodology) is that the former normally relies on sampling a relatively large number of speakers, whereas clinical concerns are often (though not always) directed towards individual clients. We concentrate in the following subsections on two areas where clinical sociolinguists have been especially active: one where the traditional random sampling approach discussed above can be used, and one where it cannot. Nevertheless, we argue that even in the latter case the insights from sociolinguistics can still be applied.

9.5.2   Sociolinguistics of Sign Language

The area of communication disorders where micro-level, or variationist, sociolinguistics has been applied most directly is that of the study of sign language.[2] This is because the physical movements that make up the signs can vary, and so different sign variables can be established, and the variants of these variables can be correlated to non-linguistic features, as with studies of phonological variation. Early work in this area is found in Woodward (1980), who found that variation in sign production was correlated with social factors, such as region, age, and ethnic background. Lucas (1989) is a collection of contributions on the sociolinguistics of sign language from both micro- and macro-sociolinguistic standpoints; and topics include discourse, language contact, language planning, and language attitude. Lucas (2001) also investigated aspects of bi- and multilingualism and sign language usage.

Other publications in the area include Lucas, Bailey, and Kelly (2005), describing some of the sociolinguistic studies undertaken on American Sign Language (ASL) and broader sociolinguistic aspects of deaf culture; and Lucas (1995) and Lucas, Bailey, and Valli (2001), reporting on some of the findings of a large-scale quantitative investigation of variation in ASL, using the Labovian model described above.

The aims of this last study were to describe phonological, morphosyntactic, and lexical variables in ASL, and their correlation with regional, age, class, and ethnicity variation. The linguistic variables included phonological ones, such as the sign DEAF, and the location of signs represented by the verb KNOW; morphosyntactic ones, in this case overt and null subject pronouns; and lexical ones.

Looking at the patterns of usage of the sign DEAF, it was found that only three of all the possible forms for this sign were extracted from the recordings, even though over a thousand instances of the sign were present in the data. The researchers note that their results indicated that variation in the form of DEAF is "systematic and conditioned by multiple linguistic and social factors, including grammatical function, the location of the following segment, discourse genre (narrative or conversation), age and region" (Lucas, Bailey, and Kelly, 2005: 257). The authors show that the results confirm the earlier finding of Lucas (1995), where it was shown that the strongest effect on a signer's choice of one of the three variants was the grammatical function of DEAF. The choice between the standard and either of the non-standard variants correlated with grammatical function and discourse genre, whereas the choice between the two non-standard variants correlated with both grammatical function and following segment. Findings showed also that non-linguistic variables were important in the choice between the variants; in particular, region and age.

Lucas, Bailey, and Kelly (2005) explain the age differences through looking at the history of ASL in schooling. The middle age group (who mostly preferred the standard variant) would have been schooled at a time when ASL had only just been recognized as a language, and thus a prescriptive approach to teaching standardized signs was in evidence. However, the older speakers had grown up in a period when ASL was not recognized, so would have lacked exposure to "correct" forms. Finally, younger speakers were educated when there was a more relaxed attitude to sign variation, so they too developed a more open attitude to non-standard variants.

9.5.3   Stylistic Variation in Clinical Data

As noted earlier, stylistic variation has long been a concern of sociolinguists, especially the formalizing effects of the interview procedures used to obtain speech data. Language interactions in the clinic often display unequal power relations (for a fuller account of this area see Damico and Ball, 2008), and together with the client paying special attention to their speech, a clinic speech style may be used that does not reflect the usage patterns in less formal interactions. A case in point is described in Müller, Ball, and Rutter (2008). This case illustrates the fact that in clinical sociolinguistics we often have to move away from studies using a large number of subjects recruited through stratified random sampling, or even from smaller social network groupings, to the single case study.

The client, called "Robert" in Müller, Ball, and Rutter (2008), was 9.8 at the time of data collection, and had received speech therapy since he was 3 years old for a variety of phonological and articulation problems. His remaining speech problem was reported by his clinician to be inconsistent productions of the target /r/. Data were collected through tape recording three tasks: first, the production of a list of 42 single words chosen to include /r/ in a variety of positions in the word, in a variety of phonetic contexts, and in words between one to three syllables long. The second task was to read the first two paragraphs of the Rainbow Passage (Fairbanks, 1960: 127). The final data type was a conversation between Robert and his clinician that lasted about 20 minutes. We will examine his realization of the target /r/ in these three styles, but also in various phonological contexts: singletons versus clusters; and the four word positions: syllable initial, word initial (SIWI), syllable initial within word (SIWW), syllable final word final (SFWF), and syllable final within word (SFWW).

A casual conversation lasting approximately 20 minutes between Robert and his clinician resulted in 33 instances of target /r/. For singleton /r/ in SIWI position (N = 5), Robert used a bilabial (1), labiodental (1), or velar approximant (3). The single target fricative+/r/ cluster in this position was realized as fricative+[ʋ]. For singleton /r/ in SIWW position the labiodental approximant predominates (N = 3), with one correct realization. In SFWW consonant sequences (N = 5), there were two omissions of target /r/, one realization as schwa, and two realization as a dark-l. In SFWF position, singleton /r/ (N = 14) is omitted eight times. In five instances, Robert used a dark-l or dark-l offglide, and in one instance, a velar approximant ([ɰ]). The use of the dark-l and the velar approxminant were also accompanied by a retracted tongue root and a velarized voice quality. SFWF target /r/-clusters (N = 4) are characterized by omission of /r/ (3), and once by the use of the dark-l offglide, again with retracted tongue root and velarized voice quality.

The distribution of Robert's realizations of target /r/ in his reading of the Rainbow Passage showed some differences to his usage in casual speech. In SIWI position /r/ is realized as a velar approximant (N = 6). However, these were produced without excessive lengthening, unlike Robert's usage in reading the word list. His SIWI clusters showed one correct target realization and two realizations of /r/ as a labiodental approximant. In SIWW position, /r/ is realized as a velar (N = 1) or a labiodental (N = 2) approximant. Syllable final /r/ is omitted (N = 5), and twice realized as a glottal stop. The retracted tongue root/velarized voice quality noted in the conversational speech and the reading of the word list did not occur in the Rainbow Passage.

Robert's reading of the word list revealed various realizations of target /r/, which patterned according to the position of the target sound, and differed from both the previous styles. For singleton /r/ in SIWI position (N = 10), Robert produced a lengthened velar approximant [ɰ] (often exceeding 300 ms). A velar approximant is an unusual realization of target /r/ in English even in disordered speech. In SIWI r-clusters (N = 3) Robert split up the cluster by the insertion of an epenthetic schwa, followed by [ɹ], and in one case of target /gr/ by [gɰ].

In SIWW position, singleton /r/ (N = 6) was regularly realized by other approximants: bilabial [β] (three times), labiodental [ʋ], labiovelar [w], and velar [ɰ] (one each). SIWW target r-clusters (N = 2) followed the pattern of SIWI clusters, that is, the breaking up of the cluster by schwa.

Singleton /r/ in SFWF position (N = 14) is most often omitted. In one case, Robert uses a dark-l, and once an l-offglide; in one case (target "car"), the preceding vowel is r-colored. Omission of /r/ is also the strategy for SFWF clusters (N = 4), and SFWW target /r/ in a consonant sequence (N = 4).

A further characteristic of Robert's output when reading the word list is the use of a velarized voice quality, which appears to originate in a retracted tongue root and was also used in the conversational style. This does not occur with target /r/ in SIWI position, but chiefly where target /r/ is in syllable-final position.

Robert's patterns of /r/ target usage reflect patterns of linguistic variation found in sociolinguistic studies: correlations with both linguistic context and with style. A clinical sociolinguistic analysis of Robert's speech, therefore, has highlighted not only the variation, but the need to bear this variation in mind in both assessment and treatment. Indeed, Müller, Ball, and Rutter (2008) speculate that the predominance of the velar approximant usage in Robert's "therapy style" (i.e. the word list) may reflect an unsuccessful attempt to teach him to produce /r/ with a bunched tongue shape.

Section Summary

- Various researchers have discussed the application of sociolinguistic methodology to clinical data.
- Variationist approaches requiring large numbers of subjects are not always feasible in clinical contexts, where single case studies may be required.
- Scholars working with American Sign Language have produced several studies of variation in sign that are closely based on sociolinguistic research methods.
- Sociolinguists' concerns with style differences are especially important to the collection of clinical data, and considerable differences may be found between different styles.

9.6   Resources

Readers interested in further resources on sociolinguistic methodology are referred to Johnstone (1999), Milroy and Gordon (2003), Tagliamonte (2006), and Bayley and Lucas (2007).

Notes

1 Linguistic variables are placed within parentheses, with the variants usually given in square brackets. So, Labov's (1966) variable (oh) had variants ranging from [ʊ³] to [ɑː].
2 This section is adapted from Damico and Ball (2005).

References

Ball, M. J. (1984). Sociolinguistic aspects of the Welsh mutation system. Unpublished doctoral dissertation, University of Wales.

Ball, M. J. (1988) Investigating performance and competence in variation studies: adapting techniques from speech pathology. In A. R. Thomas (ed.), *Methods in Dialectology*. Bristol, UK: Multilingual Matters, pp. 1–10.

Ball, M. J. (1992). Is a clinical sociolinguistics possible? *Clinical Linguistics and Phonetics*, 6, 155–160.

Ball, M. J. (1993). Initial consonant mutation in modern spoken Welsh. *Multilingua*, 12, 189–205.

Ball, M. J. (ed.) (2005). *Clinical Sociolinguistics*. Oxford: Blackwell.

Ball, M. J. (ed.) (2010). *Sociolinguistics around the World*. London: Routledge.

Ball, M. J. and Müller, N. (1992). *Mutation in Welsh*. London: Routledge.

Bayley, R. and Lucas, C. (eds) (2007). *Sociolinguistic Variation: Theories, Methods, and Applications*. Cambridge: Cambridge University Press.

Britain, D. and Matsumoto, K. (2005). Languages, communities, networks and practices. In M. J. Ball (ed.), *Clinical Sociolinguistics*. Oxford: Blackwell, pp. 3–14.

Cedergren, H. and Sankoff, D. (1974). Variable rules: performance as a statistical reflection of competence. *Language*, 50, 333–355.

Chambers, J. and Trudgill, P. (1980). *Dialectology*. Cambridge: Cambridge University Press.

Cheshire, J. (1980). *Variation in an English Dialect: A Sociolinguistic Study*. Cambridge: Cambridge University Press.

Crystal, D. (1981). *Clinical Linguistics*. Vienna: Springer.

Crystal, D. (1982). *Profiling Linguistic Disability*. London: Edward Arnold.

Crystal, D. (1984). *Linguistic Encounters with Language Handicap*. Oxford: Blackwell.

Damico, J. and Ball, M. J. (2008). Sociolinguistics. In M. J. Ball, M. Perkins, N. Müller, and S. Howard (eds), *Handbook of Clinical Linguistics*. Oxford: Wiley-Blackwell, pp. 107–129.

DeRenzi, E. and Ferrari, C. (1978). The reporter's test: a sensitive test to detect expressive disturbances in aphasics. *Cortex*, 14, 279–293.

Fairbanks, G. (1960). *Voice and Articulation Drillbook*. New York: Harper and Row.

Johnstone, B. (1999). *Qualitative Methods in Sociolinguistics*. Oxford: Oxford University Press.

Labov, W. (1963). The social motivation of a sound change. *Word*, 19, 273–309.

Labov, W. (1966). *The Social Stratification of English in New York City*. Washington, DC: Center for Applied Linguistics.

Labov, W. (1969). Contraction, deletion, and inherent variability of the English copula. *Language*, 45, 715–762.

Labov, W. (1970). The study of language in its social context. *Studium Generale*, 23, 30–87.

Labov, W. (1972). *Sociolinguistic Patterns*. Oxford: Blackwell.

Lucas, C. (ed.) (1989). *The Sociolinguistics of the Deaf Community*. San Diego, CA: Academic Press.

Lucas, C. (1995). Sociolinguistic variation in ASL: the case of DEAF. In C. Lucas (ed.), *Sociolinguistics in Deaf Communities*, vol. 1. Washington, DC: Gallaudet University Press, pp. 3–25.

Lucas, C. (ed.) (2001). *The Sociolinguistics of Sign Languages*. Cambridge: Cambridge University Press.

Lucas, C., Bailey, R., and Kelly, A. (2005). The sociolinguistics of sign languages. In M. J. Ball (ed.), *Clinical Sociolinguistics*. Oxford: Blackwell, pp. 250–254.

Lucas, C., Bailey, R., and Valli, C. (2001). *Sociolinguistics in Deaf Communities*, vol. 7, *Sociolinguistic Variation in American Sign Language*. Washington, DC: Gallaudet University Press.

Milroy, L. (1980). *Language and Social Networds*. Oxford: Blackwell.

Milroy, L. and Gordon, M. (2003). *Sociolinguistics: Method and Interpretation*. Oxford: Blackwell.

Müller, N., Ball, M. J., and Rutter, N. (2008). An idiosyncratic case of /r/ disorder: application of principles from Systemic Phonology and Systemic Functional Linguistics. *Asia-Pacific Journal of Speech, Language and Hearing*, 11, 269–281.

Oetting, J. (2005) Assessing language in children who speak a nonmainstream dialect of English. In M. J. Ball (ed.), *Clinical Sociolinguistics*. Oxford: Blackwell, pp. 190–192.

Seymour, H., Roeper, T., and de Villiers, J. (2003). *Diagnostic Evaluation of Language Variation*. San Antonio, TX: Psychological Corporation.

Tagliamonte, S. (2006). *Analysing Linguistic Variation*. Cambridge: Cambridge University Press.

Trudgill, P. (1974). *The Social Differentiation of English in Norwich*. Cambridge: Cambridge University Press.

Wardhaugh, R. (1998). *An Introduction to Sociolinguistics*. Oxford: Blackwell.

Wolfram, W. (1969). *A Sociolinguistic Description of Detroit Negro Speech*. Washington, DC: Center for Applied Linguistics.

Wolfram, W. (1993) The sociolinguistic model in speech and language pathology. In M. M. Leafy and J. L. Kallen (eds), *International Perspectives in Speech and Language Pathology*. Dublin, Ireland: Trinity College, pp. 1–29.

Woodward, J. (1980) Sociolinguistic: some sociolinguistic aspects of French and American Sign Languages. In H. Lane and F. Grosjean (eds), *Recent Perspectives on American Sign Language*. Hillsdale, NJ: Erlbaum, pp. 103–118.

10 The Recording of Audio and Video Data

Ben Rutter and Stuart Cunningham

10.1 Introduction

Researchers in clinical linguistics can adopt a variety of methodologies to describe and analyze communication impairments. These include, but are by no means limited to, speech perception tasks, conversation analysis, syntactic analysis, instrumental analysis, and acoustic phonetics. The methodology used will be determined primarily by the type of research questions being asked and the particular type of impairment being studied.

Due to the fact that many researchers in the field are concerned primarily with speech and/or language production, a large amount of clinical linguistic research involves the collection of audio or video data. This is true for acoustic phonetics, conversation analysis, and any other type of linguistic analysis using spontaneous speech production as its primary data source. Even studies using other types of data, such as X-ray, tomography, and ultrasound, can often benefit from supplementary audio recordings (e.g. Davidson, 2005).

Whenever audio and/or video data are being acquired the researcher needs to think carefully about the practices they employ. Choices made about the recording environment, the selection of equipment, and the various ways in which the data are encoded and stored can all have a bearing on the outcomes of a project (Gopal, 1995; van Son, 2005). In this chapter we explore these issues and think about how they relate specifically to research in clinical linguistics. We will focus on audio and video data and discuss some technological advances that have been made in recent years. We will also outline some good practices for the treatment, processing, storage, and archiving of audio/video data. The chapter is intended not as a prescriptive approach to audio and video research methods, but rather to highlight the

Research Methods in Clinical Linguistics and Phonetics: A Practical Guide,
First Edition. Edited by Nicole Müller and Martin J. Ball.

options that researchers have at their disposal when conducting work with audio and video data.

The chapter begins with some general remarks regarding the relationship between the purpose of a research project and the methodological choices a researcher is faced with. We then discuss audio recording in particular and outline the key components of an audio recording system. Following this we will focus on video recording and pay particular attention to the use of video for interactional studies. Finally, we look at some recommended practices for the storage and protection of data.

10.2   Audio and Video Data: Purpose and Method

The data used in clinical linguistic research are determined largely by the research questions being asked.[1] Depending on the particular focus of the analysis, audio recordings, video recordings, or a combination of the two are often necessary. Interactional studies, particularly those where non-verbal information such as gaze and proximity are of interest, will require video recording (Damico and Simmons-Mackie, 2002; ten Have, 2007). High-quality audio recordings become important whenever there is an intention to analyze speech in any sort of detail, be it impressionistically or acoustically, and accompanying video recordings will often facilitate this sort of analysis. Finally, for the linguistic analysis of syntax and semantics, audio recordings alone are often deemed sufficient, and signal quality is generally not regarded as paramount, unlike the case in phonetic research.

Whether audio recording, video recording, or a combination of the two is being used, there are a number of questions that should be addressed from the outset. A major initial consideration is whether the data will be acquired in a laboratory setting or in the field. While recordings in a lab can be controlled more easily than field recordings, a great deal of speech and language data are more suited to field recording. Ladefoged (1997), for example, outlines the importance of field research for the collection of general phonetic data and language documentation. Equally, field recordings are extremely useful in clinical linguistic research as they provide (i) naturally contextualized data, and (ii) limit the inconvenience caused for the participants. Where mobility issues accompany communication impairment field recording is particularly attractive. However, field recording severely limits the type of equipment that can be used and the extent to which environmental noise can be controlled (Ladefoged, 2003).

Where the object of analysis is linguistic rather than phonetic, as in syntactic, semantic, or pragmatic analysis, the quality of the audio data is, arguably, of less importance. However, clarity in the audio signal is always beneficial, and as a general rule it is always best to acquire an audio signal of the highest possible fidelity. Obviously, certain types of research will necessitate this more than others, and if the data are going to be analyzed acoustically then careful consideration needs to be given to signal quality (Gopal, 1995). In studying disordered speech, there is the added complication of analyzing sometimes confounding speech characteristics, such as hypernasality and other resonance disturbances (Kent *et al.*, 1999). Regardless, a number of studies (e.g. Plichta, 2004) have shown that different recording equipment can have a significant effect on the results obtained from acoustic analyses. Increasingly, journals are requiring researchers not only to report the equipment and settings they used to acquire the data but to submit only research papers in acoustic phonetics that have been carried out using particular settings.

If data are going to be transcribed phonetically then the signal needs to be clearly audible and free of background noise. A long-standing issue in the reliability of phonetic transcription has been the issue of signal quality (Shriberg and Lof, 1991), and the extent to which impressionistic phonetic transcriptions can be considered reliable is partly determined by the recordings on which they are based. Conversation analysts, on the other hand, may chose to prioritize equipment portability over auditory quality. As long as intelligibility is not affected then this is generally fine, although a recent trend in clinical conversation analysis to incorporate phonetic analysis (e.g. Rutter, 2009) means that both portability and signal quality need to be carefully balanced.

Consideration also has to be given to the number and type of speakers being recorded. If multiple speakers are contributing data that are going to be analyzed phonetically a stereo microphone can be used. If there is the potential for overlap in the speech (as is common in conversation) then two separate microphones recording on two separate channels are recommended (Harrington, 2010). This will allow the researcher to isolate the data from the individual speakers at the points of overlap. This can benefit not just the phonetic analysis but also the conversation analysis of overlapping turns. Equally, if children are involved in the study then lapel microphones or microphone-mounted vests are an option worth considering.

Finally, it is worth mentioning remote recording. It is common for speech data to be attained via telephone recordings, but it is important to bear in mind that the vast majority of methods for recording telephone signals will limit the maximum sampling rate to 8 kHz. As we discuss sampling rate later on in the chapter, it will become clear that this will have implications for the analysis of high-frequency sounds such as fricatives and affricates.

Section Summary

- Always consider the type of analysis you will be carrying out before choosing your recording equipment.
- Think about the benefits of both lab-based recordings and field recordings.
- If acoustic analysis is going to be carried out, then careful consideration needs to be given to signal quality.

10.3   Audio Recording

In this section we focus on the recording of audio data. We will outline the concept of digital signal processing, discuss the components of an audio recording system, and then look carefully at some key choices facing the researcher. The overall intention of this section is to encourage researchers to opt for the best equipment they can, aiming to capture a speech signal of the highest quality possible. However, as discussed above, we are aware that certain research projects demand this more than others and resources are often very limited.

10.3.1   Digital Audio Signals

With the rapid advance of computing technology in the last 30 years it is now likely that speech captured for the purposes of analysis will be stored on a computer in a digital format. In the following section we will describe some of the common devices for recording digital audio, but first we will describe the underlying process by which a signal in encoded and stored in a digital medium.

When we record a speech signal for analysis we use a microphone to transduce the sound pressure wave in the air into an analogue electrical signal. This analogue electrical signal is then converted into a digital signal using a process known as analogue to digital conversion (A-to-D conversion).

10.3.1.1   Sampling and quantization

There are two principal characteristics which can be said to differentiate analogue and digital signals. The first it that analogue signals are *continuous* time signals. By this, we do not mean that the signal lasts for infinite time, but rather that it has a value at every instance of its duration. Therefore, no matter what point in time we choose to try and measure the signal it will have amplitude. By contrast, a digital signal only has a value at a finite number of equally spaced moments in time.

This contrast is illustrated in Figure 10.1. In the top panel, A, a sine wave is plotted. The signal is plotted as a continuous line, which means it has a value for every point we could identify on the time axis (x-axis). In theory there are an infinite number of points on the time axis – as we could identify ever-smaller divisions of time, for example, 0.0001 s, 0.00001 s, 0.000001 s, and so on. Therefore we can say the signal is continuous in nature.[2]

In the bottom panel, B, a sine wave is also plotted. However, it is plotted only at a series of equally spaced moments in time, as these are the only moments in time for which the signal has amplitude. Just like a digital signal the wave only has amplitude at these moments in time. These points are shown in the plot by the filled circles. This is the defining property of so-called discrete time signals, of which digital signals are one such example. We refer to these equally spaced moments in time as *samples*. At all other instances in time other than the samples the signal has no value.

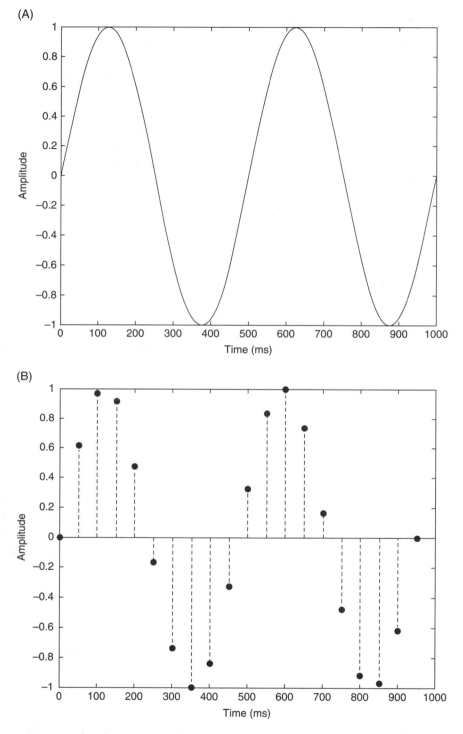

Figure 10.1 Panel A shows a plot of a sine wave. The line is continuous and indicates how an analogue signal has amplitude at every moment in time in its duration. Panel B shows the same sine wave as would be represented in a digital signal. The original signal has been sampled at a rate of 20 samples/s so the amplitude of the signal is defined only at each of these sampled points in time.

The second important thing that we can say about an analogue signal is that its amplitude values are also *continuous*. This is because, in the same way there is always an infinite number of points in time between any two points in the signal; there is also an infinite number of points between two amplitude values. For instance, the signal shown in Figure 10.1, panel A, can have an infinite range of amplitude values as there are an infinite number of values between the maximum (+1) and minimum (−1) values shown. In practice of course, it is difficult to make such accurate measurements, so we limit our measurements to a set of discrete values. This is what we do whenever we measure something; for instance, when we wish to measure a short distance we use a set of discrete values, such as millimeters or centimeters to simplify our measurement. Similarly, when we measure an analogue signal in an A-to-D conversion we say that the range of possible amplitude value we measure is quantized. That is we restrict the measurements to a set of discrete values.

Figure 10.2 shows the effect of different quantization types. We can more accurately measure a signal if we allow a greater range of possible values. So, as the size of the steps between possible values increases the resolution of the measurement decreases. This plot of a digital signal in panel A shows a much poorer signal resolution than that shown in panel B. The difference between these two plots is that in panel B the resolution is higher, and the step size between possible values is much smaller.

It is usual to express the number of levels in a particular quantization as a number of binary digits, or bits. The number of bits used in a quantization will be equal to the number of bits required to express the maximum value that a signal can represent. Typically, for most speech applications a resolution of 16 bits is sufficient. If you choose a lower bit rate you may find the range of possible amplitude values lacks precision for fine acoustic analysis (see Baken and Orlikoff, 2000: 77–79, for further detail).

10.3.1.2   Sampling rates

Having described the differences between an analogue signal and its digital counterpart, we can now see that the process of A-to-D conversion requires the analogue signal to be sampled (measured at discrete time intervals) and quantized (the measurements converted to an appropriate value). The process of A-to-D conversion is sometimes referred to as pulse code modulation (PCM), and digital output signal as a PCM signal.

The number of times the analogue signal is sampled in a second is called the *sampling rate* (expressed in samples/s) or *sampling frequency* (expressed in Hz). So, if we sampled a signal 1000 times in a second it would mean we would collect 1000 values for 1 second of signal.

When we want to record a signal we are often able to control what sampling rate we use. However, when recording and analyzing speech it is important to know what is an appropriate sampling rate to choose.

Consider what would happen if we wanted to sample a sine wave which had a frequency of 100 Hz. If we sampled at a rate of 1000 Hz (which is 1000 samples/s) each cycle of the sine wave would be represented with 10 samples in the digital signal.

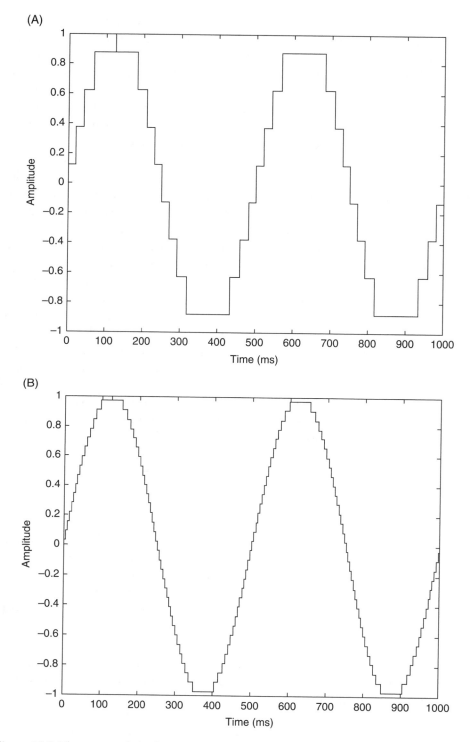

Figure 10.2 The top panel, A, shows the same sine wave shown in Figure 10.1, but quantized into a signal with only eight different amplitude levels. This results in a poor representation of the original signal. Panel B shows the signal this time quantized with 32 different amplitude levels. The resolution of the representation is much higher and captures more of the detail of the original signal.

However, if we only sample at a rate of 150 Hz, each cycle of the wave would be represented by (on average) 1.5 samples per cycles. This would be problematic as it is not possible to describe a cycle of a periodic wave with less than two samples (we need a maximum and minimum in each cycle). Therefore, the resulting digital signal would not be a sine wave with a frequency of 100 Hz, but a periodic sound with a lower frequency. Therefore the sampling rate must be at least twice the highest frequency we wish to represent. This observation is sometime referred to as the *Nyquist sampling theorem* and the highest frequency represented in a signal is referred to as the Nyquist frequency, which will be exactly half the sampling frequency (or rate).

A higher sampling rate will result in a signal containing more samples. From a storage and processing perspective it may be desirable for the files containing our signals to be as small as possible. However, if we record our signals with a lower sampling rate we know this will result in a loss in fidelity. So, what is a suitable sampling rate when recording speech?

To answer the question fully we need to know what the purpose of the recording is. If it is simply to facilitate the preparation of transcription then fidelity is not essential, and a lower sampling rate may be chosen (especially if a small portable device is being used). However, in many research projects a digital recording is made for acoustic or similar analyses. To determine an appropriate sampling rate we can ask what is the highest frequency that will be of interest when conducting such analysis? Typically, for vowels the highest frequency of interest (at least 4000 Hz) will be lower than for sounds such as fricatives and affricatives (at least 5000 Hz). However, these are not definitive, and with the fact that digital storage is relatively cheap it would be prudent to record speech signals with a sampling frequency of at least 20 kHz. This will mean that the highest frequency we can examine will be 10 kHz. Following such an approach, where equipment allows, will mean that your recorded signals will be of sufficient fidelity to be appropriate for most forms of analysis.

10.3.2 *Recording Device*

In order to capture a digital audio signal the researcher will require a recording device equipped to carry out A–D conversion. As technologies have developed and the number of options available to researchers has increased, the decision as to which recording device to use has become a difficult one. In this section we will outline some of the most frequently used recording devices and offer recommendations as to when they might be suitable for use. It should be noted that we would generally recommend an audio interface for laboratory recordings and a portable solid-state recorder for field recordings. We have, however, included mention of devices that may still be found in speech laboratories.

- *Cassette recorders*: it may be possible to still find cassette recorders in speech laboratories. Although the high-end models can record sound to a high standard we would recommend using digital recorders wherever possible. For the purpose of storage, transfer, and analysis, analogue recording devices are no longer attractive.

- *Digital audio tape*: the digital audio tape (DAT) became popular in the late 1980s and early 1990s and was used extensively by individuals who wanted to capture audio signals in the field. DAT devices are essentially digital versions of analogue cassette recorders in that they write high-quality digital signals onto magnetic tape. This can then be transferred to a computer without any loss of quality. DAT has since been discontinued by Sony, and the availability of digital audio tapes is now limited. Moreover, the introduction of solid-state recorders (see below) means that recording using DAT introduces an unnecessary step in the recording process.

- *Mini-disc*: the mini-disc was introduced in the 1990s as a medium for storing sound portably. The first generation of mini-disc stored audio in a compressed form, called ATRAC, but the high-fidelity version of the basic mini-disc format (HiMD) allowed users to record audio in uncompressed, linear PCM. The microphone input is 3.5 mm and the availability of mini-discs to record on may be limited, but an HiMD device is still a very appealing way of recording high-quality signals on an extremely small, portable device. A recommended model is the Sony MZRh1.

- *Solid-sate compact flashcard recorders*: compact flashcard recorders are probably the best option for recording outside of a lab. Like HiMD recorders, they feature input-level meters and allow the user to digitize the data using linear PCM and store it uncompressed as a WAV file. Many flashcard recorders have balanced XLR microphone inputs allowing the use of higher-quality XLR microphones (discussed below). The data are stored on a compact flashcard and can be easily transferred via a USB cable to a desktop computer. A recommended model is the Marantz PMD661.

- *Audio interfaces*: in a laboratory setting where portability is not a requirement it is preferable to record audio directly to a desktop or laptop computer. In order to do this an audio interface can be used which will allow XLR microphones to be used and recording settings to be specified. Audio interfaces are used in the music industry and can be connected to the computer using a USB or firewire connector. The MobilePre by M-AUDIO is a particularly good example of a USB-powered audio interface that could be used with a desktop computer or laptop in a lab setting.

- *Other small portable devices*: other devices that may be considered for the purpose of recording speech include digital voice recorders and portable media players such as Apple's iPod™. What these devices may offer in terms of portability and ease of use they lack in some other key areas. They typically lack input-level meters, rely on internal microphones, and will usually restrict recordings to compressed file formats (e.g. MP3). Each of these factors mean they should almost certainly be avoided if any sort of detailed (e.g. phonetic) analysis of the data is going to be carried out.

To summarize, an audio interface connected to a laptop or desktop computer is the best option for recording audio, followed by the use of a solid-state compact flashcard recorder. Both of these will allow the use of an XLR microphone and provide the option of recording audio in an uncompressed format (e.g. WAV). Audio file formats are discussed in Section 10.5.1 below, but the use of lossy[3] compression formats such as MP3 or ATRAC is not recommended if acoustic analysis is going to be carried out on the data.

10.3.3 Microphones

The selection of a recording device will determine the types of microphone available to the researcher. Some recording devices include only an inbuilt microphone, some come with 3.5 mm inputs, and the more advanced models come with XLR microphone inputs. This is the first decision surrounding microphone choice, but there several other factors to bear in mind:

- *Frequency range*: the frequency range of the microphone determines the range of frequencies it can recognize. Of particular interest here is the upper limit of this range, particularly if high-frequency sounds such as fricatives are to be analyzed. Generally, it is best to opt for a microphone with a frequency range that is at least 10 kHz at its upper-limit. A fairly "flat" frequency range is also preferable to one that adds emphasis to the lower frequencies.
- *Polar pattern*: the polar pattern, sometimes called "pick-up pattern," of a microphone refers to the area immediately surrounding the microphone, where sound is mostly likely to be picked up. The cardioid polar pattern is the most common type and is designed to pick up sound from the front in a shape similar to a heart. For single-speaker studies, this is the best option as it will be less likely to pick up environmental noise. As mentioned above, if multiple speakers are being recorded by the same microphone, an omnidirectional microphone will most likely be best as this has 360-degree sensitivity. Microphones differ in their polar pattern and it is important to check this before using them.
- *Microphone-to-mouth distance*: the potential for proximity effects is something that needs to be carefully considered, particularly if acoustic analysis going to be carried out. As a speaker naturally moves their body position their proximity to the microphone will vary. This can influence any acoustic measurements that have an intensity component to them (e.g. VOT, formant measurements, loudness). Maintaining a constant microphone-to-mouth distance is easier in experimental settings as the researcher can ask the participant to keep their head in a steady position. However, for children, speakers with a body tremor, or for any interactional studies this will prove nearly impossible. Therefore, lapel microphones or head-set microphones are a particularly good way to maintain a consistent microphone-to-mouth distance.

10.3.4 Audio Playback

For the monitoring of input levels and also for the analysis of data, a good pair of headphones is essential. Headphone selection is relatively straightforward, although there are a few factors to consider. First, it is essential to use headphones with a frequency range appropriate for the perception of speech. You will therefore want to make sure the upper limit of the range is a minimum of 8 kHz. Headphones that are *circumaural* (i.e. they sit around the ears) are generally better than *supra-aural* headphones (that sit on the ears), as they are more likely to aid in the reduction of environmental noise.

> **Section Summary**
>
> - Sampling rate determines the number of times a digital sample is taken from an analogue signal.
> - Recording devices differ according to the way in which they digitize signals, how they store them, and what type of microphones inputs they allow.
> - When selecting a microphone, consider the frequency range, the polar pattern, and the input type.

10.4   Video Recording

In this section we look at the use of video recording in clinical linguistic research. Initially we consider the sort of research questions and methodologies that might benefit from the acquisition of video data, and in Section 10.4.2 we outline some more technical issues surrounding choices of equipment and set up.

10.4.1   *Video Data in Interactional Studies*

The popularity of conversation analysis as a research method within the field of communication disorders has steadily increased over the past 20 years (Wilkinson, 2008). Particularly common has been the analysis of both verbal and non-verbal contributions within a conversation.

The use of video recording in conversation analysis seems to offer several advantages to the analyst over the use the use of purely audio data (ten Have, 2007). First, a great many visual aspects of verbal interaction can only be analyzed if video recordings are made. The direction of gaze, the use of gesture, facial expressions, and the use of proximity are all potentially interesting aspects of talk-in-interaction and all are analyzable only through the use of video data. Similarly, contextually situated interaction often uses, or indeed revolves around, physical objects in the participants' environment. The use of cues, the demonstration of referents, or the discussion of some object of joint attention can all be central to a conversation and should, if at all possible, be considered during the course of analysis.

The analysis of interactions where one or several of the interlocutors have a communication impairment can in fact add to the importance of visual information. Where speech and language production are impaired, the use of non-verbal communication can take on a more critical role than in non-impaired conversation. The use of pointing and gesturing, for example, may supplement lexical selection while the use of facial expressions or laughter may accompany particular emotional speech styles.

There are numerous studies which demonstrate the usefulness of video recorded data in clinical conversation analysis so we mention just a few particularly relevant examples here. The first, Damico and Simmons-Mackie (2002), demonstrates that the analysis of gaze/gesture can facilitate the understanding of interactions involving an individual with aphasia. The use of gaze, for example, during word-finding difficulties is argued to carry important information about floor-holding techniques and turn maintenance. Similarly, Bloch and Beeke (2008) use video recorded data to combine the analysis of turn design with the analysis of visual information such as gaze direction in episodes of co-constructed talk. Their analysis could not have been carried out in the way it was without the use of visual information.

The analysis of children's interactional patterns can also benefit from the use of video data. Children often use toys and environmental objects during interactions as so much of children's conversational speech is centered on play. Furthermore, children often learn early words and expressions with the accompaniment of exaggerated facial expressions or hand gestures (Capone and McGregor, 2004). Kidd and Holler (2009) have also shown that children use gesture to help resolve potentially ambiguous lexical items such as the homonyms 'bat' (as in baseball bat) and 'bat' (as in the mammal). All this visual information can be central to the analysis of children's interactional styles.

10.4.2 *Video data in Other Areas of Clinical Linguistics*

The analysis of human interaction naturally benefits from the analysis of video data. However, a great deal more research in clinical linguistics can be supported by video recording. The usefulness of video data for phonetic analysis, for example, has long been emphasized (Abercrombie, 1967; Kelly and Local, 1989; Ladefoged, 1997). The McGurk effect (McGurk and McDonald, 1976) suggests that a great deal of speech perception is influenced by the visual modality, and, if at all possible, video data should be combined with high-quality audio recordings. In clinical linguistic research, this has been exploited to good effect (Heselwood, 2007; Heselwood and Howard, 2008; Müller, Damico, and Guendouzi, 2006). Indeed, Heselwood (2007: 580) carried out a case study of breath control during conversational speech and concluded that "[h]ad there been no video footage and the analysis had had to be carried out entirely from an audio recording, the case study presented in this paper would not have been possible in its present form."

10.4.3 *Video Recording Considerations*

As with the development of audio recording technology, in recent years video recording devices have moved firmly into the digital domain. This means that it is likely that any video recordings you make will be in a digital format, which means they can be more easily edited and displayed on a computer. It is likely that once you have recorded a video, your first task will be to transfer it to a computer and edit it prior to analysis. You may also use the video editing software to isolate portions of particular interest which you may wish to use when reporting your study.

There are many choices of cameras and other equipment that you may use when recording video. Some of these choices will be dictated by the equipment you have available and the purpose of your recordings. However, as a rule, before you begin to use a camera you should always ensure that is compatible with your video editing software. It is the case that some cameras will store video in a format that is only compatible with particular video editing software.

Modern digital video cameras are either tape-based or tapeless. The more established tape-based cameras use MiniDV tapes to store video. It can in theory take longer to transfer recordings from these to a computer. More recent tapeless cameras may use DVDs, an internal hard disc, or memory cards to store video. It is argued that these media can make it faster to transfer video to computer for editing. However, it should be noted that it is often the case that tapeless cameras use particular formats to store the video, and most video editing software will need to convert videos into formats suitable for editing. This conversion process can often remove the time advantage claimed for tapeless devices. It is also worth noting that it is simple to archive tapes used for recording, so that you may return to the data at a later date. However, with a tapeless camera you often need to remove the video data from the device when it is full. Therefore, you will need to consider how you will archive the data by using another medium such as a DVD or a hard disc.

In terms of recording the video, it is important to consider both the lighting of participants and the positioning of the camera. There are few situations when studying human communication where it will be necessary to move the camera, so positioning the camera on a tripod will result in a stable image that will be easier to analyze. It is also worth remembering that participants may move around during a recording, so while the camera should be fixed on a tripod, the shot should be sufficiently wide to ensure an adequate "margin" in which the participants may move.

Modern cameras can accommodate a wide variety of lighting conditions, but it is important to ensure participants are lit and positioned to ensure all relevant data are captured. For instance, if you are interested in analyzing interaction and one participant is silhouetted because they are in front of an ambient light source, such as a window, it can make it difficult to observe their gaze and facial expression. Therefore, it is important to use the camera's display screen to ensure that participants are shown adequately in the shot.

Section Summary

- Video data can be a useful addition for most types of linguistic data.
- Phonetic analysis in particular has been shown to be helped by video data.
- Consider both lighting and camera position before beginning a recording.

10.5   Data Storage and Protection

10.5.1   *Audio File Formats*

We have described how an analogue signal from a microphone may be converted into a digital signal. However, we will then need to store the digital signal in an appropriate format.

Audio data files may be stored in compressed or uncompressed formats. The most common uncompressed formats for audio files are ones based on digital signals. On Windows computers these are often referred to as "wav" files (with the file extension ".wav"). On Macintosh computers these files can be referred to as "aiff" files (with the file extension ".aiff"). The formats are similar, and can support signals with a very wide range of sampling frequencies and bit rates. Therefore, they are considered to be the easiest formats for storing digital audio for research purposes.

Compressed audio formats can be described as being either *lossless* or *lossy*. A possible advantage of compressed formats is that they can take up less space than the same signals in an uncompressed format. This might be a consideration if storage space is limited, or signals have been recorded with a very high sampling frequency.

In a lossless format, unnecessary data are eliminated. In an uncompressed format, such as wav, the file of a person reading a passage from a book for 10 seconds would be the same size as 10 seconds of silence. A lossless compression algorithm will eliminate repetitive and similar values from the sequence of values in the signal. This process, however, will not affect the quality of the signal. The most common lossless audio format is FLAC.

Alternatively, a lossy compression algorithm seeks to remove the portions of the signal that might not be audible to the listener. The aim of such formats is to save space while not compromising the audio quality. The most common lossy compressed format is MP3 – which is widely used on personal music players.

The choice of appropriate format to record and store your data again is dependent on what you wish to use the data for. If a low-fidelity signal is required, simply to transcribe a conversation, then is might be possible to use a compressed format such as MP3. However, for all speech-analytical purposes it is vital to record uncompressed signals, such as WAV. This is because any compression algorithm will eliminate data. In lossy compression approaches this is usually done on the basis of which part of the signal is inaudible. Therefore, this would be an inappropriate signal on which to conduct fine-scale acoustic analysis as portions of the original speech will have been removed (see van Son, 2005).

10.5.2   Data Security and Archiving

As recordings that you make of speakers can be thought of as personal data, it is not only good research practice to store them securely, but it is likely to be demanded by the ethical codes of research conduct. Here is a list of good practice guidelines that should be observed when dealing with video and audio data:

1   Video and audio data should always be stored on a password-protected computer. With the growing use of USB data sticks to move data between computers, people often leave them in an unprotected format. However, any speech or video data collected in the course of research should always be protected by a password even if copied onto a portable device such as a USB data stick.

2   It is also good practice to be prepared for all eventualities. The catastrophic failure of a hard disk could render it impossible to recover the data from it. Therefore,

as with all types of data you store on your computer, a regular and systematic backup procedure is vital. As with copies of speech and audio data on your computer, these backups should be stored securely, by protecting them with a password and locking them in a secure place.

3   When you are collecting data it is vital that data are copied from the video or audio recording device as often as possible. This is to avoid the situation where failure or loss of the device could result in many days' worth of data being lost. Therefore, whenever possible a copy should be taken and stored in an appropriately secure place.

Once a research project is finished, you may be left with large amounts of data. You may wish to free up space on your computer and consider archiving this data. When doing so it might be worth considering what format to store the data in. Obviously you could compress the data to save space on the backup media. However, depending on the reasons you collected the data you may need to consider whether in the future further detailed acoustic analysis of the data may be required – if so, lossless compression would be appropriate. Only where the data have been used for generating transcriptions of conversations would it be appropriate to consider lossy compression. The advantage of lossless compression is that the data can be restored to the full original signal, whereas it is not possible to recover the portions that have been removed in lossy compression.

When archiving video data you might consider storing it in a digital format (on hard disks or similar), as the longevity of self-written DVDs is as yet unknown. Factory-produced DVDs and CDs are manufactured and "pressed," a process that has been shown to produce a long-lasting medium. However, discs written in a computer are produced by etching the data into a layer of dye on the disc. It is not yet known how such media will behave over long periods of time, and therefore alternative media such as hard-disk storage may be preferable.

Section Summary

- Digital signals can be stored in compressed or uncompressed formats and compressed formats can be lossy or lossless.
- WAV is an uncompressed format and is preferable to MP3, which is a lossy, compressed format.
- Always back up your data and store on a password-protected computer.

10.6   Conclusion

In this chapter we have looked at the decisions researchers must make when deciding to use audio or video data in their research. We have suggested that due to issues surrounding reliability, a general rule would be to use the best equipment available.

We have highlighted the importance of video data and outlined recent technological advances in video capturing. We have also suggested some good practices for the storing and archiving of data.

Notes

1 Issues surrounding affordability and availability of certain pieces of equipment as well as the time frame in which a project needs to be completed may also influence the selection of equipment.
2 In practice, of course, we cannot easily and accurately measure increasingly small time intervals.
3 See description of this term below in Section 10.5.1.

References

Abercrombie, D. (1967). *Elements of General Phonetics*. Chicago: Aldine.

Baken, R. J. and Orlikoff, R. F. (2000). *Clinical Measurement of Speech and Voice*, San Diego, CA: Singular/Thomson Learning.

Bloch, S. and Beeke, S. (2008). Co-constructed talk in the conversations of people with dysarthria and aphasia. *Clinical Linguistics and Phonetics*, 22, 974–990.

Capone, N. and McGregor, K. (2004). Gesture development: a review for clinical and research practices. *Journal of Speech, Language, and Hearing Research*, 47, 173–186.

Damico, J. S. and Simmons-Mackie, N. N. (2002). The base layer and the gaze/gesture layer of transcription. *Clinical Linguistics and Phonetics*, 16, 317–327.

Davidson, L. (2005). Addressing phonological questions with ultrasound. *Clinical Linguistics and Phonetics*, 19, 619–633.

Gopal, H. S. (1995). Technical issues underlying the development and use of a speech research laboratory. In A. Syrdal, R. Bennett, and S. Greenspan (eds), *Applied Speech Technology*. Boca Raton: CRC Press, pp. 315–242.

Harrington, J. (2010). *Phonetic Analysis of Speech Corpora*. Oxford: Wiley-Blackwell.

Heselwood, B. (2007). Breathing-impaired speech after brain haemorrhage: a case study. *Clinical Linguistics and Phonetics*, 21, 577–604.

Heselwood, B. and Howard, S. (2008). Clinical phonetic transcription. In M. J. Ball, M. Perkins, N. Müller, and S. Howard (eds), *The Handbook of Clinical Linguistics*. Oxford: Wiley-Blackwell, pp. 381–399.

Kelly, J. and Local, J. (1989). *Doing Phonology: Observing, Recording, Interpreting*. Manchester: Manchester University Press.

Kent, R. D., Weismer, G., Kent, I. F. *et al.* (1999). Acoustic studies of dysarthric speech: methods, progress, and potential. *Journal of Communication Disorders*, 32, 141–186.

Kidd, E. J. and Holler, J. (2009). Children's use of gesture to resolve lexical ambiguity. *Developmental Science*, 12, 903–913.

Ladefoged, P. (1997). Instrumental techniques for linguistic phonetic fieldwork. In W. Hardcastle and J. Laver (eds), *The Handbook of Phonetic Sciences*. Oxford: Blackwell, pp. 138–166.

Ladefoged, P. (2003). *Phonetic Data Analysis. An Introduction to Fieldwork and Instrumental Techniques*. Oxford: Blackwell.

McGurk, H. and MacDonald, J. (1976). Hearing lips and seeing voices. *Nature*, 264, 746–748.

Müller, N., Damico, J. S., and Geundouzi, J. A. (2006). What is transcription and why should we do it? In N. Müller (ed.), *Multilayered Transcription*. San Diego, CA: Plural Publishers, pp. 1–18.

Plichta, B. (2004). Data acquisition problems. In *Signal Acquisition and Acoustic Analysis of Speech*. Available at: http://bartus.org/akustyk/signal_aquisition.pdf (accessed April 3, 2012).

Rutter, B. (2009). Repair sequences in dysarthric conversational speech: a study in interactional phonetics. *Clinical Linguistics and Phonetics*, 23, 887–900.

Shriberg, L. and Lof, G. (1991). Reliability studies in broad and narrow phonetic transcription. *Clinical Linguistics and Phonetics*, 5, 225–279.

ten Have, P. (2007). *Doing Conversation Analysis: A Practical Guide*. London: Sage.

van Son, R. J. J. H. (2005). A study of pitch, formant, and spectral estimation errors introduced by three lossy speech compression algorithms. *Acta Acustica united with Acustica*, 91(4), 771–778.

Wilkinson, R. (2008). Conversation analysis and communication disorders. In M. J. Ball, M. Perkins, N. Müller, and S. Howard (eds), *The Handbook of Clinical Linguistics*. Oxford: Wiley-Blackwell, pp. 92–106.

11 Data Processing: Transcriptional and Impressionistic Methods

Martin J. Ball, Sara Howard,
Nicole Müller, and Angela Granese

11.1 Introduction

As noted in Chapter 10, collecting data from clients with communication disorders will usually entail making either audio or video-plus-audio recordings. However, in order to be able to describe and discuss these data, one will normally need to convert the recordings into written transcriptions, as these are much easier to access and to study. If the primary aim of a recording is the subsequent analysis of a client's speech output, then a phonetic transcription will be needed – that is, a transcription into phonetic symbols (often mediated via instrumental analysis). If the primary focus is on the client's language use, perhaps as part of a conversation, then transcription into ordinary orthography, augmented by ways of showing aspects of conversational interaction, will be more appropriate. The transcriber needs to determine the level of detail that is needed for the purpose of analyzing the data at hand, and choose the appropriate notation systems. In Section 11.2, we discuss the transcription of speech, including the use of International Phonetic Association (IPA) symbols and extended symbol sets for disordered speech and voice quality, as well as a system for including multiple layers of analysis in one transcript (a "multilayered" transcription). Section 11.3 deals with transcribing conversational interaction. Transcribing for the purpose of computer analysis is discussed in Chapter 15 of this volume, on corpora and computer archives.

Research Methods in Clinical Linguistics and Phonetics: A Practical Guide,
First Edition. Edited by Nicole Müller and Martin J. Ball.
© 2013 Blackwell Publishing Ltd. Published 2013 by Blackwell Publishing Ltd.

11.2 Transcribing Speech

11.2.1 *Principles of Phonetic Transcription*

Speech is fleeting – once the final sound waves from an utterance have died away it is no longer available for inspection. Even if we make a recording, we must then play that recording each time we wish to consider or analyze that piece of speech data. Phonetic transcription provides us with a method of creating a permanent record of a listener's auditory (and perhaps visual) impressions of a speaker's utterance, by use of special symbols. Of course, we could transcribe an utterance orthographically, but from an orthographic record there is no information about how the utterance actually sounded. Using phonetic symbols allows us to create a record which presents much more transparently detailed information about how an individual speaker produced a sound, word, or utterance, and allows us to capture significant inter- and intra-speaker differences, be they the product of regional or social accents, gender or age, pathologies of speech or language, or specific communicative contexts. In other words, in a phonetic transcription, as opposed to in orthography, there is an agreed-upon one-to-one correspondence between a particular sound or sound feature and a specific phonetic symbol or diacritic. If two speakers produce the word CAT (phonemically /kæt/) as [kʰætˀ] and [k̈aʔʰ] respectively, the phonetic transcription shows unambiguously the differences in pronunciation between the two, without having to go back to an audio or video recording.

For the purposes of clinical transcription, we make use not only of the IPA symbols (IPA, 1999) but also the symbols provided by ExtIPA (the Extensions to the International Phonetic Alphabet: Duckworth, Allen, Hardcastle, and Ball, 1990; Ball and Local, 1996) and VoQS (Voice Quality Symbols) (Ball, Esling, and Dickson, 1995). (Charts of all these symbols are included in an appendix to this chapter.) The combined resources provided by these symbol sets allows us to make written records of consonants and vowels, prosodic features such as stress, pitch, rate, and pauses, and voice quality across both typical and atypical speech production and in utterances of any size or kind, from single sounds to spontaneous connected speech. In dealing with atypical speech where we cannot make any prior assumptions about which phonological distinctions a speaker is making, or how he/she is making them, we typically make what is called an impressionistic transcription, which aims to capture as much detail about the speech behaviors as possible, prior to further analysis.

A phonetic transcription is, of course, only as good as the quality of the sound source, whether that be live or, as will generally be the case for clinical transcription, an audio or video recording. Rutter and Cunningham (Chapter 10, this volume) provide detailed information about data sampling and recording, but it is worth reminding ourselves here that most speech production, and especially atypical speech production, is simply too challenging to transcribe live *in situ* (even though listening live *in situ* is valuable in itself) (Amorosa, Wagner, von Benda, and Keck, 1985). Spending time listening, and relistening, to a good sound recording in order to produce a detailed transcription which answers the questions it was designed to answer is, indeed, time well spent (Heselwood and Howard, 2008; Perkins and Howard, 1995).

As implied by the previous statement, establishing clear aims at the outset is an important stage in the analytic process (Howard and Heselwood, 2002), irrespective of whether the transcription is being carried out for the purposes of research or of clinical assessment. Hopefully it will ensure that the exercise will yield the intended results without an unnecessary expenditure of time and effort. If, for example, I have decided that I am interested only in a child's atypical production of the sibilant fricatives from a formal assessment of single-word production, I might be well advised to focus my efforts on producing particularly narrow transcriptions of a number of tokens of /s/, /z/, /ʃ/, and /ʒ/, while largely ignoring other aspects of their speech production (for the moment, at least!). If, on the other hand, I am trying to unravel an intriguing and apparently significant relationship between atypical sibilant realizations, syllable and word contexts, and prosody, in real, spontaneous conversation, my transcription will need to be much more comprehensive (though not necessarily any less detailed) in order to provide the insights I am hoping to gain, incorporating prosodic notation as well as detailed transcription of vowel realizations, which are often neglected in clinical analysis and transcription (Howard and Heselwood, 2011).

Becoming a competent and confident transcriber requires good training and regular practice: Ladefoged (1995) suggests that an hour or two per day listening, transcribing (and producing) sounds is a reasonable expectation for the beginning phonetics student. Practice, in the complex area of clinical transcription, might not make perfect, but it is enormously helpful in honing auditory perceptual and notational skills. The act of transcription is also aided by an understanding of the reasons why it is sometimes so challenging, and the ways in which the human perceptual apparatus, by being so beautifully adapted to interpersonal communication, can be distinctly unhelpful when we try to make and record fine judgments about different aspects of speech production.

For example, the speed and accuracy of speech processing in typical human interactions is significantly aided by categorical perception, whereby listeners sort and categorize sounds according to broad phonological distinctions, rather than by their fine phonetic detail (Buckingham and Yule, 1987). In this way all kinds of variant realizations of the voiceless alveolar plosive /t/ (e.g. dentalized, retracted, glottalized, etc.) will be subsumed into the same category by the listener, and contrasted with variant realizations of, for instance, the voiceless velar plosive /k/. Whilst this "phonological" processing undoubtedly helps us in everyday interactions, it becomes such an automatic process, over the course of speech development, that it may then be hard to overcome for the purposes of narrow phonetic transcription. This is the case in the speech of some individuals with cleft palate, whose atypical realizations of /t/ and /k/ may correspond to a palatal plosive [c], which although discernible as such from instrumental analysis, may be hard to identify auditorily if the influence of categorical perception proves too great (Howard, 2011). The good news, however, is that the effects of categorical perception can be overcome by training and practice, as demonstrated in a study by Santelman, Sussman, and Chapman (1999) focusing on precisely this set of auditory distinctions in cleft palate speech.

It is also the case that visual information can sometimes mislead a transcriber, as most obviously demonstrated by the McGurk effect (McGurk and McDonald, 1976), but also revealed in studies of individuals with atypical speech production whose labial paralysis proved a significant visual distraction in the identification of place of articulation of stop consonants (Nelson and Hodge, 2000). Listeners are also susceptible to top-down processing effects produced by knowledge of the intended target and by contextual information. Ball (2008: 864) states that a clinical transcription should aim to "show the client's productions, irrespective of target," whilst also noting our human tendency to be influenced by the phonetic content expected in a typical production of a word or phrase. In a classic study of this phenomenon, Oller and Eilers (1975: 301) describe how transcribers "may perceive elements which are not present in the acoustic signal, and/or ... may fail to perceive elements which are present" in direct relation to the perceived meaning of an utterance.

A further, and obvious, challenge in transcription is to capture the ever-changing speech signal by means of a finite set of symbols arranged in a linear sequence on the page. Judicious combinations of symbols and diacritics can, however, be remarkably successful in capturing the temporal relationships between movements of the various articulators. Thus, for example, the diacritic for aspiration in the transcription of CAN /kæn/ as [kʰæ̃n] gives an indication of the timing of the onset of vocal fold vibration in relation to the release of the initial plosive and the use of the nasal tilde implies the release of velopharyngeal closure during the vowel and prior to the following nasal consonant.

Phonetic transcription has often been criticised for being subjective and for lacking the rigor of instrumental analysis. Furthermore, discussions of the value of transcription often point to the low levels of inter-transcriber agreement reported in research studies, arguing that only instrumental analysis can provide a "true" picture of speech production. Whilst fully acknowledging the challenges and limitations of narrow phonetic transcription, we should also note that a paper by Cucchiarini (1996) carefully describes how scoring transcriber agreement by symbol-to-symbol matching can sometimes be misleading in terms of representing how closely two listeners perceptions matched. Thus, for example, the transcriptions of pea /pi/ as [p˭i] (indicating that the transcriber perceives the bilabial plosive as fortis, but without aspiration) and [b̥i] (where the transcriber represents the initial consonant as a devoiced, lenis bilabial plosive) represent a fairly close consensus on the timing of vocal fold vibration in the initial plosive, but the consonant transcriptions have no symbols in common; conversely transcriptions of pea as [b̥i] and [ˌbi] (where the position of the subscript "v" symbol indicates prevoicing) look superficially similar but imply quite different auditory perceptions. Additionally, we know that sometimes in the analysis of atypical speech production there can be a strong listener consensus which is apparently negated by instrumental analysis. Howard and Heselwood (2011) discuss this phenomenon, arguing that in such cases the listener perspective (as evidenced by transcription) is every bit as important as the speaker perspective (as identified by subsequent instrumental analysis) and that the two forms of analysis should be seen as complementary and of equal value (see also Heselwood, 2009).

11.2.2 Examples of Phonetic and Multilayered Transcription

What factors must we take into consideration when undertaking a phonetic transcription of disordered speech? (See also Powell, 2001, for discussion of this area.) First, we need to decide what aspect of the speech signal we need to transcribe. If we are only interested in, for example, intonation; and if the segmental aspects of the client's speech appear within normal bounds, then it makes sense to annotate an orthographic transcription with the symbols chosen to denote intonation patterns, as in example (1) below. The speaker, referred to as "P" here, used non-normal into-nation patterns which are shown using "musical stave" notation (see Rahilly, 2006). This brief extract also illustrates a multilayered transcript layout (discussed in detail in Müller, 2006), which allows the transcriber to combine more than one level of analysis while keeping them visually separate. The left-most column indicates the line number in the transcript. The second column indicates the type of analysis: "P" stands for prosody (the feature of interest here), "O" indicates the orthographic layer; in clinical speech analysis, this is used for the target of an utterance. The "C" layer is used for clinical notes, such as atypical features.

Example (1)

	P		
2	O	L:	I says // is your heads cut?
	C		atypical pre-head; atypical head, nucleus

Speaker "N" in example (2) was male, aged 24 at the time of recording, and presented with severe stuttering behaviors which had been present since childhood. In spontaneous speech he used excessive struggle behaviors and facial grimacing. His speech was characterized by part-word repetitions of plosives and fricatives, and severe blocking on word-initial sounds. He had particular difficulty in initiating voic-ing at sentence boundaries, due to an intermittent ingressive gasp of air, or intrusive nasal snort. Ingressive airflow was also found in other situations. The multilevel transcript includes a layer labeled "S" for "segmental" – what is typically referred to as a phonetic transcript. The struggle behavior "head jerk" is included on the layer labeled "G" for "gaze/gesture", and aligned with the place where it occurs in the utterance, namely simultaneously with a repeated velopharyngeal fricative (indicated by the extIPA symbol [fŋ]; note also the use of "\" for dysfluent repetitions). The "gaze/gesture" layer also includes information on the client's eye-gaze direction here, namely to a book he is reading from. The prosody layer includes information on intensity, using the extIPA symbols "*p*" and "*pp*" (borrowed from musical notation convention for *piano* and *pianissimo*, respectively), indicating speech that is quiet compared to the surrounding speech (*p*), and even quieter than that (*pp*). The duration of the levels of intensity marked *p* and *pp* are indicated on the segmental layer by curly brackets. The prosody layer also indicates ingressive speech (marked by a down arrow), also bracketed off on the segmental layer. The speech task (reading aloud) is noted on the layer labeled "D," which stands for "discourse characteristics."

Example (2)

	G		x---------------------------*to book*---------------------------x
			head jerk
	P		*p* *pp* *pp* ↓
3	O	N:	provincial towns
	S		[p\p̺ɹəv\vɪnʃəl {t'\t'} \ {t'\t'} (.) t'\t' { t'\t' } fŋ\fŋ \ {'tãũnz }]
	D		reading aloud
	C		dysfluency v-p snort pulmonic ingressive

Key: G = gaze and gesture; P = prosody; O = orthographic; S = segmental; D = discourse; C = clinically relevant features.

Example (3) illustrates transcription of speech characterized by articulation disorder. The client ("J") was approximately 7 years old at time of data collection. He was diagnosed with a severe speech delay/disorder and mild oromotor difficulties. A prominent feature in J's speech output was the use of an approximant that was a double articulation of an unrounded bilabial and a postalveolar approximant (for detailed discussion of J's speech patterns, see Müller, Ball, and Rutter, 2006).

Example (3)

	G		x---------------------------*to therapist*---------------------------x
			pointing to picture
	P		
3	O	J:	they have to melt it, spread it
	S		[ðeɪ hʌftʊ 'meʊʔeʔ β͡ɹeʔɪʔ]
	D		picture description
	C		glottal replacement; bilabial-postalveolar approximant

Section Summary

- Clinical researchers into disordered speech will need to make use of phonetic transcription, even if their focus is on instrumental investigations.
- Clinical phoneticians may need to use the extensions to the IPA and the VoQS voice quality symbols as well as the traditional IPA.
- It is important to undertake narrow phonetic transcription and to check inter- and intra-transcriber reliability.

> - Multi-level transcriptions allow the description of segmental and suprasegmental aspects of speech along with other behaviors such as gaze and gesture.

11.3 Transcribing Linguistic Interaction

11.3.1 Conventions Used in Transcribing Conversation

In cases where the issues of interest are, for instance, conversational structure or syntactic organization, rather than speech sounds, it is appropriate to use an orthographic transcription, augmented with a set of commonly used transcriptional devices to signal aspects of a conversation that orthography cannot. In this section we will examine how to set out an orthographic transcription of linguistic interaction, and how to use the extra transcriptional devices. An important habit to acquire is to always anonymize transcripts (whether orthographic or phonetic), in order to safeguard participant confidentiality. The most convenient way to do this is by assigning (random) initials to identify speakers. Where speakers refer to others in a recording, it is often useful to assign pseudonyms: in this way, one can easily reflect the prosody and length of the recorded utterance by using a pseudonym with the same stress pattern and number of syllables: for example, a person called "Geraldine" may be referred to as "Josephine" in the transcript (see Müller, 2006). Another important principle in transcribing recordings is that a transcriber has to be faithful to the participants' words. In other words, a transcriber must not be tempted to "tidy up" or "clean up" somebody's language, even if they find the participant's language offensive or otherwise socially unacceptable (e.g. the use of swearwords, or even verbal abuse). Socially unacceptable language may be an intervention target, but it is hard to address if it is not documented in the data.

While phonetic transcripts (which are typically comparatively short, that is, rarely longer than 200 or 300 words) often don't include line numbers, it is important to number either lines or speaker turns in an orthographic transcript, since these transcripts tend to be lengthy, and line numbers help to navigate through the analysis. Example (4) shows what this looks like. As before, speakers are identified by initials.

Example (4)
001 R: hello, how are you feeling today?
002 E: oh, not so bad, you know.

In example (5), speaker E starts to speak immediately speaker R finishes without the slight pause we would assume from the transcription in (4); we show this by using the sign = at the end of R's turn and beginning of E's (this is typically referred to as "latching").

Example (5)
001 R: hello, how are you feeling today? =
002 E: = oh, not so bad, you know.

Of course, often exchanges are not as tidy as this example suggests, where speaker E begins to answer R's question only after R has finished speaking. Often we find overlaps in conversations; that is, instances where the second speaker begins to speak before the first has finished. If this had happened to the exchange given in (4) and (5), we would show this as in example (6).

Example (6)
001   R: hello, how are you feel [ing today*?
002   E: [oh, not so* bad, you know.

In this example, the square bracket [marks where the overlap commences (i.e. where the two speakers start to talk at the same time), and the asterisk shows where the overlap ends. Sometimes, one speaker's overlap can count as an interruption: that is, the first speaker can continue talking through the interruption. We can use the square bracket notation to show this as well, but if the interrupted utterance is a long one we may need to use the = notation to show that it continues over the line break. We illustrate this in example (7).

Example (7)
001   R: I was wondering how you were feel [ing, considering that it's been quite =
002   E: [oh, not so bad, you know.
003   R: = a while since the operation.

Here, we do not need to use the asterisk as the end of line 002 is assumed to mark the end of the overlap. Further, instead of using a square bracket in turn 001 and in turn 002, we can simply place a single square bracket at the point of interruption on an unnumbered line between these two turns. Other types of interlinear annotations will be looked at later.

We noted earlier that phonetic transcription can cover not only segmental aspects of speech but also the suprasegmental, also called the prosodic aspects. Prosodic features can also be included in an orthographic transcript, by using a set of conventions that are used to mark such characteristics as pitch, stress, length, loudness, and pausing. These conventions, which are (with minor variants) most often employed in Conversation Analysis (see Chapter 8 of this volume), or by transcribers schooled in this method, are shown in Table 11.1.

Using some of these conventions, we can show an extended version of our original conversation that is more fully annotated.

Example (8)
001   R: hello, (..) how are you feeling today? =
002   E: = oh, not so: bad, you know.
         (2.5)
003   R: when I heard you were ill, I was ↓flabber [gasted
004   E: [well, it was a surprise

Table 11.1 Symbols used to transcribe prosodic features in an orthographic transcript.

Symbol	Meaning	Example
.	falling intonation	you know.
,	"continuing intonation" (slight rise or fall)	not so bad,
?	rising intonation	how are you?
↑↓	a marked rise or fall on the following syllable	he said ↑what I'm ↓flabbergasted
___	underscore: added emphasis to syllable	he said ↑<u>what</u> I'm ↓<u>flab</u>bergasted
-	a cutoff of the syllable or sounds preceding hyphen	I was wondering how you were feeli-
CAPS	capitals indicate increased loudness	he said ↑<u>WHAT</u>
:	colon indicates segment length, more than one can be used	o:h no:::
(.)	a pause of one beat; (..) and (...) indicate longer pauses	hello, (..) how are you feeling today?
(2.5)	a timed pause, in seconds	not so bad, (1.5) you know.

Intelligibility is often a concern in the analysis of an interaction. When intelligibility problems are the primary concern of an analysis, then it is more appropriate to undertake a detailed phonetic transcription (where necessary, backed up with instrumental analysis), and express transcriber uncertainty through the conventions of the extIPA system (see above, and Appendix 11.B). However, it can be useful to note fluctuations of intelligibility of a recording in an orthographic transcript, too; these may be due to fluctuations in the speaker's output, for instance owing to fatigue, but external factors may also be to blame, for example overlapping speech, or background noise (which in turn can also be indicated in a transcript, see below). Guendouzi and Müller (2006) suggest the following indicators of transcriber confidence, and intelligibility.

Example (9)
(a) I was (flabbergasted)   Parentheses indicate that the transcriber is not entirely sure of the word used; this is a best guess.

(b) I was ˈfʌbɪɡɒs   Segmental transcription: an educated guess at a word is not warranted.

(c) (I was Xxx)   The entire utterance is uncertain; the final item can only be identified as three syllables, one stressed (X) and two unstressed (xx).

(d) (1.5 secs unintelligible)   Speech is present, but entirely unintelligible.

11.3.2   *Example of a Conversational Transcript*

The following transcript is taken from the third author's hitherto unpublished data, the speaker are two students (M and R), and Ms F, who is a resident in a nursing home (see also Guendouzi and Müller, 2006). The conversation was audio-recorded (with the permission of Ms F and the nursing home management) in Ms F's room, using a digital audio recorder, and a good-quality free-standing microphone placed approximately equidistant from all three speakers, who were seated in a triangle arrangement, so that each speaker could easily see the others.

In addition to the symbols indicating prosodic features listed in Table 11.1, this transcript contains a few other notational devices. An adaptation from the extIPA conventions is the use of {p, f, ...} to indicate quiet and loud speech, respectively, as in turns 2 and 17, for example. The use of *LV* in curly brackets (adapted from the extIPA conventions) indicates speech produced with a "laughing" voice quality, as of an underlying quiet chuckle, as in turns 12 and 17. Similarly *{sigh ....}* in turn 17 indicates that the portion of the utterance transcribed in brackets was produced as a sigh. Double parentheses and italics indicate transcriber comments; these can be helpful, as in turn 17, to explain why a portion of the recording remains unintelligible. Further discussion of useful transcription convention and close attention to interactional detail when transcribing can be found in Chapter 8 of this volume, on Conversation Analysis.

Example (10)
1   M   whose shoes are those.
2   F   {p huh? }
3   M   that's not- a man's shoes over there.
4   F   on-, on the porch?
5   M   by the dresser. (3.0) behind her chair.
6   F   behind that door? [behind the chair?*
7   R   [the chair*   (4.0) can you see that?
        (3.0)
8   F   bring a- a- bring one, lemme see it (get that door) *((noise as of furniture being moved))*
        (3.0)
9   M   that's a [man's shoe.*
10 R   [(x) man's shoes?*
11 F   that's a man's shoe? (6.0) oh ye:s.
        (2.5)
12 M   {LV you been havin a man caller Ms F? }
13 F   u:h no, but I have (.) my nephews be w- running around here sometimes,
14 R   m:,
15 F   they live around here you know, (5.0) but I don't have (xx X invited no man here) *((intercom announcement)) ((M chuckles, F joins in))*

16 M {LV not yet. anyway. } ((laughs))
17 F no no. (3.5) {LV got enough o'them.} ((all three laugh)) a:h lord. (6.0)
       {sigh oh yes I got enough o'them.} (6.0) (I've a xxXx) ((voices from hall
       overlap)) (3.0) but I have my nieces some time that they come make a
       round. you know and. (.) might stay overnight. {f come in,}
18 Z {f hello.}
19 R [hi,*
20 F [come* in,
21 Z {f oh that's okay I'm- I'm lookin for a patient. I'm lookin for Ms JH}.
       she's not in this room,
22 F oh.
23 M [mm.*
24 F [she's* not here.=
25 Z =okay. {forte thank you,}
       (6.0) ((Z and one other person talking))
26 F they're lookin for somebody. they're not here, (2.0) nobody here but me.
       ((Z and other person continue talking))
27 M what?
28 F I said nobody here but me and (2.0) ((2 secs noise of furniture being
       moved)) you two. you're company.
29 M yea?
       (12.5)
30 F where y'all from.
31 M I'm from O(city),
32 F that's not far from here,=
33 M =no.
34 F and where she's from- where you from honey.
35 R I'm from overseas. C(country).
36 F C(country),
37 R uhuh,
38 F overseas.
39 R yea.
40 F you visiting here,
41 R ((light laugh)) {LV I'm a student here.}
42 F huh?
43 R I'm a student (.) here.
44 F a student,
45 R yea.
46 F o:h ye:s:. (2.5) and you from,
47 R C(country).
48 F C(country).
49 R yeah.
       (3.5)
50 F ye:s:. (10.0) and how you like it over here honey.
51 R uh I like uh. (.) I like here.

> ## Section Summary
>
> - When language or interactional problems are the clinical or research focus, an orthographic transcript is more useful than a phonetic one.
> - Conversations are set out somewhat like a play script, although recall that speakers should be anonymized to safeguard confidentiality.
> - A range of symbols are available to mark aspects of interaction such as overlaps, pauses, prosodic features, or gestures, as well as non-interactional behaviors, such as coughing, etc., or extraneous factors that may influence an interaction (e.g. background noise).

11.4   Conclusion and Outlook: Why do We Transcribe, and What is a Transcript?

Transcribing in clinical practice and research is always done with a purpose in mind. While some of us may find the practice enjoyable and relaxing in its own right, we all acknowledge that transcribing is a time-consuming process that takes a considerable amount of practice. The following brief discussion and outlook on transcribing as a process and the transcript as product is based on Müller, Damico, and Guendouzi (2006), to whom readers may wish to refer for more detailed discussion. The transcriber needs to determine the amount of *detail* required for the investigation (or clinical assessment) at hand. Thus where a client's difficulties with bound morphology and limited utterance length are the focus of analysis, a faithful word-for-word transcript of what was said (taking care not to "correct" any missing morphological markers, of course), may be sufficient. At the other end of a continuum of less versus more detail are analyses of fine phonetic detail of conversational interaction that involve detailed phonetic transcription embedded in conversational transcripts, and are often combined with instrumental analyses (see e.g. Rutter, 2010). The purpose of the transcript needs to drive the process of transcribing and the level of detail included: A researcher or clinician should never be in a position where relevant aspects of an interaction, or of a speech or language sample, are lost because of a lack of detail in a transcript.

We find it useful to think of transcribing as a process of translation, from an auditory medium to a graphic one. Just as a translation of a source text is more than simply a preparation of data, but rather a process of *analysis and generation* of data, it makes sense to look at transcribing as an integral part of data analysis, and at the transcript as the record of a researcher's or clinician's dialogue with the data under investigation. A transcriber should aim for the highest possible degree of *accuracy*, within the parameters of detail required by the purpose of analysis. This includes *consistency* (or intra-transcriber reliability), as well as *reliability*, where more than one transcriber is involved in any one project. Having said that, we hold that where this choice has to be made, it is better to be honest than overly neat when transcribing: where uncertainty remains, even after consulting with other transcribers, this needs to be reflected in the transcript.

A transcript can and should, in our view, fulfill two important functions. On one hand, it is the basis for further analysis of the speech event under investigation. As such, the choices made by the transcriber, in terms of which details of the event to foreground and which to omit from the transcript, will both focus and constrain further analysis. On the other hand, a transcript is also a reader's window on the data: more often than not, readers of research in clinical linguistics and phonetics, or of clinical reports, do not have access to the "raw" data, but have to rely on reading transcripts. A reader, therefore, needs to keep in mind the transformative processes applied to the data in the construction of a transcript; in turn, a transcriber needs to make the choices made in completing the transcript transparent.

Section Summary

- Transcribing can be thought of as a process of translating details of a speech event from an auditory and/or visual medium to a graphic one.
- Transcribing should always be done with a purpose in mind, and the purpose should drive the transcriber's choices as to the type of transcript required, and the amount and types of detail included.
- Accuracy and reliability are important, but it is equally important to make uncertainty explicit.
- A transcript is both a tool for further data analysis and a reader's window on the original raw data, and on the transcriber's transformation of the original data.

11.5   Resources

11.5.1   *Further Reading*

Ball, M. J. and Müller, N. (2005). *Phonetics for Communication Disorders*. Mahwah, NJ: Lawrence Erlbaum.

Ball, M. J., Müller, N., Klopfenstein, M., and Rutter, B. (2009). The importance of narrow phonetic transcription for highly unintelligible speech: some examples. *Logopedics Phoniatrics Vocology*, 34, 84–90.

Ball, M. J., Müller, N., Klopfenstein, M., and Rutter, B. (2010). My client's using non-English sounds! A tutorial in advanced phonetic transcription. Part 2: vowels and diacritics. *Contemporary Issues in Communication Sciences and Disorders*, 37, 103–110.

Ball, M. J., Müller, N., Rutter, B., and Klopfenstein, M. (2009). My client's using non-English sounds! A tutorial in advanced phonetic transcription. Part 1: consonants. *Contemporary Issues in Communication Sciences and Disorders*, 36, 133–141.

Ball, M. J. and Rahilly, J. (1996). Acoustic analysis as an aid to the transcription of an example of disfluent speech. In M. J. Ball and M. Duckworth (eds), *Advances in Clinical Phonetics*. Amsterdam: John Benjamins, pp. 197–216.

Ball, M. J., Rahilly, J., and Tench, P. (1996). *The Phonetic Transcription of Disordered Speech*. San Diego, CA: Singular Publishing.

Rutter, B., Klopfenstein, M., Ball, M. J., and Müller, N. (2010). My client's using non-English sounds! A tutorial in advanced phonetic transcription. Part 3: prosody and unattested sounds. *Contemporary Issues in Communication Sciences and Disorders*, 37, 111–122.

11.5.2   *Details of the IA and extIPA*

The following website gives details of the IPA and extIPA: www.langsci.ucl.ac.uk/ipa/.

The IPA tutorial at the University of Victoria, British Columbia is a useful tool to familiarize oneself with IPA symbols: web.uvic.ca/ling/resources/phonlab/ipatut/index.html.

This is a classic paper by David Crystal on transcribing speech: Crystal, D. (1984). Things to remember when transcribing speech. Accessible at www.davidcrystal.com/DC_articles/Clinical28.pdf.

A list of websites linking to transcription and related software can be found in Chapter 8 of this volume.

References

Amorosa, H., von Benda, U., Wagner, E., and Keck, A. (1985). Transcribing detail in the speech of unintelligible children: a comparison of procedures. *British Journal of Disorders of Communication*, 20, 281–287.

Ball, M. J. (2008). Transcribing disordered speech: by target or by production? *Clinical Linguistics and Phonetics*, 22, 864–870.

Ball, M. J., Esling, J., and Dickson, C. (1995). The VoQS system for the transcription of voice quality. *Clinical Linguistics and Phonetics*, 25, 61–70.

Ball, M. J. and Local, J. (1996). Advances in impressionistic transcription of disordered speech. In M. J. Ball and M. Duckworth (eds), *Advances in Clinical Phonetics*. Amsterdam: John Benjamins, pp. 51–89.

Buckingham, H. and Yule, G. (1987). Phonemic false evaluation: theoretical and clinical aspects. *Clinical Linguistics and Phonetics*, 1, 113–125.

Cucchiarini, C. (1996) Assessing transcription agreement: methodological aspects. *Clinical Linguistics and Phonetics*, 19, 405–417.

Duckworth, M., Allen, G., Hardcastle, W., and Ball, M. J. (1990). Extensions to the International Phonetic Alphabet of the transcription of atypical speech. *Clinical Linguistics and Phonetics*, 4, 273–280.

Guendouzi, J. and Müller, N. (2006). Orthographic transcription. In N. Müller (ed.), *Multilayered Transcription*. San Diego, CA: Plural Publishing, pp. 19–39.

Heselwood, B. C. (2009). A phenomenalist defence of narrow phonetic transcription as a clinical and research tool. In V. Marrero and I. Pineda (eds), *Linguistics: The Challenge of*

Clinical Application (Proceedings of the 2nd International Conference on Clinical Linguistics). Madrid: Euphonia Ediciones, pp. 25–31.

Heselwood, B. and Howard, S. J. (2008). Clinical phonetic transcription. In M. J. Ball, M. R. Perkins, N. Müller, and S. J. Howard (eds), *The Handbook of Clinical Linguistics*. Oxford: Wiley-Blackwell, pp. 381–399.

Howard, S. J. (2011). Phonetic transcription for speech related to cleft palate. In S. J. Howard and A. Lohmander (eds), *Cleft Palate Speech: Assessment and Intervention*. Oxford: Wiley-Blackwell, pp. 127–144.

Howard, S. J. and Heselwood, B. C. (2002). Learning and teaching phonetic transcription for clinical purposes. *Clinical Linguistics and Phonetics*, 16, 371–401.

Howard, S. and Heselwood, B. (2011). Instrumental and phonetic analyses: the case for two-tier transcriptions. *Clinical Linguistics and Phonetics*, 25, 940–948.

IPA (1999). *Handbook of the International Phonetic Association*. Cambridge: Cambridge University Press.

Ladefoged, P. (1995). Developing phonetic skills. Proceedings of the 13th International Congress of Phonetic Sciences, Stockholm, Sweden, August 13–19.

McGurk, H. and McDonald, J. (1976). Hearing lips and seeing voices. *Nature*, 264, 746–748.

Müller, N. (ed.) (2006). *Multilayered Transcription*. San Diego, CA: Plural Publishing.

Müller, N., Ball, M. J., and Rutter, B. (2006). A profiling approach to intelligibility problems. *Advances in Speech-Language Pathology*, 8, 176–189.

Müller, N. and Damico, J. S., and Guendouzi, J. A. (2006). What is transcription and why should we do it? In N. Müller (ed.), *Multilayered Transcription*. San Diego, CA: Plural Publishers, pp. 1–18.

Nelson, M. and Hodge, M. (2000). Effects of facial paralysis and audiovisual information on stop place identification. *Journal of Speech, Language, and Hearing Research*, 43, 158–171.

Oller, D. K. and Eilers, R. E. (1975). Phonetic expectation and transcription validity. *Phonetica*, 31, 288–304.

Perkins, M. R. and Howard, S. J. (1995). Principles of clinical linguistics. In M. R. Perkins and S. J. Howard (eds), *Case Studies in Clinical Linguistics*. London: Whurr, pp. 10–35.

Powell, T. W. (2001). Transcribing disordered speech. *Topics in Language Disorders*, 21, 52–72.

Rahilly, J. (2006). Transcribing the suprasegmental level. In N. Müller (ed.), *Multilayered Transcription*. San Diego, CA: Plural Publishing, pp. 69–91.

Rutter, B. (2010). On the use of the term "repair" and its application to disordered conversational speech. *Journal of Interactional Research in Communication Disorders*, 1, 199–216.

Santelman, L., Sussman, J., and Chapman, K. (1999). Perception of middorsum palatal stops. *Cleft Palate-Craniofacial Journal*, 36, 233–242.

Appendices

The appendices contain the latest versions of the symbol charts for the International Phonetic Alphabet (IPA), the Extensions to the IPA for the transcription of disordered speech (extIPA), and the Voice Quality Symbols (VoQS), as referenced earlier in this chapter. The IPA chart is reproduced by permission of the International Phonetic Association, the extIPA chart by permission of the International Clinical Phonetics and Linguistics Association, and the VoQS chart by permission of the copyright holders.

Appendix 11.A   IPA Chart

THE INTERNATIONAL PHONETIC ALPHABET (revised to 2005)

CONSONANTS (PULMONIC)   © 2005 IPA

	Bilabial	Labiodental	Dental	Alveolar	Post alveolar	Retroflex	Palatal	Velar	Uvular	Pharyngeal	Glottal
Plosive	p b			t d		ʈ ɖ	c ɟ	k ɡ	q ɢ		ʔ
Nasal	m	ɱ		n		ɳ	ɲ	ŋ	N		
Trill	ʙ			r					R		
Tap or Flap		ⱱ		ɾ		ɽ					
Fricative	ɸ β	f v	θ ð	s z	ʃ ʒ	ʂ ʐ	ç ʝ	x ɣ	χ ʁ	ħ ʕ	h ɦ
Lateral fricative				ɬ ɮ							
Approximant		ʋ		ɹ		ɻ	j	ɰ			
Lateral approximant				l		ɭ	ʎ	L			

Where symbols appear in pairs, the one to the right represents a voiced consonant. Shaded areas denote articulations judged impossible.

CONSONANTS (NON-PULMONIC)

Clicks		Voiced implosives		Ejectives	
ʘ	Bilabial	ɓ	Bilabial	ʼ	Examples:
ǀ	Dental	ɗ	Dental/alveolar	pʼ	Bilabial
ǃ	(Post)alveolar	ʄ	Palatal	tʼ	Dental/alveolar
ǂ	Palatoalveolar	ɠ	Velar	kʼ	Velar
ǁ	Alveolar lateral	ʛ	Uvular	sʼ	Alveolar fricative

OTHER SYMBOLS

ʍ	Voiceless labial-velar fricative	ɕ ʑ	Alveolo-palatal fricatives
w	Voiced labial-velar approximant	ɺ	Voiced alveolar lateral flap
ɥ	Voiced labial-palatal approximant	ɧ	Simultaneous ʃ and x
ʜ	Voiceless epiglottal fricative		
ʢ	Voiced epiglottal fricative	Affricates and double articulations can be represented by two symbols joined by a tie bar if necessary.	k͡p t͡s
ʡ	Epiglottal plosive		

VOWELS

	Front		Central		Back
Close	i • y		ɨ • ʉ		ɯ • u
		ɪ ʏ		ʊ	
Close-mid	e • ø		ɘ • ɵ		ɤ • o
			ə		
Open-mid	ɛ • œ		ɜ • ɞ		ʌ • ɔ
	æ		ɐ		
Open			a • ɶ		ɑ • ɒ

Where symbols appear in pairs, the one to the right represents a rounded vowel.

SUPRASEGMENTALS

ˈ	Primary stress	ˌfoʊnəˈtɪʃən
ˌ	Secondary stress	
ː	Long	eː
ˑ	Half-long	eˑ
˘	Extra-short	ĕ
ǀ	Minor (foot) group	
‖	Major (intonation) group	
.	Syllable break	ɹi.ækt
‿	Linking (absence of a break)	

DIACRITICS   Diacritics may be placed above a symbol with a descender, e.g. ŋ̊

̥	Voiceless	n̥ d̥	̤	Breathy voiced	b̤ a̤	̪	Dental	t̪ d̪
̬	Voiced	s̬ t̬	̰	Creaky voiced	b̰ a̰	̺	Apical	t̺ d̺
ʰ	Aspirated	tʰ dʰ	̼	Linguolabial	t̼ d̼	̻	Laminal	t̻ d̻
̹	More rounded	ɔ̹	ʷ	Labialized	tʷ dʷ	̃	Nasalized	ẽ
̜	Less rounded	ɔ̜	ʲ	Palatalized	tʲ dʲ	ⁿ	Nasal release	dⁿ
̟	Advanced	u̟	ˠ	Velarized	tˠ dˠ	ˡ	Lateral release	dˡ
̠	Retracted	e̠	ˤ	Pharyngealized	tˤ dˤ	̚	No audible release	d̚
̈	Centralized	ë	̴	Velarized or pharyngealized	ɫ			
̽	Mid-centralized	ě	̝	Raised	e̝	(ɹ̝ = voiced alveolar fricative)		
̩	Syllabic	n̩	̞	Lowered	e̞	(β̞ = voiced bilabial approximant)		
̯	Non-syllabic	e̯	̘	Advanced Tongue Root	e̘			
˞	Rhoticity	ɚ a˞	̙	Retracted Tongue Root	e̙			

TONES AND WORD ACCENTS

LEVEL			CONTOUR		
e̋ or ˥	Extra high		ě or ˩˥	Rising	
é ˦	High		ê ˥˩	Falling	
ē ˧	Mid		e᷄ ˦˥	High rising	
è ˨	Low		e᷅ ˩˨	Low rising	
è̠ ˩	Extra low		e᷈ ˧˦˧	Rising-falling	
↓	Downstep		↗	Global rise	
↑	Upstep		↘	Global fall	

Department of Theoretical and Applied Linguistics, School of English, Aristotle University of Thessaloniki, Thessaloniki 54124, Greece.

Appendix 11.B   extIPA Chart

extIPA SYMBOLS FOR DISORDERED SPEECH
(Revised to 2008)

CONSONANTS (other than on the IPA Chart)

	bilabial	labiodental	dentolabial	labioalv.	linguolabial	interdental	bidental	alveolar	velar	velophar.
Plosive			p̪ b̪	p̟ b̟	t̼ d̼	t̪͆ d̪͆				
Nasal			m̪	m̟	n̼	n̪͆				
Trill					r̼	r̪͆				
Fricative median			f̪ v̪	f̟ v̟	θ̼ ð̼	θ̪͆ ð̪͆	h̪͆ ɦ̪͆			fŋ
Fricative lateral+median								ʪ ʫ		
Fricative nareal	m̃							ñ̥	ŋ̃	
Percussive	ʬ						ʭ			
Approximant lateral					l̼	l̪͆				

Where symbols appear in pairs, the one to the right represents a voiced consonant. Shaded areas denote articulations judged impossible.

DIACRITICS

	labial spreading	s̪		strong articulation	f͈		denasal	m̃
	dentolabial	v̪		weak articulation	v͉		nasal escape	ṽ̼
	interdental/bidental	n̪͆	\	reiterated articulation	p\p\p		velopharyngeal friction	s̴
	alveolar	t̪		whistled articulation	ṣ	↓	ingressive airflow	p↓
	linguolabial	d̼	→	sliding articulation	θs̪	↑	egressive airflow	!↑

CONNECTED SPEECH

(.)	short pause
(..)	medium pause
(...)	long pause
f	loud speech [{f laʊd f}]
ff	louder speech [{ff laʊdə ff}]
p	quiet speech [{p kwaɪət p}]
pp	quieter speech [{pp kwaɪətə pp}]
allegro	fast speech [{allegro fast allegro}]
lento	slow speech [{lento sloʊ lento}]
crescendo, ralentando, etc. may also be used

VOICING

	pre-voicing	˻z
	post-voicing	z˻
	partial devoicing	z̮ₚ
	initial partial devoicing	₍z̮
	final partial devoicing	z̮₎
	partial voicing	ꜱ̬
	initial partial voicing	₍s̬
	final partial voicing	s̬₎
=	unaspirated	p⁼
h	pre-aspiration	ʰp

OTHERS

(Ⓒ̄),(C̄),(V̄)	indeterminate sound, consonant, vowel	ⱴ	velodorsal articulation
(P̲l̲,v̲l̲s̲),(N̄)	indeterminate voiceless plosive, nasal, etc	¡	sublaminal lower alveolar percussive click
( )	silent articulation (ʃ), (m)	‼¡	alveolar and sublaminal clicks (cluck-click)
(( ))	extraneous noise, e.g. ((2 sylls))	*	sound with no available symbol

© ICPLA 2008

Appendix 11.C VoQS Chart

VoQS: Voice Quality Symbols

Airstream Types

Œ	œsophageal speech	И	electrolarynx speech
Ю	tracheo-œsophageal speech	↓	pulmonic ingressive speech

Phonation types

V	modal voice	F	falsetto
W	whisper	C	creak
V̤	whispery voice (murmur)	V̰	creaky voice
Vʰ	breathy voice	C̤	whispery creak
V!	harsh voice	V!!	ventricular phonation
V̬!!	diplophonia	V̤!!	whispery ventricular phonation
V̟	anterior or pressed phonation	W̠	posterior whisper

Supralaryngeal Settings

L̝	raised larynx	L̞	lowered larynx
Vꟹ	labialized voice (open round)	Vʷ	labialized voice (close round)
V͍	spread-lip voice	Vᶹ	labio-dentalized voice
V̺	linguo-apicalized voice	V̻	linguo-laminalized voice
V˞	retroflex voice	V̪	dentalized voice
V͇	alveolarized voice	V͇ʲ	palatoalveolarized voice
Vʲ	palatalized voice	Vˠ	velarized voice
Vʶ	uvularized voice	Vˤ	pharyngealized voice
V̙ˤ	laryngo-pharyngealized voice	Vᴴ	faucalized voice
Ṽ	nasalized voice	V͊	denasalized voice
J̞	open jaw voice	J̝	close jaw voice
J͔	right offset jaw voice	J͕	left offset jaw voice
J̟	protruded jaw voice	Θ	protruded tongue voice

USE OF LABELED BRACES & NUMERALS TO MARK STRETCHES OF SPEECH AND DEGREES AND COMBINATIONS OF VOICE QUALITY:

[ˈðɪs ɪz ˈnɔɹməl ˈvɔɪs {3V! ˈðɪs ɪz ˈveɹi ˈhɑɹʃ ˈvɔɪs 3V} ˈðɪs ɪz ˈnɔɹməl ˈvɔɪs wʌns ˈmɔɹ {L̞ 1V! ˈðɪs ɪz ˈlɛs ˈhɑɹʃ ˈvɔɪs wɪð ˈloʊɚd ˈlæɹɪŋks 1V!L̞}]

12 Data Processing: Digital Analysis of Speech Audio Signals

Mark Huckvale

12.1 Introduction

This chapter provides a practical introduction to the analysis of the phonetic properties of speech audio recordings. The chapter gives an overview of the common quantitative measures of voice pitch, voice quality, segmental quality, and prosody that can be derived from the acoustic signal.

There are many benefits to the use of acoustic analyses of clinical speech recordings compared to analyses based on symbolic transcription counts or on subjective rating scales. Speech signal analysis produces objective, quantitative data on continuous scales that are amenable to parametric statistical modeling. Recent advances in digital audio technology have made it easier to collect good quality speech recordings, which in turn have made possible finer-detailed and more reliable measurements. Corpora of clinical speech recordings are becoming more widely available, and through automated analyses can be used for much larger investigations with greater statistical power that lead potentially to new means of diagnosis, new methods for the assessment of individuals, or for the evaluation of new therapies.

In the sections below we will look at the representation of speech in computer systems, the analysis of signals, and the modeling of phonological units.

12.2 Representations

First catch your speech data. In this section we will look at how speech signals, transcripts, and acoustic parameters are stored in computer files and how we can prepare them for analysis.

Research Methods in Clinical Linguistics and Phonetics: A Practical Guide,
First Edition. Edited by Nicole Müller and Martin J. Ball.

12.2.1   *Speech Signals*

When a speech recording is digitized for manipulation by a digital computer, the continuous sound pressure signal is sliced into discrete time intervals and the amplitude of the signal in each interval is recorded as a whole number. The division into discrete time intervals is called *sampling* and is performed at a given *sampling rate* specified in terms of the number of signal samples generated per second. A very common sampling rate is 44 100 samples per second, since this was the rate chosen by Sony when the compact disc format was being designed. This is a very high rate, but it ensures that the digital signal is sampled fast enough to capture the highest sinusoidal frequencies detectable by the human ear. Mathematical analysis of sampling tells us that the highest frequency faithfully captured will be at half of the sampling rate. In practice, filters are employed in the analogue-to-digital conversion step which ensure that the analogue signal does not contain significant energy above about 0.45 of the sampling rate prior to sampling. Since speech signals have very little energy and very little phonetically useful information above 8000 Hz, sampling rates of 16 000, 20 000, or 22 050 samples/sec. are also commonly found. The lowest rate one would want to use for acoustic analysis is probably 16 000 samples/sec.

Each sample is then stored as a whole number within a limited range, and the vast majority of recordings are made with a "16-bit" range of −32 768 to +32 767 (that is −2^{15} to 2^{15}−1). This range provides a dynamic range for the sound much greater than is important for speech communication (16-bits provides a dynamic range of >90dB, whereas a typical spectrogram has a dynamic range of only 50 dB). However the extended dynamic range provided by 16-bit samples allows for a degree of protection against particularly quiet or particularly loud recordings. Although 8-bit samples and 12-bit samples are used in some telephone communication systems, these are not recommended for speech signals destined for acoustic analysis.

Because of its size, digital audio is often stored in a compressed format in which components of the sound which are less important to our perception are removed to save space. However, since acoustic analysis may be more sensitive to changes in the signal caused by lossy compression than our hearing system, it is not a good idea to use lossy compression on speech signals recorded for scientific research if it can be avoided. If lossy compression must be used, then it is advisable to maintain relatively high data rates, for example about 200 kbits/sec. This corresponds to the data rate used in minidisc recorders, and is commonly used for "transparent" coding of music. Studies have shown that such data rates have a relatively small impact on phonetic analyses (van Son, 2005).

Digital speech recordings can now be made on a wide variety of hardware devices, and this does lead to speech signals being stored in a variety of different computer file formats. The most common formats for storing uncompressed audio data are WAV, AIFF, and AU. Uncompressed data is sometimes called "PCM" data, referring to an obsolete method of encoding the bit stream over a telecom channel. A popular form of lossless compression is called "FLAC" and has its own file format supported by a few software utilities. The most popular forms of lossy compression are currently MP3, OGG, and AAC, each with its own file format. These are widely supported by media players and converters.

Digital speech recordings are also made in conjunction with video in an even wider range of devices and file types. Popular audio-video formats include: 3G2, 3GP, ASF, AVI, FLV, MOV, MP4, MPG, RM, SWF, VOB, and WMV. These are widely supported by media players and converters. Before acoustic analysis, it will be necessary to separate the audio signal from the video signal and to remove any data rate compression. Commercial media conversion tools can be purchased for this purpose, although free tools can often also be found.

12.2.2 Transcriptions

Every speech recording should be associated with some meta-data which describe who was speaking, where and when the recording was made, and how it was recorded. Additionally it may include indexical information about the speaker, such as age, sex, accent, or clinical group. It is worth emphasizing that recordings missing such data are of little use, since the goal of scientific research is not just to find the average characteristics of speech, but to explore how speech varies across individuals and situations.

A transcription of the speech in a recording can form an extremely useful element of the meta-data. Even an orthographic transcription can be used to help find recordings in a corpus on the basis of words spoken. A phonological transcription can provide an interpretation of what the speaker was trying to say, such that the realized acoustic form can be related to standard lexical forms.

A continuing challenge, and topic for debate, is whether transcripts should be "time-aligned" to the recording. That is, whether utterances or words or phonological segments should be associated with specific intervals of the audio signal. On the one hand, this provides a much finer-level indexation of the signals, such that sections corresponding to linguistic chunks can be located within a corpus automatically. In turn this might allow for automated analyses of the average signal properties across many occurrences of a word or segment. On the other hand, time alignment of transcription by hand can be very labor-intensive, and since speech signals are not really discrete sequences of sound types, the resulting alignments are somewhat arbitrary. Taken together with the likelihood of transcription variability across observers it could be argued that time-aligned narrow phonetic labels are of questionable value in most research.

A compromise position seems inevitable here. It is extremely useful to be able to find how a speaker chose to realize a particular phonological contrast through the acoustic analysis of many realized instances of that contrast. But it is extremely time-consuming and error-prone to hand-align transcription even at a phonological segment level. A balanced position is perhaps to provide an aligned utterance-level orthographic transcription such that a phonological transcription could be generated and aligned by automatic means if and when required. The automatic generation of phonological transcription from orthography is usually performed by concatenating lexical pronunciations from a dictionary. For particularly disordered speech this may not be appropriate, so a non-time-aligned phonological transcription could be

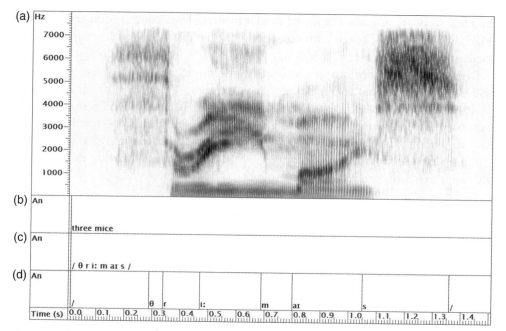

Figure 12.1 Demonstration of automatic transcription alignment: (a) an audio recording, (b) orthographic transcription entered manually, (c) automatically generated phonological transcription, (d) automatically aligned transcription. The automatic alignment is of good quality except for the boundary between silence and the initial fricative. Figure generated using the Speech Filing System.

generated manually instead. There are a number of systems for automatic alignment of transcription (see Figure 12.1 for an example). However, these systems do require good quality audio recordings, and even then the alignments may not be ideal. The trade-off is that the gain in productivity allowed by automatic alignment over hand alignments will allow much more material to be annotated, and then the increased quantity of alignments available for analysis will compensate for their poorer quality.

Many software tools also support non-linear phonological representations, most commonly through multiple "tiers" of annotation, with potential synchronization across tiers, so that a simple hierarchical structure can be represented. Levels might represent, for example, intonational phrases, accent groups, feet, syllables, onsets, rhymes, and segments. Software tools are essential to aid the construction of hierarchical annotation, particularly if each tier is also time-aligned to the signal. The advantage of providing a hierarchical context for a segment of signal is that it then becomes easier to search for and to analyze a signal form conditioned on its position within the phonological structure of an utterance (Bombien *et al.*, 2006).

12.2.3   Parameters

To make use of the results of parametric analysis of speech signals, the measurements representing, for example, voice pitch or voice regularity or formant frequencies need to be exported from signal analysis tools and imported into statistical analysis tools. Unfortunately, each signal analysis tool stores its results in its own proprietary file format, which means that it can be hard to "get at" the numerical values. Fortunately all tools have options to export parameters in a plain text format to produce files which can be opened and read by text editors, and which can be processed by text manipulation tools like *perl* or *AWK*.

For many analyses, the data format required for statistical processing consists of a table in which each row describes some event and each column represents one type of measurement of that event. A simple text file format like "comma-separated-values" or CSV is very useful here, and is reasonably well supported by spreadsheets and statistics programs. Thus it is often convenient to follow a regime: (i) export parameters from analysis tool as text, (ii) use perl or AWK to convert to CSV format, (iii) import into statistics program.

Section Summary

- Digital speech signals are typically stored as 16-bit samples, at rates higher than 16 000 samples/sec.
- Uncompressed (PCM) storage is preferred, but if lossy compression is used, it should be at a high data rate.
- Recordings should always have associated indexical information.
- Phonological-level transcriptions of the speech can be extremely useful, and tools exist to help align them to signals.

12.3 Analysis

12.3.1 *Measures of Speech Level*

A common requirement in experimental work is to measure the level of the speech signals in a recording. This is useful to ensure, for example, that different recordings can be presented to listeners at similar loudness levels. Whilst use of the RMS (root mean square) average sample value to represent loudness is widespread, it is not technically correct. When measuring level it is important to take into account the frequency range important to speech and the fact that non-speech intervals in the recording do not contribute to speech level. The ITU standard P.56 (ITU-T, 1993) provides a suitable standard for measurement of active speech level. It uses a band-pass filter to remove frequencies below 200 Hz and above 5500 Hz, and a speech activity detector to prevent silent intervals affecting the calculation of level. Once the speech levels of a set of recordings have been established by this means, they can be scaled by simple factors to equalize their levels. The active speech level should also be used when mixing speech with noise to create stimuli of a specified signal-to-noise (SNR) ratio.

Measurements of speech level made from some digitized signal will only be relative to some arbitrary reference level (such as the largest sinusoid that can be stored in a 16-bit signal). To establish the absolute sound pressure level of the signal in dBSPL (that is, sound pressure level referenced to the nominal threshold of human hearing), it is also necessary to have calibration recordings of a sound source of known level made with the same recording equipment with the same recording settings. The relative speech level of the actual recording can then be compared to the relative level of the calibration recording to establish the absolute sound pressure level at the time of recording.

12.3.2   Measures of Duration and Rhythm

Given a time-aligned phonetic transcription it is easy to extract information about the durations of segments. From these it is then straightforward to produce statistics of speaking rate or the effects of context on duration. However, the distribution of segment duration may not follow a normal shape, so it is a good idea to first apply a suitable transformation (see Figure 12.2).

Parameters which describe speech rhythm are also easy to extract from a time-aligned transcription. First the segmental transcription is simplified to a three-way classification of silence-consonant-vowel, then adjacent matching segments are collapsed into single intervals. Statistical descriptors of these intervals, such as in Table 12.1, have been studied across a number of languages (Grabe and Low, 2002; Ramus, Nespor, and Mehler, 1999).

12.3.3   Measures of Phonation Quality

Vocal fold vibration in the larynx produces air pressure fluctuations which pass along the vocal tract and propagate from the head to the microphone before being captured as a speech sound signal. A common requirement in phonetic analysis is to infer properties of the vocal fold vibration from properties of the captured signal. Broadly speaking we are interested in properties such as the repetition frequency of vibration (F0), the regularity of vibration cycles, and the quantity of turbulent noise created in the larynx during vibration.

The general approach to estimate the repetition frequency is to divide the signal into short sections (frames) and for each section look for the dominant periodicity in the waveform, then estimate the duration or frequency of that periodicity. Difficulties arise from the fact that (i) that not all signal sections will be periodic; (ii) those that are periodic may be changing in repetition frequency over the time of interest; (iii) signals may be contaminated with other noises, even with periodic signals of other repetition frequencies; (iv) signals that are periodic with interval T are also periodic with interval 2T, 3T, etc., so we need to find the smallest periodic interval or the highest repetition frequency; and (v) even signals of constant repetition frequency may be changing in other ways over the interval of interest.

A reliable way of obtaining an estimate of the dominant repetition frequency for long, clean, stationary speech signals is to use the *cepstrum*. The cepstrum is a

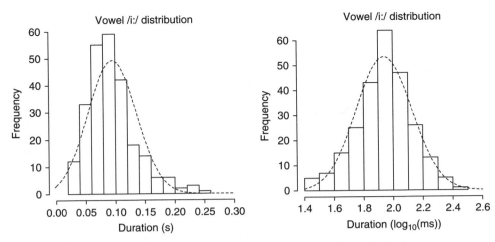

Figure 12.2 Segment durations measured in seconds are not normally distributed. Here 250 instances of /iː/ from one speaker are analyzed. When durations are measured in seconds, the shape is significantly different to normal, however when measured in terms of $\log_{10}$(ms), the distribution is better shaped.

Table 12.1   Measures of speech rhythm.

Parameter	Description
%V	Proportion of intervals that are vocalic:

$$\%V = 100 \cdot \frac{N_V}{N_V + N_C}$$

ΔV	Standard deviation of duration of vocalic intervals:

$$\Delta V = \sqrt{\frac{\sum_{i=1}^{N_V}(V_i - \bar{V})^2}{N_V}}$$

ΔC	Standard deviation of duration of consonantal intervals:

$$\Delta C = \sqrt{\frac{\sum_{i=1}^{N_C}(C_i - \bar{C})^2}{N_C}}$$

rPVI	Raw pairwise variability index. The mean absolute change in duration between adjacent vocalic intervals (or adjacent consonantal intervals):

$$rPVI = \frac{\sum_{i=1}^{N_D-1}|D_{i+1} - D_i|}{N_D - 1}$$

nPVI	Normalized pairwise variability index. The mean relative change in duration between adjacent vocalic intervals (or adjacent consonantal intervals), expressed as a percentage:

$$nPVI = \frac{100}{N_D - 1} \cdot \sum_{i=1}^{N_D-1}\left|2 \cdot \frac{D_{i+1} - D_i}{D_{i+1} + D_i}\right|$$

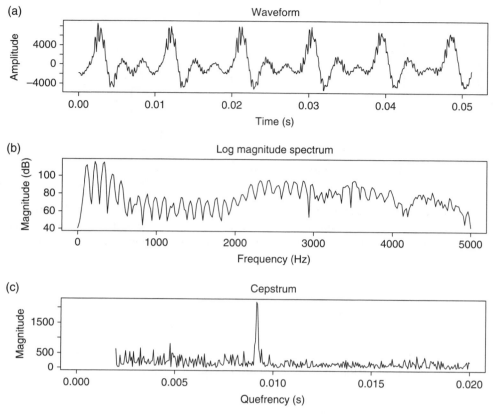

Figure 12.3 Estimation of the fundamental frequency from the cepstrum. A section of speech signal (a) is analyzed by the discrete Fourier transform and represented as a log magnitude spectrum (b). The cepstrum (c) is the discrete Fourier transform of the log magnitude spectrum. The maximum of the cepstrum in the region corresponding to 50 to 500 Hz gives the dominant repetition period, here 0.009 s or 110 Hz.

Fourier analysis of the logarithmic amplitude spectrum of the signal. For a periodic signal, the log amplitude spectrum shows many harmonics: sinusoidal frequency components of the sound that occur at whole-number multiples of the repetition (or *fundamental*) frequency. Since the spectrum then itself looks "periodic," its Fourier analysis will show a peak corresponding to the spacing between the harmonics: that is, the fundamental frequency. Effectively we are treating the signal spectrum as another signal, then looking for periodicity in the spectrum itself (Figure 12.3).

The cepstrum is so-called because it turns the spectrum inside-out. The x-axis of the cepstrum has units of quefrency, and peaks in the cepstrum (which relate to periodicities in the spectrum) are called rahmonics. To find the fundamental frequency, the cepstrum is searched for the largest peak between about 2 ms (= 500 Hz) and 20 ms (= 50 Hz). In Figure 12.3 it is easy to see how the cepstrum represents the periodicity in the log spectrum with a rahmonic at a quefrency equal to the pitch period of about 9 ms.

The cepstrum approach works best when the fundamental frequency is not changing too rapidly, when the fundamental frequency is not too high and when the

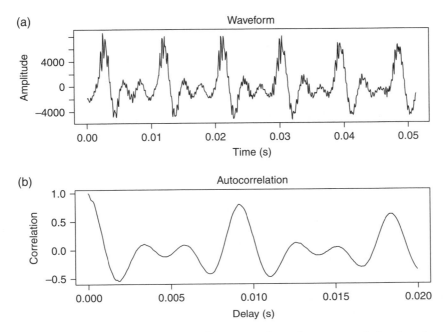

Figure 12.4 Estimation of the fundamental frequency from the autocorrelation function. A section of speech signal (a) is analyzed by calculating how well it correlates with itself over a range of signal delays (b). The maximum of the autocorrelation in the region corresponding to 50 to 500 Hz gives the dominant repetition period, here 0.009 s or 110 Hz.

signal is relatively noise-free. A disadvantage of the cepstrum is that it involves computationally expensive frequency–domain processing.

The cepstrum looks for periodicity in the log amplitude spectrum of the signal, whereas our perception of pitch is more strongly related to periodicity in the waveform itself. A means of estimating fundamental frequency from the waveform directly is to use *autocorrelation*. The autocorrelation function for a section of signal shows how well the waveform shape correlates with itself at a range of different delays. We expect a periodic signal to correlate well with itself at very short delays and at delays corresponding to multiples of pitch periods (Figure 12.4).

The autocorrelation function peaks at zero delay and at delays corresponding to ±1 period, ±2 periods, etc. We can estimate the fundamental frequency by looking for a peak in the delay interval corresponding to the normal pitch range in speech, between about 2 ms (= 500 Hz) and 20 ms (= 50 Hz).

The autocorrelation approach works best when the signal is of low, regular pitch and when the spectral content of the signal is not changing too rapidly. The autocorrelation method is prone to "pitch halving," where a delay of two pitch periods is chosen in error. It can also be influenced by periodicity in the signal caused by formant resonances, particularly for female voices, where F1 can be lower in frequency than F0.

Methods such as the cepstrum and the autocorrelation are the most popular means to estimate vocal fold repetition frequency, but need to be supplemented with heuristics to produce a relatively clean trace of F0 over time. First it is necessary to have a means for deciding when the vocal folds are vibrating, so that F0 measures

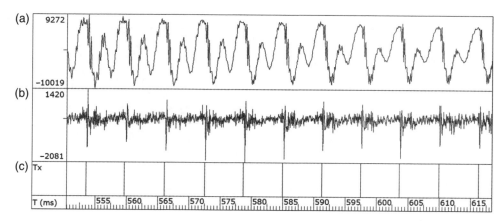

Figure 12.5 Pitch epoch location using linear prediction. An input waveform (a) is divided into short overlapping frames of about 20 ms. A linear predictor is estimated for each section. The error of prediction (b) can be used to identify the location of glottal closure events (c).

are only provided in voiced regions. Second, constraints can be applied to sequences of F0 frame estimates to limit the rate of change of F0 and ensure continuity of F0 (Talkin, 1995).

To estimate the regularity of vocal fold vibration it is useful to first delimit individual vocal fold cycles found in the speech signal. From these events, sometimes called "pitch epochs," it is possible to measure how adjacent cycles differ from one another. A number of approaches to determine the timing of each vocal fold cycle have been developed, but most start by applying a linear predictor to sections of the signal. The linear predictor, as its name suggests, tries to predict the next signal sample given a short history of the previous samples (say 10–20 samples). Since the resonances of the vocal tract passively respond to excitation, their contribution to the sound signal is fairly predictable. On the other hand, a sudden pressure change caused by rapid closure of the vocal folds is not as predictable and so the predictor works less well at this point in time. A graph of the prediction error against time typically shows a sequence of sharp pulses corresponding to the vocal fold closures. By detecting these it is possible to derive the timing of each pitch period. See Figure 12.5.

In practice, heuristics are also required to reduce the number of missed cycles and the number of false alarms (Naylor *et al.*, 2007).

There are many possible statistics of voicing irregularity that can be estimated from the delimited vocal fold cycles. These focus on jitter (period perturbations), shimmer (amplitude perturbations), or tremor (longer-term F0 variability). Some common ones are listed in Table 12.2. In the formulae, the function E() is used to represent the "expected" or mean value of its argument.

While differences in the duration or the strength of glottal cycles can be reasonably well assessed by measurements of durational or amplitude variability, it is harder to assess the amount of turbulent noise energy added to the signal during phonation. Such turbulence is commonly caused by inadequate or incomplete vocal fold adduction, such that air leaks continuously through the gap between the folds, becoming turbulent in the process. This gives rise to a perceived "breathiness" in the voice.

Table 12.2   Measures of phonation irregularity.

Parameter	Description
Relative Average Perturbation (RAP) %	Relative % variation in pitch cycle duration. Calculated as the normalized absolute difference between one cycle and the average cycle duration in a window of three cycles centered on the cycle: $$RAP = 100 \cdot E\left[\frac{\mid 2p_i - p_{i-1} - p_{i+1} \mid}{p_{i-1} + p_i + p_{i+1}}\right]$$
Period Perturbation Quotient (PPQ) %	Relative % variation in pitch cycle duration. Calculated as the normalized absolute difference between one cycle and the average cycle duration in a window of five cycles centered on the cycle: $$PPQ = 100 \cdot E\left[\frac{\mid 4p_i - p_{i-2} - p_{i-1} - p_{i+1} - p_{i+2} \mid}{p_{i-2} + p_{i-1} + p_i + p_{i+1} + p_{i+2}}\right]$$
Amplitude Perturbation Quotient (APQ) %	Relative % variation in pitch cycle amplitude. Calculated as the normalized absolute difference between the peak amplitude of 1 cycle and the average peak amplitude in a window of 11 cycles centred on the cycle: $$APQ = 100 \cdot E\left[\frac{\left\mid a_i - \frac{1}{11}\sum_{k=-5}^{+5} a_{i+k}\right\mid}{\frac{1}{11}\sum_{k=-5}^{+5} a_{i+k}}\right]$$
F0 tremor %	Average deviation from mean F0. From a sequence of F0 measurements taken on a constant pitch, express the standard deviation in F0 as a percentage of the mean F0: $$F0\ tremor = \frac{100}{\overline{F}} \cdot \sqrt{\frac{\sum_{i=1}^{N_F}(F_i - \overline{F})^2}{N_F}}$$

The measurement of added glottal turbulence is made more difficult by the presence of any other noises in the recording and by any irregularity of phonation frequency. Audio recordings are readily corrupted by broad-band noise generated by background noises such as computer fans or air-conditioning, or by the recording system itself. Acoustic measures may subsequently interpret this recording noise as glottal turbulence. In addition, if the speech signal has an irregular phonation type, then the random variation in glottal cycle duration can also be a source of signal aperiodicity that can be confused with glottal turbulence by some measures. (Michaelis, Gramß, and Strube, 1997).

Table 12.3 describes some popular measures of glottal turbulence.

As well as irregularity and noisiness, a third characteristic of phonation type related to "effectiveness" of voice is sometimes estimated from the acoustic signal.

Table 12.3 Measures of global turbulence.

Parameter	Description
Harmonic to Noise Ratio (HNR)	Looks at cycle-to-cycle variability in waveform shape. This can be performed by looking at the size of the peak in the autocorrelation function corresponding to a delay of one pitch period (r_p). Since a correlation of 1 would represent perfection, then values less than 1 can be attributed to added noise. The level of noise is then estimated as (Boersma, 1993): $$HNR(dB) = 10 \cdot \log_{10}\left(\frac{r_p}{1 - r_p}\right)$$
Cepstrum-Based Harmonics to Noise Ratio (CHNR)	An alternative method to estimate the relative amount of noise in a quasi-periodic signal using the cepstrum. The cepstrum is calculated for a piece of signal of known fundamental frequency and comb-filtered to remove the rahmonics. The modified cepstrum is then converted back to a spectral envelope and compared to the original spectrum of the whole signal to establish a periodic-to-aperiodic energy ratio (de Krom, 1993).
Normalized Noise Energy (NNE)	Ratio of energy in noise parts of spectrum to total energy in spectrum. The noise parts are found by comb-filtering the spectrum at a known fundamental frequency. The ratio is only evaluated at frequencies between 1000 and 5000 Hz (Kasuya *et al.*, 1986).
Glottal to Noise Excitation Ratio (GNE)	A measure of the correlation of energy modulations across frequency. Energy envelopes are extracted from the outputs of a bank of band-pass filters. Good correlations across different channels are used as an indicator for glottal pulsing, while weak correlations are taken to indicate noise excitation (Michaelis, Gramß, and Strube, 1997).

The idea is to capture aspects of the voice related to how well it functions to carry phonetic information from speaker to hearer. These come down to creating a sound of sufficient intensity that has energy at a wide range of frequencies.

Measuring vocal intensity really requires a recording calibrated for level in dBSPL, but since this requires special recording hardware, it is easier to look instead at how energy in the signal is distributed across frequency. This gives a relative measure independent of overall level. Some example measures of spectral energy distribution are given in Table 12.4.

Since these measures are dependent on the shape of the spectrum they will also be sensitive to the choice of speech material. Thus it is important to only look at

Table 12.4   Measures of phonation effectiveness.

Parameter	Description
Ratio of first to second harmonic amplitude (H1H2)	Ratio of amplitudes of the first and second harmonics (Holmberg, *et al.*, 1995)
Long-term average speech spectrum (LTAS)	The average speech spectrum as captured in terms of the energy in third-octave frequency bands
Spectral Slope	Slope of the long-term average speech spectrum in dB/octave calculated over the range 50–2500 Hz (Nolan, 1983: 152)
Soft Phonation Index (SPI)	Average ratio of energy in the low-frequency band (70–1600 Hz) to the high-frequency band (1600–4500 Hz)

relative differences in these parameters for recordings of the same phonetic content, say the same vowel or the same read passage.

Model-based analyses of glottal activity have also been developed. These make assumptions about the glottal system as a sound source, then attempt to estimate the parameters of the system from the acoustic signal. The Liljencrantz–Fant model of glottal area is a popular target model (Fant, Liljencrantz, and Lin, 1985; Fu and Murphy, 2004).

It is sometimes useful to explore how these parameters of irregularity, noisiness, and effectiveness co-vary with voice fundamental frequency. The phonetogram display, for example, looks at how voice intensity varies with voice pitch. The resultant displays have been used by speech-language pathologists who specialize in voice disorders to assess clients and monitor treatment efficacy (see Heylen *et al.*, 1996; Heylen *et al.*, 1998).

12.3.4   Measures of Segmental Quality

We have seen how parameters describing larynx activity can be estimated from the acoustic speech signal. The complement of these are parameters which describe how the supra-glottal vocal tract modulates the voice source or adds further sound sources to produce vowels and consonants.

The general approach to the measurement of segmental quality as opposed to phonation quality has been to first isolate the properties of the acoustic signal which have been affected by the supra-glottal tract. This is sometimes called "source-filter separation." In practice, however, separation is impossible to achieve in all situations and is always imperfect. Not only are larynx and vocal tract coupled to some degree, but some properties of the signal can also arise either glottally or supra-glottally.

Since the effect of the vocal tract on voiced non-obstruent sounds is to act as a linear filter, a common first step in analysis is to estimate the spectral envelope of the speech sound, disregarding any fine structure caused by source harmonics. The spectral envelope can then be estimated about 50–100 times per second to derive a smoothly changing description of sound quality, somewhat like a speech spectrogram.

The simplest way to produce spectral envelope data is through the use of a filterbank. This is a bank of band-pass filters each of which isolates a particular frequency region of the signal. The energy at the output of each filter channel can be estimated by rectification, smoothing and down-sampling (Figure 12.6(b)). A filterbank brings a great deal of flexibility to the analysis, since the filters need not be equally spaced, nor have constant bandwidth. A common filterbank design is modeled on auditory filter bandwidths and spacing, which gives greater spectral resolution in the lower frequencies (Holmes, 1980). Such a design is not far from a one-third octave (or one-tenth decade) filterbank used in acoustical engineering, where each filter is of constant bandwidth in log Hz. A one-third octave filterbank would represent the spectrum between 100 Hz and 8000 Hz in 19 channels.

The most popular approach to estimate the spectral envelope is through linear prediction. In the previous section linear prediction was used to find the instants of glottal excitation from the prediction error. Here we are interested in the properties of the predictor itself. Taking the error signal to be the input to a linear system which produces the observed signal, the predictor then specifies the frequency response of that system. An estimate of the spectral envelope of the signal can then be found from the filter frequency response.

To represent the spectral envelope of a speech signal up to 8000 Hz, predictors typically have 16–18 prediction coefficients, and so can be said to represent the spectral envelope in 16–18 numbers. This is similar to the third-octave filterbank, but linear prediction has an added advantage of superior rejection of the harmonic components of the voice source, particularly in the low frequencies. See Figure 12.6(c).

Once the spectral envelope has been estimated for each time interval in the signal (analysis of typically 20–30 ms sections, repeated 100 times/second) further computation is often performed to derive a small set of parameters which describe the important properties of the envelope over that interval. Since it is the locations in frequency of the peaks of the spectrum that contribute most to the perceived timbre, an obvious first choice is to reduce the envelope to a few numbers representing the location and shape of the peaks. Treating the linear predictor as a recursive filter, this reduction to peaks can be performed by analyzing the predictor using the z-transform. Under a z-transform, the frequency response of the predictor can be represented as a ratio of polynomials, and the peaks in the frequency response arise from the roots of the denominator polynomial. In short, by treating the predictor coefficients as a polynomial and solving for its roots we can model the prediction filter in terms of the frequencies and bandwidths of a small number of spectral peaks. For a signal sampled at 16000 samples/sec, a predictor with 18 coefficients might provide estimates of 8 or 9 spectral peaks between 0 and 8000 Hz.

It is very likely that for vowel sounds at least some of the peaks modeled by the predictor will correspond to resonances of the vocal tract, that is, to formants. Unfortunately the mapping can be rather variable, so one cannot rely on the fact that, for example, the lowest spectral peak corresponds to F1, or that adjacent peaks correspond to adjacent formants (see Figure 12.6(d)). Automatic algorithms employ heuristics to find good mappings between peaks and formants, but faulty assignments should always be considered a possibility. Thus when averaging across

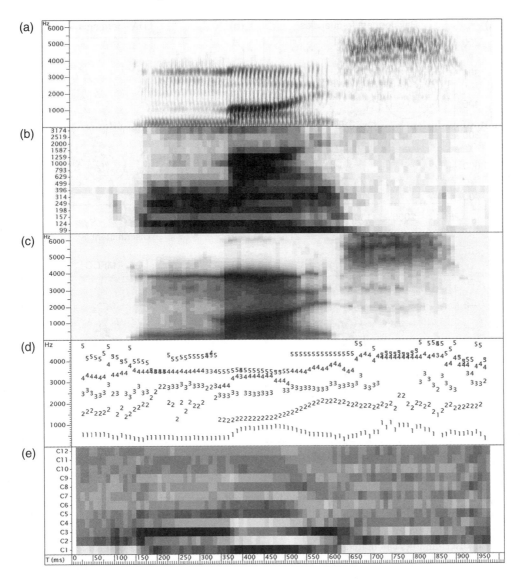

Figure 12.6 Comparison of spectral envelope representations for the word "mice."
(a) Wide-band spectrogram (DFT), (b) third-octave filterbank, (c) linear prediction
spectrogram, (d) formant frequencies, (e) Mel-scaled cepstral coefficients. Figure
generated using the Speech Filing System.

time, one might prefer a median formant frequency over a mean to reduce the influence of faulty mappings to spectral peaks.

Describing the envelope in terms of formant frequencies and bandwidths reduces the number of parameters used to describe each spectral frame from about 18 to about 8 (4 frequencies and 4 bandwidths), with only a small loss in descriptive power. An alternative is to use other transforms of the spectral envelope to derive parameters that describe the broad shape of the envelope rather than the fine detail. One way to do this is with a cosine transform of the envelope, which leads to parameters called cepstral coefficients (because of the similarity of the transformed envelope to the cepstrum).

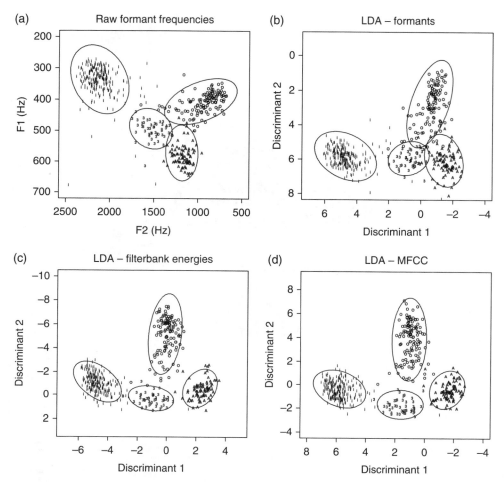

Figure 12.7 Discrimination of vowel qualities using different spectral envelope parameters. Measurements of four long monophthongal vowels from one speaker are plotted (a) in terms of the distribution of the first and second formant frequencies, (b) in terms of the first two linear discriminants calculated over all monophthongal vowels using the first three formants, (c) in terms of the first two linear discriminants calculated over all monophthongal vowels using a third-octave filterbank, (d) in terms of the first two linear discriminants calculated over all monophthongal vowels using Mel-scaled cepstral coefficients. Discrimination by formant frequencies alone is quite good, and not improved by discriminant analysis. However, discrimination is improved by the use of third-octave energies or MFCCs.

The lower cepstral coefficients model the large-scale bumps in the envelope, while the higher coefficients model the smaller details. Thus much of the detail in the shape can be captured in 10–12 coefficients. These coefficients have the bonus property that they all have similar magnitudes and are largely independent, thus making them ideal for similarity comparisons using an unweighted Euclidean metric.

One type of cepstral coefficients, very popular in speech technology, is based on the cosine transform of the energies at the output of a filterbank designed on auditory principles, this type is known as Mel-scaled cepstral coefficients, or MFCCs (Davis and Mermelstein, 1980). An example is given in Figure 12.6(e).

Spectral envelopes can also be represented using fewer parameters through statistical analysis. Here a corpus of envelopes is used to derive a set of new parameters which are linear combinations of existing parameters but which capture useful variability in the data. In this way the important variation in the envelopes can be captured in fewer coefficients per envelope. If this analysis is performed without regard to the phonetic labeling of the frames, it is called principal components analysis (PCA) and the outcome is a set of orthogonal directions within the original vector space defined by the envelope parameters. Since these directions are ordered by the degree of variability in the original corpus found along each direction, the first few directions can be chosen to capture most of the variability in the data. A similar analysis can be performed but taking into account the fact that the envelopes represent realizations of different phonetic segments. This is then called Linear Discriminant Analysis (LDA) and the outcome is a set of orthogonal directions which best separate the phonetic classes (assuming equal variance within each class). Again, the directions are ordered by their value in discriminating classes, and so the first few directions can be chosen to capture useful variation in the data. PCA and LDA are useful in exploring the changes in data sets across conditions, since they allow graphs and statistical tests to be performed in fewer measurement dimensions. However, since the principal components and the discriminants are derived from a specific corpus of data, they have no absolute, objective status unlike energies, cepstral coefficients, or formants. Figure 12.7 contrasts a scatter plot of vowels in a corpus using two formants with linear discriminants calculated from filterbank energies and Mel-scaled cepstral coefficients.

Whilst formant frequencies have found widespread use as a means to measure vowel quality, no such consensus has been achieved for the measurement of fricative quality. A number of parameters have been proposed, including spectral moments (Forrest *et al.*, 1988), dynamic amplitude and spectral slope (Jesus and Shadle, 2002). When measuring the spectral envelope of fricatives it is important to use some kind of averaging (across time or across repetition), since any single spectral slice will be strongly affected by random effects.

Section Summary

- Active speech level is the best way to measure speech signal level.
- Aligned transcriptions make it easy to extract durational and rhythmic measures.
- The cepstrum and the autocorrelation functions are commonly used to estimate voice pitch.
- Pitch epoch marking provides access to a wide range of measures of voice quality.
- The estimation of the spectral envelope is a prerequisite for analysis of segmental quality.
- The spectral envelope can be parameterized by formant frequencies, cepstral parameters or by statistical analysis.

12.4   Modeling

In the previous sections we have seen how phonetically useful parameters can be extracted from short sections of the speech signal, of perhaps 20–30 ms. However to compare the realizations of linguistic units it is necessary to find a way to model the changes in these parameters over larger time frames. We'll look first at the modeling of phonetic segments, then look at the modeling of intonational contours.

12.4.1   Modeling of Segments

Imagine a situation in which we have a set of realizations of some segment collected in some context, and another set collected in a second context and we want to investigate the change in realization due to context. Our essential strategy is to use a model of the realization of each segment and to estimate the parameters of that model from the acoustic data for each segment independently, then to determine the distribution of model parameters over all repetitions within one context, and finally submit the two distributions to statistical analysis.

A simple segment model might consist of calculating the average value of each acoustic parameter over the duration of the segment. Thus for a vowel we might calculate its mean or median formant frequencies. This simple model assumes some underlying "target" value for each acoustic parameter which has become corrupted by noise.

Another approach might be to fit a straight line to each parameter over the duration of the segment. This would provide two model parameters (a slope and a centroid) for each acoustic parameter. A third approach might be to fit a quadratic polynomial over the segment – this would generate three model parameters for each acoustic parameter. For single segments, it is unlikely that higher polynomials would be required.

An interesting alternative segment model is one which considers the segment to be "piecewise stationary," that is, composed of a sequence of steady-state pieces. The outcome is then the mean and variance for each acoustic parameter per piece (see Figure 12.8). A popular approach is to use three pieces, on the assumption that the first and last third of a segment is more strongly affected by adjacent segments than the middle third. A piecewise stationary model can be estimated from data without first deciding the duration of the respective parts. The durations can emerge from whatever division provides the best fit of the model. A piecewise stationary model of a segment is also known as a hidden Markov model or HMM. The HMM framework also leads to a statistical description across repetitions, where the means and variances on each piece capture both variability within a segment and across segments.

Given the means and variances of the model parameters collected within one context, we can now compare values across contexts to see if the form of the segment varies significantly across conditions. We might either perform a hypothesis test of difference in means for each model parameter separately, with, say, a t-test, or we can look across a number of model parameters simultaneously with a multivariate test.

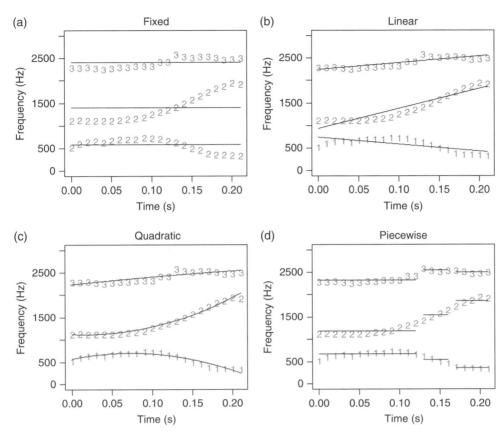

Figure 12.8 Modeling parameter dynamics over a segment with (a) a mean calculated over the whole segment (three numbers), (b) a straight line fit (six numbers), (c) a quadratic line fit (nine numbers), (d) a piecewise-stationary fit (nine numbers). Data are the first three formant frequencies for /aɪ/ diphthong.

12.4.2 Modeling of F0 Contours

While statistics about average pitch and pitch range can be estimated from averages of short-time fundamental frequency measures, the measurement of intonation requires the modeling of F0 contours over much larger time frames corresponding to syllables, prosodic feet, or intonational phrases.

Again, the general approach is to devise a model which describes the time course of F0 over a particular stretch of the signal, then to estimate the parameters of that model from the acoustic signal. There are two main types of F0 contour model: those that model the contour shape regardless of its alignment to the segmental content of the speech, and those that are anchored to the segmental content through annotations. The advantage of the former is that F0 contours can be modeled without introducing assumptions about the domains over which pitch accents operate. The advantage of the latter is that alignment makes it is easier to connect properties of pitch accents to the properties of linguistic units found in the utterance.

Models that seek only to stylize the pitch contour include the IPO (Institute for Perception Research) system ('t Hart, Collier, and Cohen, 1990) and the MOMEL (modeling melody) system (Hirst and Espesser, 1993). The IPO system models the contour as a sequence of piecewise linear segments chosen such that the stylized result should be perceptually indistinguishable from the original. The outcome of analysis is an undefined number of line segments, each with an F0 height and slope. The MOMEL system is similar but uses a quadratic spline function to model a smoothed version of the contour. The outcome of analysis are the times and heights of the "knots" which define a contour that matches the original to some degree of precision.

Models of defined regions of the contour simply seek to represent pitch movements within a given domain in a small number of parameters. The domain is typically the syllable, although larger domains are clearly possible. Most models used in speech synthesis simply measure a small number of F0 values at fixed proportions through the domain; for example, Black and Hunt (1996) use three F0 values per syllable: at the start, at the end, and at mid-vowel. In the TILT model (Taylor, 1998), each accented syllable is labeled with a "tilt event" which describes a rising–falling shape of particular degree using three parameters: amplitude, duration, and shape. Parameters for each tilt event can be calculated from the F0 contour through an analysis-by-synthesis procedure, while the contour over unaccented syllables is assumed to follow a quadratic interpolation between the tilt events. In the qTA (quantitative target approximation) model (Prom-on, Xu, and Thipakorn, 2009) the contour in each syllable is described by a pitch "target," to which the contour is said to approximate over time. The pitch target can itself be rising or falling, and the analysis procedure extracts two parameters per syllable from the F0 contour on the assumption that the contour approximates the sequence of pitch targets using a third-order critically damped system.

Section Summary

- Parameters can be summarized over the duration of a phonological segment using a model.
- It is the parameters of that model which can then be used for statistical analysis.
- Pitch contours can be stylized independently of the segmental content, or parameters can be found which describe the contour over phonological units such as syllables.

12.5   Resources

12.5.1   *Corpus Preparation Tools*

ANVIL is an audio-video annotation tool developed at DFKI, Saarbrücken, Germany (Kipp, in press). It allows for time-aligned annotation of audio and video data on multiple annotation tiers. Annotations can be imported and exported for communication with other analysis tools, and ANVIL also contains tools for some analysis of the annotations themselves, such as cross-transcriber agreement metric.

EMU is a combined annotation and database system for speech corpora originating at the Department of Linguistics, Macquarie University, Australia, but with further development at the Institute of Phonetics and Speech Processing, LMU Munich, Germany, and the Institute of Phonetics and Digital Speech Processing, CAU Kiel, Germany (Bombien *et al.*, 2006). With EMU speech signals can be annotated on multiple tiers, and the annotations stored within a relational database so that segments of speech matching phonetic criteria can be located by search patterns. EMU also contains tools for speech analysis and for statistical analysis.

Transcriber is a tool for transcription of speech recordings originally developed at LIMSI, Orsay, France (Barras, Geoffrois, Wu, and Liberman, 2000). Transcriber was designed to aid the creation of large spoken language corpora for speech technology purposes, and supports multiple levels of annotation.

WaveScroller is a tool to aid the transcription of speech signals developed at the Department of Linguistics, Northwestern University, Chicago, USA. Its design goals were to provide an interface that maximized transcription productivity and to interface to tools for automatic alignment of transcription with the audio signal.

12.5.2 *Speech Analysis Tools*

MultiSpeech and MDVP are professional tools from KayPENTAX, New Jersey, USA. MultiSpeech is a general system for speech editing, annotation, display and analysis. It supports fundamental frequency and formant estimation, as well as LPC analysis and filtering. The Multi-Dimensional Voice Profile (MDVP) software package provides a wide range of metrics for the assessment of voice in a clinical setting.

Praat is a multi-platform tool for phonetic analysis of speech signals developed at the Department of Phonetic Sciences, University of Amsterdam, the Netherlands. It contains a wide range of tools for measuring, manipulating,and synthesizing speech signals. It has a large following within the academic community and many scripts are available to extend Praat for specific phonetic modeling purposes.

Speech Analyzer is a program for speech signal display and analysis developed by SIL International, Dallas, USA. It supports the annotation of speech signals using phonetic symbols as well as formant frequency and fundamental frequency estimation.

Speech Filing System (SFS) is a wide-ranging set of tools for speech signal display and measurement largely designed and maintained by the author at the Department of Speech, Hearing and Phonetic Sciences, University College London, UK. SFS supports the acquisition, replay, display, and annotation of speech signals, tools for the processing of speech signals, as well as spectrographic and formant analysis, fundamental frequency estimation, and voice quality measurement.

WaveSurfer is a program for speech signal display, annotation, and analysis developed at the Department of Speech, Music and Hearing, KTH, Stockholm, Sweden. WaveSurfer supports a range of audio and transcription file formats, and provides facilities for spectrographic, formant and fundamental frequency analysis. Implemented within the Tcl/Tk framework WaveSurfer is multi-platform and can be extended through plug-in modules, such as provided by the Snack toolkit, below.

WinPitch is a program for speech signal annotation and analysis developed by Pitch Instruments Inc., Ontario, Canada. WinPitch supports assisted alignment of transcription and contains methods for spectrographic and fundamental frequency analysis.

12.5.3   Speech Toolkits

Edinburgh Speech Tools is a set of programs for speech signal processing developed at the Centre for Speech Technology Research, University of Edinburgh, UK. Edinburgh Speech Tools provide facilities for automated processing of signals particularly to aid in the construction of speech synthesis systems. The tools support filtering, fundamental frequency estimation, and pitch epoch marking as well as the building of classification and regression trees (CART) and weighted finite-state transducers.

Penn Phonetics Lab Forced Aligner is a trained set of hidden-Markov-models (HMMs) for automatic alignment of American English phonetic transcription developed at the Department of Linguistics, University of Pennsylvania, Philadelphia, USA.

Snack is a set of speech signal manipulation functions compatible with Tcl/Tk developed at KTH, Stockholm, Sweden. Snack provides the essential functions required to read, write, acquire, replay, and display speech signals across multiple computing platforms, and can be used as the basis for building specialised applications.

Voicebox is a set of MATLAB functions for speech signal processing developed at Imperial College London, UK. Voicebox provides reference implementations of standard signal processing algorithms, including active level measurement, linear prediction, pitch epoch detection, and noise reduction.

References

Barras, C., Geoffrois, E., Wu, Z., and Liberman, M. (2000). Transcriber: development and use of a tool for assisting speech corpora production. *Speech Communication*, 33, 5–22.

Black, A. and Hunt, A. (1996). Generating F0 contours from ToBI labels using linear regression. *International Conference on Spoken Language Processing, Philadelphia, PA, USA, October 3–6*, pp. 1385–1388.

Boersma, P. (1993). Accurate short-term analysis of the fundamental frequency and the harmonics-to-noise ratio of a sampled sound. *Proceedings of the Institute of Phonetic Sciences*, 17, 97–110.

Bombien, L., Cassidy, S., Harrington, J. *et al.* (2006). Recent developments in the Emu speech database system. In *Proceedings of the Australian Speech Science and Technology Conference. Auckland, NZ, December 2006*. Canberra: Australian Speech Science and Technology Association, CD-ROM.

Davis, S. and Mermelstein, P. (1980). Comparison of parametric representations for monosyllabic word recognition in continuously spoken sentences. *IEEE Transactions on Acoustics, Speech and Signal Processing*, 28(4), 357–366.

de Krom, G. (1993). A cepstrum-based technique for determining a harmonics-to-noise ratio in speech signals. *Journal of Speech, Hearing and Language Research*, 36, 224–266.

Fant, G., Liljencrantz, J., and Lin, Q. (1985). A four-parameter model of glottal flow. *STL-QPSR*, 26(4), 1–13.

Forrest, K., Weismer, G., Milenkovic, P., and Dougall, R. (1988). Statistical analysis of word-initial voiceless obstruents. *Journal of the Acoustical Society of America*, 84(1), 115–123.

Fu, Q. and Murphy, P. (2004). A robust glottal source model estimation technique. Paper presented at the International Conference on Spoken Language Processing, Jeju Island, Korea, October.

Grabe, E. and Low, E. (2002). Durational variability in speech and the rhythm class hypothesis. In C. Gussenhoven and N. Warner, *Papers in Laboratory Phonology 7*. Berlin: Mouton de Gruyter, pp. 515–546.

Heylen, L. G., Wuyts, F. L., Mertens, F. W., and Pattyn, J. E. (1996). Phonetography in voice diagnoses. *Acta Oto-Rhino-Laryngologica*, 50, 299–238.

Heylen, L., Wuyts, F. L., Mertens, F. *et al.* (1998). Evaluation of the vocal performance of children using a voice range profile index. *Journal of Speech, Language, and Hearing Research*, 41, 232–238.

Hirst, D. and Espesser, R. (1993). Automatic modelling of fundamental frequency using a quadratic spline function. *Travaux de l'Institut de Phonétique d'Aix*, 15, 71–85.

Holmberg, E., Hillman, R., Perkell, J. *et al.* (1995). Comparisons among aerodynamic, electroglottographic and acoustic spectral measures of female voice. *Journal of Speech and Hearing Research*, 38, 1212–1223.

Holmes, J. (1980). The JSRU channel vocoder. *Communications, Radar and Signal Processing, IEE Proceedings F*, 127, 53–60.

ITU-T. (1993). *Recommendation P 56, Objective Measurement of Active Speech Level*. Geneva: International Telecommunications Union.

Jesus, L. and Shadle, C. (2002). A parametric study of the spectral characteristics of Portuguese fricatives. *Journal of Phonetics*, 30, 437–464.

Kasuya, H., Ogawa, S., Mashima, K., and Ebihara, S. (1986). Normalized noise energy as an acoustic measure to evaluate pathologic voice. *Journal of the Acoustical Society of America*, 80(5), 1329–1334.

Kipp, M. (in press). Multimedia annotation, querying and analysis in ANVIL. In M. Maybury (ed.), *Multimedia Information Extraction. Advances in Video, Audio, and Imagery Analysis for Search, Data Mining, Surveillance, and Authoring*. Hoboken, NJ: IEEE Computer Society/John Wiley & Sons, Inc., pp. 351–367.

Michaelis, D., Gramß, T., and Strube, H. (1997). Glottal to noise excitation ratio – a new measure for describing pathological voices. *Acta Acustica*, 83, 700–706.

Naylor, P., Kounoudes, A., Gudnason, J., and Brookes, M. (2007). Estimation of glottal closure instants in voiced speech using the DYPSA Algorithm. *IEEE Transactions on Audio, Speech, and Language Processing*, 15, 34–43.

Nolan, F. (1983). *The Phonetic Bases of Speaker Recognition*. Cambridge: Cambridge University Press.

Prom-on, S., Xu, Y., and Thipakorn, B. (2009). Modeling tone and intonation in Mandarin and English as a process of target approximation. *Journal of the Acoustical Society of America*, 125(1), 405–424.

Ramus, F., Nespor, M., and Mehler, J. (1999). Correlates of linguistic rhythm in the speech signal. *Cognition*, 73, 265–292.

't Hart, J., Collier, R., and Cohen, A. (1990). *A Perceptual Study of Intonation*. Cambridge: Cambridge University Press.

Talkin, D. (1995). A robust algorithm for pitch tracking (RAPT). In W. Kleijn and K. Paliwal (eds), *Speech Coding and Synthesis*. Amsterdam: Elsevier, pp. 495–515.

Taylor, P. (1998). The Tilt intonation model. *International Conference on Spoken Language Processing. Sydney, Australia*. Canberra: Australian Speech Science and Technology Association, pp. 1383–138.

van Son, R. (2005). A study of pitch, formant, and spectral estimation errors introduced by three lossy speech compression algorithms. *Acta Acustica*, 91, 771–778.

13 Data Processing: Imaging of Speech Data

Joan Rahilly

13.1 The Background to Speech Imaging

In the broadest sense, speech imaging is a technique which provides a visual representation of the speech apparatus along with the muscular and articulatory movements involved in speech, from planning to production stages. This chapter gives an overview of the core imaging methodologies in use for investigating clinical and non-clinical speech varieties, highlights current and developing trends in the field, and indicates some specific insights gained from imaging studies which would be inaccessible using purely perceptual or acoustic methods. As far as possible in our discussion of analytic approaches, the illustrations relate to leading, commercially available technology whose details are widely available on the Internet as well as in the studies cited here. Nonetheless, the present coverage of research and development in speech imaging necessitates some reference to new instrumentation, or adaptations of existing methods, where analysts have indicated particularly promising applications for their techniques in trial. The main goal of this chapter is to provide a key to appropriate imaging techniques depending on the speech component under investigation, rather than a breakdown of the particular computing and sampling requirements of specific experimental tasks.

Many of the initiatives in speech imaging have been driven, at least in their nascent stages, by medical research wherein physicians are required to obtain pre- and post-operative information on the exact sites of lesions and tumors which affect speech mechanisms, and to evaluate effects of surgical procedures. In such cases, images of speech derived by ultrasound, for instance, have a clear diagnostic status (see, for instance, Okayhama *et al.*, 2008; Rastadmehr, Bressman, Smyth, and Irish, 2008). Further medical reasons for and applications of speech imaging have obvious links with speech and language therapy and clinical speech research. These include the

Research Methods in Clinical Linguistics and Phonetics: A Practical Guide,
First Edition. Edited by Nicole Müller and Martin J. Ball.
© 2013 Blackwell Publishing Ltd. Published 2013 by Blackwell Publishing Ltd.

charting of movements involved in speech dynamics, such as in motor deficits following stroke, in wider neuromuscular deficits (see, for instance, Jiang, 2008) and swallowing disorders (illustrated in Steele and Van Lieshout, 2004, 2009). This facility for providing insights into dynamic aspects of speech production and the interacting mechanisms involved, rather than more traditional static accounts of individual gestures, is one of the main benefits of imaging work. Of course, not all speech imaging is carried out for clinical or therapeutic purposes. Some of the work referred to in this chapter capitalizes on imaging approaches for examining speech features in areas such as professional voice use, second language learning, and sociolinguistic variation. Increasingly, as speech-imaging technology advances in complexity and the range of potentially relevant insights expands, research in the area tends to be conducted by multidisciplinary teams with expertise in physiology and computing, for example, as well as in speech science.

Leaving aside, for the moment, the variety of approaches involved in speech imaging and the issue of how close their "representation" might be to articulatory configurations (a photographic image of the vocal folds, for example, is more direct than a graph-type arrangement from which vocal fold patterns may be inferred), we begin by outlining the domain, role, and value of imaging as a central pursuit in modern phonetics.

Section Summary

- Speech imaging provides a visual representation of the speech apparatus, including information on the muscular and articulatory movements involved in speech, from planning to production stages.
- Imaging is applied in medical and speech therapy contexts, and in work involving non-clinical aspects of speech variation.

13.2   What is Speech Imaging? Parameters for Analysis

The impetus behind all imaging analyses in phonetic study is the need to make speech events amenable to visual inspection, that is, to allow observation by sight, which, in turn, enables appropriate charting of those events as a basis for subsequent investigation. Within the fields of clinical speech and language work, and in speech analysis more generally, the methods involved vary considerably in terms of their complexity of experimental design, architecture, and build, as well as equipment cost. Nonetheless, some basic elements are essential to all set-ups: a monitoring, recording or photographic device for capturing the relevant aspects in the speech production chain, combined with software and hardware which decodes and processes the data and presents the user with visually meaningful results. Various reasons exist for employing imaging approaches in speech studies, including the need to establish empirical bases for clinical and therapeutic work, and the opportunity for supplementing impressionistic and acoustic findings.

It is worth pointing out that all areas of phonetic analysis, whether presented in imaging terms or not, presuppose an explicitly visual charting of speech events. One is reminded of Bell's (1867) efforts towards a transcription system for making speech *visible*, and, while his proposed symbol set is idiosyncratic, his aim to "*depict* the organic positions and actions that produce the sounds of the symbols" (p. 15; my italics) indicates the interface role served by visual records as a means for conveying auditorily salient events. Furthermore, the sort of information made available in a reliable phonetic transcription, produced by impressionistic means using agreed IPA symbols, provides a picture or a visual medium which can be decoded by trained users and reassembled into a reasonably close version of the original sample. Indeed, our understanding of articulatory categories draws on the established correlations between sounds and visual maps which allow analysts to conceptualize and diagram vocal tract contact patterns and trajectories. In experimental phonetics, too, we approach speech data by way of the observable acoustic signal, and we infer particular articulatory categories and patterns of intersegmental co-ordination based on the arrangement of frequency patterns within spectrograms and pitch traces. For beginning students in acoustic analysis, there often exists a comforting circularity in deriving a visual representation which seems to bear a direct relationship to given sound categories, so they are often gratified when a spectrogram allows them to "see," as it were, the presence of Fundamental Frequency (F_0) in what they have already identified as a "voiced" sound. However, it is important to realize that, while the visual aspect of acoustic analysis can be a useful parse for speech data, we should not expect it to constitute an easy means of proof or denial of success in perceptual analysis. The untrained user who finds no visible trace of F_0 for a sound segment which they have transcribed as voiced will be at a loss, without an understanding of how issues such as co-articulation and VOT affect archetypal patterns. In other words, aspects of data which are presented as visual records, including those mediated by acoustic analysis methods, must be interpreted in the light of appropriate phonetic knowledge. As we will show in the course of this chapter, the same caveat applies to the interpretation of speech imaging data. Nowhere is it suggested that imaging studies should take the place of, or are necessarily more reliable than perceptual evaluation. Hypernasality, for example, is the focus of considerable attention in speech imaging (for a detailed review of the methods in use, see Shprintzen and Marrinan, 2009), but Vogel, Ibrahim, Reilly, and Kilpatrick (2009), in their study of hypernasality in children with cleft lip and palate, state that "[p]erceptual judgement remains the primary means of evaluating levels of nasality in children with CLP" (p. 1640).

As indicated above, mainstream approaches to speech imaging take indirect and direct forms. We use "indirect" to refer to schematized representations of the speech components and movements in question, derived by electronic monitoring of vocal activity, and "direct" to indicate a true image acquired by photographic means, or scans of various sorts. Investigators often combine both types of approach; Engwall (2002), for instance, in a study which models lingual configurations and dynamics, uses direct and indirect methods in pursuit of a three-dimensional model of tongue movement. While something of an oversimplification, it is fair to say that indirect and direct approaches in speech imaging often characterize two-dimensional (2D) and three-dimensional (3D) accounts respectively, and they also often form the basis for static and dynamic investigations, again respectively. In summary, set alongside impressionistic and acoustic analysis, imaging approaches illuminate the underlying relationship between the speech signal and the organs and articulators, made visible directly or indirectly, which produced it.

While our interests in this chapter relate mainly to the role of imaging techniques in clinical and research contexts, from the perspective of the investigator, it is also important to highlight the application of imaging for biofeedback purposes. Visual representations of speakers' own output are known to facilitate improvement and enhance therapy in, for instance, Down syndrome children (Cleland *et al.*, 2009), apraxic conditions (Morgan and Vogel, 2008), and various types of misarticulation (McAuliffe and Cornwell, 2008). For professional voice users, too, imaging technology offers a central method for creating awareness of speech parameters (see, for example, Dejonckere, 2000; Fourcin, Abberton, Miller, and Howells, 1995).

We now move on to deal with specific methods in speech imaging. The relevant techniques are considered here in terms of their relationship to specific and key points in the speech production chain, although some methodologies allow a broad range of speech features to be imaged. Hence, we begin with neuroimagery and explain ways in which links between the brain and speech behavior are typically profiled. From there, we move on to look at imaging methods which have been developed for examining vocal tract regions, nasal and oral airflow, and, finally, attention is given to imaging resources for charting lingual patterns in relation to other articulators. We should note from the outset, though, that there is an inevitable crossover between techniques. For example, depending on the nature of the research task, the case of a speaker who presents with excessive nasality may be studied usefully using imaging for nasal airflow, or scans of velopharyngeal structure, or endoscopic investigation.

Section Summary

- Imaging approaches require a monitoring, recording or photographic device for capturing relevant aspects of speech, software and hardware which decodes and processes the data and presents the user with visually meaningful results.
- Speech imaging takes direct and indirect forms, depending on whether they produce schematized representations or true images.
- Imaging has an analytic role for investigators and a biofeedback role for speakers.

13.3 Neuroimagery: Charting Brain Activity in Speech Production

Neuroimagery is the technique intended for viewing areas of the brain musculature which are activated during language tasks. Its underpinnings lie in the late nineteenth century, when the aphasia studies conducted by Broca (1861) and Wernicke (1874) enabled associations to be made between lesions in the brain and impairments in language production and perception. By way of autopsy studies on speakers with a known language disorder who were discovered to have abnormalities in a certain region of the cortex, Broca and Wernicke were able to conclude that the language task in question was localized in that part of the brain and, therefore, that given areas of the brain were specialized for language production and reception (see also Posner, 1988). While such work was foundational for an understanding of the neural basis of speech, Blank *et al.* (2002) note that early studies highlighted "ill-defined" (p. 1829) regions of the brain, and that some crucial areas went unidentified.

While X-ray photography for neuroimaging, and for imaging other physiological structures, was in common usage throughout the twentieth century, it has become rather outmoded, first because of its relatively poor quality when seen alongside digital images and also due to what may be unacceptable levels of radiation exposure for subjects under investigation (see Baer, Gore, Boyce, and Nye, 1987). Developments in X-ray technology which have made their way into current speech imaging work include microbeam displays for tracking articulatory movement, and these will be discussed later in this chapter (see Section 13.7). Current approaches to mapping brain activity during speech tasks have been developed within the discipline of Functional Neuroimaging, the two main strands of which are functional magnetic resonance imagery (fMRI, where the "functional" aspect refers to imaging undertaken during the performance of a particular speech task) and positron emission tomography (PET). Both methods rely on a system of electrical stimulation of blood flow to acquire data, but there are some key differences between them. PET employs a so-called "tracer," that is, a radioactive substance which is inserted into the bloodstream and causes radioactive transmission to emanate from areas of higher bloodflow and, therefore, greater activity. PET produces what Fiez (2001) refers to as "pictures of the distribution of radiation" (p. 446). fMRI, on the other hand, relies on magnetic forces to register comparatively strong or weak bloodflow as a result of oxygen content in the blood. It is fMRI which has become the neuro-imaging method of choice for most investigators, largely because it is capable of sampling at much higher rates than PET. Fiez notes that, in a two-hour session, for example, PET can produce 10 images, compared to the fMRI capacity for generating more than 1000. While it is preferred, too, for reasons of financial expediency and because it is less invasive than PET, Fiez offers some potential pitfalls regarding the use of fMRI in speech-specific work:

One problem is that the scanner is noisy, which can make studies that hinge upon subtle differences in auditorily presented stimuli difficult to implement. A second problem is

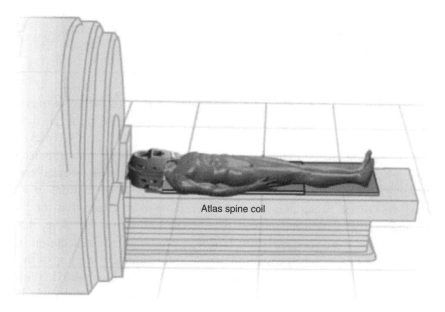

Atlas spine coil

Figure 13.1 Experimental set-up for fMRI.

that speaking leads to movements of the sinus air cavities, and this can lead to disruptions in the magnetic signal, causing speech-related artifacts in the data. A third problem is that the signal generated in response to a single stimulus item is potentially smaller than it is in PET. This may be an important constraint for studies in which only a limited number of well-controlled stimulus items are available, as is often the case in language studies. Fortunately, recent methodological advances have made all of these problems tractable, and so this issue will be less of a concern in the future.

(Fiez, 2001: 448–449)

Figure 13.1 shows the typical scanning chamber used to produce fMRI images. In this case, the patient is fitted with a head and neck coil, in order to minimize head movement, while Figure 13.2 shows sample fMRI scans for a pediatric patient.

Neuroimaging studies of speech have been used to monitor brain activity across a wide variety of language tasks, such as the patterns and extent of neural impulses in children's phonological inconsistency (Bolger *et al.*, 2008), phonological behavior in adults (Gitelman *et al.*, 2005), acquired language disorders (Ramage, Kiran, and Robin, 2008), stuttering and altered speech rhythm (De Nil, Sasisekaran, Pascal, and Van Lieshout, 2008), foreign accent syndrome (Luzzi *et al.*, 2008), and bilingualism (Liu, Hu, Guo, and Peng, 2010). Complementary to the work which has elucidated the neural basis for speech problems, imaging approaches have emphasized some interdependence between speech and brain activity by stimulating particular parts of the brain into triggering changes in speech behavior (Ingham, Cykowski, Ingham, and Fox, 2008, for instance, used this technique to produce stuttering).

In addition to establishing the set of neural networks that are activated during speech production, the neuroimaging literature gives specific consideration to the

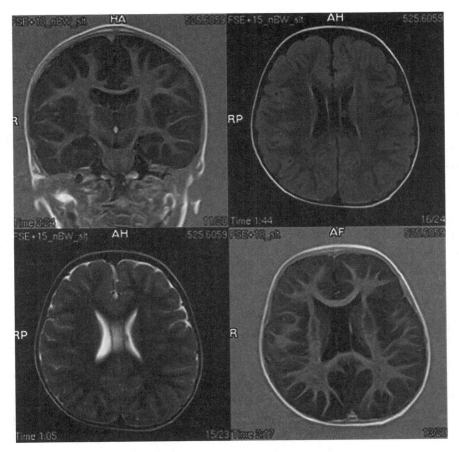

Figure 13.2 fMRI scans of activity in the brain of a pediatric patient.

role of the auditory cortex at the level of auditory feedback not just for perception of heard voices, but for fine-tuning of one's own speech (see Formisamo, De Martino, Bonte, and Goebel, 2008; Guenther, 2008). Along somewhat similar lines, Watkins, Smith, Davis, and Howell (2008) note the potential of neuroimaging for revealing interconnections between the precise areas of the brain involved in production and perception, with some regions performing a dual role.

While acknowledging the presupposition which underlies neuroimaging for speech, that is, that speech can indeed by mapped onto neural areas and mechanisms, analysts should be wary of assuming consistent, direct, or localized correlations. Guenther (2008), in his wide-ranging review of the history, background, and major trends in neuroimaging, emphasizes the need for cautious interpretation:

[S]uch studies are notoriously difficult to interpret, for several reasons. First, rarely do different patients have lesions in precisely the same region of the cortex. Second, most lesions span several cortical areas and thus affect a number of neural systems, not just the system involved in a particular task such as speech production (which in itself actually involves several different brain regions). Third, spared portions of cortex often will take over functions formerly performed by the damaged portion. Fourth, considerable variability may exist in the location of a particular brain function … Finally, higher-level language functions such as grammatical processing appear to involve large expanses of cortex spanning multiple cortical lobes.

(Guenther, 2008: 6)

The problem is, perhaps, no thornier than any interpretative task wherein the analyst is required to generate data and make appropriate inferences regarding the significance of that data. Guenther's points, however, serve as a useful warning in an analytic area where we may be tempted to interpret images as somehow objective or absolute. In other words, speech imaging may get us closer to the speech mechanisms than we can manage with auditory and acoustic methods, but we must remain vigilant and informed in our interpretations.

We now move on to look at the role of speech imaging in revealing activity in the vocal tract, beginning with a consideration of typical approaches to imaging the lower tract and vocal fold activity.

Section Summary

- Neuroimagery maps areas of the brain which are involved in speech production, as well as auditory perception and auditory feedback.
- fMRI methods, which tend to be preferred by analysts over PET approaches, enable insights into brain activation patterns which underlie clinical and non-clinical aspects of phonological behavior.
- Caution must be exercised in our interpretation how neural activity relates to speech components, given the multi-functionality of a number of neural regions.

13.4   Imaging the Lower Vocal Tract

Most imaging work in clinical speech studies focus on the larynx and the upper vocal tract, with the latter extending into the nasal and oral cavities. Nonetheless, the role of the sub-laryngeal lower vocal tract is also considered, usually in terms of MRI-based studies dealing with pharyngeal structures, and principally for the purpose of medical investigations of laryngeal cancer and consequences of larynx removal. Kazi, Rhys-Evans, and Nutting (2009), for instance, are interested in tracheoesophageal speech after laryngectomy, and Magen, Kang, Tiede, and Whalen (2003) look at the effects of pharyngeal wall movement on phonation amongst patients with velo-pharyngeal difficulties. Figure 13.3 shows a sample MRI image of the pharynx area.

Pharyngeal imaging is not restricted to clinical speech cases, though, and there are several accounts dealing with issues of expansion and constriction of the pharynx in

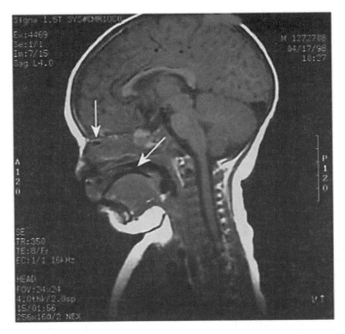

Figure 13.3 MR image (courtesy of University of Oxford Phonetics Laboratory).

normal speech as revealed by MRI. Echternach *et al.* (2010), for example, use the technique to examine lower- as well as upper-tract frequencies and transitions, including those brought about by widening of the pharynx, in adult female singers. Also working with singers, Gullaer, Walker, Badin, and Lamalle (2006) use MRI to document activity of the interpharyngeal muscles, as a biofeedback means for heightening singers' awareness of vocal technique. Further MRI-derived insights into the pharynx as resonator have been facilitated by work on pharyngeal narrowing in throaty voice quality (Laukkanen, 1996), on pharynx shape and volume in voiced and voiceless fricatives (Proctor, Shadle, and Iskarous, 2010), in vowels (Whalen *et al.*, 1999), and on articulatory movements more generally (Inoue *et al.*, 2006). Finally, Vorperian and Kent (2007) and Vorperian *et al.* (2005) use MRI to provide useful normative data on developing vocal tract length as a whole in childhood.

While MRI methods for investigating the lower vocal tract have yielded important results and insights, the technique is likely to be prohibitively expensive in the case of relatively routine investigations of velopharyngeal activity. Rowe and D'Antonio (2005), for instance, note that, as an alternative to MRI, nasendoscopic methods are also in frequent use for the clinical evaluation of velopharyngeal function. Endoscopic methods for revealing velopharyngeal function involve the insertion of a flexible tube with attached imaging device through the nostrils and rearwards into the velopharynx area. The endoscope is then linked with a computer interface and monitor enabling live viewing of pharyngeal effects by physician and patient or other user, and offering the chance to store stretches of speech for reviewing. The experimental set-up shown in Figure 13.4 is common to endoscopic techniques for viewing the pharynx and the larynx.

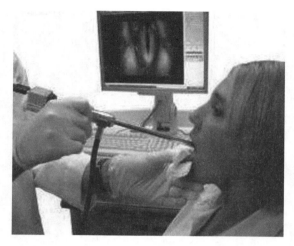

Figure 13.4 Experimental set-up for endoscopic examination (courtesy KayPENTAX).

For Section 13.5, we now shift our attention to the larynx and to the ways in which imaging techniques have advanced our understanding of laryngeal structure and function, and of the role of the larynx in voice production more generally.

> **Section Summary**
>
> • Lower-vocal tract imaging focuses on the role of the pharynx in clinical cases involving, for example, velopharyngeal inadequacy and in post-laryngectomy contexts. For non-clinical speech, images of pharyngeal widening and contraction facilitate work on phonation, voice quality, and segmental volume, with reference to a wide range of subjects.
> • MRI investigations of the lower vocal tract entail considerable expense, compared to endoscopic methods.

13.5   Larynx Imaging

Given the central function of the larynx in speech production, in terms of controlling phonation and voice quality settings, it will come as no surprise that considerable research effort has been expended on deriving detailed images of the larynx. Mirroring distinctions which we have used earlier in this chapter, the main approaches to larynx imaging are known as "direct" and "indirect." Direct methods are those in which endoscopy is used, sharing the same system referred to above for pharynx observation except that, rather than nasal insertion of a flexible tube, a rigid tube is inserted orally. Mehta and Hillman (2008) offer a helpful summary and review of recent advances in endoscopy for voice assessment, and note that increasingly high-speed capture "provide[s] new insights into relationships between vocal fold tissue motion and sound production" (p. 213).

The facility for creating stroboscopic sequences of images of the larynx tends to be bundled with endoscopic hardware and software. A useful description of stroboscopy, also known as videostroboscopy is provided by Kazi, Rhys-Evans, and Nutting (2009) and the relevant section is worth quoting at some length because it also warns against inappropriate interpretations of stroboscopic data in cases where aperiodic voices are the object of investigation:

> The frequency of the examinee's sustained voice is picked up by a microphone and ... trigger[s] the stroboscopic light source. When the vocal vibrations are periodic and the frequency of light flashes is equal to the vocal frequency, it will produce a clear still image of the vibratory cycle. When the frequency of the flashes is slightly less than the vocal fold vibration ... the illusion of slow motion is obtained. While videostroboscopy greatly enhances the diagnostic sensitivity of laryngoscopy, its interpretation is dependent upon the skill and experience of the performing clinician and, more specifically, that of the diagnostic interpreter.
>
> (Kazi, Rhys-Evans, and Nutting, 2009: 122).

In order to overcome difficulties of interpretation when presented with irregular voicing patterns, analysts tend to align stroboscopic images with a glottal waveform derived by way of a complementary but indirect system known as electrolaryngology, electrolaryngography, or electroglottography (the first two are usually abbreviated to ELG, and the third to EGG). While the terms are almost synonymous, the key difference between ELG and EGG is that ELG measurements operate along a positive scale while EGG uses a negative one (for a description of the scales involved, see Herbst, Howard, and Schlömicher-Thier, 2010).

> The underlying principle was invented by Fabre [1957] as a noninvasive method to measure variations in contact area between the two vocal folds as a function of time. A small, high-frequency current, usually having a frequency between 300 kHz and 5 mHz, is passed between two electrodes that are placed externally on each side of the thyroid cartilage at larynx level. Because human tissue is a fairly good electrical conductor compared to air, the opening and closing of the vocal folds will cause variations in the electrical impedance across the larynx, resulting in a variation in current flow between the electrodes if the voltage between them is kept constant. The variation in current flow is interpreted in terms of changes in vocal fold contact area.
>
> (Herbst, Howard, and Schölmicher-Thier, 2010: 70–1)

Overall, the set of indirect techniques for imaging speech behavior involving the application of surface electrodes in the area under investigation come under the heading of electromyography (EMG; Gentil and Moore (1997) provide an excellent introduction to the principle of EMG). The leading larynx-specific application of EMG has been developed by Fourcin and his colleagues (see, for instance, Fourcin, 2000) and takes the form of the Laryngograph, that is, the trading name for their ELG system. Since 1973, the Laryngograph team have been providing, enhancing, and expanding hardware and software for monitoring vocal fold contact. Figure 13.5 shows their core hardware component, the Laryngograph microprocessor unit with attached electrodes.

The electrodes are applied to the speaker's neck at the level of the thyroid cartilage, and the role of the system is to uncover what Fourcin refers to as the "true frequency"

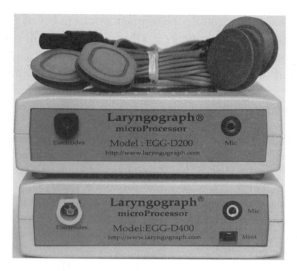

Figure 13.5 The Laryngograph microprocessor and electrodes (courtesy Laryngograph).

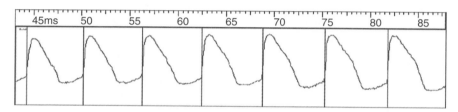

Figure 13.6 Laryngograph output showing Lx waveform (courtesy Laryngograph; Fourcin 2000).

of vocal fold vibration (p. 103). The significance of "true" here points toward the fact that, while F_0 tends to be interpreted as an average measurement and implies regularity of vocal fold vibration, there may well exist between-cycle differences in glottal opening patterns which are concealed in overall average measures. The Laryngograph, then, separates the laryngeal waveform into a number of component levels, including the average rate of vibration as it is normally understood. While Fx indicates standard average frequency measures, Lx gives a period-by-period indication of vocal fold contact patterns, and Tx refers to the timing of the individual glottal openings. Furthermore, Qx is a particular measure of voice quality, described by Fourcin *et al.* (1995) as "the ratio of the closed phase of vocal fold vibration to the total period of time between two successive epochs of excitation" (p. 103). Figure 13.6 shows a sample time-aligned Lx waveform produced by Laryngograph.

As indicated above, the combination of simultaneously derived laryngeal waveforms with stroboscopic images allow a clear view of how vocal fold contact patterns align with closure and opening phases of individual cycles. Figure 13.7 provides an eight-frame breakdown of a single glottal cycle, for modal voice, aligned with the Lx waveform, revealing a detailed pattern of vocal fold symmetry or regularity throughout the gesture. The vertical line within each frame marks the point at which the strobe was fired to produce the image. In the case of a disordered speaker, one would expect the Lx waveform to be rather less regular.

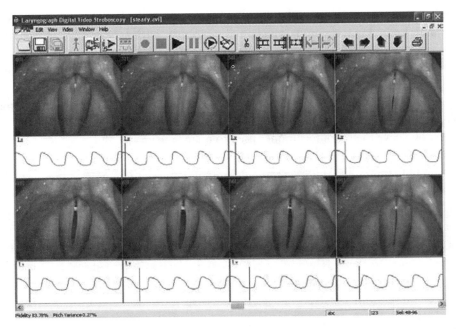

Figure 13.7 Laryngeal waveform aligned with stroboscopic images (courtesy Laryngograph).

ELG/EGG techniques have been widely applied in clinical and non-clinical work, largely for the investigation of voice quality characteristics, pitch traits, and articulatory properties in which laryngeal timing and degree of contact play an important role (see Dejonckere, 2000). Aspects of dysphonia, too, are amenable to ELG analysis. Fourcin (2000), for instance, uses laryngography to uncover phonation features in a patient whose pitch, following removal of a vocal cyst, was judged to be abnormally high. Manickam, Moore, Willard, and Slevin (2005) also offer a convenient perspective on the use of ELG in the quantification of dysphonia in the case of laryngeal cancer. Ma and Love (2010) employ EGG to evaluate age and gender effects on phonation, and Johnstone and Scherer (1999) apply EGG for examining the glottal correlates of perceived emotional speech. ELG has been used, too, in the profiling of language-specific glottal traits (Mooshammer, 2010), as well as how those traits relate to wider sociolinguistic effects within the language, including reference to the effects of smoking on laryngeal activity (Guimarães and Abberton, 2005). Orlikoff, Deliyski, Baken, and Watson (2009) consider the speed of vocal fold adduction as a component of vocal attack in voice disorders.

Since its inception, ELG has offered a particularly useful biofeedback mechanism for speakers. Most obviously, perhaps, laryngography has been used as an effective tool in enabling deaf speakers to conceptualize their output in pitch production (Fourcin, Abberton, and Ball, 1975, offer an early explanation of the beneficial effects). Visual feedback on the Lx waveform has been shown, too, to have positive effects for singers (Howard, 1995) and other professional voice users (Rossiter and Howard, 1996) who wish to alter their phonatory behavior. Nonetheless, the success of ELG displays as a remediation tool is known to be closely associated with the level of instruction, training, and practice provided for the subject (Herbst, Howard, and Schlömicher-Their, 2010, consider training effects in the case of a speaker with breathy voice, in particular). We should note, too, that while ELG techniques were originally limited to viewing laryngeal habits in the restricted contexts of sustained phonation on single vowels, the technology now routinely allows users to expand the analysis to connected speech tasks and, according to Ma and Love (2010), to produce more accurate and realistic measures. The ability to consider increasingly longer-term dynamic aspects of laryngeal behavior is facilitated by ongoing development of high speed digital imaging (HSDI) methods (see Yan, Damrose, and Bless, 2007).

We now leave the set of techniques used to image the larynx and consider available methods for charting nasal and oral airflow.

Section Summary

- Methods for imaging the larynx can be direct, involving endoscopic and stroboscopic investigation, or indirect, wherein patterns of electrical activity are gathered and presented as waveforms.
- Combinations of stroboscopic images with larynx waveforms provide a valuable perspective on aperiodic voice.
- Larynx imaging is used as a helpful method for providing visual feedback in clinical situations, and in a range of vocal therapy contexts.

13.6   Imaging Nasal and Oral Airflow

Some consequences of the velopharyngeal and laryngeal incompetence mentioned above include the inability to create, balance, and maintain appropriate levels of oral and nasal air pressure, and many of the findings point compellingly to the need for imaging approaches. A considerable body of work exists in relation to speakers' inability to distribute and manage airflow in cleft palate speech (see, for instance, Haapenen, 1992; Sell, Harding, and Grunwell, 1999), where reconstructive velo-pharyngeal surgery may be undertaken to remediate the problem. Maxillofacial surgery, too, has been shown to result in a variety of pressure-related articulation problems (Main, Kelly, and Manley, 1999), and the typical speech movement difficulties associated with the dysarthrias also affect speakers' ability to manage nasal to oral pressure ratios (Wenke, Theodoros, and Cornwell, 2010). Much non-clinical work has concentrated on relative nasality and orality distribution in a variety of languages (see, for instance, Brunnegård and Van Doorn, 2009; Lee, Brown, and Gibbon, 2008; Prathanee, Thanaviratananich, Pongjunyakul, and Rengpatanakij, 2003). The relevant literature, whatever the precise orientation, acknowledges that nasality is not easy to rate perceptually, and that opinion differs significantly among listeners regarding its effects. For example, in a study of perceptions of cleft palate speech, Brunnegård, Lohmander, and Van Doorn (2009) note that it tends to be characterized by hypernasal resonance, nasal air emission, and nasal turbulence, with hypernasality being the most marked feature and evocative of negative and problematic ratings. Nonetheless, the authors refer to problems of listener sensitivity as a key variable in judging particular components of nasality:

> The clinical experience is that mild hypernasality or audible nasal air emission and/or nasal turbulence is frequently considered acceptable and many times not even noticed by the client and their parents. However, we also occasionally encounter the opposite situation where an SLP has judged that the hypernasality or audible nasal air emission and/or nasal turbulence is mild or infrequent but the parents or the client consider it a problem.
> (Brunnegård, Lohmander, and Van Doorn, 2009: 659)

Along similar lines, Lee, Brown, and Gibbon (2008), in a study of perceptions of nasality in English and Cantonese speakers, also note the low inter-judge reliability measures for trained student listeners, and moderate reliability for non-experts. While auditory and instrumental approaches may provide important basic perceptual insights on problems of excessive or reduced nasality, therefore, imaging analyses offer finer-grain detail which enhances existing knowledge and sheds new light on velopharyngeal function.

In order to assess extent of nasal airflow, available imaging techniques typically deal with feature known as nasalance, that is, the ratio of nasal to oral sound pressure. Nasalance extraction tends to be performed using the of the KayPENTAX Nasometer, shown in Figure 13.8, a headset with an attached plate, positioned at the mouth and below the nostrils, for separating nasal and oral airflow, and microphones for recording nasal and oral components of speech. The Nasometer is linked to a computer interface, shown in Figure 13.9, which provides continual visual feedback for the speaker throughout the experimental task, thereby encouraging speakers to manipulate the features of speech which create impressions of hypernasality (see Wenke, Theodoros, and Cornwell, 2010). The system also generates figures for charting normative versus disordered measures and pre–post operative states. While the Nasometer is the system most commonly in use for clinical and research purposes, Awan, Bressman, Sader, and Horch (1999) also report on their lower-cost version in development, called NasalView. Their analysis produced statistically robust measures of nasalance but, given that substantial differences existed between NasalView- and Nasometer-derived analysis, and the need for comparability of results, the Nasometer remains the imaging method of choice.

As well as imaging techniques for assessing nasal airflow, there are also conditions in which it is important to monitor airflow more generally in terms of speed, timing, direction, volume, and stricture. Given the need to perform something of a balancing act between the features of speech which impinge upon efficient aerodynamics of speech, including F_0, the management of airflow is known to be particularly problematic for stutterers and among childhood apraxics (Sealey and Giddens, 2010), for dysarthric speakers, and in cases of auditory deprivation (Svirsky, Lane, Perkell, and Wozniak, 1992). In addition, Grolman *et al.* (2008) indicate that lower overall energy typifies airflow patterns in patients' speech following laryngectomy, and Holmberg, Oates, Dacakis, and Grant (2009) discuss airflow as a relevant variable in male-to-female transsexual voices. In relation to non-clinical cases, Koenig, Lucero, and Mencl (2008) refer to the "aerodynamic adjustments" required for /h/ voicing and devoicing, and Boucher (1999) discusses stricture force in reiterated syllables for French and English and its co-ordination with airflow timing patterns. The technique

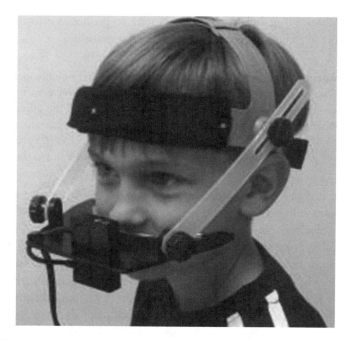

Figure 13.8 The Nasometer (courtesy KayPENTAX).

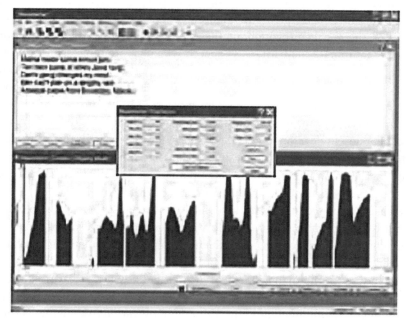

Figure 13.9 Sample screen output from the Nasometer (courtesy KayPENTAX).

employed for measuring overall patterns in airflow is known as aerometry and, while Hillman (2004) notes that the aerometry-based literature lags somewhat behind that for other imaging approaches, and that it is beleaguered by a lack of

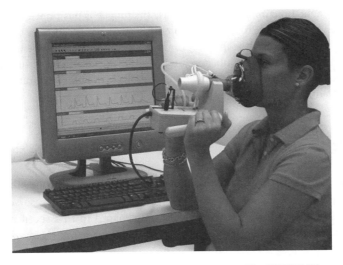

Figure 13.10 The Phonatory Aerodynamic System (courtesy KayPENTAX).

standardized procedures and small sample sizes, it is possible to identify the emerging gold-standard method in the Phonatory Aerodynamic System (PAS), as shown in Figure 13.10. As well as PAS's ability to measure sound pressure levels, recent developments to the system permit the integration of EGG data to the analytic task, all of which are displayed simultaneously on screen.

Section Summary

- Appropriate control of nasal and oral airflow and nasalance (i.e. the ratio of nasal and oral airflow) is required for normal speech production.
- The Nasometer measures nasal airflow, while the Phonatory Aerodynamic System (PAS) provides data on oral sound pressure levels.
- EGG data may be combined with information from PAS, in order to synchronize images of glottal activity with accompanying airflow patterns.

13.7   Imaging the Tongue

Given the centrality of the tongue in speech production, it will come as no surprise that attempts and developments in imaging lingual activity constitute a major ongoing research effort. One of the key contributors to tongue imaging (Stone, 2005) explains the relationship of the tongue to other areas in the vocal tract, and its importance for a range of speech and non-speech behaviors. She indicates the particular difficulties involved in tongue imaging as follows:

Measuring tongue function is difficult because the tongue is positioned deep within the oral cavity and inaccessible to most instruments. To directly measure the tongue requires a device to be inserted into the mouth. Any transducer used within the mouth must be unaffected by temperature or moisture, and should not disturb the tongue's motion. This last requirement is so problematical that very little tongue measurement was done until the advent of indirect imaging techniques.

(Stone, 2005: 5)

13.7.1   Palatography

The methods for measuring tongue function referred to by Stone, that is, those in which a device is inserted into the oral cavity, in addition to those which use non-invasive "indirect" imaging methods, will be discussed in this section. We begin by looking at work which charts linguo-palatal contact, and move on to consider ultrasound techniques.

Methods for imaging tongue–palate contact come under the general category of "palatography" and have been in use, in various stages of sophistication, for some time and with varying emphases. One major distinction amongst palatographic approaches is whether they provide a single image of a given articulatory gesture, or a series of images indicating linguo-palatal changes over time; the methods are known, respectively, as static or dynamic palatography. The static approach is described by Anderson (2008):

Static palatography essentially involves painting a speaker's tongue or palate with a nontoxic marking material, after which the speaker utters a word containing the speech sound in question. During the articulation, marking material is transferred to the opposite articulator. This contact pattern is videotaped and the speaker then rinses his or her mouth with water.

(Anderson, 2008: 2)

Dynamic palatography, on the other hand, involves monitoring of tongue movement by way of electrodes embedded in a plastic custom-made palate, hence the more usual term for dynamic palatography is electropalatography (EPG), with "palatometry" also used. It is tempting to infer that EPG is the obvious and natural imaging method, compared to the static method, given the former's ability to trace aspects of tongue dynamics. Nonetheless, one should note that static palatography remains a cost-effective alternative and may be the only practical system available in the fieldwork context, as indicated by Anderson. Most clinical and research work, however, uses an EPG system whose origins lie in the late 1970s and 1980s (see, for instance, Hardcastle, 1972; Hardcastle *et al.*, 1989) and which is in continual development. The plastic palate, or pseudo-palate, is cast from a mould, usually constructed in a dental laboratory, of the upper teeth and palate, with the location of electrodes on the pseudo-palate corresponding to key areas of linguo-palatal activity, namely the upper front teeth, the alveolar/postal-veolar region, and palatal and velar regions. In the UK and USA, two EPG systems are dominant in the research and SLT contexts. For the UK, the system developed in Reading University and Queen Margaret College, now in its third iteration, is

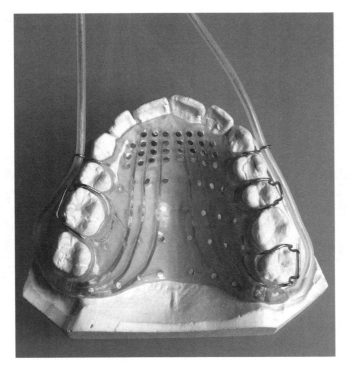

Figure 13.11 The Articulate Instruments EPG pseudo-palate. (Courtesy of Articulate Instruments Ltd)

the main one. The so-called "Reading" palate, now produced by Articulate Instruments Ltd and shown in Figure 13.11, contains 62 electrodes and is held in place in the mouth by clips. In the USA, KayPENTAX were early market leaders, with their production of a fully plastic system which enclosed the teeth and registered contact patterns by way of 96 electrodes. While the company no longer produces pseudo-palates, they continue to provide a palatometer database, containing normative EPG traces for any point selected in the sample. Figure 13.12 illustrates a sample palatometer screen in which /t/ is chosen as the segment for viewing.

As portions of the tongue touch sections of the palate, the electrodes in that section are fired and the activation patterns are registered by the linked computer in terms of a stylized palate arrangement. Sample stylized patterns for /t/ and /s/ are illustrated in Figure 13.13.

In the USA, the LogoMetrix system is in frequent use. It operates with 118 electrodes which are glued to the pseudo-palate rather than embedded in it (see, for instance, Dromey and Sanders, 2009). Variants on the main EPG methods include a battery-powered portable training system which operates as a self-contained device without the need for a computer, and is typically used where speech and language therapists are required to conduct home visits. A Japanese variant on EPG also exists (see Suzuki *et al.*, 1995), known as the Rion system and consisting of 63 electrodes in a palate which is not custom-made. While the cost of the Rion system is considerably

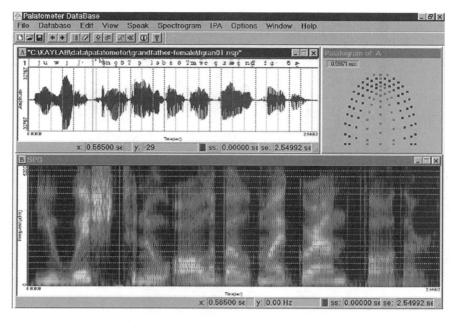

Figure 13.12 The Palatometer database, showing /t/ (courtesy KayPENTAX).

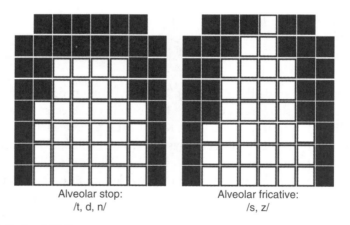

Figure 13.13 Stylized EPG patterns.

lower than that entailed by other devices, the disadvantage is that important speaker-specific palatal architecture affecting patterns of lingual contact may be missed. Given the range of structural variation that exists in EPG systems, too, it is important to be cautious regarding comparability of results produced by different systems. Suzuki *et al.*'s (1995) description of the design aspects of the Rion system includes a useful caveat:

> In the Reading system, electrodes are placed according to anatomical landmarks to enable comparisons of contact patterns to be made between different speakers. The Japanese system uses a set of standard templates with electrodes fixed in place and a

best fit for an individual palate is chosen. One consequence is that often there is a considerable gap between the most posterior electrodes and the junction between the hard and soft palates. The different criteria for electrode placement in the two systems needs to be taken into account when comparing tongue contact patterns for the Japanese and British subjects.

(Suzuki et al., 1995: 240)

EPG studies are undertaken for a variety of purposes, with the majority oriented towards cleft palate speech and functional articulation disorders. Howard (1998), for instance, looks at speech production in a child with Pierre Robin Sequence (PRS), a condition in which cleft palate and tongue posture pose problems. Following surgery, Howard notes that the speech of individuals with PRS varies depending on whether a tracheostomy has been performed and, for the child in her study who did indeed undergo a tracheostomy, EPG confirms problems in "achieving specific articulatory movements, particularly those involving the tongue" (p. 159). The child in question exhibited particular issues with place and manner of articulation, mostly involving segments with tongue tip and blade articulations; /s/ and /ʃ/, for instance, were typically realized palatals or velars. Howard uses EPG, therefore, to support the statement that the segments produced indicate "specific anatomical or neuromuscular lingual impairment" (p. 163). Howard and Varley (1995) use EPG to examine tip/blade and tongue body systems and confirm that, for the speaker under investigation, the secondary importance of the latter indicates absence of precise articulatory control. The value of EPG for uncovering and treating characteristics of stuttering behavior has been confirmed by Wood (1995), for example, who looked at contact patterns and dynamics for alveolar stops and fricatives and found that stutterers increased their tongue–palate contact for alveolar stops. The patterns uncovered by EPG investigation, therefore are twofold: they provide information on articulatory configurations, but also enable a wider-reaching view of overall muscular tension in the speech system. In the case of a functional articulation problem, Gibbon and Hardcastle (1995) note distortions including excessive contact between the tongue and the palate for /s/ and lateralized versions of /ʃ/ and /tʃ/.

The biofeedback role provided by EPG is crucial in therapeutic contexts, and has met with considerable success (see Gibbon and Paterson, 2006). For Down syndrome (DS) children, Cleland *et al.* (2009) highlight the particular issue of relatively small oral cavity characteristic of DS, and larger relative space occupied by the tongue, combined with motor control problems. For Cleland *et al.* (2009) and Gibbon, McNeill, Wood, and Watson (2003), therapy sessions in which DS speakers viewed the relevant palatograms resulted in significant improvement in articulation. In the case of hearing loss, too, Pratt (2007) demonstrates the successful effect of EPG feedback on the integration of labial sounds into the subject's system. Other positive results for EPG have been reported by Hartelius, Theodoros, and Murdoch (2005) for dysarthria following brain injury.

For monitoring production in developmental and acquired conditions, such as hearing impairment, glossectomy cases, and neurological problems, EPG has also proved fruitful (for an overview of applications, including non-clinical cross-linguistic and articulatory studies, see Gibbon, 1996; Gibbon *et al.*, 1998, and Suzuki *et al.*, 1995). It is also important to note that a number of EPG studies have enabled investigators to uncover patterns which had been previously unsuspected. Ball and Lowry (2001) note, for instance, the role of EPG images in revealing patterns not revealed in an impressionistic approach, "simply because some articulatory gestures may be 'hidden' (or overlaid) by others, and because the same (or very similar) acoustic patterns may be produced by different configurations of the vocal organs" (p. 50) and Gibbon and Hardcastle (1995) note that, while some of the sounds produced by their subjects are perceptually similar, EPG reveals a range of distortions, including /t/ retraction in one speaker.

As indicated above, EPG affords numerous insights into lingual activity, but there are some areas in which it is appropriate to problematize the technique. For example, while an EPG frame in a given sequence gives an indication of contact patterns at that time, and the sequence itself provides an overview of movement from one frame to the next, there can be no indication of the precise inter-frame dynamics. Furthermore, it is not possible to discern exactly which portion of the tongue is making contact during a given gesture (see Kelly, Main, Manley, and McLean, 2000), and what portions may be redundant or involved in a secondary capacity. In other words, EPG may occasionally mask elements whose details are required for informing diagnosis and therapy. Occasionally, the contact patterns as revealed by EPG may be close to non-existent, so that its clinical role is less than immediately useful. MorganBarry's (1995) study of a child with extreme dysarthria provides an EPG trace for "cat" in which there is almost complete absence of contact, and she concludes that lingual issues resulting from velopharyngeal problems are less amenable to productive EPG work. Obviously, too, one should not expect detailed pictures of linguo-palatal contact from areas not covered by electrodes, with velar regions, for example, being difficult to track (see Gibbon *et al.*, 2003). Other problematic issue affecting EPG use are the gagging reflex sometimes brought about by the palate insertion or sustained use (Pratt; 2007; Wrench, 2007), and issues of generalizability (Pratt, 2007). For these reasons, speech pathologists often have recourse to methods which enable complementary analyses of lingual activity.

Section Summary

- One type of lingual imaging consists of electropalatography (EPG), allowing patterns of tongue–palate contact to be viewed. The dominant EPG system requires a "pseudo-palate" containing electrodes which are activated when relevant areas are touched by the tongue. The highlighted patterns are then viewed on-screen.
- EPG sometimes permits hidden linguo-palatal patterns to be revealed, but there are aspects of articulation which cannot be revealed by EPG, including information on the precise area of the tongue involved.

13.7.2   *Lingual Kinematics: EMA and Ultrasound*

The section on EPG above indicates the range of work which has been undertaken in order to chart aspects of lingual articulations in clinical and non-clinical speech varieties. While EPG provides crucial information on the areas of the tongue involved in the production of speech sounds, on linguo-palatal contact and on the tongue's configuration as it progresses through connected speech, other important aspects are not amenable to EPG investigation. Horn *et al.* (1999c) indicate the need for an imaging method which allows "a direct and reproducible representation of any path of movement over a period of time with defined measuring points" (p. 351). Combined information on path and speed of movement is known as kinematics (for a detailed description of lingual kinematics, see Bartle-Meyer, Goozee, and Murdoch, 2009). In particular, we may need to know about the precise nature of interactions between the tongue and other articulators, such as the jaw. The technique which allows investigators to track movement as it occurs simultaneously inside and outside the vocal tract is known as electromagnetic articulography (EMA) or electromagnetic midsagittal articulography (EMMA), with both terms referring to a procedure which involving a tracking mechanism consisting of electromagnetic transmitter and receiver coils. While the methods are similar, "EMMA" contains a direct reference to the location of the coils, that is, along the midsagittal plane. Typically in past studies, three transmitter coils were used, positioned on a helmet worn by the speaker, in front of the forehead, the jaw, and neck. Up to five detector coils were placed and fixed with surgical glue on the relevant articulators, usually the upper and lower lips, mandible, tongue tip, and tongue dorsum. For these older EMA variants, the coils were wired to the recording and monitoring unit of the device, but current technology forgoes the helmet and coils, and uses sensors which transmit ultrasonically to the receiving processor. Further EMA developments include the facility for measuring movement in three dimensions, in terms not just of two interacting articulators, but including the angle of that interaction. Horn *et al.* (1999a and 1999b), for instance, used EMA to look at tongue malfunction in the case of tongue thrust and in swallowing along the dimensions of "distances, angles and courses of time intervals" (1999b: 357). Schiller, van Lieshout, Meyer, and Levelt (1999), similarly, used displacement and velocity data in his consideration of intervocalic consonant realization relative to within-syllable location. EMA images and measurements help inform decisions on whether, for example, a given speech disorder is the result of anatomic structure defects or caused by a developmental issue. Figure 13.14 shows the EMA unit developed by Carstens, in which the speaker under investigation can move freely and wirelessly within the sensor unit.

An EMA-derived kinematic profile for repetitions of /ba/, /bi/, and /bu/ is shown in Figure 13.15, with one sensor on the tongue, two at the lower jaw and one at the lower lip.

For an analysis which combines EPG and EMA in order to highlight articulatory detail, see Moen and Simonsen (2007), for example.

Figure 13.14 The EMA unit (courtesy Carsten).

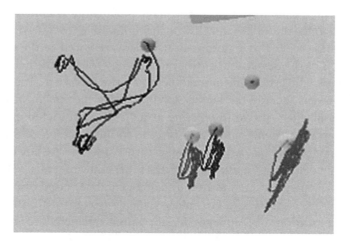

Figure 13.15 Kinematic profile, via EMA (courtesy Carsten).

Also used for imaging tongue kinematics is ultrasound, frequently known as sonography. Ultrasound images are generated by a probe placed under the chin which projects rays up to the tongue (see Stone, 2005). Unlike EMA methods, wherein a limited number of sensors track movement relative to other articulators, ultrasound measures soft-tissue activity throughout the tongue, yielding a comprehensive view of lingual movement, extending to the root, and from a

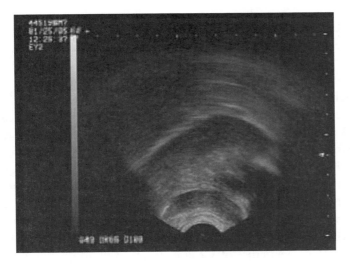

Figure 13.16 Ultrasound image of the tongue (courtesy Tim Bressmann).

number of planes or viewing angles. Figure 13.16 shows an ultrasound image of the tongue.

Ultrasound constitutes a less expensive alternative to EMA, and its reliability is proven (see Hardin and Frisch, 2005). For patients with partial glossectomies, it offers the facility for registering movement and velocity in available portions of the tongue and, according to Rastadmehr *et al.* (2008) the technique can help "develop a better under-standing of the biomechanical effects of a lingual resection and reconstruction" (p. 724). It is also a non-invasive method for examining swallowing disorders (Sonies, Chi-Fishman, and Miller, 1991) and sucking mechanisms in babies (Weber and Woolridge, 2008). As well as being an analytic and diagnostic tool, ultrasound has been shown to be an effective in offering visual feedback for speech therapeutic ends (Modha, Bernhardt, Church, and Bacsfalvi, 2008). It is worth noting, too, that Stone and Lundberg (1996) have developed an imaging technique which aligns ultrasound with EPG traces, thereby combining perspectives on detailed lingual configurations and contact patterns.

Section Summary

- Electromagnetic articulography (EMA/EMMA) allows lingual movement to be tracked precisely in relation to other articulators.
- Ultrasound imaging techniques permit a detailed view of soft-tissue activity in all areas of the tongue.
- EMA and ultrasound allow analysts to produce images of articulatory movement and speed of movement.

13.8   Multipurpose Analysis: The Visi-Pitch

While most of the imaging systems discussed here are tailor-made for investigating specific speech tasks and specific areas in the speech production chain, there is one imaging device which has achieved prominence because of its applicability for a range of tasks. The Visi-Pitch, produced by KayPENTAX, allows the analysis of a range of parameters such as phonation, pitch, intensity, and timing features. Nonetheless, it tends to be used primarily for biofeedback purposes, as a provider of real-time visual and auditory feedback, whereby the user can map his or her own patterns against stored examples or those of the therapist. Loeb and Allen (1993), for instance, report on use of Visi-Pitch for modeling intonation contours, and a sample intonation modeling screen is shown in Figure 13.17.

The highly interactive nature of VisiPitch is achieved, too, by on-screen games in which particular movements required for the game are controlled by vocal means. The manufacturers note that it has applications in a range of voice disorders, motor speech problems, articulation training, and professional use of voice. In the research context, it has been used profitably for the investigation of diadochokinesis, that is, the ability to produce alternating syllables at appropriate speeds, by Padovani, Gielow, and Behlau (2009) and Prathanee *et al.* (2003), amongst others.

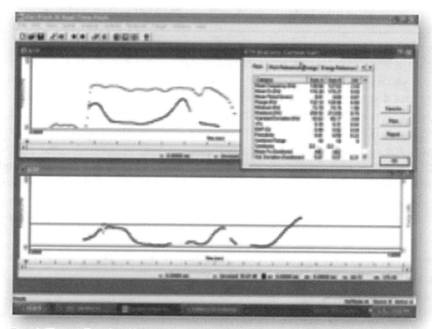

Real-Time Pitch allows clients to monitor pitch and amplitude as they speak. Speech productions can be compared both graphically (using split screen) and quantitatively.

Figure 13.17 Visi-Pitch trace for modeling intonation contours (courtesy KayPENTAX).

13.9   Conclusion

This chapter has provided an overview of the main imaging techniques currently in use for investigating speech production characteristics, in a variety of clinical and non-clinical contexts. Many of the references cited in the course of this chapter will equip researchers with excellent breadth and understanding of relevant imaging methods, and the Suggestions for Further Research section (13.10) offers suggestions for acquiring further information on the techniques already introduced, and advice on pursuing areas not discussed in detail here.

13.10   Resources

- Baken and Orlikoff's (2000) chapter on speech movements provides a comprehensive and detailed account of a wide range of imaging techniques.
- One of the most comprehensive reviews of fMRI techniques in use up to the end of the twentieth century and their application is provided by Kent (1998). George, Vikingstad, Silbergleit, and Cao (2007) also offer a useful account of brain imaging.
- For a brain imaging account which includes PET techniques, in addition to the MRI approaches highlighted here, see Narayana *et al.* (2010).
- A technical overview of MRI systems is available at http://www.toshiba-medical. eu/en/Our-Product-Range/MRI/Technologies/.
- For a discussion of X-ray techniques, touched upon only briefly here, see Ball and Gröne (1997).
- The application of EMG approaches to speech recognition contexts is illustrated by Denby *et al.* (2010).
- In order to develop familiarity with endoscopic techniques for imaging the pharynx, larynx and velopharynx, a DVD intended for medics and SLTs is likely to be invaluable (Hapner, 2010). Along similar lines, Sapienza and Ruddy's (2009) DVD provides splendid images using many of the techniques discussed here on examinations, with particular reference to voice disorders. High-quality endoscope images are also available in Sataloff, Hawkshaw, and Eller (2007).
- McLeod and Singh (2009a, 2009b) offer static images of speech sounds, derived from ultrasound, EPG, front-of mouth photographs and schematic drawings of the midsagittal section. Their aim is to facilitate clinicians' and patients' understanding of all relevant components of segments, and to provide a complement to students' impressionistic phonetic analysis.

References

Anderson, V. B. (2008). Static palatography for language fieldwork. *Language Documentation and Conservation*, 2(1), 1–27.

Awan, S., Bressman, T., Sader, R. and Horch, H. (1999). Measures of RMS nasalance using NasalView in patients undergoing secondary osteoplasty. In B. Maassen and P. Groenen (eds), *Pathologies of Speech and Language*. London: Whurr, pp. 333–341.

Baer, T., Gore, J. C., Boyce, S., and Nye, P. W. (1987). Application of MRI to the analysis of speech production. *Magnetic Resonance Imaging*, 5(1) 1–7.

Baken, R. J. and Orlikoff, R. F. (2000). *Clinical Measurement of Speech and Voice*, 2nd edn. San Diego: Singular.

Ball, M. J. and Gröne, B. (1997). Imaging techniques. In M. J. Ball and C. Code (eds), *Instrumental Clinical Phonetics*. London: Whurr, pp. 194–227.

Ball, M. J. and Lowry, O. (2001). *Methods in Clinical Phonetics*. London: Whurr.

Bartle-Meyer, C. J., Goozee, J. V., and Murdoch, B. E. (2009). Kinematic investigation of lingual movement in words of increasing length in acquired apraxia of speech. *Clinical Linguistics and Phonetics*, 23(2), 93–121.

Bell, A. M. (1867). *Visible Speech*. London: Simpkin, Marshall and Co.

Blank, S. C., Scott, S. K., Murphy, K. *et al.* (2002). Speech production: Wernicke, Broca and beyond. *Brain*, 125, 1829–1838.

Bolger, D. J., Hornickel, J., Cone, N. E. *et al.* (2008). Neural correlates of orthographic and phonological consistency effects in children. *Human Brain Mapping*, 29, 1416–1429.

Boucher, V. (1999). Effects of stricture-force changes on the coordination of oral and glottal aperture motions in normal speech. In B. Maassen and P. Groenen (eds), *Pathologies of Speech and Language*. London: Whurr, pp. 292–298.

Broca, P. (1861). Perte de la parole. Ramolissement chronique et destructions partielle du lobe antérior gauche du cerveau. *Bulletin de la Société d'Anthropologie*, 2, 235–238.

Brunnegård, K., Lohmander, A., and Van Doorn, J. (2009). Untrained listeners' ratings of speech disorders in a group with cleft palate: a comparison with speech and language pathologists' ratings. *International Journal of Language and Communication Disorders*, 44(5), 656–674.

Brunnegård, K. and Van Doorn, J. (2009).Normative data on nasalance scores for Swedish as measured on the Nasometer: influence of dialect, gender, and age. *Clinical Linguistics and Phonetics*, 23(1), 58–69.

Cleland, J., Timmins, C., Wood, S. W. *et al.* (2009). Electropalatographic therapy for children and young people with Down's syndrome. *Clinical Linguistics and Phonetics*, 23(12), 926–939.

Dejonckere, P. H. (2000). Perceptual and laboratory assessment of dysphonia. *Otolaryngologic Clinics of North America*, 334, 731–750.

Denby, B., Schultz, T., Honda, K. *et al.* (2010). Silent speech interfaces. *Speech Communication*, 52, 270–287.

De Nil, L. F., Beal, D. S., Lafaille, S. J. *et al.* (2008). The effects of simulated stuttering and prolonged speech on neural activation patterns of stuttering and nonstuttering speakers. *Brain and Language*, 107, 114–123.

De Nil, L. F., Sasisekaran, J., Pascal, H. H. M., and Van Lieshout, P. S. (2005). Speech disfluencies in individuals with Tourette syndrome. *Journal of Psychosomatic Research*, 58, 97–102.

Dromey, C. and Sanders, M. (2009). Intra-speaker variability in palatometric measures of consonant articulation. *Journal of Communication Disorders*, 42, 397–407.

Echternach, M., Sundberg, J., Arndt, S. *et al.* (2010). Vocal tract in female registers – a dynamic real-time MRI study. *Journal of Voice*, 24(2), 133–139.

Engwall, O. (2002). Tongue talking: studies in intraoral speech synthesis. Doctoral dissertation, Stockholm University.

Fiez, J. A. (2001). Neuroimaging studies of speech: an overview of techniques and methodological approaches. *Journal of Communication Disorders*, 34, 445–454.

Formisamo, E., De Martino, F., Bonte, M., and Goebel, R. (2008). "Who" is saying "what"? Brain-based decoding of human voice and speech. *Science*, 322(5903), 970–973.

Fourcin, A. (2000). Voice quality and electrolaryngography. In R. D. Kent and M. J. Ball (eds), *Voice Quality Measurement*. San Diego, CA: Singular Publishing, pp. 285–306.

Fourcin, A., Abberton, E., and Ball, V. (1975). Voice and intonation – analysis, presentation and training. In Ben A. G. Elsendoorn, Frans Coninx, and Annelies Brekelmans (eds), *Interactive Learning Technology for the Deaf*. Berlin: Springer-Verlag, 1993.

Fourcin, A., Abberton, E., Miller, D., and Howells, D. (1995). Laryngography. *European Journal of Disorders of Communication*, 30, 101–115.

Gentil, M. and Moore, W. H. (1997). Electromyography. In M. J. Ball and C. Code (eds), *Instrumental Clinical Phonetics*. London: Whurr, pp. 30–37.

George, K. P., Vikingstad, E., Silbergleit, R., and Cao, Y. (2007). Brain imaging in acquired language disorders. In A. F. Johnson and H. B. Jacobson (eds), *Medical Speech-Language Pathology: A Practitioner's Guide*. New York: Thieme Medical, pp. 19–52.

Gibbon. F. (1996). Bibliography of electropalatographic (EPG) studies in English (1957–2006). Edinburgh: Speech and Hearing Sciences, Queen Margaret University College.

Gibbon, F. and Hardcastle, B. (1995). A study of obstruent sounds in school-age children with speech disorders using electropalatography. *European Journal of Disorders of Communication*, 30, 213–225.

Gibbon, F. and Paterson, L. (2006). Therapy outcomes in Scotland. A survey of speech and language therapists' views on electropalatography. *Child Language Teaching and Therapy*, 22(3), 275–292.

Gibbon F., McNeill, A. M., Wood, S. E., and Watson, J. M. (2003). Changes in linguapalatal contact patterns during therapy for velar fronting in a 10-year-old with Down's syndrome. *International Journal of Language and Communication Disorders*, 38(1), 47–64.

Gibbon, F., Whitehill, T., Hardcastle, W. J. *et al.* (1998). Cross-language (Cantonese/English) study of articulation error patterns in cleft palate speech using EPG. In W. Ziegler and K. Deger (eds), *Clinical Phonetics and Linguistics*. London: Whurr, pp. 167–178.

Gitelman, D. R., Nobre, A. C., Sonty, S. *et al.* (2005). Language network specializations: an analysis with parallel task designs and functional magnetic resonance imaging. *NeuroImage*, 26, 975–985.

Grolman, W., Eerenstein, S. E., Tange, R. A. *et al.* (2008). Vocal efficiency in tracheoesophageal phonation. *Auris Nasus Larynx*, 35, 83–88.

Guenther, F. H. (2008). Neuroimaging of normal speech production. In R. J. Ingram (ed.), *Neuroimaging in Communication Sciences and Disorders*. San Diego, CA: Plural Publishing, pp. 1–51.

Guimarães, I. and Abberton, E. (2005). Fundamental frequency in speakers of Portuguese for different voice samples. *Journal of Voice*, 19(4), 592–606.

Gullaer, I., Walker, R., Badin, P., and Lamalle, L. (2006). Image, imagination, and reality: on effectiveness of introductory work with vocalists. *Logopedics, Phoniatrics, Vocology*, 31(2), 89–96.

Haapanen, M. L. (1992). Nasalance scores in patients with a modified Honig velopharyngeal flap before and after operation. *Scandinavian Journal of Plastic and Reconstructive and Hand Surgery*, 26, 301–305.

Hapner, E. (2010). *Training and Interpretation of FEES*. San Diego, CA: Plural Publishing, DVD.

Hardcastle, W. J. (1972). The use of electropalatography in phonetic research. *Phonetica*, 25, 197–215.

Hardcastle, W. J., Jones, W., Knight, C. *et al.* (1989). New developments in electropalatography: a state-of-the-art report. *Clinical Linguistics and Phonetics*, 3, 1–38.

Hardin, S. M. and Frisch, S. A. (2005). Reliability of measurements from ultrasound images. *Journal of the Acoustical Society of America*, 118(3), 2023.

Hartelius, L., Theodoros, D., and Murdoch, B. (2005). Use of electropalatography in the treatment of disordered articulation following traumatic brain injury: a case study. *Journal of Medical Speech – Language Pathology*, 13(3), 189–204.

Herbst, C. T., Howard, D., and Schlömicher-Thier, J. (2010). Using electroglottographic real-time feedback to control posterior glottal adduction during phonation. *Journal of Voice*, 24(1), 72–85.

Hillman, R. E. (2004). Aerodynamic assessment of vocal function. In R. D. Kent (ed.), *The MIT Encyclopedia of Communication Disorders*. Cambridge, MA: MIT Press, pp. 7–9.

Holmberg, E. B., Oates, J., Dacakis, G., and Grant, C. (2009). Phonetograms, aerodynamic measurements, self-evaluations, and auditory perceptual ratings of male-to-female transsexual voice. *Journal of Voice*, 24, 511–522.

Horn, H., Göz, G., Bacher, M. *et al.* (1999a). Variability of tongue movement during normal swallowing and tongue-thrust. In B. Maassen and P. Groenen (eds), *Pathologies of Speech and Language*. London: Whurr, pp. 360–364.

Horn, H., Göz, G., Bacher, M. *et al.* (1999b). Variability of tongue movement during speaking sequences in diagnosis of tongue thrust. In B. Maassen and P. Groenen (eds), *Pathologies of Speech and Language*. London: Whurr, pp. 355–359.

Horn, H., Scholl, T., Ackermann, H. *et al.* (1999c). Registration of lip and tongue movement with a new electromagnetic articulography instrument. In B. Maassen and P. Groenen (eds), *Pathologies of Speech and Language*. London: Whurr, pp. 351–354.

Howard, D. M. (1995). Variation of electrolaryngographically derived closed quotient for trained and untrained adult female singers. *Journal of Voice*, 9(2), 163–172.

Howard, S. (1998). A perceptual and electropalatographic case study of Pierre Robin Sequence. In W. Ziegler and K. Deger (eds), *Clinical Phonetics and Linguistics*. London: Whurr, pp. 157–164.

Howard, S. and Varley, R. (1995). Using electropalatography to treat severe acquired apraxia of speech. *European Journal of Disorders of Communication*, 30(2), 246–255.

Ingham, R. J., Cykowski, M., Ingham, J. C., and Fox, P. T. (2008). Neuroimaging contributions in developmental stuttering theory and treatment. In R. J. Ingham (ed.), *Neuroimaging in Communication Sciences and Disorders*. San Diego, CA: Plural Publishing, pp. 53–85.

Inoue, M. S., Ono, T., Honda, E. *et al.* (2006). Application of magnetic resonance imaging movie to assess articulatory movement. *Orthodontics and Craniofacial Research*, 9, 157–162.

Jiang, J. (2008). *Vocal Fold Dynamics: Phonation Mechanism, Aerodynamics, Impact Stress and Mucosal Wave*. San Diego, CA: Plural Publishing, DVD/ CD-ROM.

Johnstone, T., and Scherer, K. R. (1999). The effects of emotions on voice quality. In J. Ohala, Y. Hasegawa, M. Ohala *et al.* (eds), *Proceedings of the XIVth International Congress of Phonetic Sciences, San Francisco*. Berkeley, CA: Department of Linguistics, University of California at Berkeley, pp. 2029–2032.

Kazi, R., Kanagalingam, J., Venkitaraman, R. *et al.* (2009). Electroglottographic and perceptual evaluation of tracheoesophageal speech. *Journal of Voice*, 23(2), 247–254.

Kazi, R., Rhys-Evans, P., and Nutting, C. M. (2009). The great debate: stroboscopy vs. high-speed imaging for assessment of alaryngeal phonation. *Journal of Cancer Research and Therapeutics*, 5, 121–123.

Kelly, S., Main, A., Manley, G., and McLean, C. (2000). Electropalatography and the Linguagraph system. *Medical Engineering and Physics*, 22, 47–58.

Kent, R. D. (1998). Neuroimaging studies of brain activation for language, with an emphasis on functional magnetic resonance imaging: a review. *Folia Phoniatrica et Logopaedica*, 50(6), 291–304.

Koenig, L. L., Lucero, J. C., and Mencl, W. E. (2008). Laryngeal and aerodynamic adjustments for voicing versus devoicing of /h/: a within-speaker study. *Journal of Voice*, 22(6), 709–20.

Laukkanen, A. (1996). Physical variations related to stress and emotional state: a preliminary study. *Journal of Phonetics*, 24, 313–335.

Lee, A., Brown, S., and Gibbon, F. E. (2008). Effect of listeners' linguistic background on perceptual judgements of hypernasality. *International Journal of Language and Communication Disorders*, 43(5), 487–498.

Loeb, D. F and Allen, G. D. (1993). Preschoolers' imitation of intonation contours. *Journal of Speech and Hearing Research*, 36, 4–13.

Liu, H., Hu, Z., Guo, T., and Peng, D. (2010). Speaking words in two languages with one brain: neural overlap and dissociation. *Brain Research*, 1316, 75–82.

Luzzi, S., Viticchi, G., Piccirilli, M. *et al.* (2008). Foreign accent syndrome as the initial sign of primary progressive aphasia. *Journal of Neurology, Neurosurgery and Psychiatry*, 79, 79–81.

Ma, E. P. and Love, A. L. (2010). Electroglottographic evaluation of age and gender effects during sustained phonation and connected speech. *Journal of Voice*, 24(2), 146–152.

McAuliffe, M. J. and Cornwell, P. L. (2008). Intervention for lateral /s/ using electropalatography (EPG) biofeedback and an intensive motor learning approach: a case report. *International Journal of Language and Communication Disorders*, 43(2), 219–229.

McLeod, S. and Singh, S. (2008a). *Seeing Speech: A Quick Guide to Speech Sounds*. San Diego, CA: Plural Publishing.

McLeod, S. and Singh, S. (2008b). *Speech Sounds: A Pictorial Guide to Typical and Atypical Speech*. San Diego, CA: Plural Publishing.

Magen, H. S., Kang, A. M., Tiede, M. K., and Whalen, D. H. (2003). Posterior pharyngeal wall position in the production of speech. *Journal of Speech, Language and Hearing Research*, 46(1), 241–251.

Main, A., Kelly, S., and Manley, G. (1999). Articulation difficulty following maxillofacial surgery: a single case study. In B. Maassen and P. Groenen (eds), *Pathologies of Speech and Language*. London: Whurr, pp. 299–306.

Manickam, K., Moore, C., Willard, T., and Slevin, N. (2005). Quantifying aberrant phonation using approximate entropy in electrolaryngography. *Speech Communication*, 47, 312–321.

Mehta, D. D. and Hillman, R. E. (2008). Voice assessment: updates on perceptual, acoustic, aerodynamic and endoscopic imaging methods. *Current Opinion in Otolaryngology and Head and Neck Surgery*, 16, 211–215.

Modha, G., Bernhardt, B. M., Church, R., and P. Bacsfalvi (2008). Case study using ultrasound to treat /ɹ/. *International Journal of Language and Communication Disorders*, 43(3), 323–329.

Moen, I. and Simonsen, H. G. (2007). The combined use of EPG and EMA in articulatory descriptions. *International Journal of Speech-Language Pathology*, 9(1), 120–127.

Mooshammer, C. (2010). Acoustic and laryngographic measures of the laryngeal reflexes of linguistic prominence and vocal effort in German. *Journal of the Acoustic Society of America*, 127(2), 1047–1058.

Morgan, A. T. and Vogel, A. P. (2008). Intervention for childhood apraxia of speech. *Cochrane Database of Systematic Reviews*, issue 3. DOI: 10.1002/14651858.CD006278.pub2.

MorganBarry, R. A. (1995). EPG treatment of a child with the Worster–Drought syndrome. *European Journal of Disorders of Communication*, 30, 256–263.

Narayana, S., Fox, P. T., Zhang, W. *et al.* (2010). Neural correlates of efficacy of voice therapy in Parkinson's disease identified by performance-correlation analysis. *Human Brain Mapping*, 31, 222–236.

Orlikoff, R. F., Deliyski, D. D., Baken, R. J., and Watson, B. C. (2009). Validation of a glotto-graphic measure of vocal attack. *Journal of Voice*, 23(2), 164–168.

Padovani, M., Gielow, I., and Behlau, M. (2009). Phonarticulatory diadochokinesis in young and elderly individuals. *Arqivos de Neuro-psiquiatria*, 67(1), 58–61.

Posner, M. I., Petersen, S. E., Fox, P. T., and Raichle, M. E. (1988). Localization of cognitive operations in the human brain. *Science*, 240, 1627–1631.

Prathanee, B., Thanaviratananich, S., Pongjunyakul, A., and Rengpatanakij, K. (2003). Nasalance scores for speech in normal Thai children. *Scandinavian Journal of Plastic and Reconstructive and Hand Surgery*, 37, 351–355.

Pratt, S. R. (2007). Using electropalatographic feedback to treat the speech of a child with severe-to-profound hearing loss. *Journal of Speech-Language Pathology and Applied Behavior Analysis*, 2, 213–237.

Proctor, M. I., Shadle, C. H., and Iskarous, K. (2010). Pharyngeal articulation in the produc-tion of voiced and voiceless fricatives. *Journal of the Acoustical Society of America*, 127(3), 1507–1518.

Ramage, A. E., Kiran, S., and Robin, D. A. (2008). Has imaging advanced the science in aphasiology? A critical review of neuroimaging research in acquired adult language dis-orders. In R. J. Ingham (ed.), *Neuroimaging in Communication Sciences and Disorders*. San Diego, CA: Plural Publishing, pp. 155–192.

Rastadmehr, O., Bressmann, T., Smyth, R. and Irish, J. C. (2008). Increased midsagittal tongue velocity as indication of articulatory compensation in patients with lateral partial glos-sectomies. *Head and Neck*, 30(6), 718–726.

Rossiter, D. and Howard, D. M. (1996). ALBERT: a real-time visual feedback computer tool for professional vocal development. *Journal of Voice*, 10(4), 321–336.

Rowe, M. R. and, D'Antonio, L. L. (2005). Velopharyngeal dysfunction: evolving develop-ments in evaluation. *Current Opinion in Otolaryngology, Head and Neck Surgery*, 13(6), 366–370.

Sapienza, C. and Ruddy, B. (2009). *Visual Examination of Voice Disorders*. San Diego, CA: Plural Publishing, DVD.

Sataloff, R., Hawkshaw, M. and Eller, R. (2007). *Atlas of Laryngoscopy*, 2nd edn. San Diego, CA: Plural Publishing.

Schiller, N. O., Van Lieshout, P. H., Meyer, A. S. and Levelt, W. J. M. (1999). Does the syllable affiliation of intervocalic consonants have an articulatory basis? Evidence from electro-magnetic midsagittal articulography. In B. Maassen and P. Groenen (eds), *Pathologies of Speech and Language*. London: Whurr, pp. 343–349.

Sealey, L. R. and Giddens, C. L. (2010). Aerodynamic indices of velopharyngeal func-tion in childhood apraxia of speech. *Clinical Linguistics and Phonetics*, 24, 417–430.

Sell, D., Harding, A., and Grunwell, P. (1999). GOS.SP.ASS.'98: an assessment for speech disorders associated with cleft palate and/or velopharyngeal dysfunction (revised). *International Journal of Language and Communication Disorders*, 34(1), 17–33.

Shprintzen, R. J and Marrinan, E. (2009). Velopharyngeal insufficiency: diagnosis and management. *Current Opinion in Otolaryngology and Head and Neck Surgery*, 17(4), 302–307.

Sonies B., Chi-Fishman, G., and Miller, J.-L. (1991). Ultrasound imaging and swallowing. In B. Jones (ed.), *Normal and Abnormal Swallowing: Imaging in Diagnosis and Therapy*, 2nd edn. Berlin: Springer-Verlag, pp. 119–136.

Steele, C. M. and Van Lieshout P. H. (2004). Use of electromagnetic midsagittal articulography in the study of swallowing. *Journal of Speech, Language and Hearing Research*, 47(2), 342–352.

Steele, C. M. and Van Lieshout P. (2009). Tongue movements during water swallowing in healthy young and older adults. *Journal of Speech, Language and Hearing Research*, 52(5), 1255–1567.

Stone, M. (2005). A guide to analysing tongue motion from ultrasound images. *Clinical Linguistics and Phonetics*, 19(6/7), 455–501.

Stone, M. and Lundberg, A. (1996). Three-dimensional tongue surface shapes of English consonants and vowels. *Journal of the Acoustical Society of America*, 99(6), 3278–3737.

Suzuki, N., Wakumoto, M., Michi, K. *et al.* (1995). Cross-linguistic study of lateral misarticulation using electropalatography. *European Journal of Disorders of Communication*, 30, 237–245.

Svirsky, M. A., Lane, H., Perkell, J. S., and Wozniak, J. (1992). Effects of short-term auditory deprivation on speech production in adult cochlear implant users. *Journal of the Acoustical Society of America*, 92(3), 1284–1300.

Vogel, A. P., Ibrahim, H. M., Reilly, S., and Kilpatrick, N. (2009). A comparative study of two acoustic measures of hypernasality. *Journal of Speech, Language and Hearing Research*, 52(6), 1640–1651.

Vorperian, H. K. and Kent, R. D. (2007). Vowel acoustic space development in children: a synthesis of acoustic and anatomic data. *Journal of Speech, Language and Hearing Research*, 50, 1510–1545.

Vorperian, H. K., Kent, R. D., Lindstrom, M. J. *et al.* (2005). Development of vocal tract length during early childhood: a magnetic resonance imaging study. *Journal of the Acoustical Society of America*, 117(1), 338–350.

Watkins, K. E., Smith, S. M., Davis, S., and Howell, P. (2008). Structural and functional abnormalities of the motor system in developmental stuttering. *Brain*, 131, 50–59.

Weber, F. and Woolridge, M. W. (2008). An ultrasonic study of the organization of sucking and swallowing by newborn infants. *Developmental Medicine and Child Neurology*, 28(1), 19–24.

Wenke, R. J., Theodoros, D., and Cornwell, P. (2010). Effectiveness of Lee Silverman Voice Treatment (LSVT) on hypernasality in non-progressive dysarthria: the need for further research. *International Journal of Language and Communication Disorders*, 45(1), 31–46.

Wernicke, C. (1874). *Der Aphasische Symptomencomplex*. Breslau (Wrocław), Poland: Cohn and Weigert.

Whalen, D. H., Kang, A. M., Magen, H. S. *et al.* (1999). Predicting midsagittal pharynx shape from tongue position during vowel production. *Journal of Speech, Language and Hearing Research*, 42, 592–603.

Wood, S. E. (1995). An electropalatographic analysis of stutterers' speech. *European Journal of Disorders of Communication*, 30, 226–236.

Wrench, A. A. (2007). Advances in EPG palate design. *Advances in Speech-Language Pathology*, 9(1), 3–12.

Yan, Y., Damrose, E., and Bless, D. (2007). Functional analysis of voice using simultaneous high-speed imaging and acoustic recordings. *Journal of Voice*, 21(5), 604–616.

14 Data Analysis and Interpretation: Statistical Methods

Eleonora Rossi

14.1 Doing Statistics: Probability, Hypothesis Testing, Type I Error, Type II Error

Researchers make use of statistics to test the probability that differences in the compared distributions are due to real differences between samples, rather than being due to chance. Investigators usually start with a research question which leads them to formulate specific hypotheses in order to test different theories of interest. Typically, a null hypothesis (H_0) and an alternative hypothesis (H_a) best describe the expectations of a research question. The H_0 is the hypothesis that is being tested with a test of significance, and it is usually a statement of no effect, or no difference in the distribution between two (or more) groups or two (or more) conditions. The H_a is the hypothesis that states that there is a true effect or a significant difference in the distributions. The H_0 and the H_a are validated with statistical tests that vary according to the design of the experiment (as outlined in the next sections). There are two types of errors that can happen while accepting or rejecting the H_0. *Type I error* happens when the H_0 is rejected by the experimenter (even while H_0 is actually true), consequently leading the experimenter to erroneously conclude that there is a significant difference between the observed means. Conversely, *Type II error* happens when the experimenter accepts the H_0 (while the H_0 is not true), incorrectly assuming that there is no difference between the two means. The *α-level* is an arbitrary cut-off point set by the experimenter (usually $\alpha = 0.05$, or $\alpha = 0.01$) that defines the level of accepted error in the estimation. For example an α-level of 0.05 implies that a result is accepted under the assumption that there is a 5% probability that a Type I error occurs (a probability small enough to be accepted). All statistic tests (see further, below) provide two values that are particularly important to determining the outcome of a statistic test: a test statistic and a relevant probability value, or *p-value*.

Research Methods in Clinical Linguistics and Phonetics: A Practical Guide,
First Edition. Edited by Nicole Müller and Martin J. Ball.
© 2013 Blackwell Publishing Ltd. Published 2013 by Blackwell Publishing Ltd.

The test statistic values vary according to each particular distribution of reference. For example, in a chi-squared distribution, which is the distribution of reference for the chi-squared test, or in an F distribution used for example in ANOVAs (see Section 14.5 in this chapter), the test statistics can only assume values > 0, while in a t distribution the values of t can span from $-\infty$ to $+\infty$. The *p-value* is the probability, calculated under the assumption that H_0 is correct, that the test's statistics take a value that is as extreme as or more extreme than the actual observed value. The smaller the p-value, the stronger the evidence against H_0. In other words, the p-value represents the probability to make a Type I error. Therefore, the smaller the p-value, the better! Importantly, if the p-value exceeds the set α-level, H_0 should be accepted and therefore H_a should be rejected.

14.2   Units of Statistical Analysis: Variables

In statistics, a *variable* is a measurement or a property which takes different values, and it constitutes the main focus of statistical analysis. Variables can be *numeric* (for example, Reaction Times in ms, vowel duration in ms) or *categorical* (nominal), that is, a category and not a number, for example the color of the eyes (brown/blue), a specific impairment status that can be relevant to the analysis (i.e. participants with a hearing impairment vs. hearing participants; linguistic status, monolingual, bilingual). Categorical variables can be further subdivided into purely categorical or ordinal. Purely categorical variables, like the color of the eyes, cannot be ranked or ordered, while ordinal categorical variables can be ordered. For example, people with dysarthria can be categorized according to the severity of their symptoms, into mild, moderate, and severe.

In formal experiments, researchers usually label variables as *dependent* and *independent*. Dependent variables are the ones that are measured during a formal experiment, that is, the variables on which the hypothesis is tested. Independent variables, on the other hand, are the ones that can be manipulated by the experimenter or that are defined by the characteristics of the populations under investigation. For example, Janse (2009) tested neighborhood density effects on lexical decision performance in two groups of aphasic speakers (15 non-fluent Broca's aphasics, and 12 fluent Wernicke's aphasics) and an aged-matched control group. The material included 80 non-words, half of which were classified as having a high number of real-word neighbors, and the other half having a low number of real-word neighbors. To counterbalance for lexical status, an additional 80 words were added to the stimuli. Participants listened to all the material, and their task was to perform a lexical decision (i.e. to decide whether a string of sounds is a real word or not) as quickly and as accurately as possible. In this example, the two dependent variables under investigation are one nominal variable, that is, accuracy (correct/incorrect) and a continuous numeric one, that is, the speed of response – RTs – which is usually measured in milliseconds (ms). The independent variables are two nominal variables: (1) group (Broca's aphasics, Wernicke's aphasics, and controls), and (2) neighborhood density (high vs. low). Note that the variable "group" is not directly manipulated by the experimenter, but is chosen on purpose to test the experimenter's predictions (in this case the prediction is that Broca's and Wernicke's aphasics are differentially impaired in lexical access). Instead, the variable "neighborhood density" is directly manipulated by the experimenter by virtue of creating ad hoc experimental material. Finally, very often, independent variables are defined as *factors* having a specific number of *levels*. In the previous example, there were two independent variables (now factors), "group" and "neighborhood density." The first factor (group) is defined by having three levels which correspond to each group of interest: (1) Broca's, (2) Wernicke's, and (3) controls. The second factor (neighborhood density) has only two levels: (1) high neighborhood density, and (2) low neighborhood density. In a later section, I will illustrate how factors are used in more complex statistical models.

14.3 Descriptive Statistics

One of the biggest challenges in clinical research is the large variability in the linguistic performance observed within and across individuals, variability that may be mirrored in a large variation in data distribution. Very often the large variability in performance is intrinsically linked to the nature of clinical populations, and as such has to be considered highly informative. However, extreme variability might be a problem for the application of ad hoc statistical analyses. In fact, if the distribution of the dependent variable(s) is not normal (I will explain later on in detail what this concept entails), or if the number of tested participants is too low to be able to produce reliable effects, *parametric statistics* (i.e. the branch of statistics that assumes that data come from a probability distribution) cannot be applied. Therefore, before performing any analysis it is always good practice to observe the pattern of a distribution to determine whether it is normal or whether it deviates from normality. How is it possible to determine whether a distribution is normal? Before answering this question, some fundamental terms have to be introduced.

Each numeric distribution can be described by *measures of central tendency*: the *mean*, *median*, and *mode*, and *measures of spread*: the *range*, the *deviation*, the *variance*, and the *standard deviation* (SD).

- Mean: the average across individual scores of a measure. The mean can be heavily influenced by extreme values and outliers.
- Median: the middle observation in a group of scores when the values are ordered from highest to lowest. The median is not heavily influenced by extreme values or outliers.
- Mode: the value that occurs most often in a distribution. Usually the mode represents the peak of the distribution. In cases in which there are two or more frequently observed values, the distribution can have two modes (often referred to as bi-modal distribution).
- Range: the range between the minimum and the maximum score.

- Deviation, variance, and standard deviation (SD): each observation (y_i) in a sample deviates from the sample mean (Y). The *deviation* of an observation from the sample mean is defined as the difference between them, i.e. (y_i − Y). The *variance* is defined as the average of all squared deviations, that is, the variance represents the average of the squared distances from the mean. However, the variance might be difficult to interpret as a measure, since it uses squared deviations. Easier to interpret is the *standard deviation* (SD). The SD is the positive square root of the variance, and it indicates how much a score deviates from the mean in standardized values. The SD is calculated using the following formula:

$$\sigma = \sqrt{\frac{\sum (y_i - Y)^2}{n - 1}}$$

- Standard normal distribution (SND), outliers: An *SND* distribution is characterized by the mean, median, and mode roughly coinciding, and by being unimodal, that is, with one central peak only, having a mean of 0 and an SD of 1. An SND distribution is represented by a bell-shaped graph. In an SND approximately 68% of the data fall between +1 and −1 SD from the mean; 95% of the data fall between +2 and −2 SD from the mean, and all or nearly all data fall between +3 or −3 SD from the mean. By definition, values that are above or below 3 SD from the mean are considered *outliers*.

Histograms, quantile plots, and box plots allow researchers to visually inspect the distribution of variables, and are particularly informative regarding their normality. For example, the visual inspection of a histogram reveals whether the distribution is symmetrical and unimodal, and shows the frequency for each value in the data set (Figure 14.1(a)). A box plot is very useful in visually determining the median of a distribution and its symmetry. In fact, in a box plot the median is represented by the line that dissects the box. Moreover, 50% of the distribution is represented in the box, and the lines that depart from the box (denoted as "whiskers") show the values including the maximum and the minimum values (Figure 14.1(b)). Any extreme values or outliers lie beyond the whiskers. Extreme values and outliers are denoted differently depending on the software used. For example, the statistical software IBM SPSS (see Section 14.6 on "Doing Stats") indicates extreme values with a circle, and clear outliers with a star. Finally, in a normal quantile plot, theoretical quantiles and sample quantiles are plotted together. If the distribution is roughly normal, the datapoints in a quantile plot should be aligned on a line. Examples of a normal distribution plotted in a histogram, box plot, and a quantile plot are shown in Figure 14.1(a), (b), and (c), respectively.

If the observed distribution is non-symmetric (i.e. skewed to the right or to the left), or bimodal (i.e. with two modes or peaks), this is a sign revealing non-normality. Excellent reviews and examples for normal and non-normal distributions can be found in Agresti and Finley (2008). The next section introduces the concepts of skewed distributions and outliers, as well as frequently used techniques to deal with these particular cases.

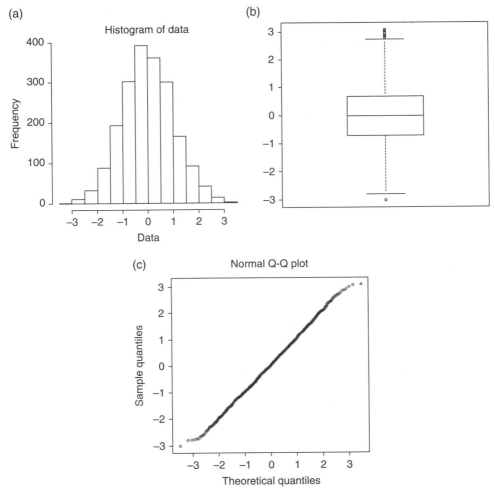

Figure 14.1 Plotting a normal distribution (a) histogram; (b) box plot; (c) quantile plot.

Section Summary

- Measures of central tendency are: mean, median, and mode.
- Measures of spread are: range, deviation, variance and standard deviation (SD).
- Standard normal distribution (SND): in a SND distribution mean, median and mode roughly coincide. An SND has a mean of 0 and a SD of 1.
- Descriptive statistics: Describes the main parameters of a distribution in terms of measures of central tendency and spread. Histograms, box plots, and quantile plots are useful to visually inspect distributions.

14.4   Skewed Distributions, Outliers, and Data Trimming

As mentioned above, a skewed distribution is by definition abnormal. However, some distributions are skewed by nature, and it is therefore important to be able to recognize them. For example, the distribution of RTs is typically skewed to the right, as participants may be faster or slower but they will never be faster than 0 ms (the value 0 being already an improbable one for any conscious cognitive process in response to a stimulus). A prototypical example of a right-skewed distribution is presented in Figure 14.2(a), in which the mean of the distribution is at 468 ms. However, it has a clear right tail with observations up to 1800 ms. When faced with this type of data there can be two possible approaches. The first is to apply a natural logarithm transformation to the raw data to revert the extreme values towards normality, as shown in Figure 14.2(b). Alternatively, the median value can be used as a measure of central tendency (instead of the mean), as it is less sensitive to extreme values or outliers. For example, for the dataset exemplified in Figure 14.2(a), the median value is 419, which is clearly closer to the center of the distribution. Both approaches are useful.

Outliers are observations that greatly deviate from the mean of a distribution, even more than extreme values do. Including outliers in the analysis can be very misleading, as they will directly influence the mean value. However, outliers are present in almost any experimental dataset, and it is therefore good practice to be able to deal with them. This is particularly true when collecting data from clinical populations, whose intrinsic characteristics might lead to recording extreme values. Outliers can be subdivided into two types: absolute and relative. Absolute outliers can be defined as values that are not representative of a true linguistic or cognitive process, and they should be recognized and removed even before applying any transformation on the data. Absolute outliers can be due to failures with data-recording mechanisms. For example, during a word-naming task in which the goal is to measure voice onset time (VOT), if the microphone is not correctly triggered, the result could either be an excessive delay or an excessively early VOT measurement which will not be representative of the participant's true performance. Moreover, absolute outliers are datapoints that fall outside a possible range of values (e.g. RTs, VOTs) representing any real linguistic/ cognitive process, and they can be determined by deciding an arbitrary cutoff value depending on the nature of the task. For example, if we were to analyze behavioral responses during a lexical decision task (in a normal population) measured recording RTs when participants press a response key, all the measurements above 3000 ms should be considered absolute outliers, as responses slower than 3000 are not representative of a real cognitive performance (i.e. participants might be sleepy and RTs might slow down). Importantly, before deciding any absolute cutoff values, it is crucial to perform a descriptive analysis of the data to have a sense of the overall distribution.

Once absolute outliers are trimmed, relative outliers can be eliminated. Relative outliers are observations that may largely deviate from the mean, but that can still be considered the reflection of a real linguistic/cognitive behavior. As such, it is important to decide whether they should be kept in for analysis, or whether they should be

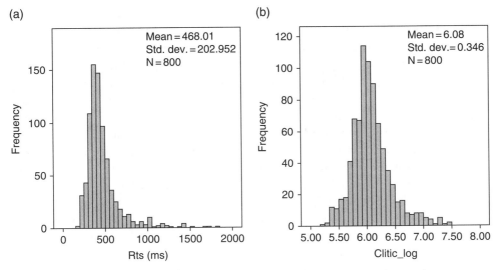

Figure 14.2 (a) A right-skewed distribution. (b) The same distribution after applying a natural logarithmic transformation.

eliminated. The cutoff point for trimming relative outliers is variable, at times being +2.5 or –2.5 SD from the mean for each single participant (Maloney, Risko, O'Malley, and Besner, 2009; Martens and De Jong, 2006) or more conservative +2 or –2 SD from the mean (Munro, Derwing, Clifford, and Burgess, 2010). One of the consequences of extreme data trimming is that the power of the data analysis will diminish. Once again, one of the common techniques to avoid this problem is using the median (instead of the mean) or using the natural logarithm to normalize the distribution. For an overview of how to treat outliers (especially referring to RTs) see Ratcliff (1993).

Section Summary

- Some distributions are naturally skewed to the right, for example RTs (reaction Ttimes) or VOT (voice onset times). For these types of distributions valuable approaches are: (1) using the natural logarithm of the data, and/or (2) using the median as the measure of central tendency (instead of the mean).
- Outliers (absolute and relative) and extreme values are datapoints that strongly deviate from the mean of the distribution.

14.5   Parametric and Non-parametric Statistics

One of the main challenges of scientific research is determining which statistical approach is the most appropriate for the data under investigation, and this choice is heavily influenced by the experimental design and by the type of data that is collected. As we saw earlier, parametric statistics is based on the assumption that the observed data come from a normal distribution, and can be safely applied when the sample size is sufficiently large. In other words, parametric statistics makes more assumptions concerning the distribution, and as a result produces more accurate estimates when applied correctly and appropriately. If the assumptions underlying parametric statistics are not met, it is not appropriate to apply those statistical analyses, as the results can be very misleading (besides violating the core principles of statistical analysis). For example, if a descriptive analysis reveals that the distribution of interest is not normal, or if the sample size is too limited to safely apply parametric statistics, there are two possible approaches. The first is to directly apply *non-parametric statistics*, that is, statistical tests that are not based on the assumption of normality. The second approach (most useful when the sample size is large enough, but the distribution is not normal) is to determine whether the data can be trimmed or cleaned in order to normalize the distribution, and therefore allow the application of parametric statistics and gain in power, as illustrated in a previous section of this chapter. To summarize, if the sample size is too limited or if the data cannot be normalized with cleaning and trimming procedures, non-parametric statistics should be applied. In this section, I will illustrate parametric and non-parametric statistic tests that are frequently used in clinical linguistics and phonetics, and I will provide examples of their application.

One widely used statistic is the t-statistic. A *two sample t-test* is used when the experimenter is interested in comparing whether two independent groups of participants show the same behavior when the variable of interest is a numeric variable. In other words, the two-sample t-test compares whether mean scores from two independent groups are equal or different. For example, a hypothetical study might want to compare at which point in the frequency band a group of children with severe hearing loss and a group of normally hearing children begin to perceive sounds. The experimenter collects data from a total of 60 children, 30 per group. During the experiment participants listen to tones at various frequencies and their task is to press a response button as soon as they hear a sound. Both groups of participants hear the same set of stimuli. In this case the H_0 will state that there is no difference between the two group means, that is, $H_0: \mu_1 = \mu_2$ while the H_a (the hypothesis that is actually tested) states that there is a significant difference between the two means, that is, $H_a: \mu_1 \neq \mu_2$. The formula to calculate the two-sample t-statistic is shown below:

$$t = \frac{\mu_1 - \mu_2}{\sqrt{\dfrac{s_1^2}{n_1} + \dfrac{s_2^2}{n_2}}}$$

where μ_1 is the mean of scores for group 1 and μ_2 is the mean of scores of group 2. At the denominator are the estimates for the two SD for the two groups. The two-sample t-statistics draws its values from the t distribution which by definition has k degrees of freedom, which are usually calculated automatically by the statistical softwares. However, the rule of thumb for calculating the degrees of freedom for a t distribution is to take the smaller value between $n_1 - 1$ and $n_2 - 1$. For this specific example, k = 29.

A variant of the t-statistic that is widely used in the clinical literature is the *paired t-test*. Paired t-tests are used when comparing a specific set of variables measured in the same participants over time (e.g. in two separate experimental sessions), for example to determine whether a specific treatment or intervention has a positive effect. In this case the statistical test does not compare two means from two different groups, but instead computes the difference between two different means within the same subjects. For example, Fridriksson and colleagues (2007) tested whether a group of anomic aphasic patients would benefit from being treated either with a semantic-based anomia treatment or with a phonological-based anomia treatment. The group of participants consisted of three aphasic speakers who were tested before and after the treatment using the Philadelphia Naming Task. Results revealed that two patients' naming abilities significantly improved after treatment, whereas there was no difference for one patient, revealing overall that the treatment had a significant effect. Similarly, a series of paired t-tests were used to determine whether a group of infants discriminate between minimal pairs and whether their performance changed between one of the testing blocks and the last habituation block (Fennel and Werker, 2003). The paired comparisons result showed that there was a significant difference between the testing blocks and the habituation block, with a p-value < 0.001.

When research is aimed at comparing one specific measure in more than two groups (i.e. when each experimental condition is tested in three different groups), a t-test (and t distribution) is not suitable anymore. Instead a single ANOVA (analysis of variance) which is based on the F statistic is the most suitable analysis in order to compare three independent groups. The idea behind ANOVA is that in order to determine whether there is a difference among populations' means the variation *among* the means of the groups is compared with the variation *within* each group, therefore performing an analysis of variance. In similar fashion to what was described for the t-test, the null hypothesis in an ANOVA states that there is no difference between the means observed in the three groups, that is, H_0: $\mu_1 = \mu_2 = \mu_3$ while the alternative hypothesis states that there is a significant difference between the three means, i.e. H_a: $\mu_1 \neq \mu_2 \neq \mu_3$. Note, however, that in contrast to hypothesis testing using a two-sample t-test, the ANOVA H_a is fairly generic. In other words, it simply states that the means between the three groups are different, without making any claim about what might be driving a potential significant difference. Specifically, this will need to be reported in a separate set of hypotheses that will be tested with a priori *simple comparisons* in case there are specific hypotheses about which are the groups that differ. In case there are no a priori hypotheses for the pattern of difference post-hoc analyses (for example Tukey's test) can be performed to determine which means are different from one another. To exemplify the use of ANOVA, let's recall the example used when describing a two-sample t-test. In that example the perception of frequencies via the use of pure tones was tested in a group of children with severe hearing loss and a group of normally hearing children. Now, a group of children with cochlear implants is added to the study. In this scenario, a single ANOVA is the most appropriate analysis to be used for investigating whether the means measured from the three independent groups differ. Similar to this example the experimental design followed by Maassen *et al.* (2001) exemplifies the use of a single ANOVA paradigm. In their experiment the authors assessed the ability to identify and discriminate voicing and place of articulation in three independent groups of children: one group of eight children diagnosed with developmental dyslexia, and two control groups, that is, one group matched in age and the other one matched for reading abilities. Very frequently, however, experimental designs are more complex, and include not only comparing the performance of two or more experimental groups for a single variable, but also designs in which two (or more) groups of participants provide measurements for all experimental conditions. In this case a *repeated-measures ANOVA* (part of the mixed-design analysis of variance) is the most appropriate analysis to perform.

Let's illustrate the use of repeated-measures ANOVA. One experiment is designed to determine whether dyslexic children can successfully discriminate between pairs of phonemes, and specifically to determine whether different places of articulation may play a role in this process. To address this research question, a group of dyslexic children and a group of non-dyslexic children are tested using a phoneme categorization task in which pairs of phonemes are modified along two variables: manner of articulation, for example plosive versus fricative (i.e. /p/ versus /f/), and place of articulation (for example bilabial or labiodental). All the auditory stimuli pairs in all conditions are presented in a randomized order and participants are asked to press a response button to determine whether the two sounds are the same or not. Accuracy and RTs for the response will be recorded. For this example, the statistical analysis will need to account for all the following factors: (1) determine whether different places and manners of articulation play a role in performing phoneme discrimination; (2) determine whether the two experimental groups differ in how accurately they can determine whether the two phonemes are equal or distinct (accuracy being a categorical dichotomous variable characterized by 1 – correctly judged, and 0 – incorrectly judged); and (3) determine whether the two groups differ in how fast they can make this decision (RTs being a numeric variable). Critically, given that both groups of participants provide data on all experimental conditions, a repeated-measures ANOVA analysis will be used. For this specific example, several *factors* will need to enter into the analysis. Specifically, "place of articulation" and "manner of articulation" are considered *within subject* factors, given that all participants in both groups are exposed to all experimental conditions. The variable "group," instead, is referred to as a *between subject* variable, given that it is a variable that identifies each group of participants.

Even though repeated-measures ANOVAs are still widely used, since about the turn of the century a more statistically robust procedure has been applied: *multi-level modeling* (MLM), or mixed-effects modeling. In fact, repeated-measures ANOVAs rely on some strong assumptions that are often violated, among which is the assumption of sphericity, that is, the assumption that the variances for each pair of difference scores are equal. Another assumption that is often violated is the assumption that there should not be missing datapoints. Instead, MLM does not rely on these assumptions, and is characterized as a more robust model. I will not explain in detail here how MLM works; however, several handbooks are available, and a useful introduction to MLM applied to linguistic data is provided by Quené and van den Bergh (2004).

One of the questions that often arises in experimental research is whether two variables are correlated, that is, whether there is a linear association between two numerical variables. In order to determine this, researchers use correlation

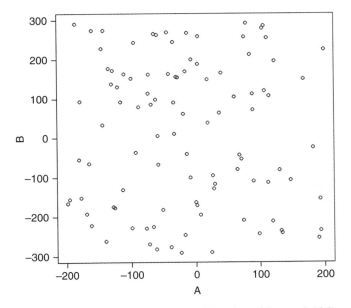

Figure 14.3 Plot of a correlation between two variables (A and B r = –0.035).

analysis, which tells whether two numeric variables are correlated in linear dependence. The *Pearson correlation coefficient* (r) can have values between –1 and +1. A positive value of r signifies a positive correlation between the two variables, while a negative value indicates a negative correlation. The more r approaches the 0 value, the less correlation there is between the two variables. For example, if we simulate two random samples (A and B), and we run a correlation analysis, r = –0.035, this tells us that there is absolutely no correlation between the two variables, as can be observed from the dispersion of datapoints in Figure 14.3. It is important to remember, however, that correlation does not entail causation. In other words, if two variables are correlated (in a positive or negative way) no inference can be made about the nature of their correlation.

All the models and statistics described up to now rely on the assumption that the distribution is normal, and that the number of observations (n) is large enough. However, if the assumptions of normality or sample size and/or other assumptions underlying the use of parametric tests are violated, non-parametric statistics must be used. Non-parametric tests (or assumption-free tests) are tests that rely less restrictively on distributional assumptions than their parametric counterparts. Most non-parametric tests rely on performing the analysis not on the actual data, but on ranked data. Working on ranked data partly solves the issues of non-normality. The reminder of this section briefly introduces the most frequently used non-parametric tests. One of these is the Mann–Whitney U-test (the non-parametric counterpart of a two-sample t-test), which is used when the assumptions required for parametric statistics are violated. For example, Kuruvilla, Murdoch, and Gozée (2008) investigated spatial and temporal phonetic measures using electropalatography in a group of dysarthric patients who had suffered traumatic brain injury, and compared the data to a group of neurologically intact participants. However, the collected data were revealed to have violated the assumption of normality (assessed using the Shapiro–Wilk test that is available through the major statistical programs). Similarly, Rossi and Bastiaanse (2008) compared one group of aphasic speakers against one control group on the production of different types of verbs. Given that the data from the group of aphasic speakers violated the assumptions of normality, the Mann–Whitney U-test was applied in order to compare the two groups.

When comparing more than two independent groups, and when some of the assumptions underlying one-way ANOVA are violated, it is best to use the non-parametric version of the one-way ANOVA, that is, the Kruskal–Wallis test. This test is based on the same basic idea of ranking data in order to avoid non-normality in the distribution. The non-parametric version of the Pearson correlation coefficient (r) is the *Spearman's rank correlation coefficient (ρ)*. Once again, this test relies on ranked data in order to compensate for the non-normality of the distributions. The Spearman's correlation coefficient is a measure of statistical dependence between two numeric variables, and its values range between –1 and +1.

A further powerful statistical test that is very often used in clinical research is the chi-square test. One of the primary characteristics of this test is that it is used to analyze nominal (or categorical) data sets (instead of numeric variables), and it allows to compare whether two or more sets of categorical variables are associated, that is to say, there is no specific information on the direction of the association (the direction of the association is usually clear by looking at the descriptive statistics). The null hypothesis (H_0) for a chi-square test states that there is no association between the two variables, while the alternative hypothesis (H_a) states that there is a significant association between the two variables. The chi-square test is based on the chi-square distribution, which can assume different functions according to the degree of freedom (df), however only assuming positive values. The rationale behind the chi-square test can be explained using *contingency tables*. Contingency tables plot the number of observations for different groups and different variables of interest. For example, Stow and Dodd (2005) investigated whether there is a difference in the number of referrals to speech pathologists between monolingual and bilingual children – two categorical variables. One of the research questions investigated in this study specifically asked whether there is a difference between the number of males and females referred – a categorical variable – in the two populations. The relevant contingency table plots the raw number of observations for each group:

	Monolingual	*Bilingual*	*Total*
Female	46	32	78
Male	90	57	147
Total	136	89	225

The chi-square statistic (χ^2) relies on the difference between the number of actual observations and the number of observations that would be expected under the assumption that H_0 was true (i.e. under the assumption of no association), as shown in the following formula:

$$\chi^2 = \sum \frac{(Observed\ count - Expected\ count)^2}{Expected\ count}$$

where "observed" represents the observed sample count, "expected" the expected count for the same cell. From the formula, it is clear that the chi-square statistic can only assume positive values, as the nominator is always a squared value. For the chi-square statistic the degrees of freedom are calculated as follows: df = (r–1) (c–1), "r" being the number of rows and "c" the number of columns in the contingency table. The results for the example below show that there is no association between group and gender revealing that there is no significant difference in the number of males and females referred in the two groups (χ^2 = 0.034, df = 1, p = 0.853).

Section Summary

- Parametric statistics: based on the assumption that data come from a normal distribution. If this assumption is violated, non-parametric statistics can be used to perform analyses.
- Non-parametric statistics: not based on the assumption of normality. Primarily useful for small samples and for when assumptions of normality are badly violated.

Frequently used parametric tests:
- Two-sample t-test, paired t-test, one-way ANOVA (comparison among three independent groups), repeated-measures ANOVA, Pearson's correlation coefficient.

Frequently used non-parametric tests:
- Mann–Whitney U-test, Kruskal–Wallis test, Spearman's rank correlation coefficient, chi-square test.

14.6   "Doing Stats": Available Software

Researchers are often faced with large datasets to analyze, from multiple participants and multiple studies. Moreover, it should be clear at this point that performing the sort of statistical analyses just described by hand would be close to impossible (even if for very small samples and for easier analyses it would certainly be possible, it not very practical). Fortunately, there are by now a large number of statistical programs and software packages that can perform all sorts of statistical analyses, from simple (but fundamental!) descriptive analyses to very complex models (as for example repeated-measures ANOVAs or correlation analyses). Some of them are commercial, while others are open-source and freely downloadable from the Internet. In what follows, I will focus on and describe computer programs that are often used in psycholinguistics and clinical linguistics, and more generally in the cognitive sciences. One of the most popular statistical programs is IBM SPSS – Statistical Package for the Social Sciences – (previously known as PASW or SPSS). IBM SPSS has to be purchased, but most universities and research institutions purchase collective licenses, allowing the affiliated investigators to use it. One of the main advantages of IBM SPSS is that it is moderately user-friendly thanks to its graphical user interface that makes extensive use of menus to perform a very large number of statistical analyses. For more advanced users, IBM SPSS provides the opportunity to write scripts using its syntax language, which is useful to automate repetitive analyses and to perform additional options that are not available via the menu interface. One of the major drawbacks of IBM SPSS is that the steps needed to prepare the data to perform a specific analysis via the menu interface can be quite laborious. However, IBM SPSS is probably the best tool for researchers who are at a beginner/ intermediate level of knowledge and intend to perform statistical analyses without stepping into more serious programming. I recommend *Discovering Statistics using SPSS* (Field, 2005) as a tool to consolidate some statistical concepts, and as an excellent guide for people who are learning IBM SPSS.

A widely used, freely available statistics tool is available from the R-project website (www.r-project.org). The major difference between IBM SPSS (and other graphics- and menu-driven software packages) is that R does not provide any menu user interface, but it is actually operated through a computer programming language. As such, R is extremely flexible for data manipulation and permits researchers to perform ad hoc statistical analyses that may diverge from the standard procedures. Even if at first sight learning a programming language may scare many users, to learn at least the basics of R can be very useful, especially if the objective is to use statistical analyses for more complex studies, for example, studies involving ERPs or eye-tracking data. Investing some time at the beginning may save more time later! The R development team provides an online manual that can be found on the website. There are also two books that may serve as an initial guide to the use of R: *Introductory Statistics with R* (Dalgaard, 2008), and *Analyzing Linguistic Data: A Practical Introduction to Statistics Using R* (Baayen, 2008).

Besides IBM SPSS and R there are many other statistics programs that will fit the specific needs and preferences of different investigators. Among other commercial packages specializing in statistics that use a graphic interface are Statistica and Minitab. Both software packages are commercial and can be purchased via dedicated websites (see section summary box). MATLAB (which is part of MathWorks) is another very powerful programming language that can perform a variety of operations on large matrices of data. The use of MATLAB goes beyond statistical analysis, as it allows to program entire experimental paradigms, beginning with the presentation of experimental stimuli. However, MATLAB requires building strong programming skills, which may take a user a while to acquire.

Section Summary

Sources for available software packages:

- IBM SPSS: www.spss.com/software/statistics
- R: www.r-project.org
- Statistica: www.statsoft.com
- Minitab: www.minitab.com
- MATLAB: www.mathworks.com/products/matlab.

14.7   Conclusion

In this brief chapter I have reviewed the most important concepts related to statistic analysis as a tool for analyzing clinical data. In particular, I have focused on two characteristics typical of data coming from clinical populations, that is, variability and non-normality, trying to provide some practical tools to approach these issues. However, statistics and applied statistics are fields in constant evolution. It is therefore always good practice to keep up to date with new statistical methodologies that might be particularly suitable to approach data analysis.

References

Agresti, A. and Finley, B. (2008). *Statistical Methods for Social Sciences*, 4th edn. Upper Saddle River, NJ: Prentice Hall.

Baayen, R. H. (2008). *Analyzing Linguistic Data: A Practical Introduction to Statistics Using R*. Cambridge: Cambridge University Press.

Dalgaard, P. (2008). *Introductory Statistics with R*. New York: Springer.

Fennel, C. T. and Werker, J. F. (2003). Early word learners' ability to access phonetic detail in well-known words. *Language and Speech*, 46(2/3), 245–264.

Field, A. (2005). *Discovering Statistics Using SPSS*, 2nd edn. London: Sage.

Fridriksson, J., Moser, D., Bonilha, L. et al. (2007). Neural correlates of phonological and semantic based anomia treatment in aphasia. *Neuropsychologia*, 45(8), 1812–1822.

Janse, E. (2009). Neighbourhood density effects in auditory non-word processing in aphasic listeners. *Clinical Linguistics and Phonetics*, 23(3), 196–207.

Kuruvilla, M. S., Murdoch, B. E., and Gozée, J. V. (2008). Electropalatographic (EPG) assessment of tongue-to-palate contacts in dysarthric speakers following TBI. *Clinical Linguistics and Phonetics*, 22, 703–725.

Maassen, B., Groenen, P., Crul, T. et al. (2001). Identification and discrimination of voicing and place-of-articulation in developmental dyslexia. *Clinical Linguistics and Phonetics*, 4, 319–339.

Maloney, E., Risko, E. F., O'Malley, S., and Besner, D. (2009). Tracking the transition from sublexical to lexical processing: on the creation of orthographic and phonological lexical representations. *Quarterly Journal of Experimental Psychology*, 62, 858–867.

Martens, V. E. G. and de Jong, P. F. (2006). The effect of word length on lexical decision in dyslexic and normal reading children. *Brain and Language*, 98(2), 140–149.

Munro, M. J., Derwing T. M., Clifford, S., and Burgess, C. S. (2010). Detection of nonnative speaker status from content-masked speech. *Speech Communication*, 52, 626–637.

Quené, H. and van den Bergh, H. (2004). On multi-level modeling of data from repeated measures designs: a tutorial. *Speech Communication*, 43, 103–121.

Ratcliff, R. (1993). Methods for dealing with reaction time outliers. *Psychological Bulletin*, 114(3), 510–532.

Rossi, E. and Bastiaanse, R. (2008). Spontaneous speech in Italian agrammatic aphasia: a focus on variability and verb production. *Aphasiology*, 22, 347–362.

Stow, C. and Dodd, B. (2005). A survey of bilingual children referred for investigation of communication disorders: a comparison with monolingual children referred in one area in England. *Journal of Multilingual Communication Disorders*, 3, 1–23.

15   AphasiaBank: Data and Methods

Brian MacWhinney, Davida Fromm, Audrey Holland, and Margaret Forbes

15.1   Introduction

Recent years have seen a rapid growth in the use of computerized databases throughout the sciences. In the area of language studies, many of these databases involve the collection of large amounts of either spoken or written language. These collections, called corpora, are then accessed over the Internet and subjected to a variety of analyses for language structure, function, and content. The conditions of access to these corpora vary widely. However, some corpora, such as those in the CHILDES or TalkBank databases, are freely open to all researchers.

Typically, individual corpora have been collected and organized with a specific set of research questions in mind. For example, the CHILDES database includes corpora from children growing up in bilingual families in which care has been taken to collect the two languages when used either separately or together (Yip and Matthews, 2007). Other corpora may focus on the use of language in classrooms (Goldman *et al.*, 2007) or doctor-patient interaction (Frederiksen *et al.*, 2004).

Corpora can be subjected to a wide variety of analyses. One can study changes in language over time during language learning (Brown, 1973) or recovery (Feldman *et al.*, 1994). Corpora may be sampled systematically across different social situations or levels (Labov, 2001) or using different elicitation formats (Schober and Conrad, 2006). The analyses can be conducted through methods as diverse as computer modeling (MacWhinney and Leinbach, 1991), microgenetic analysis (Siegler, 2006), Conversation Analysis (MacWhinney and Wagner, 2010), and computational linguistic methods for automatic grammatical analysis (MacWhinney, 2008).

Research Methods in Clinical Linguistics and Phonetics: A Practical Guide,
First Edition. Edited by Nicole Müller and Martin J. Ball.
© 2013 Blackwell Publishing Ltd. Published 2013 by Blackwell Publishing Ltd.

15.2 AphasiaBank

Some research areas have made more extensive use of corpora than others. One area that has benefitted particularly from the availability of open-access corpora has been the field of child language research. In this area, over 3500 articles have been published using the CHILDES database (http://childes.psy.cmu.edu). CHILDES is an international cooperative venture, involving some 3000 users located in over 30 countries. Most new empirical studies of child language production rely on the analysis of data from the CHILDES database and the majority of theoretical papers on language that make reference to production data are now based on the use of the CHILDES database (MacWhinney, 2010). The system provides users access to a set of programs (CLAN), a database (CHILDES), a transcription system (CHAT), documentation, and a mailing list (Info-CHILDES) for communicating on problems in language analysis. The form of these tools has been shaped by continual input from active members of the system.

The AphasiaBank project seeks to extend the methods and procedures developed in the CHILDES system to the study of language in aphasia. To achieve this, the AphasiaBank project has developed a shared database of multimedia interactions for the study of communication in aphasia. This database now provides both a powerful platform for improving our understanding of aphasia and its treatment. In this chapter we will describe the goals of the project, the process of development, and the various analyses that are being conducted on the data. These analyses will illustrate a wide-ranging set of new tools for the analysis of language production in aphasia. By improving access to a shared database on aphasia, we can achieve a rapid improvement in the empirical grounding of work in this field. Together, the new database and the new analytic system will be able to support a major revolution in this field.

The organization of AphasiaBank began with a planning meeting of 20 senior aphasia researchers in 2005 who agreed on the need for a shared protocol, a shared database, and increased availability of computational tools for the aphasia research community. After funding was awarded in 2007, we developed the testing protocol and began collecting data from research and clinical aphasia centers around the USA. To date, the database includes over 120 participants with aphasia from 10 different sites and just over 100 non-aphasic adults from 3 sites. The core database has been limited (with few exceptions) to individuals whose aphasia results from a stroke that can be verified through neuroimaging or a clear medical diagnosis. The current samples are all in English, with additional new samples being collected in Cantonese, Mandarin, German, and Swedish.

Section Summary

- Electronic corpora that are openly available over the Internet are providing an increasingly powerful research tool for various areas in language studies. Recently, the AphasiaBank project has extended these methods to the study of aphasia.

15.3 Goals

The overarching goal of work in AphasiaBank is the construction of methods for improving patient-oriented treatments in aphasia. To reach that goal, we must solidify the empirical database supporting our understanding of communication in aphasia. The consortium of aphasia researchers that has been involved in this project throughout its inception and development has continued to contribute to a shared conceptual and methodological framework that drives the collecting, recording, transcribing, and coding of language samples. The nine specific aims of AphasiaBank are:

1 Protocol standardization. We have developed a standardized data collection protocol that is being implemented at all consortium sites. Use of this standardized protocol guarantees maximal comparability across data sets.

2 Database development. We are compiling data from a large number of participants. Transcripts are done using the CHAT system (MacWhinney, 2000) and linked to the digitized audio and video.

3 Analysis customization. Using the current CLAN programs (MacWhinney, 2000) as a basis, we have constructed a set of tools for the analysis of multimedia transcripts on the levels of phonology, lexicon, morphology, syntax, discourse, and pragmatics.

4 Measure development. We use the annotations produced by these tools to automatically compute measures that were otherwise being coded by hand. We are also developing new measures based on automatically constructed annotations.

5 Syndrome classification. Using these new measures and the growing database, we are working with consortium members and statistical consultants to develop new approaches to syndrome-based patient classification and diagnosis.

6 Support for qualitative analysis. We are supporting qualitative analysis on three levels. First, the CLAN editor supports standard Conversation Analysis (CA) transcription. Second, we have formalized a set of coding systems specific to communications involving persons with aphasia. Third, we are promoting a system to provide web-based collaborative commentary on conversational interactions.

7 Characterization of recovery processes. We will develop microgenetic methods such as time sequential analysis and growth curves to trace changes across time in both individual participants and groups of participants.

8 Evaluation of treatment effects. We will develop methods that allow us to evaluate the effectiveness of specific aphasia rehabilitation treatments and we are beginning to get repeated measures at yearly intervals from some participants.

9 Johnny Appleseed. We are disseminating these new tools through personal contact, annual workshops, journal publications, conference presentations, the AphasiaBank Google Group, and downloads available over the Internet.

Section Summary

- The goals of AphasiaBank are protocol standardization, database development, analysis customization, measure development, syndrome classification, support for qualitative analysis, characterization of recovery processes, evaluation of treatment outcomes, and dissemination of methods.

15.4 Protocol Standardization

Based on extensive input from consortium members and pilot work, we have established a uniform AphasiaBank protocol. This protocol, along with demographic forms, demographic spreadsheets, tests, and stimuli, is available at the AphasiaBank website (http://www.talkbank.org/AphasiaBank). The protocol consists of four different discourse genres: personal narratives, picture descriptions, story telling, and procedural discourse. A script was developed to keep the prompts consistent across investigators. The script includes a second-level prompt to use if a participant does not respond in 10 seconds. A troubleshooting script is also available for participants who still cannot respond and need additional prompting with simplified questions. The discourse protocol is administered in one session and is recorded on video. The investigator makes every effort to be as silent as possible while giving maximal non-verbal encouragers to the participants. Participants are given as much time as they need for their responses.

The personal narratives are elicited by asking the participants with aphasia about their speech, their stroke, their recovery, and an important event in their lives. Non-aphasic participants are asked about an illness or injury, their recovery from that illness or injury, any experience they have had with people who have trouble communicating, and an important event in their lives.

For the picture descriptions, participants are shown three black-and-white drawings. They are asked to look at the picture and tell a story with a beginning, middle, and end. The first picture stimulus is a four-paneled picture of a child playing with a soccer ball and breaking a window, the second is a six-paneled picture of a child refusing an umbrella and getting caught in the rain, and the third is the Nicholas and Brookshire (1995) picture of a cat stuck in a tree. A fourth picture, a color photograph of a flood-rescue scene, was used for the first two years of the project and then discontinued because many participants were having trouble interpreting the picture.

For the story-telling task, participants are shown a paperback picture book of Cinderella, with the words covered. They are told to look through the book to remember how the story goes. Then the book is taken away and they are asked to tell as much of the story as they can.

Finally, the procedural discourse task involves asking the participants to describe how they would make a peanut butter and jelly sandwich. (Test sites outside the United States may substitute another simple food preparation.) A stimulus picture

Table 15.1   Demographic and test data for AphasiaBank participants.

	Aphasia n=102	on-Aphasia n=102
Age – mean (s.d.)	63.8 years (12.9)	60.9 years (17.0)
Gender	35 females	55 females
	67 males	47 males
Handedness	88 right	88 right
	8 left	10 left
	5 ambidextrous	3 ambidextrous
	1 unknown	
Education	15.6 years (3.0)	15.1 years (2.3)
Time post-onset	6.8 years (5.9)	
Type of aphasia (by WAB)	34 Anomic	
	26 Broca	
	14 Conduction	
	10 Wernicke	
	9 not aphasic	
	5 Transcortical Motor	
	2 Global	
	1 Transcortical Sensory	
	1 unavailable	
WAB AQ score	68.73 (21.19)	

with photographs of peanut butter, bread, and jelly is available for use with participants who need extra help.

In addition to the discourse protocol, four tests are administered to participants with aphasia: (1) the Aphasia Quotient (AQ) subtests from the Western Aphasia Battery, Revised (WAB; Kertész, 2007); (2) the short form of the Boston Naming Test, Second Edition (Kaplan, Goodglass, and Weintraub, 2001); (3) the Verb Naming Test from the Northwestern Assessment of Verbs and Sentences, Revised; and (4) the AphasiaBank Repetition Test, developed to assess word-level and sentence-level repetition skills. All testing, with the exception of the WAB, is recorded on video. The non-aphasic participants are tested with the Mini-Mental State Exam (Folstein, Folstein, and Fanjiang, 2002) and the Geriatric Depression Scale (Brink *et al.*, 1982) to rule out cognitive impairment and depression. All test results are entered into a master spreadsheet that is password protected on the AphasiaBank website and available to AphasiaBank members.

Finally, in addition to the discourse protocol and the testing, investigators collect extensive demographic information about all participants. Fifty-one fields of data in the demographic spreadsheet include variables such as gender, date of birth, race, handedness, education, occupation, language status (monolingual, childhood bilingual, etc.), aphasia etiology, aphasia duration, aphasia type, site of lesion, motor status, depression, dysarthria, apraxia of speech, history of neurological conditions, and history of communication disorders. Table 15.1 provides a snapshot from June 2010 on a selection of test and demographic variables.

> **Section Summary**
>
> • AphasiaBank uses a uniform protocol for the collection of discourse and demographic data, as well as testing of participants. The AphasiaBank protocol and demographics collection methods are available on the web at http://www.talkbank.org/AphasiaBank.

15.5 Transcribing

All discourse samples are transcribed in the CHAT format (MacWhinney, 2000). CHAT is a transcription format that has been developed over the last 30 years for use in a variety of disciplines such as first-language acquisition, second-language acquisition, classroom discourse, and Conversation Analysis. The CHAT transcription format is designed to operate closely with a set of programs called CLAN, which is also described in MacWhinney (2000). These programs, along with electronic versions of the manual, can also be downloaded from the AphasiaBank website at http://talkbank.org/AphasiaBank.

The CLAN programs permit the analysis of a wide range of linguistic and discourse structures. Transcription in CHAT is facilitated by a method called Walker Controller, which allows the transcriber to continually replay the original audio record. This method is built into the CLAN program and the editing of transcripts relies on the CLAN editor facility. One direct result of this process is that each utterance is then linked to a specific region of the audio or video record. This linkage can be useful for verification of transcription accuracy and for later phonological, gestural, or conversational analysis. A transcription training manual was prepared specifically for AphasiaBank purposes and posted at the website. Following the guidelines set by Berndt *et al.* (2000), utterances are segmented based on the following hierarchy of indices: syntax, intonation, pause, and semantics. Many students and research assistants in our facility and others have been trained to transcribe reliably and every transcript is reviewed by at least two transcribers for accuracy. For the aphasia transcripts, one of those reviewers is always speech-language pathologist.

The following CHAT fragment from the elman07a file in AphasiaBank displays some of the basic CHAT coding conventions for marking linguistic behaviors such as word repetitions ([/]), fillers (&), and gestures (&=).

```
(1)   *INV:   what kinds of things have you done to try to get better
              since your stroke ?
      *PAR:   &uh &=shrugs hell I don't know.
      *PAR:   I suppose &uh everything [/] &uh everything better all the
              time.
```

At the end of each line, there is a round bullet symbol that contains information regarding the time value for the beginning and end of the utterance. Usually, this bullet is closed. However, if you wish to see these values, the bullet can be expanded to display the times, as shown here:

```
(2)   *INV:   what kinds of things have you done to try to get better
              since your stroke ? •244832_249548•
      *PAR:   &uh &=shrugs hell I don't know. •249548_257129•
      *PAR:   I suppose &uh everything [/] &uh everything better all
              the time. •257129_261774•
```

> **Section Summary**
>
> • AphasiaBank transcription relies on the CHAT data format as formalized
>   in the CHAT manual available from http://talkbank.org/AphasiaBank.

15.6   Error Coding

Errors are coded at both the word and sentence level by speech-language pathologists. For word-level errors, we have developed a hierarchical system to capture errors in six categories: phonology, semantics, neologism, dysfluency, morphology, and formal lexical features. Within each category, errors are coded further to capture whether the error was a word or non-word, whether the target was known or unknown, whether a suffix was missing, and more. Errors that are not real words are transcribed using IPA. The error code can also indicate if the error was repeated or changed (retraced) by the speaker within the utterance by added "-rep" or "-ret", respectively, to the error code. Examples 3a–f illustrate the six word-level error types.

(3a)   Neologism, unknown target [* n:uk]:
```
       *PAR:   and of course she has a fancy ɹup@u [* n:uk].
```

(3b)   Phonological error, real word, target known [* p:w]:
```
       *PAR:   and she went to the [/] &uh the mall [: ball] [* p:w].
```

(3c)   Phonological error, non-word, target known [* p:n]:
```
       *PAR:   peanut bʌθɚ̞@u [: butter] [* p:n] and sɛlɪ@u [: jelly]
               [* p:n] sæmɪtʃ@u [: sandwich] [* p:n].
```

(3d)   Semantic error, related word, known target [* s:r]:
```
       *PAR:   and the &m mother has two daughters himself [: herself]
               [* s:r].
```

(3e) Semantic error, unknown target [* s:uk]:
    PAR: and they get married and live everyone [s:uk] you
           know.

(3f) Morphology error, overregularized [* m:=s]:
    PAR: &uh my second third and fourth childs [m:=s]
           were &=laughs + ...

The reader will note that these examples included some CHAT symbols that had not yet been covered: @u for "Unicode" is appended to all IPA productions; intended (target) words, if known, are placed next to the error production as [: target]; errors are coded as [* error code] immediately following the target word, if known, or the error itself; and +... at the end of an utterance indicates trailing off.

In addition to these six categories of word-level codes, there are several utterance-level codes that are marked at the ends of utterances, as illustrated in 4a–c:

(4a) Agrammatism [+ gram]:
    *PAR: yeah &=finger:write May twenty fifth two thousand one
           I [/] I &s I [/] I am a stroke. [+ gram]

(4b) Empty speech [+ es]
    *PAR: &uh I went to my &=sighs whatever &=laughs. [+ es]

(4c) Jargon [+ jar]
    PAR: if I could ɹeɪv@u [: x@n] [n:uk] it I guess I can
           bɹæm@u [: x@n] [* n:uk] it. [+ jar]

15.7 Analyses

15.7.1 CLAN

Once files have been transcribed in CHAT, users can run a wide variety of CLAN analysis programs. There are 29 CLAN programs, each with a wide variety of functions and options. String-search programs can compute frequency counts, key-word and line profiles, mean length of utterance, mean length of turn, type–token ratios, maximum word-length counts, maximum utterance-length histograms, vocabulary diversity, and so on. It is worth noting that there are several fields for demographic information to be included in the header lines of a transcript. This allows for the analysis outputs to include that information or for analyses to be conducted on particular subsets of the data, for example males versus females or just participants with Wernicke's aphasia.

15.7.2 Extensible Markup Language (XML)

The TalkBank project, which includes AphasiaBank as well as several other shared databases, has constructed Java-based tools that convert CHAT files to XML. The XML format facilitates systematic analysis, display, and searching of data over the web, but it is intended for reading by programs, not by humans. These XML files can then be reformatted back to CHAT and the initial and final versions compared to guarantee the accuracy of the roundtrip. Only when the roundtrip runs without differences can we accept the data into TalkBank. The process of converting the database to XML was completed in 2004, after nearly three years of work. An important outcome of this conversion has been the full systematization of the coding system and an increase in the consistency of the database. In addition, we were able to convert a wide range of discrepant font and character encoding systems to a consistent Unicode format. This was particularly important for Asian languages that use non-Roman characters, but it was also useful for special Roman characters with diacritics in languages such as French, German, and Spanish.

15.7.3   GEM

When transcribing language samples that include various tasks, headers marked by @G or "gem headers" are used to mark the beginning of a new task. In AphasiaBank, for instance, some of the headers are @G: Umbrella (for the refused umbrella picture stimulus) and @G: Cinderella (for the Cinderella story telling). For example, if you wanted to look at the Cinderella portion of a transcript only and you wanted the participants' lines only, you would use this command:

```
gem +sCinderella +t*PAR +n +d1 +f *.cha.
```

The result would be new gem files in legal CHAT format with file names, line numbers, and identification codes for each original CHAT file in the folder. If you wanted to do this on multiple folders, you simply need to add +re to the command line.

15.7.4   *Lexical and Morphological Coding*

CLAN has a subprogram called MOR that applies part-of-speech taggers for English, Spanish, German, French, Italian, Japanese, Cantonese, and Mandarin. The results of these taggers are then disambiguated using the statistical disambiguator called POST (Parisse and Le Normand, 2000) that uses the context before and after the word to assign part-of-speech to ambiguous cases. The transcript then appears with a new tier, %mor, under each speaker tier that gives the lexical and morphological coding for each word on the main speaker tier. These morphological codes can then be used to automatically compute indices such as DSS (Developmental Sentence Score; Lee, 1966), IPSyn (Index of Productive Syntax; Scarborough, 1990), and a simple version of LARSP (Language, Assessment, Remediation, and Screening Procedure; Crystal, Fletcher, and Garman 1976).

The following example transcript shows a block of conversation that has been automatically supplemented with a %mor line in which each word of the main line is given a full morphological analysis.

```
(5)   *INV:   can you tell me more &=ges:more about it ?
      %mor:   aux|can pro|you v|tell pro|me adv|more prep|about
              pro|it ?
      *PAR:   well my stroke started on [//] &uh &w (.) one night and
              I did not think it was too bad.
      %mor:   co|well   pro:poss:det|my   n|stroke   v|start-PAST   pro:
              indef|one n|night conj:coo|and pro|I aux|do&PAST neg|not
              v|think pro|it v:cop|be&PAST&13S adv:int|too adj|bad.
      *PAR:   well it started at noon actually.
      %mor:   co|well pro|it v|start-PAST prep|at n|noon
              adv:adj|actual-LY.
      *PAR:   and then I went out with my friends and &uh they were
              concerned because I was driving erratically.
      %mor:   conj:coo|and adv:tem|then pro|I v|go&PAST adv:loc|out
              prep|with
              pro:poss:det|my   n|friend-PL   conj:coo|and   pro|they
              aux|be&PAST
              part|concern-PERF conj:sub|because pro|I aux|be &PAST&13S
              part|drive-PROG adv:adj|erratic-AL-LY.
```

In this sample, the main speaker tier is followed by the %mor tier. On the main speaker tier, [/] indicates repetition, [//] indicates revision, (.) indicates a short pause, & is used before fillers and word fragments, and &= is used before gestures. On the %mor line, the part of speech (e.g. "aux" for auxiliary, "pro" for pronoun, "v" for verb) comes before the vertical bar and the word used by the speaker from the main tier. Suffixes are attached to the word (e.g. &PAST for irregular past, -PL for regular plural, -PROG for progressive).

In this example, the %mor line was created automatically through these three computer commands:

```
mor *.cha
post *.cha
check *.cha
```

The first command runs the MOR grammar for English on the basic transcript file. This grammar can be downloaded from http://childes.psy.cmu.edu/morgrams/. The second command automatically disambiguates alternative readings inserted by MOR. The third command checks to make sure that the output is complete and syntactically accurate. For more information on the development and inner workings of MOR, POST, and CHECK, the reader is encouraged to read MacWhinney (2008).

15.7.5 *Lexical Diversity Analysis*

A glossary of CLAN commands for some basic types of analyses was developed and posted at the AphasiaBank website. The commands included in the glossary were intended to serve as a template to allow aphasia researchers to explore the wide variety of analyses that are possible. For example, to analyze lexical diversity, a researcher could use the command:

```
vocd +r6 +t*PAR *.cha
```

to calculate VOCD (VOCabulary Diversity) in the participants' utterances for all of the CHAT files within a folder. The +r6 part of the command is used to exclude retracings (revisions) from the calculation. VOCD was developed by Malvern *et al.* (2004) as a replacement for the type/toke ratio (TTR) measure, which fails to correct for sample size. The TTR is a simple ratio of the types of words used by a speaker in a transcript over the total number of words in the transcript. For example, if the speaker uses 30 different words and produces a total output of 120 words, then the TTR is 30/120 or 0.25. However, small transcripts often have inaccurately high TTR ratios, simply because they are not big enough to allow for word repetitions. VOCD corrects this problem statistically for all but the smallest samples (for details, see the CLAN manual available online at http://childes.psy.cmu.edu/). One can compute VOCD either from the main speaker line or the %mor line in the CHAT transcript. However, the goal of both TTR and VOCD is to measure lexical diversity. For such analyses, it may not be appropriate to treat variant inflected forms or derivations of the same base (e.g. marry, remarry, and married) as different. To avoid this problem, one can compute VOCD from the %mor line using this command to control the filtering of affixes:

```
vocd +t%mor -t* +s"*|*-%%" +s"*|*&%%" *.cha.
```

It may also be necessary to exclude other unwanted items such as neologisms or unintelligible utterances, which can be done by adding those exclusions to the CLAN command.

Fergadiotis, Wright, and Capilouto (2010) used the VOCD command to determine if productive vocabulary differs across discourse types in non-aphasic young adults (20–29 years old, n=43) and older adults (70–79 years old, n=43). (These participants are part of the non-aphasic corpus in the AphasiaBank database.) Results indicated that lexical diversity was influenced by discourse type and age. For both groups, the lexical diversity hierarchy was the same, with procedural discourse yielding the least lexical diversity, personal recounts the greatest, and single picture description and story telling falling in-between. Age was a factor for the procedural discourse and personal recounts, with older adults producing significantly greater lexical diversity than the younger adults. It would be interesting to conduct these types of analyses on the discourse samples from participants with aphasia to add to our understanding of discourse and the influence of the various methods used for its evaluation and treatment.

15.7.6 *MORtable*

A relatively new CLAN analysis program, MORTABLE, was developed to create a table of parts of speech and bound morphemes. The command

```
mortable +t*PAR +u *.cha
```

generates a file that can be opened directly as an Excel spreadsheet. The columns of this spreadsheet provide the following information:

- identifying information from the header lines in the CHAT transcript (e.g. participant ID, gender, type of aphasia);
- parts of speech frequency information for wh-words, adjectives, adverbs, auxiliaries, complements, conjunctions, determiners, infinitives, modals, nouns, negations, prepositions, pronouns, possessive pronouns, reflexive pronouns, quantifiers, and verbs; and
- bound morpheme frequency information for third-person singular irregular, past irregular, third-person singular regular, past regular, comparative, superlative, irregular plural, regular plural, possessive, past participle irregular, past participle regular, present participle.

15.7.7 *Lexical Frequency Analysis*

Lexical frequency analyses have been conducted to examine the Cinderella storytelling lexicons in participants with and without aphasia (MacWhinney *et al.*, 2010). The following FREQ command was used to compute the frequencies of word form occurrences on the %mor line of Cinderella gem files:

```
freq +t%mor -t* +s@r-*,o-% +u +o +fS *.gem.cex
```

This command has eight segments, the meanings of which are:

```
freq            activates the FREQ command
+t%mor          includes information from the %mor line
-t*             excludes information from the main speaker line
+s@r-*,o-%      finds all stems and ignores all other markers
+u              merges all specified files together
+o              sorts output by descending frequency
+fS             sends output to a file
*.gem.cex       runs the command on all files with that extension.
```

The resulting CLAN output lists the frequencies of each word used in the participants' stories. When the story transcripts include errors for which the intended target is known (e.g. sippers for slippers), the analysis will be based on tallies of the intended word (slippers). One can also decide whether to exclude various tokens that are counted as words, such as neologisms, unintelligible words, onomatopoeia, and letters (of the alphabet). If, for example, one wanted to exclude neologisms and unintelligible words, one would include –s@"l–neo,l–unk" in the command line.

The results of this analysis showed that non-aphasic speakers (n=25) generated 839 different word types and a cumulative total of 13 309 words; participants with aphasia (n=24) generated 526 word types and a cumulative 5330 tokens.

Examination of the word totals showed that, for each group, roughly a third of the words occurred only once, another third occurred from two to four times, with the remaining third occurring five times or more. Although this wide range of lexical diversity is of interest in itself, the core ideas of the Cinderella story appear to be captured in the 306 words that occurred at least five times in the non-aphasic sample. These words included nouns, verbs, adjectives, and adverbs.

To create a target lexicon, we narrowed our focus to nouns and verbs. To search for nouns only, the following command was used:

```
freq +t%mor +t*PAR -t*+o +s@r-*,|-n:*,|-n,o-% +u *.gem.cex
```

The primary modification to this command from the previously explained command is the addition of |-n:*,|-n which finds all nouns, including proper nouns, compound nouns, and nouns with prefixes, still collapsing them across stems. To search for verbs, the command used these +s switches to search for verbs, auxiliaries and participles:

```
+s@r-*,|-v*,o-% +s@r-*,|-aux*,o-% +s@r-*,|-part*,o-%
```

The results showed that speakers with aphasia produced only two-thirds as many different word types as did the non-aphasic speakers, with less than half the number of tokens. Non-aphasic speakers used 80 nouns and 71 verbs at least five times. In comparison, speakers with aphasia used 34 nouns and 36 verbs five times or more, reflecting the far more restrictive lexical diversity imposed by aphasia. Nevertheless, 76% of the nouns used by the aphasic speakers also appeared in the non-aphasic lexicon.

The 10 most frequently occurring nouns in both the non-aphasic and the aphasic samples had six words in common: Cinderella, ball, prince, slipper, mother/stepmother, and sister/stepsister. The four other most frequent nouns in the aphasia stories were man, shoe, girl, and home, which are not as tightly and specifically linked to the Cinderella story as are the four other words from the top 10 nouns in the non-aphasia stories, which were dress, fairy, daughter/stepdaughter, and godmother.

There were eight verbs in common among the "top 10" of the aphasia and non-aphasia story samples, and all 33 verbs used by speakers with aphasia were found in the non-aphasic lexicon. Gordon (2008) tracked the usage of 11 light verbs (be, have, come, go, give, take, make, do, get, move, and put). All of these, with the exception of "move" and "get," occurred in the aphasic sample, whereas only six of them appeared in the non-aphasic lexicon. The fact that the non-aphasic verb lexicon (71 verbs) was more than twice as large as the sample provided by speakers with aphasia (33 verbs) supports the argument that speakers with aphasia are in general more reliant on light verbs, showing more limited diversity for verbs. It is important to note that these analyses were conducted on 25 speakers with various types of aphasia, but with a greater representation of speakers with anomia and conduction aphasia and only a few individuals with Broca's aphasia.

To illustrate the application of these findings on an individual basis, MacWhinney *et al.* (2010) examined Cinderella lexicons for two speakers with different aphasia types and severities. Speaker 1 has severe Wernicke's aphasia (WAB AQ=28.2) as a result of a stroke. He was 4 years post-onset of his aphasia, and had received both individual and group therapy since that time. Speaker 2, although scoring above the WAB cut-off for aphasia, has persistent mild word-finding problems. He displays many hesitancies and false starts of the type that characterize speakers with anomia. One of the authors (ALH) has followed this individual since his stroke approximately 10 years ago. Throughout the decade, he has received extensive individual and group treatment, and has made significant progress in rehabilitation. These two fluent speakers represent extremes of the aphasia severity scale, and should not only contrast with each other in their Cinderella narratives, but Speaker 2 should also more closely approximate the non-aphasic speech sample than he does the aphasic sample overall. If there is merit in comparing such individuals to non-aphasic speakers, then their similarities and differences from the normal lexicon should become apparent.

Results revealed that Speaker 1's total speech output for the Cinderella story was 107 words, representing 59 different word types. Accordingly, his TTR (0.55) is considerably higher than the aphasic mean TTR (0.41). In fact, Speaker 1 used 42 words of his 107-word narration only once. Largely, this reflects his unfocused and neologistic output. However, as mentioned earlier, the TTR measure fails to correct for sample size. Using the version of VOCD built into CLAN, we found that his lexical diversity score was 45.95. However, seven of his "words" were in fact neologisms for which no clear referent could be identified. Only three nouns (Cinderella, home, party) and three verbs (go, have, think) from his sample also appeared in the non-aphasic lexicon.

In contrast, Speaker 2's narrative was both longer and much more clearly related to the lexicon of the non-aphasic speakers. It included 96 word types and 263 tokens, with a resultant TTR of 0.36 and lexical density of 31.11, almost precisely the non-aphasic mean for TTR (0.35) and lexical density. Even though his narrative was relatively brief, it provided a substantially correct summary of the Cinderella story. (It is interesting to note that it also contained some words that were not in the non-aphasic lexicon at all, but were used appropriately. These included "lowly", "envious", and "smitten".)

This research demonstrates that many of the methods for studying lexical patterns from the language-acquisition research tradition can be applied directly to the study of lexical usage in participants with aphasia. The Cinderella story, for example, has frequently been used in aphasia research (Faroqi-Shah and Thompson, 2007; Rochon *et al.*, 2000; Stark and Viola, 2007; Thompson *et al.*, 1997). Both Rochon *et al.* and Thompson *et al.* have developed general systems for scoring narrative productions that have been applied to the Cinderella transcripts of individuals with aphasia. However, a surprising oversight in past research has been the lack of a non-aphasic standard for comparison. Without a baseline for how non-aphasic speakers narrate Cinderella, it is difficult to understand how measures of severity relate to normal expectations, and to evaluate the extent to which aphasic speakers can recover function. Furthermore, the various analyses of production in the Cinderella task have focused primarily on the construction of measures of morphosyntactic control. These measures include a wide diversity of counts of grammatical structures, inflectional processes, and sentence patterns. However, with the exception of a recent analysis by Gordon (2008), there has been relatively little attention to the analysis of the use of specific lexical items that play a role within the story of

Cinderella. Hopefully, awareness of the tools described here can stimulate increased attention to patterns of lexical frequency, lexicon development, and lexical diversity in aphasia.

15.7.8 COMBO

This CLAN command can be used to search for a connected string of words. For example, to examine the use of "once upon a time" or "happily ever after" in Cinderella stories by aphasic and non-aphasic participants, one could use the following commands:

```
combo +t*PAR +re +d1 +sonce^upon^a^time *.cha
combo +t*PAR +re +d1 +shappily^ever^after *.cha.
```

In 120 aphasia samples, "once upon a time" occurred one time; in 101 non-aphasic samples it occurred 16 times. "Happily ever after" occurred 11 times in the 120 aphasic samples and 75 times in the 101 non-aphasic samples. In some of the aphasia samples, it should be noted, the productions were not error-free. Here are examples of some of the paraphasic errors observed:

```
*PAR:  they live hevry [: happily] [* n:k] ever after.
*PAR:  &uh and they're &maf haffiply [: happily] [* n:k] ever after.
```

Further investigations into idioms and formulaic speech are underway and should provide insight into the relative preservation or loss of these linguistic elements in aphasic discourse.

15.7.9 Error Analysis

As mentioned above, AphasiaBank transcripts include a large number of word-level and sentence-level error codes. In CLAN, the FREQ command can be used to list and count each of these errors. CLAN can produce the results in a variety of ways. For example, using the +d2 option in the CLAN command sends the output to an Excel file. For word-level errors, using the +d6 option outputs the error production, the target word (if known), and the transcript file name. To search for semantic errors, one can use the following FREQ command:

```
freq +s"[\* s*]" +t*PAR +d6 adler12a.cha.
```

The output from this command looks as follows:

```
4 [* s-ret]
2 he [: she] [* s-ret]
1 she [: he] [* s-ret]
1 guy [: woman] [* s-ret]
```

```
3 [* s]
1 floor [: ground] [* s]
1 she [: he] [* s]
1 sandwich [: bread]
```

In these sample outputs, the [* s] means the error was a semantic paraphasia; the [*s-ret] means the participant retraced (revised) the semantic paraphasia within the utterance. All other CHAT coding symbols should already be familiar to the reader.

If more information about the error is desired, one can use the +d option, which outputs the selected errors with their frequencies and the filename and transcript line number where the error occurs. It also displays the actual transcript line from the file with the error so it can be seen in context. From this CLAN output, one can triple click on the filename information line and bring up onto the computer screen the whole transcript with the relevant line highlighted for even fuller context.

MacWhinney *et al.* (2010) illustrated a very simple example of tracking errors in the Cinderella story using the following command to trace variant forms of production of the word "Cinderella":

```
freq +s"Cinderella" +t*PAR +u *.gem.cex.
```

This command tracks both correct uses of "Cinderella" and incorrect forms with the replacement code [: Cinderella] when the intended target was "Cinderella". The results included paraphasic errors such as Cinderenella, Cinderlella, Cilawella, Cilawilla, Cilawillipa, and Secerundid.

More investigations of word-level and sentence-level errors are underway and planned. Ideas for future studies have been posted at the AphasiaBank website. Within the domain of errors, we intend to delve further into the nature of paraphasic errors and the relative advantages of common coding systems. Neologistic errors (non-word errors that are not phonologically related to a known the target word) can be examined to determine what attributes permit listeners to grasp meaning in some cases but not in others. The range of questions that can be posed to these data, using these tools, is practically limitless.

Section Summary

- AphasiaBank data can be analyzed by CLAN programs for errors, morphosyntax, lexical frequencies, syntactic patterns, and discourse patterns.

15.8   Syndrome Classification

Several classifications systems have been described and used over the many decades of aphasia research (Geschwind, 1979; Luria and Hutton, 1977; Schuell, 1974).

These systems have also received extensive criticism (e.g. Caramazza, 1984; Schwartz, 1984; Sundet and Engvik, 1985). In AphasiaBank, participants are being classified in two ways: by the WAB and by their clinician. The eight possible WAB types are: Anomic, Conduction, Transcortical Sensory, Wernicke, Broca, Isolation, Transcortical Motor, and Global. They are based on the participants' scores on subtests in the domains of Spontaneous Speech Fluency and Information Content, Auditory Comprehension, Repetition, and Naming. Clinicians use their judgment and experience to identify the aphasia type, usually resulting in one of the same eight possible types used by the WAB.

We have conducted principle components and k-means analyses on the current AphasiaBank database to examine the agreement between clinician types and WAB types, where and why the disagreements occur, and what types of analyses and variables (e.g. adding discourse and error measures to the traditional measures of fluency, comprehension, naming, and repetition) may help improve the classification. One initial finding was that there are nine participants who perform above the WAB cutoff for any aphasia type but who are still deemed to be Anomic by their clinicians. A second finding is that patients classified as Broca's aphasics by clinicians fall into two different clusters in the statistical analysis, as found earlier by Sundet and Engvik (1985). To complete a full classificatory analysis requires as large a dataset as possible in order to properly classify types such as conduction. Moreover, we believe that further work needs to be done in terms of evaluating clinician judgments, as well as their match to WAB type (Swindell, Holland, and Fromm, 1984). Overall, the construction of syndrome classification continues to be a work in progress and a long-term goal of the study.

15.9   Content Analysis

The interview data can also be subjected to content analyses for features such as attitudes and coping strategies (Pennebaker, Francis, and Booth, 2001). An example of content analysis of the database makes use of the GEM command to extract a section of the discourse sample in which participants with aphasia (n=71) were asked about their speech (Fromm *et al.*, 2011). Specifically, at the beginning of the testing session, participants were asked, "How do you think your speech is these days?" Responses to this question were coded by two researchers, revealing that positive responses accounted for 59% of all responses, followed by average or mixed responses (18%), negative responses (17%), and unclear/jargon responses (6%). Aphasia severity was significantly associated with the nature of the response, with higher WAB AQ scores in the positive group. Aphasia type and time post-onset were not significantly associated with the nature of response. Research of this type provides insight into aphasia participants' perceptions of their condition and can inform treatment designed to help individuals with aphasia capitalize on or develop resilience.

15.10 Profiles of Recovery Processes

We have only just begun to get repeated measurements on participants to start examining changes over time. The plan is to compare quantitative discourse measures before and after the administration of different types of treatments to evaluate their impact on recovery.

15.11 Conclusion

AphasiaBank provides both a rich database and powerful analysis techniques for improving our understanding of aphasia and its treatment. As this database grows in coverage for patient types, ages, and languages, we will be able to ask increasingly powerful questions. We encourage researchers to collect new data using the standard protocol and to contribute these data to the shared database. We also encourage researchers to use the tools that are available to conduct increasingly sophisticated studies of communication in aphasia.

References

Berndt, R., Wayland, S., Rochon, E. *et al.* (2000). *Quantitative Production Analysis: A Training Manual for the Analysis of Aphasic Sentence Production*. Hove, UK: Psychology Press.

Brink, T. L., Yesavage, J. A., Lum, O. *et al.* (1982). Screening tests for geriatric depression. *Clinical Gerontologist*, 1, 37–44.

Brown, R. (1973). *A First Language: The Early Stages*. Cambridge, MA: Harvard University Press.

Caramazza, A. (1984). The logic of neuropsychological research and the problem of patient classification in aphasia. *Brain and Language*, 21, 9–20.

Crystal, D., Fletcher, P., and Garman, M. (1976). *The Grammatical Analysis of Language Disability*. London: Edward Arnold.

Faroqi-Shah, Y. and Thompson, C. K. (2007). Verb inflections in agrammatic aphasia: encoding of tense features. *Journal of Memory and Language*, 56, 129–151.

Feldman, H., Janosky, J. E., Scher, M. S., and Wareham, N. L. (1994). Language abilities following prematurity, periventricular brain injury, and cerebral palsy. *Journal of Communication Disorders*, 27, 71–90.

Fergadiotis, G., Wright, H. H., and Capilouto, G. J. (2010). Productive vocabulary across discourse types. Paper presented at the Clinical Aphasiology Conference, Isle of Palms, SC, May 23–27.

Folstein, M., Folstein, S., and Fanjiang, G. (2002). *Mini-Mental State Examination*. Lutz, FL: Psychological Assessment Resources, Inc.

Frederiksen, C., Donin, J., Koschmann, T., and Kelson, A. M. (2004). Investigating diagnostic problem solving in medicine through cognitive analysis of clinical discourse. Paper presented at the Society for Text and Discourse, Chicago, August 1–4.

Fromm, D., Holland, A., Armstrong, E. *et al.* (2011). "Better but no cigar": persons with aphasia speak about their speech. *Aphasiology*, 25(11), 1431–1447.

Geschwind, N. (1979). Specializations of the human brain. *Scientific American*, 241(3), 7–16.

Goldman, R., Pea, R., Barron, B., and Derry, S. (eds) (2007). *Video Research in the Learning Sciences*. Mahwah, NJ: Lawrence Erlbaum Associates.

Gordon, J. (2008). Measuring the lexical semantics of picture description in aphasia. *Aphasiology*, 22, 839–852.

Kaplan, E., Goodglass, H., and Weintraub, S. (2001). *Boston Naming Test*, 2nd edn. Austin, TX: Pro-Ed.

Kertész, A. (2007). *Western Aphasia Battery*. San Antonio, TX: PsychCorp.

Labov, W. (2001). *Principles of Linguistic Change*, vol. 2, *Social Considerations*. Oxford: Blackwell.

Lee, L. (1966). Developmental sentence types: a method for comparing normal and deviant syntactic development. *Journal of Speech and Hearing Disorders*, 31, 331–330.

Luria, A. R. and Hutton, J. T. (1977). A modern assessment of the basic forms of aphasia. *Brain and Language*, 4, 129–151.

MacWhinney, B. (2000). *The CHILDES Project: Tools for Analyzing Talk*, 3rd edn. Mahwah, NJ: Lawrence Erlbaum Associates.

MacWhinney, B. (2008). Enriching CHILDES for morphosyntactic analysis. In H. Behrens (ed.), *Trends in Corpus Research: Finding Structure in Data*. Amsterdam: John Benjamins, pp. 165–198.

MacWhinney, B. (2010). Computational models of child language learning. *Journal of Child Language*, 37, 477–485.

MacWhinney, B., Fromm, D., Holland, A. *et al.* (2010). Automated analysis of the Cinderella story. *Aphasiology*, 24, 856–868.

MacWhinney, B. and Leinbach, J. (1991). Implementations are not conceptualizations: revising the verb learning model. *Cognition*, 29, 121–157.

MacWhinney, B. and Wagner, J. (2010). Transcribing, searching and data sharing: the CLAN software and the TalkBank data repository. *Gesprächsforschung*, 2, 1–20.

Malvern, D., Richards, B. J., Chipere, N., and Durán, P. (2004). *Lexical Diversity and Language Development*. New York: Palgrave Macmillan.

Nicholas, L. and Brookshire, R. (1995). Presence, completeness and accuracy of main concepts in the connected speech of non-brain-damaged adults and adults with aphasia. *Journal of Speech and Hearing Research*, 38, 145–156.

Parisse, C. and Le Normand, M. T. (2000). Automatic disambiguation of the morphosyntax in spoken language corpora. *Behavior Research Methods, Instruments, and Computers*, 32, 468–481.

Pennebaker, J. W., Francis, M.E., and Booth, R. J. (2001). *Linguistic Inquiry and Word Count (LIWC): A Computerized Text Analysis Program*. Mahwah, NJ: Lawrence Erlbaum Associates.

Rochon, E., Saffran, E., Berndt, R., and Schwartz, M. (2000). Quantitative analysis of aphasic sentence production: further development and new data. *Brain and Language*, 72, 193–218.

Scarborough, H. S. (1990). Index of productive syntax. *Applied Psycholinguistics*, 11, 1–22.

Schober, M. and Conrad, F. (2006). Does conversational interviewing reduce survey measurement error? *Public Opinion Quarterly*, 61, 576–602.

Schuell, H. (1974). *Aphasia Theory and Therapy*. Baltimore: University Park Press.

Schwartz, M. (1984). What the classical aphasia categories can't do for us, and why. *Brain and Language*, 21, 3–8.

Siegler, R. S. (2006). Microgenetic analyses of learning. In D. Kuhn and R. S. Siegler (eds), *Handbook of Child Psychology*, vol. 2, *Cognition, Perception, and Language*. Hoboken, NJ: John Wiley & Sons, Inc., 464–510.

Stark, J. A. and Viola, M. S. (2007). Cinderella, Cinderella! Longitudinal analysis of qualitative and quantitative aspects of seven tellings of Cinderella by a Broca's aphasic. *Brain and Language*, 103, 234–235.

Sundet, K. and Engvik, H. (1985). The validity of aphasic subtypes. *Scandinavian Journal of Psychology*, 26, 219–226.

Swindell, C., Holland, A., and Fromm, D. (1984). Classification of aphasia: WAB type versus clinical impression. Paper presented at the Clinical Aphasiology Conference, Seabrook Island, SC, May 20–24.

Thompson, C. K., Ballard, K. J., Tait, M. E. *et al.* (1997). Patterns of language decline in nonfluent primary progressive aphasia. *Aphasiology*, 11, 297–321.

Yip, V. and Matthews, S. (2007). *The Bilingual Child: Early Development and Language*. Cambridge: Cambridge University Press.

16 Disseminating Research: Reading, Writing, and Publishing

Sharynne McLeod

16.1 Introduction

The previous chapters have provided guidelines for undertaking research in the field of clinical linguistics and phonetics. Once new knowledge has been generated through research it is important to disseminate findings with others to change understanding and practice. Dissemination of findings can occur within public, professional, and academic contexts via the Internet, presentations, and publications. Ultimately, publishing research in journal articles and books enables the creation of a permanent and accessible record. Longevity of research is typically achieved through such avenues and once work is published, people from across the globe can draw on these findings to create new ideas, understandings, and directions. Therefore, researchers should think about the message they wish to convey through their research: "What is your dialogue with the future?"

This chapter outlines how to read and critique research, then how to write for publication in order to disseminate research findings. The chapter is written for people undertaking research (particularly research students and beginning researchers) as well as consumers of research (students, researchers, and clinical practitioners).

16.2 Finding and Reading Literature

Reading previous research enables an understanding of disciplinary traditions, new techniques, and perspectives. Reading previous research also ensures that research is

Research Methods in Clinical Linguistics and Phonetics: A Practical Guide,
First Edition. Edited by Nicole Müller and Martin J. Ball.
© 2013 Blackwell Publishing Ltd. Published 2013 by Blackwell Publishing Ltd.

not being replicated, and enables contextualization of work through the literature review (Blaxter, Hughes, and Tight, 2006). The first step is to find appropriate research to read.

16.2.1   Finding Literature

There are a number of journals that publish papers in the field of clinical linguistics and phonetics (Table 16.1). Some are research-focused (e.g. *Journal of Speech, Language, and Hearing Research, Clinical Linguistics and Phonetics*) while others are more clinically focused (e.g. *Journal of Clinical Practice in Speech-Language Pathology*). Some relate to acquired communication disorders (e.g. *Aphasiology*), and some relate to children's communication (e.g. *Language, Speech, and Hearing Services in Schools*). Some mainly publish research undertaken using qualitative methodologies (e.g. *Journal of Interactional Research in Communication Disorders*), whereas others publish both experimental and qualitative methodologies (e.g. *International Journal of Speech-Language Pathology*).

It is useful to sign up for automated content alerts to relevant journals (Table 16.2). This service provides an email each time a new issue of a journal is published, and some also provide email alerts when manuscripts are published online ahead of publication. Regular updates also enable an understanding of each journal's culture, including the type of manuscripts that are published, so that when it is time to submit a journal manuscript a range of possible journal locations is known.

Abstracting and indexing databases provide search engines to scour journals for relevant content. Table 16.3 lists abstracting and indexing databases that are relevant to the field of clinical linguistics and phonetics. Some of these services require a subscription, typically made through a university or hospital library. Other services are free; for example, the most accessible general service is Google Scholar (scholar. google.com). It is useful to work with a reference librarian, particularly when beginning research, in order to assist with refining database searches. Reference librarians will assist with finding key terms and constructing Boolean searches (e.g. combining more than one search term) to make searching efficient and effective. Carefully designed searches ensure that key articles are not missed, and irrelevant articles are less likely to be accessed. It is possible to save search strategies so that search engines will regularly update the findings from a search by email.

16.2.2   Managing Literature

It is useful to catalogue relevant articles for future access. Most researchers use bibliographic software such as EndNote® or ProCite® to manage and organize literature. Most online sites of clinical linguistics and phonetics journals have a feature whereby metadata (including authors' names, title, journal title, volume number, page numbers, abstract, and Digital Object Identifier (DOI®)) can be automatically downloaded into bibliographic software without retyping. Creating a personalized keyword list within bibliographic software enables searching for

Table 16.1 Journals that publish papers in the area of clinical linguistics and phonetics.

Journal title	Acronym	Website	ISSN
1. American Journal of Speech-Language Pathology	AJSLP	ajslp.asha.org	1058-0360, 1558-9110
2. Aphasiology	–	www.tandf.co.uk/journals/pp/02687038.html	0268-7038, 1464-5041
3. Applied Psycholinguistics	APS	journals.cambridge.org/action/displayJournal?jid=APS	0142-7164
4. ASHA Leader	–	www.asha.org/leader.aspx	1085-9586
5. Asia Pacific Journal of Speech, Language and Hearing	APJSLH	www.pluralpublishing.com/journals_APJ.htm	1361-3286
6. Augmentative and Alternative Communication	AAC	informahealthcare.com/aac	0743-4618
7. Child Language Teaching and Therapy	CLTT	clt.sagepub.com/	0265-6590, 1477-0865
8. Clinical Linguistics and Phonetics	CLP	informahealthcare.com/clp	0269-9206, 1464-5076, 1476-9670
9. Communication Disorders Quarterly	CDQ	cdq.sagepub.com/	1525-7401, 1538-4837, 1093-5703
10. Communication Disorders Review	CDR	www.pluralpublishing.com/journals_CDR.htm	1933-2831
11. Contemporary Issues in Communication Science and Disorders	CICSD	www.nsslha.org/publications	1092-5171
12. Evidence-Based Communication Assessment and Intervention	EBCAI	www.informaworld.com/ebcai	1748-9539, 1748-9547
13. Folia Phoniatrica et Logopaedica	FPL	www.karger.com/fpl	1021-7762, 1421-9972, 0015-5705
14. International Journal of Language and Communication Disorders	IJLCD	informahealthcare.com/lcd	1368-2822, 1460-6984
15. International Journal of Speech-Language Pathology	IJSLP	informahealthcare.com/ijslp	1754-9507, 1754-9515
16. Journal of Child Language	JCL	journals.cambridge.org/jcl	0305-0009, 1469-7602

#	Journal	Abbr.	URL	ISSN
17.	Journal of Clinical Practice in Speech-Language Pathology	JCPSLP	www.speechpathologyaustralia.org.au/publications/jcpslp	1441-6727
18.	Journal of Communication Disorders	JCD	www.journals.elsevier.com/journal-of-communication-disorders/	0021-9924, 1054-8505
19.	Journal of Interactional Research in Communication Disorders	JIRCD	www.equinoxjournals.com/ojs/index.php/JIRCD	2040-5111, 2040-512X
20.	Journal of the International Phonetic Association	JIPA	journals.cambridge.org/ipa	0025-1003, 1475-3502
21.	Journal of Linguistics	JL	journals.cambridge.org/action/displayJournal?jid=LIN	0022-2267, 1469-7742
22.	Journal of Medical Speech-Language Pathology	JMSLP	cengagesites.com/academic/?site=3802	1065-1438
23.	Journal of Speech, Language, and Hearing Research	JSLHR	jslhr.asha.org/	1092-4388, 1558-9102
24.	Language, Speech, and Hearing Services in Schools	LSHSS	lshss.asha.org/	0161-1461, 1558-9129
25.	Logopedics Phoniatrics Vocology	LPV	informahealthcare.com/lpv	1401-5439, 1651-2022
26.	New Zealand Journal of Speech-Language Therapy	NZJSLT	www.speechtherapy.org.nz/about-nzsta/publications-1/nzsta-journal	1754-9507, 1754-9515
27.	Seminars in Speech and Language	SSL	www.thieme-connect.de/ejournals/toc/ssl	0734-0478, 1098-9056
28.	South African Journal of Communication Disorders/Die Suid-Afrikaanse Tydskrif vir Kommunikasie-afwykings	SAJCD	www.sajcd.org.za	0379-8046
29.	Topics in Language Disorders	TLD	journals.lww.com/topicsinlanguagedisorders	0271-8294, 1550-3259
30.	Topics in Stroke Rehabilitation	TSR	thomasland.metapress.com/content/300381/	1074-9357

Sharynne McLeod

Table 16.2 Online journal content alerting services.

Publisher	Representative journals*	Website
American Speech-Language-Hearing Association (ASHA)	AJSLP, JSLHR, LSHSS	journals.asha.org/cgi/alerts/etoc
Cambridge Informahealthcare	APS, JIPA, JCD AAC, CLP, IJLCD, IJSLP, LPV	www.cambridge.org/alerts/ informahealthcare.com/page/services/ alertingservices
Karger	FPL	content.karger.com/services/alert.asp#01
Lippincott Williams and Wilkins	TLD	journals.lww.com/topicsinlanguage disorders/pages/etoc.aspx
Psychology Press/ Taylor and Francis	EBCAI, Aphasiology	www.psypress.com/emails/
Sage	CDQ, CLTT	www.sagepub.com/emailAlerts.sp
Thieme	SSL	www.thieme-connect.de/ejournals/ alerts_confirm

* Journal acronyms are explained in Table 16.1.

Table 16.3 Abstracting and indexing databases pertaining to clinical linguistics and phonetics.

Abstracting and indexing	Acronym	Website
1. Applied Social Sciences Index and Abstracts	ASSIA	www.csa.com/factsheets/ assia-set-c.php
2. Bibliography of Linguistic Literature	BLLDB	www.blldb-online.de
3. Campbell Collaboration		campbellcollaboration.org
4. Child Development Abstracts	CDA	www.informaworld.com/smpp/ title~content=t714859093
5. Cochrane Collaboration	Cochrane	www.cochrane.org
6. Cumulative Index to Nursing and Allied Health Literature	CINAHL	www.ebscohost.com/cinahl/

Table 16.3   (cont'd).

Abstracting and indexing	Acronym	Website
7. Current Contents® - Social and Behavioral Sciences		www.ovid.com/site/catalog/ DataBase/924.jsp
8. EBSCO Host: Health Source – Nursing/ Academic edition	EBSCO online	www.ebscohost.com/
9. Education Resources Information Centre	ERIC	www.eric.ed.gov/
10. EMBASE/Excerpta Medica	EMBASE	www.embase.com/
11. European Reference Index for the Humanities	ERIH	www.esf.org/research-areas/ humanities/erih-european-reference-index-for-the-humanities.html
12. Linguistic Abstracts		www.linguisticsabstracts.com/ help.aspx
13. Linguistic and Language Behavior Abstracts	LLBA	www.csa.com/factsheets/ llba-set-c.php
14. Medline®		www.proquest.com/en-US/ catalogs/databases/detail/ medline_ft.shtml
15. Psychological Database for Brain Impairment Treatment Efficacy	PsycBITE	www.psycbite.com/
16. PsycINFO	PsycINFO	www.ovid.com/site/catalog/ DataBase/139.jsp
17. Social Sciences Citation Index®	SSCI/ISI	thomsonreuters.com/products_ services/science/science_ products/a-z/ social_sciences_citation_index#
18. SciSearch®: A Cited Reference Science Database	SciSearch	library.dialog.com/bluesheets/ html/bl0034.html
19. SCOPUS®		info.scopus.com/
20. Speech Pathology Database for Best Interventions and Treatment Efficacy	SpeechBITE	www.speechbite.com/

relevant articles. It is also useful to save copies of articles by author's surname and year of publication that can be attached to the bibliographic software entry of that article to increase accessibility.

16.2.3   *Reading Literature*

16.2.3.1   *Review papers: literature that summarizes the state of the art*

A recent meta-analysis, review paper, or tutorial on the topic of interest is a good starting point. Such literature provides an overview of the state of the art of the topic and may also describe the historical trajectory of thought within a field. Journals such as *Seminars in Speech and Language* and *Topics in Language Disorders* frequently publish review papers; however, most journals publish at least some. If a relevant recent tutorial paper cannot be found, then a book chapter summarizing recent literature is a good alternative; see for example the *The Handbook of Clinical Linguistics* (Ball *et al.*, 2008). If a general overview article cannot be found, then a *current* textbook used by linguistics, phonetics, or speech-language pathology students is useful.

16.2.3.2   *Reading literature in depth*

There are four approaches to reading literature in depth, and each is relevant at different stages. The first approach is to categorize literature into levels of relevance, the second is to read the work of a few key authors, the third is to undertake a conceptual literature review, and the fourth is to critique individual research articles. Each of these approaches will be covered in turn.

Determine the relevance of literature   The English philosopher Francis Bacon (1561–1626) was credited with saying "Some books are to be tasted, others to be swallowed, and some few to be chewed and digested." This maxim is very true when reading research literature (e.g. books and journal articles). Findley (1989) suggested that students and their supervisors/advisers categorize literature into levels of relevance with respect to the research topic: A = highly relevant; B = less relevant, but still important; C = "articles that leave you with a nagging feeling that you should have read them" (p. S17); X = "don't want to read, not relevant, never will be relevant" (p. S17). A articles should be read (perhaps more than once), B articles should be skimmed, and abstracts of the C articles should be read. The X articles may yet become useful if one's research focus changes (particularly once research data has been obtained).

Reading the work of prominent authors   Reading articles from one or two prominent researchers, including letters to the editor and forums where their work has been debated, should provide an understanding of how researchers have systematically built knowledge over time as well as an in-depth understanding of a researcher's perspective.

Undertaking a conceptual literature review   Instead of (or as well as) reading the work of key researchers, an alternative approach to reading is to categorize literature around a particular topic or concept. To begin, read category A articles (the highly relevant ones) and write notes or key words on the front page of each. Next, list major points from these articles and sort these points into an order that makes sense. Then use the key words, concepts, and points to construct a classification framework or a concept map. Finally construct a table listing the author and year under each conceptual category. At times, portions of the conceptual literature review may be included as a table or appendix within a research article. One example is found in table 1 of Harrison and McLeod (2010). The columns of this table were the risk and protective factors identified from the literature for childhood speech and language impairment and the rows were relevant studies. Each cell included either yes/no/unknown to indicate whether or not the factor was found to be a significant risk in the cited research. This conceptual review was then used to identify key risk factors for subsequent data analysis.

Critiquing individual research articles   Critiquing individual articles enables researchers to "chew and digest" both content and methodology. During a critique of individual articles, take into account distinctions between published and unpublished papers, peer-reviewed and non-reviewed papers, contemporary and classic works, introductory and overview texts, edited collections, literature reviews, methodological writings and between primary, secondary, and tertiary sources (Blaxter et al., 2006). Some of these works are more credible and have undergone more extensive peer-review processes than others. However, one should aim for the majority of key articles to be gleaned from international peer-reviewed journals (see Table 16.1).

There are numerous formats within research and psychology texts for reviewing individual articles (e.g. Leedy and Ormrod, 2010; Schiavetti, Metz, and Orlikoff, 2011). For example, Schiavetti and colleagues provide checklists for rating the introduction, method, results, and discussion of studies. Rosenfeld (2010) gives an outstanding overview for those involved in formal peer review for journal manuscript submissions; however, his advice is also relevant when reviewing individual articles, as well as when preparing work for publication.

Recent international attention to evidence-based practice (EBP) has resulted in publication of guidelines for determining the methodological rigor of intervention studies (Lohr, 2004), including within the profession of speech-language pathology. Checklist forms titled Critical Appraisal of Treatment Evidence (CATE) and Critical Appraisal of Systematic Review of Meta-analysis (CASM) are included in Dollaghan (2007) to evaluate the quality of peer-reviewed publications. The EBP website SpeechBITE (www.speechbite.com) states that it provides a "catalogue of Best Interventions and Treatment Efficacy across the scope of Speech Pathology practice" and "methodological ratings are included to allow you to discern the scientific quality of each research study." Other sites containing EBP reviews include: www.cochrane.org; campbellcollaboration.org; and guideline.gov.

16.2.3.3   Note taking

It is important to keep notes while reading to enable ready recall to articles when writing a literature review. Some people prefer to take notes in a book or folder, with a page for each article read. Others prefer to use index cards, documenting the reference and key points. Many people write directly on hard copies of articles, making notes and highlighting different issues in different colours. Others find it useful to list references in concept maps drawn on a whiteboard, paper, or even using concept mapping software. Some people like to keep (and even publish) an annotated bibliography of their readings (Küster, 1999). Many researchers use their bibliographic database program (e.g. Endnote® or Procite®) to take notes, as well as keep a list of the references they have read. The notes sections of these programs allow for large slabs of text or quotes to be inserted; which is subsequently useful for pasting into a literature review. The search function of these bibliographic programs is multi-layered to enable searching for words anywhere within the entry.

16.2.3.4   Reviewing literature at different stages and for different purposes

Literature will be read differently throughout the research process. According to Blaxter *et al.* (2006: 101) at the *beginning* of research, one should read "in order to check what other research has been done, to focus your ideas, shape your hypotheses and explore the context for your project"; *during* research, "to keep you interested and up to date with developments, to help you better understand the methods you are using and the field you are researching, and as a source of data"; and *after* research, "to see what impact your own work has had and to help you develop ideas for further research projects." In addition, reading should include general books on research (e.g. Grbich, 1999; Minichiello *et al.*, 2004; Portney and Watkins, 2008), research texts specifically written for fields relating to clinical linguistics and phonetics (including this one; L. Nelson, 2008; Schiavetti *et al.*, 2011), accounts of research methods; for example, books about writing qualitative research (Higgs, Horsfall, and Grace, 2009) and texts that support academic writing (e.g. Higgs *et al.*, 2008; Taines, 2007; Thomas, 2000).

Section Summary

- Find literature: in journals, via abstracting and indexing databases, librarians.
- Manage literature: using bibliographic software such as EndNote® or ProCite®.
- Categorize literature: according to relevance.
- Read and critique literature: reviews, papers by key researchers, and relevant papers.
- Take notes: to construct a conceptualization of the field.

16.3   Writing Up Research

According to the American Psychological Association (2010) there are five frequently published types of articles: empirical studies, literature reviews, theoretical articles, methodological articles, and case studies. Empirical studies report original research and typically are presented in four sections: introduction, method, results, discussion. Literature reviews critically evaluate previously published research. Theoretical articles are written to advance theory by examining the internal consistency and external validity of a theoretical construct. Methodological articles present new or revised methodologies and focus on the method and data analysis. Case studies illustrate a problem by drawing on data from individuals, communities or organizations (Barlow, Nock, and Hersen, 2009). Within the field of clinical linguistics and phonetics articles of each of these types appear; however, empirical studies are the most common, followed by literature reviews (sometimes referred to as tutorials). Since the introduction section of empirical studies includes a literature review, we will now consider how to write a literature review, and then consider additional components of writing empirical studies.

16.3.1   *Writing a Literature Review*

The basic principles of writing a literature review apply whether writing a literature review as a stand-alone review, or at the beginning of a project, thesis, dissertation, book chapter, or journal article.

16.3.1.1   *Types of literature reviews*

There are three main types of literature reviews: systematic reviews, meta-analyses, and narrative reviews. The first two are formalized genres typically used for writing stand-alone literature reviews. The third type may also be a stand-alone review, but typically is used when writing the introduction to an empirical study. Systematic reviews provide evidence-based inferences after a comprehensive search of all available evidence. According to Collins and Fauser (2004: 103) "The systematic review attempts to reduce reviewer bias through the use of objective, reproducible criteria to select relevant individual publications and assess their validity." Three informative methodological papers to assist with writing systematic reviews are Marshall *et al.* (2011), Reeves *et al.* (2002), and Turner *et al.* (2007). Recent examples of systematic reviews in clinical linguistics and phonetics are Law *et al.* (2000) and Fey *et al.* (2011). Meta-analyses include a statistical synthesis of data from previously published studies (often relying on data from randomized controlled trials) that have been selected often within a systematic review (Turner *et al.*, 2007). Examples of meta-analyses in fields related to clinical linguistics and phonetics are Casby (2001), Law, Garret, and Nye (2004), and H. Nelson *et al.* (2006). Finally, narrative reviews are the most common type of literature reviews encompassing the breadth and varying quality of available research. As Collins and Fauser (2004: 104) state, "[n]arrative reviews generally are comprehensive and cover a wide range of issues within a given topic, but they do not necessarily state or follow rules about the search for evidence." Recent examples of narrative reviews include Baker and McLeod (2011) and Chi-Fishman (2005).

16.3.1.2   *The macrostructure of a literature review*

When writing a literature review, particularly as the introduction to a project, thesis, dissertation, or journal article, it is useful to consider the funnel approach to writing. That is, one starts with broad information that is known by any reader and systematically narrows the focus until the reader has been led to the research question posed. Swales (1990) proposed a three-phased framework titled Create a Research Space (CARS) as a structure for a literature review. He proposed the first part of the literature review should *establish the territory* by showing that the general area is important, central, interesting, problematic, and/or relevant. In this section, introduce and review previous research. Second, *establish a niche*. That is, indicate a gap in the previous research, raise a question about it, or aim to extend previous knowledge. Finally, *occupy the niche* by outlining the purpose or nature of the research, and indicate the structure of the paper (Swales, 1990).

A literature review should be comprehensive yet selective. It should not just be a description of what has gone beforehand, but should critique the state of the art. Critique may also extend to individual articles or methodologies; is more often directed towards concepts (identified in a conceptual review of the literature) supported by examples and details. Findings from different studies should be integrated by comparing and contrasting them. A clear and persuasive expression of purpose should build throughout the literature review, culminating in the need for the study and the research questions (Brown, Rogers, and Pressland, 1994).

16.3.2   *Writing the Method, Results, and Discussion*

The research and its findings are described in the method, results, and discussion sections. The genre of writing of these sections will depend on the type of research (e.g. qualitative vs. experimental) and the type of publication (project, thesis, dissertation, book chapter, journal article).

The method should provide a detailed description of how the study was conducted and give enough information for it to be replicated (if this is methodologically appropriate). It is useful to use headings such as Participants, Sampling, Measurements/ Instruments, Procedure, Reliability (where appropriate), and Data Analysis. The results section should clearly present the data and analyses, typically using the research questions as the guiding framework. Rosenfeld (2010: 483) suggests that a well-written results section is a "logical and orderly blend of numbers and narrative with supporting tables and figures." The discussion should evaluate and interpret the

Table 16.4 Components of a typical journal article.

Component	Subcomponents and comments
Title	Write a clear summary statement of approximately 10–12 words
Abstract	Briefly describe the context, purpose, method, results, and conclusions
Key words	Select up to 5 key words
Introduction	Include a general statement of the problem, literature review, study rationale, and research questions (and hypotheses if appropriate)
Method	Describe participants (sample size, characteristics, selection criteria), materials/instruments, procedure (tasks and protocol), reliability and validity, and data analysis. Some journals also require a statement regarding ethical approval for the study
Results	Structure according to the research questions. Describe and present data clearly
Discussion	Summarize the results in relation to the research questions. Describe the relationship of the results to previous research, limitations of the research study, implications of the research (theoretical, clinical, and practical) and directions for future research. Provide concluding comments
Acknowledgments	Include only if appropriate. Acknowledge the funding source and collaborators/supporters who are not authors
References	Adhere strictly to the specified referencing style for the journal you submit to (for both in-text citations and the list of references)
Appendices	Include only if appropriate. This could contain participant data that is too extensive for an in-text table or additional information about stimulus materials, procedures and protocols (e.g. sample questions from the research questionnaire)
Tables and figures	Use tables and figures sparingly but cleverly to illustrate the data and key concepts

results in light of previous research and indicate limitations and implications for clinical practice (if appropriate) and future research. Sometimes in qualitative research the results and discussion sections are combined. A summary of key components for an empirical research article is included in Table 16.4. For additional information, the STROBE statement (Strengthening the Reporting of Observational Studies in Epidemiology; Vandenbroucke *et al.*, 2007; von Elm *et al.*, 2007) includes a checklist to enable research to "be reported transparently so that readers can follow what was planned, what was done, what was found, and what conclusions were drawn" (von Elm *et al.*, 2007: 806). Although the STROBE statement has specifically been designed for cohort, case-control, and cross-sectional studies, many of the recommendations are appropriate across experimental studies in the field of clinical linguistics and phonetics. In order to look at good examples of writing it is a good idea to ask colleagues for their favorite articles (including ones outside of the topic area). Award-winning manuscripts can be viewed by looking at the annual recipients of the ASHA journals Editors' Awards and many journal websites include a list of the most downloaded and most cited articles.

16.3.3   *The Microstructure of Writing*

It is essential to ensure that the primary content is accurate and well crafted, as outlined above; however, the stylistic microstructure is almost as important. The language, paragraphing, style, grammar, punctuation, word choice, spelling, and format should be considered carefully. *The Publication Manual of the American Psychological Association* (APA, 2010) is a definitive source of information on the stylistic features of writing in many disciplines. Many journals within the field of clinical linguistics and phonetics use this manual as the basis for the formatting of text, referencing, tables, and figures. Even if the APA style for referencing is not used, the APA manual contains a comprehensive and extremely informative chapter (chapter 8) on the publication process. Other texts, including *Usage and Abusage* (Partridge, 1973), provide guidelines for word choice, and syntactical construction.

All sources of literature should be present, correctly acknowledged, and correctly referenced using the recommended style (e.g. APA, 2010). Never underestimate the importance of attention to detail when it comes to referencing. Appropriate use of capitalization, italicization, and punctuation is appreciated by journal editors, reviewers, copy-editors and typesetters. It is not just a courtesy to use the recommended style, but also ensures that the publication process is more streamlined and readers can easily locate referenced sources.

For those not from an English-speaking background, it is important that the manuscript is read and checked by someone from an English-speaking background with knowledge of academic writing skills and, if possible, knowledge of clinical linguistics and phonetics. There are professional organizations that can provide this service for a fee.

16.4   Publishing Research

Publishing research is an important part of the research process. As mentioned at the beginning of this chapter, publication enables research to be widely accessed (across the world and into the future) so that others can benefit and facilitate their own research and practice. Rightly or wrongly, "professionals with strong publication records are often considered to have more competence and expertise than their less published counterparts" (Fine and Kurdek, 1993: 1141). Thus, alongside planning, conducting, and writing research it is useful to consider where to publish it. This simultaneous consideration is important so that the methods, analyses, and foundational literature that underpin research align with those of the publication venue. The most accessible publishing venue for researchers is to submit a manuscript to a journal, since, typically, book chapters are written either by invitation from the editor or after presentation of a paper at a conference (e.g. Windsor, Kelly, and Hewlett, 2002).

16.4.1   Writing a Journal Manuscript

16.4.1.1   Selecting a journal

The first step in writing a journal manuscript is to select the venue. The list of journals found in Table 16.1 can assist consideration of the most appropriate venue. However, even if one key venue is selected, it is useful to have a few additional venues in mind in case the research focus changes, or the work is rejected from the first choice. There are different techniques for determining the quality of journals. Some abstracting and indexing services (Table 16.3) such as Medline and PsycINFO have strict criteria for acceptance, so only journals deemed to be of high quality are included in these databases. Some countries also rate journal quality. For example, the European Reference Index for the Humanities (ERIH) publishes a ranked list of journals. The Social Sciences Citation Index applies another technique for determining journal quality: the number of citations is used as an indicator of quality. It publishes the average number of citations per manuscript in the journal over a particular time period (usually a year). Currently, within the field of clinical linguistics and phonetics, most journals have a citation rate between 0.5 and 2.0. However, the most important determinant of the venue for submitting one's work is whether the research fits within the remit of the journal and will be useful to the journal's readership.

16.4.1.2   Authorship

Deciding on the authorship of the manuscript (including the order of names) is also important. Within the field of clinical linguistics and phonetics, single-authored papers are rare. Multi-authored papers are the most common; typically with two to five authors. Justice (2010: 1) suggested that authorship is a "highly subjective issue, because knowing whether a person should be represented as an author of a work can often be unclear and even ambiguous." It is important to discuss authorship at the beginning of the research, a long time before writing for publication begins, and to be familiar with guidelines for deciding on authorship within the institution (university, hospital), profession, country, and the broader research community (e.g. see APA, 2010: 18–19). Decisions regarding authorship should include consideration of input into the conceptualization, design, conduct, and writing of the research.

When research is undertaken within a research degree, decisions regarding authorship (e.g. inclusion or exclusion of students and their supervisors/advisers) as well as the authorship order can be complex and grounded in discipline traditions. The Vancouver protocol states that "Authorship credit should be based on 1) substantial contributions to conception and design, acquisition of data, or analysis and interpretation of data; 2) drafting the article or revising it critically for important intellectual content; and 3) final approval of the version to be published. Authors should meet conditions 1, 2, and 3" (International Committee of Medical Journal Editors, 2009). This protocol has been adopted by many universities throughout the world across most disciplines. Authorder® (www.authorder.com) provides a tool to enact the Vancouver protocol for deciding on authorship order on publications.

Fine and Kurdek (1993) present case studies and a discussion listing two important ethical dilemmas: when faculty take undeserved credit as an author, and when students are given undeserved credit as an author. They conclude their discussion with a number of helpful guidelines for determining authorship. The first is: "To be included as an author on a scholarly publication, a student should, in a cumulative sense, make a professional contribution that is creative and intellectual in nature, that is integral to completion of the paper, and that requires an overarching perspective of the project." The second: "Authorship decisions should be based on the scholarly importance of the professional contribution and not just the time and effort made" (Fine and Kurdek, 1993: 1145).

16.4.1.3   Components of a manuscript

When writing a journal article it is easy to overlook the importance of spending time composing the title and abstract. However, consumers' decisions regarding whether to read an article are frequently based on the title and abstract. Therefore, a title should be clear, brief, and interesting. It should contain key words that others will typically use to search when looking for research in that field. It should be honest, yet capture readers' attention. Words that are unnecessary in the title include, for example: "a study of" or "preliminary findings." When writing the abstract, similarly chose the words carefully. Rosenfeld (2010: 483) suggests that a good abstract should provide a "stand-alone 'snapshot' of the manuscript." Some journals (e.g. *International Journal of Language and Communication Disorders*) require a structured abstract (using headings such as Purpose, Methods, Results, Conclusions), whereas other journals just specify the number of words. As a rule of thumb, the abstract should have one sentence for each of the following: context, purpose, method, results, and conclusions (see APA, 2010: 26–27, for different types of manuscript abstracts).

Another important consideration is selection of key words. Key words enable others to locate research on a particular topic. Reference librarians can provide advice about key words used within the discipline of clinical linguistics and phonetics and also locate the key words for other similar papers. It makes sense to use similar key words across papers so that people can locate other papers on the same topic.

The guidelines above for writing a literature review, method, results, and discussion apply to writing these elements within a journal article. When composing a journal submission Table 16.4 may be useful as a checklist. In order to be published, work must make a *new* contribution to the literature. Research that presents new solutions to problems is more likely to be published than research that presents what is already known. Most clinical linguistics and phonetics journals require an international focus. Localized work that is not contextualized within the world's literature rarely will be published. Table 16.5 presents a checklist and procedure for the journal submission process.

16.4.2   Responding to Feedback

Within the field of clinical linguistics and phonetics, feedback after a journal submission can be extensive. Some journals provide feedback from the editor, associate editor, and up to four independent reviewers. The extent of feedback should not be alarming, but rather be seen as instructive. Often it is useful to number each of the editors' and reviewers' comments so that if more than one has commented on the same topic they can be cross-referenced. In responding to reviewers' feedback always be courteous and always be thorough (provide a line-by-line response). There is no need to agree with everything, but everything should be addressed and responded to. If you do not agree with a reviewer's suggestion, justify your decision not to make the changes, preferably with research evidence. Indeed Frey (2003: 205) wrote a provocative paper encouraging authors to disregard the advice of reviewers if appropriate and suggested "this reduces intellectual prostitution and produces more original publications."

16.4.3   If a Paper is Rejected

Most seasoned researchers know: some papers get rejected from journals. There are many reasons for this, and not all relate to the quality of research. As Culatta (1984) indicated, reasons why articles were not published in ASHA journals have included: that they were inappropriate for the journal (21% of rejected articles), there were writing-style flaws (17.5%), they did not make a meaningful contribution to current knowledge (16.5%), there was inadequate research design (14%), inadequate sampling (11.7%), overgeneralization from data (10.5%), and the research question was not answered (8.2%). If a paper was rejected because it was inappropriate for that particular journal, it can be submitted to another journal. However, if a paper was rejected because of perceived flaws, the feedback from the reviewers deserves close attention. Ask senior colleagues for advice about the feedback to assist with the revision. Sometimes it may be appropriate to resubmit a substantially revised version of the paper to the same journal as a new submission, but often it is better to consider another journal to which to submit a revised manuscript. Remember that the field of clinical linguistics and phonetics is small. If the original journal editor gave feedback on how to improve a manuscript and this feedback is not addressed before submitting the manuscript to another journal, it is quite possible that the next journal editor may invite the same reviewer to review the

Table 16.5 Journal submission process.

---

1   Select the most appropriate journal for your work
  • Read the aims and scope of the journal. Read a range of other articles from the journal. Look at the society/association attached to the journal and attend its conference(s) if appropriate. Look at publications by the *current* editor and editorial board (in other journals)

2   Prepare your manuscript for submission to the chosen journal
  • Assess your work: Does your manuscript present high quality and rigorous research? Does your manuscript provide new information? Have you contextualized your work with an international audience in mind? Have you contextualized your work by considering (and citing) other papers published in the chosen journal?

3   Download the instructions for authors and follow them
  • Make sure the author guidelines are followed exactly with respect to: abstract style and length, length of the paper (check whether the recommended length includes title page, abstract, text, references, appendices, tables, and figures), preparation of tables and figures, whether figures and tables should be at the end or in separate documents, referencing style (correct referencing is *very important*), inclusion of audio or video content, recommended font (if your manuscript includes phonetic symbols), identification of authorship on the title page (some journals require double-blind peer review)

4   Submit your article to the journal
  • Submission usually occurs directly to the editor or via an online submission process

5   Wait for the peer review process to occur
  • The process typically involves three stages: the editor considers whether the manuscript is appropriate for the peer-review process. If so, it is sent for peer review often by two international experts. The editor considers the reviewers' responses and makes a recommendation that may be: accept without changes (this is *extremely rare*), minor revision, major revision, reject. Some journals may also recommend major revision + second review, or reject + resubmit

6   Make the recommended changes
  • If invited, make revisions suggested by the editor(s) and reviewer(s). Write a comprehensive letter/table addressing each of the reviewers' comments and resubmit the manuscript

7   Wait for the editorial decision
  • Once again, the editor considers whether the paper requires additional peer review, and makes a recommendation to the author. It is very common for additional changes to be requested

8   Wait for publication process
  • If the editor accepts the manuscript, then the manuscript is copy-edited and typeset by the publisher. Typically page proofs are sent to authors for checking with a tight timeline. Eventually the paper will be published (often this occurs online ahead of hard-copy publication)

Table 16.5   (cont'd).

---

9   After publication
 • Congratulate (and reward) yourself. Share your publication with your support crew and other people who may be interested. After a while, check to see
   if it has been cited (e.g. via Google Scholar, SCOPUS, or Social Sciences
   Citation Index). Start the process again

---

manuscript. Journal editors and reviewers do not appreciate authors who do not
acknowledge and respect the time it takes to provide advice to authors.

16.4.4   Publishing from Projects, Theses, or Dissertations

Traditionally, research as part of a higher degree is submitted as a dissertation (this
term now will be used to encompass the terms "project", "thesis", and "dissertation").
However, the investment of time and effort by the researcher, supervisors/advisers,
and research participants should not result in the publication of a "limited edition
book" that is read only by examiners. In order to ensure wider access to students'
research some universities require students to submit a copy of their dissertation to
their library. Others encourage digital submission of dissertations and there are a
number of digital repositories of dissertations including:

 • ProQuest UMI Dissertation Publishing (www.proquest.com/en-US/products/
   dissertations/).
 • Networked Digital Library of Theses and Dissertations (www.ndltd.org/).
 • Dissertation.com (www.dissertation.com/browse.php).

A number of universities enable students to present a dissertation by publication.
This format often starts with a synopsis, then includes journal articles on a similar
topic that have been submitted or published by the author of the dissertation, and
concludes with a discussion that ties the work together and specifies the unique
contribution of the body of work.

Regardless of whether a dissertation is submitted in the traditional format, the
first step to publication may be to present work at a local, national, and or
international conference. Conference presentations not only assist in clarifying
thinking, but also provide feedback from people in the audience. Sometimes journal
editors or editorial board members are in the audience and can give feedback
regarding the suitability of submission to journals. In order to select the most appropriate venue(s) for publishing, the reference list of a dissertation is a useful starting
point. What journals have been read and cited? What journals does a department or
university subscribe to, and which journals do you receive automated content
alerts from?

In a dissertation students *need to prove* they know what they are writing about.
In a journal article it is expected that authors *already know* what they are writing

about. Consequently, a journal article should contain a thorough description and contextualization of the research, but every detail does not need to be justified and explained. Furthermore, think about publishing one or two good papers from a dissertation rather than carving it up into a number of smaller papers dealing with very small components of the research (described as "salami science": Hoit, 2007: 94).

16.4.5   Final Thoughts about Writing

Writing is not only an end product, but also an important part of the research process. Lee and Boud (2003: 187) have stated that "writing is best seen as a starting point, rather than an end point, of the research process and hence fostering academic writing is a useful place to do research development work." Consequently, writing does not always come easily. Justice (2009: 307) suggests four strategies to facilitate writing: "block out writing time ... write with others ... set realistic deadlines ... break written deliverables into small manageable tasks." It is helpful to talk about research with colleagues, family, and friends; ideas will become clearer because of the need to rephrase information for different audiences. Young researchers can volunteer to be peer reviewers for conferences and journals to enhance skills at critiquing research. Finally, celebrate when research is published, and if possible track citations to determine engagement and critique by other researchers. As we started this chapter, so we will end: publications are a dialogue with the future. What do you want to say?

> **Section Summary**
>
> - Select: the most appropriate journal for your publication.
> - Spend time: on the title and abstract.
> - Write the literature review: establish your territory, establish a niche, and occupy the niche (Swales, 1990).
> - Write the method, results, and discussion: provide enough detail so it can be replicated.
> - Pay attention to details: including grammar, punctuation, word choice, and formatting of references.
> - Publish research: and learn from the reviewers' comments.

Acknowledgments

Support to write this chapter was provided by the Australian Research Council Future Fellowship (FT0990588). Earlier sections of this manuscript were based on McLeod (2002) and have been used with permission from the publisher.

References

American Psychological Association (APA) (2010). *Publication Manual of the American Psychological Association*, 6th edn. Washington, DC: APA.

Baker, E. and McLeod, S. (2011). Evidence-based practice for children with speech sound disorders: a narrative review. *Language, Speech, and Hearing Services in Schools*, 42, 103–139.

Ball, M. J., Perkins, M. R., Müller, N., and Howard, S. (eds) (2008). *The Handbook of Clinical Linguistics*. Oxford: Wiley-Blackwell.

Barlow, D. H., Nock, M. K., and Hersen, M. (2009). *Single-Case Experimental Designs: Strategies for Studying Behavior Change*, 3rd edn. Boston, MA: Allyn and Bacon.

Blaxter, L., Hughes, C., and Tight, M. (2006). *How to Research*, 3rd edn. Maidenhead, UK: Open University Press.

Brown, R. F., Rogers, J. D., and Pressland, A. J. (1994). Create a clear focus: the "big picture" about writing better research articles. *American Entomologist*, 40, 144–146.

Casby, M. W. (2001). Otitis media and language development: a meta-analysis. *American Journal of Speech-Language Pathology*, 10(1), 65–80.

Chi-Fishman, G. (2005). Quantitative lingual, pharyngeal and laryngeal ultrasonography in swallowing research: a technical review. *Clinical Linguistics and Phonetics*, 19(6/7), 589–604.

Collins, J. A. and Fauser, B. C. J. M. (2004). Balancing the strengths of systematic and narrative reviews. *Human Reproduction Update*, 11(2), 103–104.

Culatta, R. A. (1984). Why articles don't get published in ASHA. *ASHA Leader*, March, 25–27.

Dollaghan, C. A. (2007). *The Handbook of Evidence-Based Practice in Communication Disorders*. Baltimore, MD: Paul H. Brookes Publishing.

Fey, M. E., Richard, G. J., Geffner, D. *et al.* (2011). Auditory processing disorder and auditory/language interventions: an evidence-based systematic review. *Language, Speech, and Hearing Services in Schools*, 42(3), 246–264.

Findley, T. W. (1989). The conceptual review of the literature or how to read more articles than you ever want to see in your entire life. *American Journal of Physical Medicine and Rehabilitation*, 70, S17–S22.

Fine, M. and Kurdek, L. (1993). Reflections on determining authorship credit and authorship order on faculty–student collaborations. *American Psychologist*, 48, 1141–1147.

Frey, B. S. (2003). Publishing as prostitution? Choosing between one's own ideas and academic success. *Public Choice*, 116(1/2), 205–223.

Grbich, C. (1999). *Qualitative Research in Health: An Introduction*. St Leonards, Australia: Allen & Unwin.

Harrison, L. J. and McLeod, S. (2010). Risk and protective factors associated with speech and language impairment in a nationally representative sample of 4- to 5-year-old children. *Journal of Speech, Language, and Hearing Research*, 53(2), 508–529.

Higgs, J., Ajjawi, R., McAllister, L. *et al.* (2008). *Communicating in the Health Sciences*, 2nd edn. South Melbourne: Oxford University Press.

Higgs, J., Horsfall, D., and Grace, S. (eds) (2009). *Writing Qualitative Research on Practice*. Rotterdam, the Netherlands: Sense Publishers.

Hoit, J. D. (2007). Salami science. *American Journal of Speech-Language Pathology*, 16(2), 94–95.

International Committee of Medical Journal Editors (2009). *Uniform Requirements for Manuscripts Submitted to Biomedical Journals: Ethical Considerations in the Conduct and Reporting of Research: Authorship and Contributorship*. Accessible at http://www. icmje.org/ethical_1author.html (accessed July 6, 2011).

Justice, L. (2009). Don't forget to write. *American Journal of Speech-Language Pathology*, 18(4), 307–308.

Justice, L. (2010). Authorship intricacies. *American Journal of Speech-Language Pathology*, 19(1), 1–2.

Küster, J. M. (1999). Bibliographies: works in progress. *ASHA Leader*, 41(6), 63.

Law, J., Boyle, J., Harris, F. *et al.* (2000). Prevalence and natural history of primary speech and language delay: findings from a systematic review of the literature. *International Journal of Language and Communication Disorders*, 35(2), 165–188.

Law, J., Garrettt, Z. and Nye, C. (2004). The efficacy of treatment for children with developmental speech and language delay/disorder: a meta-analysis. *Journal of Speech, Language, and Hearing Research*, 47(4), 924–943.

Lee, A. and Boud, D. (2003). Writing groups, change and academic identity: research development as local practice. *Studies in Higher Education*, 28(2), 187–200.

Leedy, P. D. and Ormrod, J. E. (2010). *Practical Research: Planning and Design*, 9th edn. Boston, MA: Allyn and Bacon.

Lohr, K. N. (2004). Rating the strength of scientific evidence: relevance for quality improvement programs. *International Journal for Quality in Health Care*, 16(1), 9–18.

McLeod, S. (2002). How to review a mountain of literature. *ACQuiring Knowledge in Speech, Language and Hearing*, 4, 18–20.

Marshall, J., Goldbart, J., Pickstone, C. and Roulstone, S. (2011). Application of systematic reviews in speech-and-language therapy. *International Journal of Language and Communication Disorders*, 46(3), 261–272.

Minichiello, V., Sullivan, G., Greenwood, K. M., and Axford, R. (eds) (2004). *Handbook of Research Methods for Nursing and Health Sciences*, 2nd edn. Frenchs Forest, Australia: Pearson Education.

Nelson, H. D., Nygren, P., Walker, M., and Panoscha, R. (2006). Screening for speech and language delay in preschool children: systematic evidence review for the US Preventive Services Task Force. *Pediatrics*, 117, e298–e319.

Nelson, L. (2008). *Research in Communication Sciences and Disorders: Methods for Systematic Inquiry*. San Diego, CA: Plural Publishing.

Partridge, E. (1973). *Usage and Abusage*. London: Penguin Books.

Portney, L. G. and Watkins, M. P. (2008). *Foundations of Clinical Research: Applications to Practice*, 3rd edn. Upper Saddle River, NJ: Prentice Hall.

Reeves, S., Koppel, I., Barr, H. *et al.* (2002). Twelve tips for undertaking a systematic review. *Medical Teacher*, 24, 358–363.

Rosenfeld, R. M. (2010). How to review journal manuscripts. *Otolaryngology – Head and Neck Surgery*, 142, 472–486.

Schiavetti, N., Metz, D. E., and Orlikoff, R. F. (2011). *Evaluating Research in Communicative Disorders*, 6th edn. Boston, MA: Allyn and Bacon.

Swales, J. M. (1990). *Genre Analysis: English in Academic and Research Settings*. Cambridge: Cambridge University Press.

Taines, C. (2007). *A Practical Guide to Writing for Psychology*. Sydney: McGraw Hill.

Thomas, S. A. (2000). *How to Write Health Science Papers, Dissertations, and Theses*. New York: Livingstone.

Turner, H. M., Nye, C., Ortiz, M. *et al.* (2007). Producing systematic reviews of interventions in speech-language pathology: a framework for sustainability. *Evidence-Based Communication Assessment and Intervention*, 1(4), 201–212.

Vandenbroucke, J. P., von Elm, E., Altman, D. G. Altman *et al.* [STROBE Initiative] (2007). Strengthening the Reporting of Observational Studies in Epidemiology (STROBE): Explanation and elaboration. *PLoS Medicine*, 4(10), 1628–1654.

von Elm, E., Altman, D. G., Egger, M. *et al.* [STROBE Initiative] (2007). Strengthening the Reporting of Observational Studies in Epidemiology (STROBE) statement: guidelines for reporting observational studies. *British Medical Journal*, 335, 806–808.

Windsor, F., Kelly, L., and Hewlett, N. (eds) (2002). *Themes in Clinical Phonetics and Linguistics*. Hillsdale, NJ: Lawrence Erlbaum.

Index

References to tables are given in **bold** type and to figures in *italic* type

Research Methods in Clinical Linguistics and Phonetics: A Practical Guide,
First Edition. Edited by Nicole Müller and Martin J. Ball.
© 2013 Blackwell Publishing Ltd. Published 2013 by Blackwell Publishing Ltd.